DATE DUE

FEB 2 7 1992	

Jewellery Gallery Summary Catalogue

Shirley Bury FSA

Deputy Keeper
Department of Metalwork

VICTORIA AND ALBERT MUSEUM

The Jewellery Gallery in the Victoria and
Albert Museum: a Visual Catalogue.
Published by Emmett Microform. Available
in the V&A Shop from October 1983.

This is a Visual Catalogue illustrating, in
colour on microfiche, all the jewellery
exhibited in the Jewellery Gallery. It follows
the same order and arrangement as the
Summary Catalogue, making them ideal
companion publications. Only the Local and
Traditional Jewellery and Costume
Jewellery, which will be included in later
microfiche publications, and snuff boxes etc.
have been excluded.

ISBN 0 905209 29 X

Designed by Leonard Lawrance.
Printed and bound by Four Winds Press,
Hampton, Middlesex.

Published by the Victoria and Albert
Museum,
London SW7 2RL.

INTRODUCTION

This summary catalogue is in effect the second edition of the Jewellery Gallery handlist compiled for the reopening of the Gallery after the installation of new cases in 1972. The handlist was printed solely for use in the Gallery, but the Department of Metalwork received so many requests for copies that it was decided to make the next version available for purchase. The opportunity occurred rather earlier than was expected, for late in 1977 we had to close the Gallery and remove the contents to enable various complex works to be carried out. The Gallery closed on a high note with a memorial exhibition to Dame Joan Evans, our learned and generous benefactor, who two years earlier had commuted her loan collection of jewellery into a gift. Many of her pieces, described as in a 'private collection', are illustrated in her magisterial *History of Jewellery, 1100-1870* (first edition, 1953; new edition, 1970).

Before she died in 1977 Dame Joan, with great magnanimity, gave us permission to integrate her jewellery, hitherto shown as an entity, into the main collection. This has now been accomplished. The rearrangement was an incentive to re-examine most of the main collection, including the impressive group of late eighteenth and nineteenth century jewellery bequeathed to the Museum in 1951 by Lady Cory. There are stories still extant of Lady Cory appearing at first nights at Covent Garden before the last world war ablaze with parts of the collection. She clearly adored wearing her purchases, but it was her percipience in collecting Victorian jewellery, a field which then attracted little serious attention, which has made her bequest of such value to the Museum, for it laid the foundation of a good and increasingly comprehensive coverage of nineteenth century work.

The Museum could scarcely have been more fortunate in its two chief twentieth century benefactors, for Dame Joan's interests were centred on the Middle Ages and the Renaissance. Her ventures into the nineteenth century were few in number, though significant. Thus the Evans and Cory collections complement each other, and indeed, the major gifts made in the nineteenth century. Among the latter is the fine collection of precious stones mounted in rings (shown in Case 31), which was bequeathed to the Museum in 1868 by the poet and cleric, the Rev. Chauncey Hare Townshend. Some items can be traced back to the early years of the nineteenth century when they belonged to Henry Philip Hope, brother of the antiquary and writer Thomas Hope. The Museum has continued to be fortunate in attracting gifts, each piece in its diverse ways invaluable to the collection. It is impossible here to cite all the donors, though they are acknowledged in the catalogue. Mention must however be made of the splendid necklace and earrings, part of Napoleon's marriage gift in 1806 to Stéphanie de Beauharnais, the future Grand Duchess of Baden (Case 17, Board F, no. 2), which were presented in 1978 by the Countess Margharita Tagliavia.

The study of jewellery has made great strides in recent years partly as a result of loan exhibitions such as Princely Magnificence, organised by my colleague Anna Somers Cocks in the Museum in 1980. Her catalogue, published under the same title, has become an essential work of reference. The publication of catalogues of permanent collections is equally important. Among those which have already appeared is that of the Walters Art Gallery, Baltimore, which came out in 1979, while the British Museum is about to publish the collection given by Professor and Mrs Hull Grundy. Gerald Taylor of the Ashmolean Museum tackled the rings given to the V & A by Dame Joan Evans in his catalogue of an exhibition to which we were among the principal lenders. The exhibition was held at the Ashmolean and Goldsmiths' Hall in 1978 (G. Taylor and D. Scarisbrick, *(Finger Rings from Ancient Egypt to the Present Day)*. I have made consistent use of this catalogue in working through our rings: any departure from Gerald Taylor's text must be on my own head, as are some departures from the attributions made by Charles Oman in his *Catalogue of Rings* [in the V & A], 1930. The Papal 'Ring of the Fisherman' (Case 1, Board E, no.69) is now thought to be a seal, and the ring formerly associated with Mary, Queen of Scots and Lord Darnley (Case 33, Board H, no. 25), is, it is suggested, an original sixteenth century ring with later embellishments. A selection of jewellery with revised ascriptions is shown on two boards (Case 21, Board F and Case 34, Board J); taken together, they are a striking testimony to the conscientious re-creation of old techniques and styles by nineteenth century goldsmiths.

The present catalogue, a much enlarged and revised version of the handlist of 1972, with a few illustrations to give the flavour of the collection, represents a further stage in the progression towards a comprehensively documented publication, an ideal that will only be achieved when the requirements of use in the Jewellery Gallery are not paramount. In order to keep the publication down to a portable size, a selective system of description and comment has been adopted. Some categories have fared better than others. Few additions have been made to the watches, to the Ancient Egyptian and Classical jewellery (which the Museum possesses without making it the subject of research), and to the local and traditional jewellery. Discrimination has also been practised in the main collection of jewellery, some pieces being given a fuller description than others, partly on account of their importance, partly to incorporate new information. The addition of later (usually French) marks on old pieces has also been noted, as indicating the movement of the specimens concerned from one country to another. Cuts of diamonds are described, since they have played a crucial part in the development of jewellery design; space has precluded a similar treatment being accorded to coloured stones.

It must also be stressed that the arrangement of the catalogue is entirely governed by the display, which makes a strict chronology impossible for aesthestic and practical reasons. The central cases in the gallery further dislocate the overall chronological sequence. The watches, for instance, are divided between Cases 1 and 2 (both wall-cases) and 9 (a central case). Renaissance jewellery is shown in Cases 12 and 13 (wall-cases) and in Cases 25, 26 and 28 (centre-cases), which is less odd when you are actually in the Gallery because the latter cases are seen to be adjacent to the former. Case 24, which contains work dating from the late nineteenth and the twentieth century, is contiguous to Cases 21, 22 and 23, where articles of the same date can be seen. The disposition of the cases can be studied in the diagram below.

No task of this kind can be undertaken without assistance. I am much indebted to my colleagues Claude Blair, Anna Somers Cocks, Marian Campbell, Ronald Lightbown, John Mallet, A.R.E. North, Michael Snodin and Charles Truman in matters of scholarship, and to Frances Bryant, Martin Chapman, Jane Stancliffe and Eric Turner for their practical help. John Cherry, Hugh Tait, Judith Rudoe and Timothy Wilson, all of the Department of Medieval and Later Antiquities at the British Museum, gave useful advice, as did Reynold Higgins, formerly of the Greek and Roman Department of the British Museum, Charlotte Gere, Jack M. Ogden, Geoffrey Munn, Brigitte Marquardt and other fellow-members of the Society of Jewellery Historians. E. Allan Jobbins of the Geological Museum gave unstinting and authoritative help in identifying stones, correcting among other things the early twentieth attributions of the Townshend Collection. John Goodall made important contributions to the identification of armorials, and the ring collection has gained from his examination. In 1972 the task of arranging the jewellery was carried out in the Jewellery Gallery itself, with the assistance of Deirdre O'Day. This time round Françoise B. de B. Crichton worked with me for three years in a secure store in the Museum still redolent of the chemicals used to preserve the tapestries stored in it some fifteen years earlier. There the jewellery was rearranged on paper templates cut to the size of the boards in the Gallery, and the objects re-examined and listed before being carried off in batches to be photographed and cleaned, the latter operation being carried out under the supervision of David Northrop of the Conservation Department. In the final stages of checking the prepared text against the objects, many of my colleagues in the Department of Metalwork lent a hand; apart from those named above, I am grateful to Philippa Glanville, Elaine Barr and Jean Schofield.

Shirley Bury

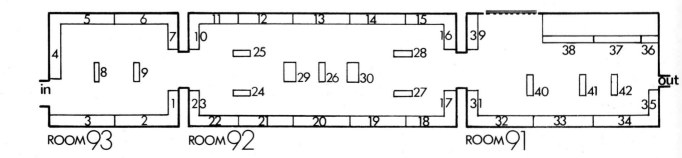

THE ORIGINS OF THE WATCH

Case 1 Board A

(Asterisks denote that the object is illustrated)

GERMAN WATCHES:
16th and 17th centuries

Watches seem to have been introduced in the early years of the sixteenth century in Germany, as a result of the solution, probably in Nuremberg, of the problem of scaling down clock mechanisms to a size convenient for carrying about the person. Germany remained the leading centre for production until towards the middle of the seventeenth century, when the watchmakers of Blois established French supremacy. The watch trade, however, flourished in many countries.

1 WATCH
Signed: *Johannes Buz* (Augsburg). Engraved and gilt brass case with enamelled silver dial. The four dials have astronomical significance.
GERMAN: first half of 17th century.
3236-1856

2 WATCH
Cast, pierced and chased gilt brass case. (The movement does not belong).
GERMAN: second half of 16th century.
Bernal Collection
2369-1855

3 CASE OF A CLOCK WATCH
Cast, pierced and chased brass; formerly gilt.
GERMAN: late 16th century.
Bequeathed by Miss Ethel Gurney
M.177-1939

4 WATCH
Cast, pierced and chased case of gilt brass, with St George and the Dragon.
GERMAN: second half of 16th century.
The case bears the maker's mark HVG, for Hans Grüber of Nuremberg, with the inscription: *'Für Grüber.'*
31-1866

5 WATCH
Cast, pierced and chased case of gilt copper.
GERMAN: second half of 16th century.
Given by Miss G.M. Pratt
M.1-1957

6 WATCH
Signed: *Johann Kessborer Vlm.* Engraved silver case.
GERMAN: second half of 17th century.
137-1907

7 WATCH
Signed: *Conradt Kreizer.* Case of gilt brass, crystal and blue glass panels.
GERMAN: early 17th century.
Bernal Collection
2352-1855

8 CASE OF A CLOCK WATCH
Cast, pierced and chased gilt brass.
GERMAN: late 16th century.
Soulages Collection
5713-1859

Case 1 Board B

ENGLISH WATCHES:
17th century

9 WATCH AND PAIR-CASE
Signed: *Edmund Bull Fleetstreete fecit.* Watch-case silver, with engraved brass dial. Silver pair-case.
ENGLISH: early 17th century.
45-1876

10 WATCH
Signed: *Edm. Day London* (defaced). Case of pierced and engraved gilt brass with silver dial-ring. Engraved with the arms of Stephens (of Colchester and Arden, Essex), granted 1592. Chain of cast gilt brass. The movement partly renewed.
ENGLISH: about 1600.
1137-1905

11 WATCH
Signed: *N. Ridgdale.* Silver case and gilt brass dial, both engraved.
ENGLISH: early 17th century.
Bernal Collection
2365-1855

*12 WATCH
Signed: *David Ramsay me fecit.* Case and dial of silver, parcel-gilt, and gilt brass.
ENGLISH: early 17th century.
Spitzer Collection
Lent from the Salting Bequest
M.558-1910

13 WATCH
Signed: *Ro. Grinkin, London.* Case and dial of engraved silver and gilt brass.
ENGLISH: about 1640.
Lent by Miss I. de B. Lockyer

4

*14 WATCH
Signed: *Ri Barnes at Worcester.* Case
and dial of engraved silver and gilt
brass.
ENGLISH: early 17th century.
921-1855

15 WATCH
Signed: *Eduardus East Londini.*
Case of crystal and engraved gilt
brass; dial of engraved gilt brass and
silver.
ENGLISH: about 1640.
Given by Miss Eva Mᵃ Earle of Great
Yeldham
M.360-1927

16 WATCH
Signed: *W. Houllgatt att Ipswich.*
Case of silver and gilt brass, with gilt
brass dial, both engraved.
ENGLISH: early 17th century.
45-1894

17 WATCH
Signed: *T. Chamberlin fecit.* Case of
pierced and engraved gilt brass with
silver dial.
ENGLISH: about 1600.
8535-1863

18 WATCH
Signed: *Edm. Bull in Fleetstreet
Fecit.* Case and dial of engraved gilt
brass and silver.
ENGLISH: early 17th century.
418-1893

19 WATCH
Signed: *Henry Grendon at ye
Exchange Fecit.* The case silver,
parcel-gilt, in tulip form, the dial
engraved.
ENGLISH: first half of 17th century.
Dunn Gardner Collection
549-1902

20 WATCH AND PAIR-CASE
Signed: *R. Crayle.* Silver watch-case;
leather pair case.
ENGLISH: early 17th century.
M.270-1923

21 WATCH
Signed: *Eduardus East Londini.*
Case and dial of painted enamel and
gilt brass.
ENGLISH: about 1640.
Bequeathed by Miss Charlotte
Frances Gerard
14-1888

22 WATCH AND PAIR-CASE
Signed: *William Knottesford,
London.* Pierced and engraved gold.
ENGLISH: (inner case), London
hallmarks for 1683-84, goldsmith's
mark, crowned ND in monogram;
(pair-case), London, 1695-96,
goldsmith's mark, RB.
Brooke Gift
298-1864

23 WATCH AND PAIR-CASE
Enamelled and engraved gold; the
movement renewed.
ENGLISH: mid 17th century.
64-1896

*24 WATCH AND PAIR-CASE
Enamelled gold; the movement, dial
and silver pair-case later. Engraved
on the pair-case are the Stuart Royal
Arms in Garter, with crested helm
and supporters, and monogram C.R.
with the defaced inscription: *This
watch was a present from ye King to
The Earl of Menteith.*
ENGLISH: early 17th century.
It would appear that the watch
belonged originally to Charles I
(beheaded 1649), and was later
presented by Charles II to William
Graham, 19th Earl of Menteith
(1661-94).
446-1884

25 WATCH
Signed: *Simon Hackett Londini.*
Enamel and gilt brass.
ENGLISH: mid 17th century.
74-1866

26 WATCH
Signed: *Markwick Londini.* Silver.
Pair-case of brass, covered with
tortoiseshell set with silver-gilt studs
and plaques.
ENGLISH: late 17th century.
Goldsmith's mark, W.F.
1148-1893

27 WATCH
Signed: *Jose(ph)Knibb London.*
Engraved and pierced silver.
ENGLISH: second half of 17th
century.
1138-1905

28 WATCH
Signed: *Quare London.* Engraved
and pierced silver.
Pair-case of brass, originally leather-
covered, studded with silver.
ENGLISH: second half of 17th
century.
Alfred Williams Hearn Gift
M.131-1923

29 WATCH
Signed: *Josephus Quash Londini.*
Engraved silver.
ENGLISH: mid 17th century.
122-1908

30 WATCH
Signed: *Eduardus East Londini.*
Engraved and pierced silver, with
gilt brass dial.
ENGLISH: mid 17th century.
Schloss Collection, Paris
200-1908

31 WATCH AND PAIR-CASE
Signed: *Johannes Bayes Londini.*
Silver, parcel-gilt, pierced and
engraved. Pair-case of brass covered
with tortoiseshell set with silver-gilt.
ENGLISH: third quarter of 17th
century.
395-1888

32 WATCH
Signed: *Simon Hackett Londini fecit.*
Engraved and pierced silver.
ENGLISH: mid 17th century.
7-1894

Case 1 Board E

WATCH BALANCE BRIDGES, WATCH KEYS, AND SEALS:
17th and 18th centuries.

All seals are intaglios, that is, the design is cut into the surface of the metal or stone, so that the device appears in relief on the impression.

33 WATCH
Signed: *Henry Terold of Ipswich Fecit.* Silver, chased in relief.
ENGLISH: about 1640.
M.61-1954

34 WATCH AND PAIR-CASE
Signed: *Fr. Stamper London.* Silver, the pair-case of brass covered with tortoiseshell inlaid with silver.
ENGLISH: late 17th century.
46-1905

35 WATCH
Signed: *Ric Colston London.* Silver. Pair-case of brass, covered with tortoiseshell inlaid with silver, including the arms of Strickland.
ENGLISH: late 17th century.
Brooke Gift
635-1864

36-46 WATCH BALANCE BRIDGES
Silver and silvered brass, pierced and engraved.
FRENCH: 17th and 18th century.
396-398-1878

47-57 WATCH-KEYS OF VARIOUS MATERIALS
WEST EUROPEAN: 16th-19th century.
5752-1859, 851-1864, M.216-1919, 1098-1868, 844e-1864, 328a-1897, 844a-1864, 1098a-1868, 556b-1901, M.20-1957, M.21-1957

58 SEAL
Enamelled gold, engraved with a running greyhound on a wreath, the crest of Smith of Wiltshire, and inscribed: *Pray for J.S.*
ENGLISH: about 1600.
Given by Dame Joan Evans, P.P.S.A.
M.96-1962

59 SEAL
Gold; arms of Brooke impaling Vaughan or Parry.
ENGLISH: late 17th century.
Brooke Gift
692-1864

60 SEAL
Enamelled gold, set with a spinel ruby intaglio of a laureate classical head.
ENGLISH: second half of 17th century.
Dug up in 1950 on the site of new government offices in Whitehall, and given by H.M. Ministry of Works.
M.61-1953

61 SEAL
Quartz intaglio bust of Galileo; gold mount.
ITALIAN: the intaglio 17th century; the mount later.
Given by Miss Anna Newton, a collateral descendant of Sir Isaac Newton, its former owner.
1632-1903

62 SEAL
Gold; unidentified coat of arms.
ENGLISH: last third of 17th century.
Given by Dame Joan Evans, P.P.S.A.
M.235-1975

63 SEAL
Gold; unidentified coat of arms.
ENGLISH: last third of 17th century.
Given by Dame Joan Evans, P.P.S.A.
M.237-1975

64 SEAL
Gold; arms of a female member of the Heningham family of Suffolk.
ENGLISH: late 17th century.
S.H.J. Johnson Bequest
M.2-1958

65 SEAL
Sapphire intaglio of the arms of Craddock of Staffordshire; gold mount.
ENGLISH: late 17th century.
623-1894

66 SEAL
Sard intaglio of the arms of Craye, of Wickford, Isle of Ely; gold mount.
ENGLISH: early 18th century.
Given by Mill Stephenson Esq., F.S.A.
M.832-1927

67 SEAL
Cornelian intaglio of an unidentified coat of arms; enamelled gold mount.
FRENCH or GERMAN: late 17th century.
Given by Dame Joan Evans, P.P.S.A.
M.104-1975

68 SEAL
Cornelian intaglio, possibly of Diomedes and the Palladium; enamelled gold mount.
The intaglio ROMAN: 2nd or 3rd century AD; the mount 2nd half of 17th century.
Bernal Collection
2287-1855

69 SEAL
Bloodstone intaglio of St. Peter in a
boat, drawing a net; gold mount.
ITALIAN: about 1780.
The handle of the seal adapted to
make it appear that the piece is an
unused Ring of the Fisherman, that
is, a ring with which every Pope is
invested on election, set with an
intaglio such as this and engraved
with his name. On the Pope's death
the ring is formally broken.
The adaptation probably pre-dates
the acquisition of the piece as a ring
by Edmund Waterton, the antiquary
whose collection was largely acquired
by the Museum in 1871.
749-1871

70 SEAL
Cornelian intaglio of the arms of
Clarke, of Gloucestershire and
London; gold mount.
ENGLISH: early 18th century.
Given by Mill Stephenson, Esq.,
F.S.A.
M.833-1927

71 SEAL
Crystal intaglio of Venus and Cupid;
gold mount.
ENGLISH: early 18th century.
Brooke Gift
694-1864

72 SEAL
Amethystine quartz intaglio of Zeus;
gold mount.
ENGLISH: early 18th century.
Given by Mill Stephenson Esq.,
F.S.A.
M.835-1927

73 SEAL
Crystal intaglio of the arms of
Barbor, of Stamford, London, or
Bury St. Edmunds; gold mount.
ENGLISH: 18th century.
Given by Miss M. Blencowe
890-1894

CASE 1
BOARD B
NO 12

CASE 1
BOARD C
NO. 24

CASE 1
BOARD B
NO. 14

OBJECTS OF VERTU:
16th-early 18th century
The term is used to denote small items of luxury

WATCHES (mainly DUTCH):
17th century

FRENCH WATCHES:
17th century

1 CUP AND COVER
Agate, mounted in enamelled gold.
FRENCH: mid 17th century.
870-1882

2 CUP
The bowl agate, the stem formed by a silver-gilt female figure with a dog; the foot, also silver-gilt, enriched with rubies and emeralds set in openwork silver foliage.
GERMAN: first half of 18th century.
868-1882
Nos. 1 & 2, Jones Collection

3 BOX
Crystal, with enamelled gold mounts.
FRENCH: 17th century.
405-1854

4 SHIP
Ivory, with gold rigging and enamelled gold rails; gold mounts set with rose-cut diamonds.
GERMAN: second half of 17th century.
Bequeathed by Dr. W.L. Hildburgh
M.343-1956

5 CASKET
Silver-gilt, mounted with emeralds in enamelled settings.
SOUTH GERMAN: 17th century.
Alfred Williams Hearn Gift
M.114-1923

6 LION RAMPANT
Gold and enamel lion on heliotrope rock work base and ebonised stand.
SOUTH GERMAN: 16th century.
Lent anonymously

7 CYLINDRICAL BOX AND COVER
Enamelled gold, with brilliant-cut diamonds in silver settings and four rubies.
GERMAN (Saxony): about 1710.
Made by Johann Melchior Dinglinger (1664-1731).
Given by Dame Joan Evans, P.P.S.A.
M.121-1975

8 WATCH
Signed: *Claude Pascal fecit A La Haye.* Pierced and engraved gold over enamel.
DUTCH: third quarter of 17th century.
Lent from the Salting Bequest
M.561-1910

9 WATCH
Signed: *Claude Pascal A La Haye.* Enamelled and gilt pierced brass.
DUTCH: mid 17th century.
2362-1855

10 WATCH AND PAIR-CASE
Signed: *Benjamin Lysle fecit Rotterdã.* Silver, chased in relief.
Pair-case of leather-covered brass studded with silver.
DUTCH: mid 17th century.
2357-1855

11 WATCH
Signed: *Pieter Visbach IIaghe.* Enamelled and gilt brass.
DUTCH: mid 17th century.
2370-1855
Nos. 9-11, Bernal Collection

12 WATCH
Signed: *Mathys Bockels Haerlm.* Silver and silver-gilt; partly filigree.
DUTCH: mid 17th century.
43-1876

13 WATCH-CASE
Enamelled and gilt brass.
TURKISH (Constantinople): second half of 17th century.
425-1889

14 WATCH
Signed: *Gribelin A Blois.* Engraved gilt brass and silver.
FRENCH: dated 1614.
1066-1853

15 WATCH
Crystal and gilt brass.
FRENCH: early 17th century.
1669-1855

16 WATCH
Signed: *Charles Perras A Bloys.* Enamelled gilt brass.
FRENCH: early 17th century.
Bernal Collection
2353-1855

17 WATCH
Signed: *Sonnerau A La Rochelle.* Crystal and gilt brass.
FRENCH: early 17th century.
278-1894

18 WATCH
Signed: *Charles Perras A Bloys.* Engraved silver and gilt brass.
FRENCH: early 17th century.
Lent from the Salting Bequest
M.559-1910

19 WATCH
Signed: *H.G.R.* (mark of Hans Reinhold of Strasburg).
Agate and enamelled gold, set with garnets.
FRENCH: second quarter of 17th century.
2360-1855

*20 WATCH
Signed: *N.R.* Crystal and cast and chased brass.
FRENCH: first half of 17th century.
2356-1855
Nos. 19 & 20, Bernal Collection

21 WATCH (inside pair-case)
Signed: *Estienne Hubert A Rouen.* Silver and gilt brass. Pair-case of leather-covered brass studded with silver.
FRENCH: second half of 17th century.
M.135-1923

FRENCH WATCHES:
about 1640-1700

22 WATCH
Signed: *N. Lemmaindre A Blois.*
Silver and gilt brass.
FRENCH: first half of 17th century.
M.132-1923
Nos. 21 & 22, Alfred Williams Hearn
Gift

23 WATCH
Signed: *C. Cameel A Strasburg.*
Engraved silver and gilt brass.
FRENCH: early 17th century.
2354-1855

24 WATCH
Signed: *Pierre Combret A Lyon.*
Silver case formed as a cockle-shell
and engraved silver and gilt brass
dial.
FRENCH: first half of 17th
century.
2364-1855
Nos. 23 & 24, Bernal Collection

25 WATCH AND PAIR-CASE
Signed: *G. Seney orloger du Roi A
Rouen.* Engraved gilt brass and
crystal. Silver pair-case.
FRENCH: first half of 17th century.
1668-1855

26 WATCH
Signed: *Noel Hubert A Rouen.*
Engraved and pierced silver and
gilt brass.
FRENCH: early 17th century.
Bernal Collection
2363-1855

27 WATCH
Signed: *Charles Barras A Bloys.*
Engraved silver.
FRENCH: early 17th century.
394-1888

28 WATCH
Signed: *Nicolas Gando.* Engraved
silver with enamel dial.
FRENCH: third quarter of 17th
century.
Lent from the Salting Bequest
M.562-1910

*29 WATCH
Signed: *Du Val A Paris.* Copper,
embossed and formerly gilt.
FRENCH: late 17th century.
Evan Roberts Gift
M.177-1915

*30 WATCH
Signed: *Goullons A Paris.* Enamelled
copper-gilt. The enamelled decora-
tion, which includes the Virgin and
Child and portraits of Louis XIII and
Cardinal de Richelieu, attributed to
Henri Toutin (1614-1683).
FRENCH: about 1640.
7543-1861

31 WATCH-CASE
Painted enamel on gold; the
Adoration of the Magi. Mounted
in gold as a brooch in the mid
19th century.
FRENCH: about 1660-70.
M.35-1971

32 WATCH
Signed: *D. Millard A Paris.* Chased
silver.
FRENCH: about 1700.
1363-1904

33 WATCH
Signed: *Du Hamel A Paris.*
Enamelled gold.
FRENCH: mid 17th century.
Schloss Collection
205-1908

34 WATCH
Signed: *H. Collomby A Huninguen*
(Alsace). Enamelled copper.
FRENCH: second half of 17th
century.
Halliburton Collection
636-1868

35 WATCH AND PAIR-CASE
Signed: *Pierre Paris A Nantes.*
Chased silver. Pair-case of leather-
covered brass, studded in silver.
FRENCH: second half of 17th
century.
Shoppee Collection
556-1901

36 WATCH
Signed: *Phillippe Greban A Paris.*
Engraved and pierced silver.
FRENCH: second half of 17th
century.
Brooke Gift
300-1864

37 WATCH
Signed: *Gribelin A Paris.* Chased
brass, formerly gilt.
FRENCH: late 17th century.
139-1907

38 WATCH
Signed: *Vincent Constentin A
Dieppe.* Engraved and chased
silver.
FRENCH: second half of 17th
century.
Schloss Collection
203-1908

39 WATCH
Signed: *Iosve Panier A Paris.* Chased
brass, formerly gilt.
FRENCH: about 1700.
M.93-1909

SWISS WATCHES:
about 1600-1700

40 WATCH
Signed: *Henry Ester.* Silver and
copper-gilt, in the form of a swan.
FRENCH or SWISS (Ester's
nationality is disputed): about 1600.
758-1864

41 WATCH AND PAIR-CASE
Signed: *Meylin a Zurich.* Chased
silver. The decoration of the pair-
case includes the mounted figure of
William III, King of England
(reigned 1689-1702).
SWISS: about 1700. Goldsmith's
mark, A H crowned.
464-1880

42 WATCH
Signed: *Pierre Duhamel* (Geneva).
Case of copper-gilt, enamelled by
Pierre Huaud (père).
SWISS: 1680.
2371-1855

43 WATCH AND PAIR-CASE
The movement signed: *Jean de
Choudens* (Geneva). Copper-gilt case,
enamelled and signed: *Les deux frère
huaut pintre de son A.E. a berlin*
(Jean Pierre and Ami Huaud of
Geneva). Pair-case of leather-covered
brass studded with gilt brass.
SWISS: probably between 1682 and
1686. 2361-1855
Nos. 42 & 43, Bernal Collection

44 WATCH
Case of copper-gilt enamelled with
scenes including Roman Charity,
and signed: *Les deux freres Huaud
Les jeunes* (Jean Pierre and Ami
Huaud of Geneva).
SWISS: probably between 1682 and
1686.
Joicey Bequest
M.208-1919

45 WATCH
Case of copper-gilt enamelled with
scenes including Roman Charity,
and signed: *Huaud Le puisné fecit*
(Jean Pierre Huaud of Geneva).
SWISS: about 1680 (the movement
later).
From the old Geological Museum,
Jermyn Street
4858-1901

46 WATCH
The movement signed: *Baccuet.* Case
of copper-gilt enamelled by Jean
Pierre and Ami Huaud of Geneva
with scenes including Roman
Charity.
SWISS: about 1686.
Given by Miss G.M. Pratt
M.3-1957

47 THE HOPE VASE   9
Bloodstone cup; silver-gilt base;
enamelled gold mounts; representing
the legend of Perseus and
Andromeda.
Designed in about 1854 by Louis-
Constant Sévin (1821-1888); the
hardstone carved by J.V. Morel
(1794-1860), the head of the firm
responsible for making the piece.
FRENCH (Paris): about 1854-55; the
base of the hardstone signed:
MOREL/1855.
Executed for Henry Thomas Hope
(1808-1862), collector and luminary of
the Society of Arts, and member of
the jury for the goldsmithing section
in the great Exhibition of 1851. The
two putti perched on the rim of the
cup hold globes (from Hope's
armorials) and his family motto: *AT
SPES NON FRACTA.*
The vase was exhibited at the Paris
Universal Exhibition of 1855 by J.-
V.Morel, goldsmith and lapidary,
who was awarded a gold medal by
the jury.
Lent anonymously

10

48 NAUTILUS-SHELL CUP
The shell (damaged) engraved with
insects and scrolls in the manner of
Jean Bellekin (1597-1636) of
Amsterdam. Mounted in gold,
enamelled with black insects and
scrolls on a white ground.
Probably DUTCH: about 1610-30.
M.179-1978

**49 TWO-HANDLED CUP
AND COVER**
Gold, engraved with the arms of Sir
William Bowes of Streatlam Castle,
Co. Durham (1389-1460?).
ENGLISH: London hallmarks for
1675-76; maker's mark, IB above a
crescent and two pellets.
Lent anonymously

**50 TWO-HANDLED CUP
AND COVER**
Gold, engraved with the English
Royal Arms and the Arms of the City
of Edinburgh.
SCOTTISH: about 1750; maker's
mark, KD.
Lent anonymously

**51 TRAVELLING CUTLERY
SET**
With box for condiments and an egg
cup. Three coloured gold and
platinum.
SOUTH GERMAN: third quarter of
18th century.
Lent anonymously

*52 NAUTILUS CUP
Nautilus shell mounted in gold, set
with onyx, chalcedony and paste
intaglios of Eros, Hercules, Diana,
Roman soldiers, and Bacchic scenes,
attributed to the Italian workshop of
the Pichler family; the base and
cover mother-of-pearl.
POLISH (Warsaw): signed: *J.
MARTIN FAIT A VARSOVIE LE 26
AOUT 1770.*
From 1769-91 Jean Martin was Court
Jeweller to King Stanislaus
Augustus (1764-95) in Warsaw. The
cup, one of Martin's first
commissions from the King, is
recorded in the royal accounts as
having been ordered in 1770; it was
clearly designed as a vehicle for
cameos.
M.281-1921

*53 CLOCK-WATCH
Gilt metal, with mother-of-pearl
medallion set with two onyx cameos of
the Roman Emperors Augustus
Caesar (died 14 AD) and Vespasian
(died 79 AD), on gilt trophies; in the
centre, a bust of Minerva mounted in
gold; on the summit, a crown set with
rose-cut diamonds; the whole set
round with coloured stones.
GERMAN (Zerbst and Hall): the
watch signed inside: *Du Thuillay A
Hall;* the medallion signed inside:
J.S. Meyer, Zerbst, 1788.
Johann Salomon Mayer of Zerbst
(Anhalt), goldsmith, became master
in 1763.
7677-1861

54 TWO GOA-STONE HOLDERS
Pierced and chased gold egg-shaped
containers, with scrolling decoration,
on gilt metal tripod stands.
? ENGLISH (London): late 17th or
early 18th century.
Goa-stones, glossy balls concocted
from bezoar-stones (accretions from
the stomach or intestines of
ruminatives), ambergris, musk,
precious stones and pearls ground
into powder, gold leaf and other
ingredients, were invented by a
Florentine lay-brother in the
Portuguese colony of Goa in the
seventeenth century. Much prized in
Europe as a prophylactic and
medicine, they were taken both
externally and internally. For
internal consumption, scrapings
were taken from the balls and
dissolved in a liquid.
The stones were costly and were
clearly thought to merit expensive
containers; there is a similar holder
in the Wellcome Collections, Science
Museum, and another in the Hull
Grundy Collection, British Museum.
781, 782-1891

55 GOA-STONE HOLDER
Pierced gold spherical container, set
with ruby pastes; inside is a Goa-
stone, showing signs of having been
scraped.
INDO-PERSIAN (Moghul): 17th
century.
Given by the Royal Asiatic Society
M.604-1924

PERSIAN ENAMELS:
19th century

SEALS AND OBJECTS OF VERTU:
mid 18th-early 19th century

56 PAIR OF EARRINGS
Painted enamel on gold.
PERSIAN: third quarter of 19th century.
Given by Mr. Dennis Martin
M.90 & a-1969

57 SEAL
Bloodstone, mounted in a six-sided handle of enamelled gold; the seal of Charles James Mathews, actor and dramatist (1803-1878).
The seal ENGLISH, the handle PERSIAN: 19th century.
Jones Collection
936-1882

58 KNIFE-SHEATH
Velvet-covered wood, mounted in enamelled gold.
PERSIAN: early 19th century.
888-1874

59 TWO MEDALLIONS
Painted enamel on gold, inscribed.
PERSIAN: 19th century.
8454-5-1863

60 PAIR OF EARRINGS
Enamelled gold, set with pearls and precious stones.
PERSIAN: about 1840.
515 & a-1874

61 PAIR OF MEDALLIONS
Painted enamel on gold, representing the Waq-waq tree, on which grew the heads of men and beasts.
PERSIAN: third quarter of 19th century.
Given by Mr. Dennis Martin
M.91 & a-1969

The male fashion for wearing fob seals pendent from the waist, which reached its peak early in the nineteenth century, is reflected in the objects on this board. Most examples were designed to be worn in this manner, though a few (such as no. 75) are desk seals. Women took to hanging seals on their neckchains in the 1820s and 30s.

62 SEAL
Cornelian intaglio bust of Achilles, after a work by Charles Brown (1749-95) which was exhibited at the Royal Academy 1771; gold mount.
ENGLISH: ? after 1771.
Robinson Collection
141-1879

63 SWIVEL SEAL
Bloodstone intaglio probably showing the embarkation of Louis XVIII in France on the restoration of the Bourbon monarchy.
Signed: *Parry F* (ecit); gold mount
ENGLISH: after 1815, the seal handle about 1760, and presumably re-used.
Parry was an English gem-engraver working in the first half of the 19th century.
Bernal Collection
2285-1865

64 SEAL
Crystal intaglio with a coat of arms, possibly of Hoskins, of Oxted, Surrey; gold mount.
ENGLISH: mid 18th century.
119-1864

65 SEAL
Revolving three-sided crystal, one intaglio face with Diana, the second with Sir Kenrick Clayton's monogram, his wife's initials on the third with his coat of arms (he succeeded to the title in 1744); gold mount. Sir Kenrick Clayton died in 1769; his wife in 1774.
ENGLISH: mid 18th century.
Given by Mrs O.C. Leveson-Gower
M.6-1972

66 SEAL
Cornelian intaglio with the arms of Hutchinson, later Synge-Hutchinson, of Castle Sallah, Wicklow, Ireland.
ENGLISH: late 18th century.
Brooke Gift
689-1864

67 SEAL
Sard intaglio with the arms of ? Blackmore of London; gold mount.
ENGLISH: late 18th century.
M.836-1927

68 SEAL
Agate intaglio with the arms of ? Baker, of Battle, Sussex; gold mount.
ENGLISH: late 18th century.
M.830-1927
Nos. 64 & 65, given by Mill Stephenson Esq., F.S.A.

69 SEAL
Cornelian intaglio of the head of Antinous; gold mount.
ENGLISH: late 18th century.
Brooke Gift
693-1864

70 SEAL
Cornelian intaglio with the arms of Leslie and Abernethy; gold mount.
ENGLISH: late 18th century.
Given by Mill Stephenson Esq., F.S.A.
M.843-1927

71 SEAL
Cornelian intaglio with the arms of Townsend, of Ellerton Hall, Stafford; gold mount.
ENGLISH: late 18th century.
Given by Miss Anna Newton
1635-1903

72 SEAL
Cornelian intaglio of the head of Mars, after the original by Charles Brown exhibited at the Royal Academy, 1781; gold mount.
ENGLISH: after 1781.
Bequeathed by Mrs. A.B. Woodcroft
477-1903

73 SEAL
Cornelian intaglio with a coat of
arms impaling Ingleby or
Spendelow; gold mount.
ENGLISH: early 19th century.
Given by Mill Stephenson, Esq.,
F.S.A.
M.834-1927

*74 SEAL
Revolving three-sided topaz, one
intaglio face with the Battle of
Trafalgar (1805); gold mount.
ENGLISH: about 1815.
Bequeathed by Miss P.M. Sheward
M.105-1945

75 TRIPLE SEAL
In the form of an ivory hand clasping
a cylinder, a seal at each end; with a
cuff of gold, mounted with moss
agate, its base also a seal.
ENGLISH: about 1820.
M.8-1972

76 SEAL
Cornelian intaglio of a female head,
mounted in gold with enamelled
forget-me-not decoration; bloodstone
handle in the form of a parrot.
ENGLISH: about 1820.
Given by Dame Joan Evans, P.P.S.A.
M.236-1975

77 SWIVEL SEAL
Jasper intaglio with the initials
FB and the arms of Boscawen
impaling Glanville for Frances
Glanville (d.1805), who married
in 1742 Admiral Edward Boscawen
(1711-1761); gold mount.
ENGLISH: about 1760.
Given by Mrs. O.C. Leveson Gower
M.52-1974

78 SEAL
Onyx intaglio of a Bacchante; the
mount of hardstones, diamond
sparks, coloured stones and gold and
silver, in the form of a blackamoor
with a turban. The intaglio late
ROMAN: perhaps 2nd century AD,
the mount probably GERMAN: third
quarter of 18th century.
Bernal Collection
2286-1855

79 SEAL
Cornelian intaglio of the Priapic
Festival, after a lost original
formerly in the Stosch Collection;
gold mount set with point-cut
diamonds, rubies, emeralds; and
three miniatures in the manner of
Van Blarenberghe, of a French Royal
accouchement, the acknowledgement
of the child, and a Royal procession.
FRENCH: late 18th century; illegible
mark on the suspension ring.
Given by Dame Joan Evans, P.P.S.A.
M.59-1962

80 SEAL
Sardonyx intaglio bust of Ceres
veiled, attributed by Bracci to the
Roman gem-engraver Flavio Sirletti,
though the Raspe-Tassie catalogue
(no.1882) suggests that it is by L.
Natter (1705-1763); gold mount.
WEST EUROPEAN: second third of
18th century.
Medina and Bessborough Collections
Lent from the Salting Bequest
M.557a-1910

*81 KNIFE
The handle of enamelled gold
bearing a partly-defaced inscription,
of which only: *IENNE BERLV ...
1637,* can be read. On the blade is the
cutler's mark, a fleur-de-lis over a
chevron, and the dagger mark of the
London Cutlers' Company.
The handle FRENCH or ENGLISH:
dated 1637; the blade English; early
18th century.
M.11-1971

82 SCISSORS CASE
Painted enamel flowers on gold.
DUTCH: mid 17th century.
29-1866

83 WRITING TABLETS
The tablets ivory, in enamelled gold
covers set with emeralds and rubies.
Outside, Joseph thrust into the well
by his brethren and Joseph and his
brethren on the Journey into Egypt;
inside, two landscape scenes.
DUTCH: second half of 17th century.
Given by Mrs Carew from the
Farquhar Matheson Collection
M.283-1921

84 SEALING-WAX CASE
Silver-gilt, decorated with enamel
and surmounted by a polychromed
ivory bust said to be of Louis XIV
(1638-1715).
Possibly GERMAN: about 1670.
Webb Collection
247-1874

85 SCENT FLASK
Gold, enamelled with birds and
flowers.
DUTCH: mid 17th century.
221-1865

CASE 2
BOARD C
NO. 20

CASE 2
BOARD H
NO. 53

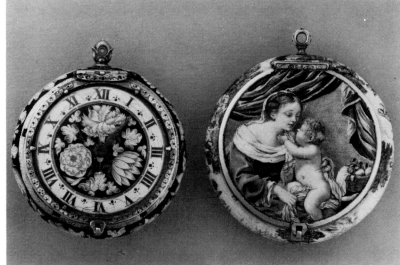

CASE 2
BOARD D
NO. 30

CASE 2
BOARD K
NO. 74

CASE 2
BOARD H
NO. 52

CASE 2
BOARD K
NO. 81

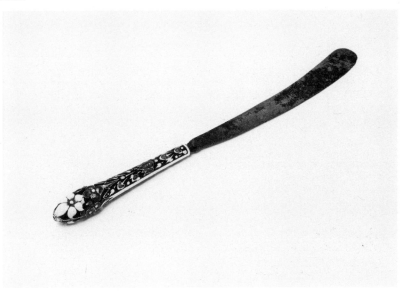

FRENCH WATCHES
AND OTHER
GOLDSMITH'S WORK:
2nd half of 18th century

14

By the early eighteenth century watches were worn on elaborate chatelaines formed of decorative panels suspended from belt hooks (a later example is shown as no.5). Besides watches, chatelaines supported watch keys, seals, etuis (cases containing articles such as toothpicks, scissors, bodkins, pencils and ivory writing tablets) and other small 'toys' or trinkets.

*1 ETUI
Coloured gold.
FRENCH (Paris): 1771-5. Maker's mark of Nicolas Durier.
Paris marks for 1768-75 and 1771-2.
Jones Collection
941-1882

2 WATCH
Signed: *Vauchez A Paris*. Enamelled and coloured gold.
FRENCH: late 18th century.
Joicey Bequest
M.196-1919

3 WATCH
Signed: *Herbeau A Paris*. Enamelled and coloured gold.
FRENCH: second half of 18th century.
Joicey Bequest
M.285-1919

4 WATCH
Signed: *J. Romilly A Paris*. Coloured gold.
FRENCH: second half of 18th century. Casemaker's mark: IT crowned.
Given by Miss Elizabeth A. Chilcote
373-1908

*5 WATCH AND CHATELAINE
Signed: *Julien le Roy A Paris*. Gold set with topazes and table- and brilliant-cut diamonds.
FRENCH: about 1760.
Bequeathed by Mrs. Hornby Lewis
M.16-1932

6 WATCH
Signed: *Vauchez A Paris*. Enamelled copper-gilt, set with pastes.
FRENCH: late 18th century.
1301-1871

7 WATCH
Signed: *L'Epine A Paris*. Enamelled and coloured gold, set with pastes.
FRENCH: late 18th century.
Casemaker's mark: DL.
Evan Roberts Gift
M.165-1915

8 WATCH
Signed: *Gregson Horr du Roy A Paris*. Enamelled gold.
FRENCH (Paris): mark for 1789.
Casemaker's mark of Jean-Jacques Le Bain.
Joicey Bequest
M.195-1919

9 SEALING-WAX CASE
Enamelled gold.
FRENCH (Paris): 1773-81. Maker's mark unidentified.
Paris marks for 1768-75, and 1773-4, and 1775-81.
Given by Mrs. Samuel S. Joseph
M.175-1941

The boxes shown in cases 3-7, though often denominated snuff boxes, were made for a variety of purposes. Some were intended for sweetmeats, face patches, rouge or powder; others, bearing portraits of the donor or recipient, represent a traditional type of royal or diplomatic gift. Most boxes however carried snuff, the powdered tobacco which was in vogue from the seventeenth to the nineteenth century. Gold snuff boxes were made in Italy before 1636, but most surviving specimens date from the eighteenth and early nineteenth centuries. All the resources of the goldsmith's and lapidary's art were lavished on the boxes, which were a fashionable accessory for both men and women.

The complex system of marking French plate in force before the Revolution of 1789 derived from the controls which were legally exercised by a variety of officials and contracted tax-collectors.
The addition of later marks to pre-Revolutionary gold plate (and jewellery) indicates that the pieces concerned were subject to French census controls or were re-submitted by importers, dealers or auctioneers to their local assay office as a necessary preliminary to sale in France.

Case 3 Board B

FRENCH BOXES:
about 1747-1781

10 BOX
Coloured gold, with enamels of
peasant interiors after
David Teniers I (1610-1690).
FRENCH (Paris): 1759-62. Maker's
mark of Jean Ducrollay.
Paris marks for 1756-62 and 1759-60.
Presented to David Garrick by the
Duke of Parma in 1764. A portrait
under the lid perhaps early 19th
century.
Given by Mrs. Wilhemina Caroline
Garrick
310-1885

*11 BOX
Gold, set with panels of sealing-wax
red lacquer, on which are mounted
medallions of amorini and other Neoclassical motifs.
FRENCH (Paris): 1769-1781. Maker's
mark of R.-J. Auguste.
Paris marks for 1768-1775, 1769-71,
1770-71, 1775-81; a provincial
countermark for 1781-3, and later
marks for 1819-38 and 1838 onwards.
W.W. Aston Bequest
M.137-1917

*12 BOX
Enamelled gold.
FRENCH (Paris): 1747-50. Maker's
mark of Paul Robert.
Paris marks for 1744-50, 1747-8, the
discharge mark for old works for
1756-62, and French import marks
for 1838 onwards.
Given by Mrs Samuel S. Joseph
M.166-1941

*13 BOX
Gold, with enamel paintings of
figures in landscapes, signed: *Le
Sueur.*
A miniature in the lid inscribed:
*John, Marquis of Granby to Brice
Fisher Esq., 1764.*
FRENCH (Paris): 1750-56. Maker's
mark of Jean Ducrollay.
Paris marks for 1750-56, 1750-51,
1756-62, 1762-68.
Jones Bequest
910-1882

14 BOX
Coloured gold, with trophies.
FRENCH (Paris): 1763-68. Maker's
mark of D.F. Poitreau.
Paris marks for 1762-68 and 1763-64.
W.W. Aston Bequest
M.120-1917

15 BOX
Gold, chased with flowers and
ribbons. Inside, a miniature portrait
of Grace Carteret, Countess of Dysart
(1729-55), by C.F. Zincke (1683-1767).
FRENCH (Paris): 1749-50.
Paris marks for 1744-50 and 1749-50.
From Ham House
H.H.460-1948

16 BOX
Coloured gold; chased medallion on
lid.
FRENCH (Paris): 1772-75. Maker's
mark of Pierre-André Barbier.
Paris marks for 1768-75 and 1772-73.
George Mitchell Bequest
175-1878

Case 3 Board C

FRENCH BOXES:
about 1745-1783

17 BOX   15
Coloured gold; medallions with
trophies.
FRENCH (Paris): 1774-81. Maker's
mark of Melchior-René Barre.
Paris marks for 1768-1775, 1774-75
and 1775-81.
George Mitchell Bequest
170-1878

18 BOX
Gold, with paintings in oil of
figures in landscapes, after
Teniers.
FRENCH (Paris): 1781-83. Maker's
mark of J.-F. Garand.
Paris marks for 1780-81, 1781-83 and
1797-1809; marks for 1819-1838.
W.W. Aston Bequest
M.134-1917

19 BOX
Coloured gold, machine-engraved.
FRENCH (Paris): 1771-75. Maker's
mark of J.-J. Barrière.
Paris marks for 1768-75 and 1771-72.
180-1864

20 BOX
Gold, set with panels of Japanese
lacquer.
FRENCH (Paris): 1767-68. Signed:
Drais a Paris (Pierre-François Drais).
Paris marks for 1762-68 and 1767-68.
Acquired with funds from the W.B.
Sutherland Bequest with the aid
of a contribution from Messrs.
S.J. Phillips.
M.38-1956

21 BOX
Gold and mother-of-pearl.
FRENCH (Paris): 1745-46.
Paris marks for 1744-45 and 1745-46.
W.W. Aston Bequest
M.117-1917

Case 3 Board D

FRENCH BOXES:
about 1745-1768

22 BOX
Gold, inlaid with chinoiserie designs
in mother-of-pearl.
FRENCH (Paris): 1749-50. Maker's
mark illegible.
Paris marks for 1744-45 and 1749-50.
Given by Mrs. Samuel S. Joseph
M.168-1941

23 BOX
Coloured gold, chased with land-
scapes.
FRENCH (Paris): 1757-62. Maker's
mark of Jean Ducrollay.
Paris marks for 1757-58 and 1756-62.
Given by Colonel F.R. Waldo-
Sibthorp
1959-1898

24 BOX
Coloured gold, machine-engraved.
FRENCH (Paris): 1767-68. Maker's
mark of J.-J. Barrière.
Paris marks for 1762-68 and 1767-68.
Alfred Williams Hearn Gift
M.121-1923

25 BOX
Coloured gold, with an enamelled
plaque of putti.
FRENCH (Paris): 1765-68. Maker's
mark of J.M. Tiron.
Paris marks for 1765-66 and 1762-68.
156-1878

26 BOX
Gold, inlaid with chinoiserie designs
in mother-of-pearl.
FRENCH (Paris): 1745-50.
Paris marks for 1744-50, 1745-46 and
1746-47.
163-1878
Nos. 25 & 26, George Mitchell
Bequest

Case 3 Board E

FRENCH:
about 1750-1783

27 BOX
Enamelled gold, with hairwork and
miniatures on ivory of the Princesse
de Lorraine (lid), Prince de Lorraine
(bottom), and the Prince de Lambesc,
Duc de Vaudemont, Princesse de
Carignan and Princesse Charlotte,
Abbesse de Remiremont (sides).
FRENCH (Paris): 1781-83. Maker's
mark of L. Cousin.
Paris marks for 1781-82 and 1781-83.
98-1865

28 BOX
Enamelled gold (damaged).
FRENCH (Paris): 1753-56. Maker's
mark of Claude Lissonet.
Paris marks for 1750-56 and 1753-54.
George Mitchell Bequest
265-1878

29 BOX
Enamelled gold, with a miniature of
the Marriage of Perseus and
Andromeda.
FRENCH (Paris): 1777-81. Maker's
mark of L. de Roussy (Roussy du
Nord).
Paris marks for 1775-81 and 1777-78.
M.132-1917

30 BOX
Enamelled gold.
FRENCH (Paris): 1750. Maker's
mark of M.-R. Hallé.
Paris marks for 1744-50 and 1750-52.
M.115-1917
Nos. 29 & 30, W.W. Aston Bequest

31 BOX
Gold, with enamelled subjects after
H.F. Gravelot (1699-1773).
FRENCH (Paris): 1750. Maker's
mark of Pierre-Etienne Buron.
Paris marks for 1744-50 and 1750-56.
Lent anonymously

Case 3 Board F

FRENCH BOXES:
about 1763-1789

32 BOX
Coloured gold.
FRENCH (Paris): 1789-89.
Paris marks for 1783-89, 1787-88, and
1789.
Swedish marks, probably dating
from the early 19th century.
George Mitchell Bequest
174-1878

33 BOX
Coloured gold.
FRENCH (Paris): 1764-65. Maker's
mark of Charles Le Bastier.
Paris marks for 1762-68 and 1764-65.
The interior is numbered 1153.
Lent anonymously

34 BOX
Coloured gold, with trophies.
FRENCH (Paris): 1776-81. Maker's
mark of Jean Louis Désir.
Paris marks for 1775-81 and 1776-67.
Bequeathed by Captain Walter
Dasent, R.N.
M.350-1940

35 BOX
Gold, enamelled and set with a
miniature, surrounded by pastes.
FRENCH (Paris): 1763-68. Maker's
mark of J.-J. Barrière.
Paris marks for 1762-68 and 1763-64.
Given by Mrs. Samuel S. Joseph
M.164-1941

Case 3 Board G

FRENCH BOXES:
about 1740-1781

36 DOUBLE BOX
Agate, mounted in enamelled gold.
FRENCH (Paris): 1740-44. Maker's
mark of Noël Hardivilliers.
Paris marks for 1738-44 and 1740-42.
W.W. Aston Bequest
M.111-1917

37 BOX
Gold, enamelled and set with a
miniature after Rosalba Carriera
(1675-1757).
FRENCH (Paris): 1778-81. Maker's
mark of J.B. Marvint.
Paris marks for 1775-81 and 1778-89;
marks for 1819-38.
Jones Collection
927-1882

38 BOX
Coloured gold, set with a miniature
portrait of a lady by C.F. Zincke
(1683-1767), dated 1717.
FRENCH (Paris): 1771-72. Maker's
mark of Charles Alexandre
Bouillerot.
Paris marks for 1768-75, and 1771-72.
George Mitchell Bequest
151-1878

39 BOX
Gold and mother-of-pearl; shell
motifs.
FRENCH: (Paris): 1743-44.
Paris marks for 1738-44 and 1743-44.
Lent anonymously

Case 3 Board H

FRENCH WATCHES AND OTHER ARTICLES:
about 1748-1790

40 FRUIT-KNIFE
Gold and steel blades, with a gold-
mounted lacquer handle.
FRENCH (Paris): 1760-62.
Paris marks for 1756-62 and 1760-61;
warranty mark for 1847 onwards.
Jones Collection
861-1882

41 WATCH
Signed: *Vauchez A Paris*. Enamelled
copper-gilt studded with pastes.
FRENCH: late 18th century.
Bequeathed by Miss Louisa M.
Westmacott
309-1885

42 WATCH
Signed: *Lesser A Paris*. Copper-gilt,
enamelled and set with pastes.
FRENCH: about 1790. Casemaker's
mark: LETO.
181-1864

43 WATCH
Signed: *Jln Le Roy A Paris*.
Enamelled and coloured gold.
FRENCH: mid 18th century.
M.200-1919

**44 PAIR OF EMBOSSED
PLAQUES**
Gilt metal; Rococo compositions with
figures.
FRENCH: mid 18th century.
M.309 & a-1919

45 EMBOSSED PLAQUE
Gilt metal; a love scene.
FRENCH (Paris): 1748. Signed and
dated by P. Suther (a Swede working
in Paris).
M.310-1919
Nos. 43-45, Joicey Bequest

*46 MEMORANDUM BOOK
Panels of Japanese lacquer, mounted
in gold, with a gold pencil. Inside,
enamelled miniatures, probably 19th
century, of Ninon de Lenclos (1616-
1706) and Elizabeth Hamilton,
Comtesse de Grammont (1641-1708).
FRENCH (Paris): 1761-62. Maker's
mark of J.M. Tiron.
Paris marks for 1756-62 and 1761-62.
The pencil marked 1750-56.
Jones Collection
954 & a-1882

17

47 WATCH
Signed: *Nl. Balthazard A Paris*.
Gold; the reverse with an enamelled
figure group, including an artist.
FRENCH: second half of 18th
century. Casemaker's mark, crossed
keys.
1306-1871

48 WATCH
Signed: *Jln Le Roy A Paris*.
Enamelled gold, set with pearls.
FRENCH: late 18th century.
Joicey Bequest
M.189-1919

49 WATCH
Signed: *Jean Fazy*. Coloured gold
and enamelled gilt copper, set with
pastes.
FRENCH: second half of 18th
century.
Bolckow Bequest
742-1890

50 NEEDLE-CASE
Agate, mounted in coloured gold.
FRENCH or ENGLISH: about 1750.
W.T. Johnson Bequest
M.1781-1944

Case 3 Board I

FRENCH BOXES:
about 1762-1790

51 BOX
Tortoise-shell, painted and mounted with gold.
FRENCH (Paris): the gold mounts struck with Paris marks for 1771-81.
Murray Bequest
M.1033-1910

52 BOX
Vernis Martin, mounted in gold, set with a miniature of the Empress Maria Theresa (1717-1780).
FRENCH (Paris): 1762-68.
Paris marks for 1762-68; French mark introduced in 1864 for imported articles.
223-1878

53 BOX
Horn, inlaid and mounted with coloured gold; tortoise-shell lining.
FRENCH (Paris): 1776-81.
Paris marks for 1775-81 and 1776-67.
230-1878
Nos. 52 & 53, George Mitchell Bequest

54 BOX
Lacquer and coloured gold, set with a portrait of a lady, dating about 1710.
FRENCH (Paris): 1776-81.
Paris marks for 1775-81 and 1776-77.
128-1865

55 BOX
Vernis Martin, mounted in gold and lined with tortoise-shell; set with a miniature of a 17th century Countess of Southesk.
FRENCH: late 18th century.
224-1878

56 BOX
Horn, striped with coloured gold, the lid set with an enamelled portrait under glass of a lady, dating about 1760.
FRENCH (Paris): 1768-75.
Paris marks for 1768-75.
229-1878
Nos. 55 & 56, George Mitchell Bequest

Case 3 Board J

FRENCH BOXES:
about 1746-1781

57 BOX
Gold.
Probably FRENCH (Paris): 1746-50.
Maker's mark, PT.
Paris marks for 1744-50 and 1746-47.
W.W. Aston Bequest
M.131-1917

58 BOX
Gold, engraved and enamelled.
FRENCH (Paris): 1753-56. Maker's mark of Noël Hardivilliers.
Paris marks for 1750-56 and 1753-54.
Given by Mrs. Samuel S. Joseph
M.169-1941

59 BOX
Gold.
FRENCH (Paris): 1775-81. Maker's mark of J.-C. Genu.
Paris marks for 1775-81 and 1775-76.
Sold by Granchez at 'Le Petit Dunkerque', a fashionable shop in Paris.
George Mitchell Bequest
168-1878

60 BOX
Silver-gilt and mother-of-pearl.
FRENCH (Paris): 1757-62.
Paris marks for 1756-62 and 1757-58.
M.120-1923

61 BOX
Iron, mounted and overlaid with silver-gilt and mother-of-pearl, set with enamelled plaques.
FRENCH (Paris): 1750-56.
Paris marks for 1750-56.
M.117-1923
Nos. 60 & 61, Alfred Williams Hearn Gift

Case 3 Board K

FRENCH BOXES:
about 1775-1789

62 BOX
Gold, with paintings on ivory under glass of the sale of Cupids.
FRENCH (Paris): 1789. Maker's mark of Jean-François Morand.
Paris marks for 1789.
M.142-1917

63 BOX
Gold, decorated with lacquer and mother-of-pearl, set with a miniature painting by E. Leguay.
FRENCH (Paris): 1775-81. Maker's mark unidentified.
Paris marks for 1775-81 and 1775-76.
M.148-1917
Nos. 62 & 63, W.W. Aston Bequest

64 BOX
Gold, set with panels painted in grisaille.
FRENCH (Paris): 1789. Maker's mark of Jean-François Morand.
Paris marks for 1789.
216-1878

65 BOX
Enamelled gold.
FRENCH (Paris): 1787-89. Maker's mark of J.-E. Blerzy.
Paris marks for 1783-89 and 1787-88.
267-1878
Nos. 64 & 65, George Mitchell Bequest

66 BOX
Gold, set with panels painted in grisaille.
FRENCH: (Paris): 1789. Maker's mark of Jean-François Morand.
Paris marks for 1789.
Given by Mrs. Carew from the Farquhar Matheson Collection
M.306-1921

67 BOX
Gold, chased, enamelled and set with pearls.
FRENCH (Paris): 1785-89. Maker's mark of Pierre-Claude Pottiers.
Paris marks for 1783-89 and 1785-86.
George Mitchell Bequest
266-1878

Case 3 Board L

FRENCH BOXES:
about 1768-89

68 BOX
Enamelled gold, set with a miniature
of a man in a green coat by
J.-B. Weyler (1749-91).
FRENCH (Paris): 1789.
Paris marks for 1783-89 and 1789;
warranty marks for 1838-47.
Given by Mrs. Samuel S. Joseph
M.162-1941

69 BOX
Coloured gold, enamelled and set
with crystals, enclosing a miniature,
a bust of a woman in a yellow dress.
FRENCH (Paris). 1787-89.
Paris marks for 1783-89 and 1787-88;
Paris import mark for 1864 onwards.
Henry L. Florence Bequest
M.228-1917

70 BOX
Enamelled gold, set with rose-cut
diamonds and a 19th century
miniature of the Duchesse de Sully.
FRENCH (Paris): 1783-89. Maker's
mark of J.-E. Blerzy.
Paris marks for 1783-84 and 1783-89;
Viennese duty mark for 1806-7.
George Mitchell Bequest
237-1878

71 BOX
Gold, enamelled and set with panels
of children painted in grisaille.
FRENCH (Paris): 1770-75. Maker's
mark of J.-J. Barrière.
Paris marks for 1768-75 and 1770-71;
warranty marks for 1838-47.
Jones Collection
913-1882

72 BOX
Gold, set with panels of *Vernis
Martin*; the lid set with a late 18th
century enamelled medallion of a
classical subject.
FRENCH (Paris): 1768-75. Maker's
mark of Charles le Bastier.
Paris marks for 1768-75.
George Mitchell Bequest
241-1878

Case 3 Board M

FRENCH BOXES:
about 1781-89

73 BOX
Rock-crystal, mounted in gold, and
set with a miniature signed: *Weiler*
(J-B Weyler 1747-1791).
FRENCH (Paris): 1781-83.
Paris marks for 1781-83 and 1781-82;
warranty marks for 1847 onwards.
M.147-1917

74 BOX
Enamelled gold, set with an enamel
after J-B. Greuze (1725-1805) of a girl
lamenting a dead bird.
FRENCH (Paris): 1783-89. Maker's
mark of A.-G. Turmine.
Paris marks for 1782-83 and 1783-89.
M.145-1917
Nos. 73 & 74, W.W. Aston Bequest

75 BOX
Gold, with panels of amorini painted
in grisaille.
FRENCH (Paris): 1783-89. Maker's
mark of A.-G. Turmine.
Paris marks for 1783-89 and 1783-89.
Jodrell Collection
500-1890

Case 3 Board N

FRENCH BOXES:
about 1775-1830

76 BOX
Tortoise-shell, mounted in gold, set
with a Roman mosaic of two storks,
after the antique.
FRENCH: Paris marks for 1797-1809.
Maker's mark, AT.
Roman mosaics are composed of
minute tesserae of coloured glass or
ceramic.
Given by Mrs. Carew from the
Farquhar Matheson Collection
M.289-1921

77 BOX
Tortoise-shell, japanned and
mounted in gold, set with a painting
of a battle scene under glass.
FRENCH (Paris): 1775-81.
Paris marks for 1775-81; discharge
mark for 1789, possibly indicating
that the box was repaired at this
date.
Murray Bequest
M.1035-1910

78 BOX
Tortoise-shell, mounted in enamelled
gold and set with a Florentine mosaic
of a basket of flowers.
FRENCH: Paris marks for 1797-1809.
Maker's mark of F.N. Duprez.
Florentine mosaic *(commesso di
pietre dure)* is a marquetry of
coloured hardstones.
Given by Mrs. Carew from the
Farquhar Matheson Collection
M.293-1921

79 BOX
Gold, enamelled and set with agate
panels.
FRENCH: Paris marks for 1798-1809.
Maker's mark of Adrien-Jean-
Maximilien Vachette. Inscribed on
the rim: *Vachette, Bijoutier, a Paris*
and *Or a 22 Karats*.
Vachette, well known as a box-maker
under Napoleon, employed craftsmen
whose skills were acquired during the
reign of Louis XVI.
Lent anonymously

80 BOX
Gold, set with panels of Roman glass.
FRENCH: post-Revolutionary Paris
marks and marks for 1819-38.
Maker's mark of Vachette. Inscribed
on the rim: *Vachette Bijer a Paris*
and *22 k.5*.
Lent anonymously

20   **81 BOX**
Mother-of-pearl, studded with gold
discs (piqué work); mounted in
coloured gold and set with applied
cartouches of gardening subjects in
gold.
FRENCH (Paris): about 1750.
Austrian import marks for 1862-72.
George Mitchell Bequest
212-1878

Case 4 Board A

FRENCH WATCHES:
18th century

1 WATCH AND PAIR-CASE
Signed: *De la Vieville a Dieppe.*
Pierced and engraved silver. Pair-
case of leather-covered brass
mounted in silver.
FRENCH: early 18th century.
1379-1901

2 WATCH
Signed: *Le Coeur L'ainé A Paris.*
Enamelled gold.
FRENCH: Paris marks for 1783-4.
Given in accordance with the wishes
of the late Miss Bernardine Hall
M.60-1914

3 WATCH
Silver-gilt and enamelled copper.
FRENCH: second half of 18th
century.
M.245-1919

4 WATCH
Signed: *Gédéon Fontaine.* Coloured
gold with enamelled decoration.
FRENCH: mid 18th century.
Casemaker's mark, RC crowned.
M.284-1919

**5 WATCH AND CHATELAINE
WITH WATCH KEY AND SEAL**
Enamelled gold. Watch signed:
Adamson et Millenet A Paris.
FRENCH: Paris mark for 1775-76.
M.295-1919

6 WATCH AND PAIR-CASE
Signed: *Dumollin A Calais.* Gold
with pair-case of gilt and enamelled
copper.
FRENCH: mid 18th century.
M.258-1919

7 WATCH
Signed: *Jln. Le Roy A Paris.*
Enamelled gold and gilt copper.
FRENCH: mid 18th century.
M.252-1919
Nos. 3-7, Joicey Bequest

8 WATCH
Signed: *Juln. Le Roy A Paris.* Gold
and bloodstone.
FRENCH: about 1760.
Given by Miss G.H. Pratt
M.II-1957

9 WATCH
Signed: *Dardenne à Orleans.* Chased
silver.
FRENCH: second quarter of 18th
century.
H. Batsford Bequest
M.51-1953

10 CALENDAR WATCH
Coloured gold.
FRENCH: late 18th century.
Joicey Bequest
M.249-1919

Case 4 Board B

FRENCH BOXES:
about 1795-1850

11 BOX
Tortoise-shell, mounted in coloured
gold.
FRENCH: about 1820.
Given by Colonel F.R. Waldo-
Sibthorp
1960-1898

12 BOX
Silver, gilt and nielloed. (Niello
is a black composition used to
accentuate engraved designs).
FRENCH: about 1850. Maker's mark
of Louis-Alexandre Bruneau.
Paris warranty mark for 1838
onwards.
Bequeathed by Miss J.A.F.V. Scott
M.2-1964

13 BOX
Gold, enamelled in imitation of
niello; the lid with applied and
enamelled gold flowers, set with rose-
cut diamonds.
FRENCH: about 1840. Paris
warranty marks for 1838 onwards.
262-1878

14 BOX
Gold and painted mother-of-pearl.
FRENCH: post-Revolutionary Paris
marks and marks for 1819-38.
Maker's mark of A.A. Héguin.
Further marks indicate that the box
was later imported into Russia.
213-1878
Nos. 13 & 14, George Mitchell
Bequest

15 BOX
Tortoise-shell, mounted in gold, set
with a Roman mosaic of the Bay of
Naples.
FRENCH: Paris marks for 1797-1809.
Maker's mark, possibly of A.A.
Héguin.
Given by Mrs. Carew from the
Farquhar Matheson Collection
M.297-1921

16 BOX
Tortoise-shell, mounted in gold and
set with a miniature of Venus and
her nymphs.
FRENCH: post-Revolutionary Paris
marks and marks for 1809-19 and
1819-38. Maker's mark of P.A.
Montaubon.
George Mitchell Bequest
202-1878

FRENCH BOXES:
early 19th century

22

17 BOX
Tortoise-shell, set with a Roman
mosaic of the Forum, Rome, in a gold
frame.
FRENCH: Paris warranty mark for
1838-47 on a silver-gilt hinge.
Maker's mark, P.D.O.
Given by Mrs. Carew from the
Farquhar Matheson Collection
M.288-1921

18 BOX
Enamelled gold, set with pearls;
? Minerva and Ceres.
FRENCH: 1804-09.
Post-Revolutionary Paris mark and
marks for 1797-1809. Maker's mark,
ELB. Inscribed: *446/ No. 13/
Marguerite, Joaillier de la Couronne
de leurs Majtes Imples et Royles*
[Napoleon I (1769-1821) and his
Empress, Josephine].
Marguerite was the nephew and
successor of Foncier, a jeweller
long associated with the
Beauharnais family.
Given by Mrs. Carew from the
Farquhar Matheson Collection
M.296-1921

19 BOX
Enamelled gold, set with a
chalcedony intaglio of a Roman
emperor driven in a chariot by
Victory.
FRENCH: post-Revolutionary Paris
marks and warranty marks for 1847
onwards. Maker's mark, L.-A.-F.
Ricart.
Given by Colonel F.R. Waldo-
Sibthorp
1964-1898

20 BOX
Gold, enamelled and set with a
miniature on ivory, perhaps of the
Comtesse de Grignan (daughter of
Madame de Sévigné).
FRENCH: about 1780. Later Paris
warranty marks for 1838-47.
Jones Collection
926-1882

21 BOX
Enamelled gold, set with brilliant-cut
pastes and a miniature of Napoleon I
(1769-1821), who gave it to Captain
Ussher of H.M.S. Undaunted at
Portoferrajo, Elba, 27th May, 1814.
FRENCH: post-Revolutionary Paris
marks and marks for 1809-19.
Given by Mr. Arthur Ussher
560-1908

22 BOX
Gold, set with brilliant-cut diamonds
in the form of the initial of Napoleon
I, within an enamelled border.
FRENCH: Paris marks for 1797-1809.
Maker's mark, ELB. Inscribed:
*Etienne Nitot et Fils Joailliers
Bijoutiers de S.M. Impce et Reine a
Paris.*
Nitot made much of the Crown
jewellery for the coronation of
Napoleon and Josephine in 1804.
W.W. Aston Bequest
M.122-1917

23 BOX
Gold, engraved and enamelled, set
with an onyx cameo signed: *Garelli*
(Giovanni Garelli, 1782-1834).
FRENCH: Paris marks for 1809-19.
Maker's mark of L.-A.-F. Ricart.
Said to have been given by Napoleon
I to his sister Marie Annonciade
Caroline 1782-1839, wife of Joachim
Murat, created King of Naples in
1808.
Murray Bequest
M.1039-1910

24 BOX
Chased gold, decorated with blue
translucent enamel. On the lid, an
enamelled miniature of a natural
child of Louis XIV (1643-1715).
FRENCH: Paris marks for 1809-19
and warranty marks for 1838-47. Pre-
and post-Revolutionary maker's
marks of A.-J.-M. Vachette. Signed
on the rim: *Vachette et Ouizille
Bijoutiers du Roi a Paris.*
Jones Collection
906-1882

Case 4 Board D

FRENCH BOXES:
first half of 19th century

25 BOX
Tortoise-shell, mounted in gold and
set with a 19th century miniature of
Monsieur de Pontchartreux.
FRENCH: post-Revolutionary Paris
marks and marks for 1819-38 and
1838-47. Maker's mark of A.-J.-M.
Vachette. Signed on the rim:
Vachette a Paris.
929-1882

26 BOX
Tortoise-shell, mounted in gold. On
the lid, an enamelled miniature of
Henrietta, Duchesse d'Orléans,
(1644-70), daughter of King Charles I,
probably after Petitot (1607-1691).
FRENCH: about 1820. Maker's mark
of P.A. Montaubon.
Viennese marks for 1824-66;
the gold rim inscribed: *Piote a
Vienne No. 684*.
932-1882

27 BOX
Tortoise-shell, mounted in gold and
set with miniatures in oil of
landscapes and figures, signed: *F.
Guerin* (working 1791).
FRENCH: Paris warranty marks for
1838-47. Maker's mark of A. Leferre.
900-1882

28 BOX
Tortoise-shell, mounted in gold. On
the lid, an enamel miniature of
Arthur Wellesley, 1st Duke of
Wellington (1769-1852), signed *IP* (J.
Parent)
Inscribed inside: *from the Earl of
Yarmouth to Dr. Chermside, Paris,
Augte 1823*.
FRENCH: post-Revolutionary Paris
marks and marks for 1809-19.
Maker's mark of A.A. Héguin.
Francis Seymour-Conway, Earl of
Yarmouth (1777-1842), a noted roué
and collector, became the 3rd
Marquis of Hertford; Dr. Chermside
was physician to the English
Embassy, Paris.
904-1882

29 BOX
Tortoise-shell, mounted in gold. On
the lid, a miniature on vellum of
Madame Scarron, afterwards
Madame de Maintenon (1635-1719).
FRENCH: Paris marks for 1809-19.
928-1882
Nos. 25-29, Jones Collection

30 BOX
Tortoise-shell, mounted in gold, set
with early 19th century miniatures of
Johannes Steiger of Bern (d.1581)
and his wife, Barbara (d.1566).
FRENCH: post-Revolutionary Paris
marks and Paris marks for 1809-19,
1819-38 and 1847 onwards. Maker's
mark, CP.
George Mitchell Bequest
204-1878

31 BOX
Tortoise-shell, mounted in gold and
set with a miniature of Louis XIV,
after a painting at Versailles, signed:
J. Parent 1817.
FRENCH: post-Revolutionary mark
and Paris marks for 1809-1819.
Jones Collection
899-1882

Case 4 Board E

SWISS BOXES:
18th century

32 BOX
Coloured gold.
The experiments of the Montgolfier
brothers in about 1783 are
commemorated in the balloon in the
central trophy on the lid.
SWISS: late 18th century.
George Mitchell Bequest
172-1878

33 BOX
Coloured gold, machine-engraved
and set with pearls.
SWISS: late 18th century.
Alfred Williams Hearn Gift
M.122-1923

34 BOX
Coloured gold, chased and engraved.
SWISS: about 1760.
George Mitchell Bequest
167-1878

35 BOX
Coloured gold, set with diamond
chips, emeralds and rubies.
SWISS: about 1760-80.
Imitation Paris marks, a Dutch
import mark for 1814-1953 and
French import marks introduced in
1864.
Given by Colonel Waldo-Sibthorp
1966-1898

36 BOX
Enamelled gold.
SWISS (Geneva): 1783-90. Maker's
mark of Jean Georges Rémond.
W.W. Aston Bequest
M.129-1917

37 BOX
Enamelled gold.
Swiss (Geneva): late 18th century.
Maker's mark of Bautte et Moynier.
Henry L. Florence Bequest
M.227-1917

38 BOX
Enamelled gold.
SWISS: late 18th century. Maker's
mark, D & C.
W.W. Aston Bequest
M.130-1917

39 BOX
Coloured gold.
SWISS: about 1760-80. Maker's mark,
DMC.
George Mitchell Bequest
171-1878

Case 4 Board F

SWISS BOXES:
late 18th century

40 BOX
Enamelled gold.
SWISS: late 18th century. Maker's mark, RPC crowned.
M.211-1919

41 BOX
Enamelled gold. Inscribed inside: *If thou wilt, remember, and if thou wilt, forget.*
SWISS (Geneva): 1790-1800. Maker's mark of Georges Rémond et Cie.
M.287-1919
Nos. 40 & 41, Joicey Bequest

42 BOX
Enamelled gold.
SWISS (Geneva): late 18th century. Maker's mark, LFT (LFT is a well-known, but unidentified, Geneva goldsmith).
Imitation French marks for 1773-74; genuine Paris marks for 1847 onwards.
George Mitchell Bequest
269-1878

43 BOX
Enamelled gold, the lid set with a porcelain plaque.
SWISS: late 18th century.
W.W. Aston Bequest
M.151-1917

44 BOX
Gold, decorated with enamel *en camaieu*.
SWISS: late 18th century.
Imitation Paris marks for 1770.
George Mitchell Bequest
268-1878

Case 4 Board G

SWISS BOXES:
late 18th century

45 BOX
Enamelled gold.
SWISS: late 18th century.
St. Petersburg mark for 1825.
George Mitchell Bequest
240-1878

46 BOX .
Gold, chased, engraved and enamelled.
SWISS (probably Geneva): late 18th century. Maker's mark, AI.
Imitation Paris marks.
George Mitchell Bequest
155-1878

47 BOX
Enamelled gold, set with pearls and a miniature of Maria Isabella, Duchess of Rutland (1756-1831), after Richard Cosway (1740-1821).
SWISS: late 18th or early 19th century.
Struck with marks for objects made in Switzerland under French jurisdiction, 1798-1809.
W.W. Aston Bequest
M.118-1917

48 BOX
Enamelled gold.
SWISS: late 18th century. Maker's mark illegible.
Imitation Paris marks for 1762-68; genuine Paris warranty marks for 1847 onwards.
Given by Mrs. Samuel S. Joseph
M.170-1941

Case 4 Board H

FRENCH WATCHES AND OTHER ARTICLES:
about 1747-1867

49 LOCKET
Enamelled gold, set with pearls and an embossed medallion on the back.
FRENCH: Paris marks for 1797-1809.
Given by Dame Joan Evans, P.P.S.A.
M.46-1962

50 WATCH
Spurious signature: *Breguet A Paris*.
Enamelled gold.
FRENCH: early 19th century.
Joicey Bequest
M.289-1919

51 MEMORANDUM BOOK
Gold, ivory, hardstone and mother-of-pearl.
FRENCH (Paris): 1747-50. Maker's mark of Thomas-Pierre Breton.
Paris marks for 1744-50 and 1747-48.
This item was given by Beau Brummell (George Bryan Brummell, 1778-1840) to Lady Harriet Villiers, later Lady Bagot, in 1805.
Lent anonymously

52 WATCH
Signed: *Breguet et Fils* (Paris).
FRENCH: about 1820.
Given by Mrs. Weymouth
269-1903

53 WATCH
Signed: *Berthoud Frères* (Paris).
Enamelled gold.
FRENCH: second quarter of 19th century.
Given by Miss G.M. Pratt
M.17-1957

54 WATCH
Signed: *Guyerd et ainé A Paris*.
Enamelled gold.
FRENCH: Paris marks for 1819-38.
Evan Roberts Gift
M.166-1915

55 NEEDLE-CASE
Coloured gold.
FRENCH (Paris): 1789-1809. Maker's mark of T.F. Pillieux.
Paris marks for 1789 and 1797-1809.
Begun in the year of the Revolution and presumably set aside for several years.
Alfred Williams Hearn Gift
M.77-1923

56 WATCH
Signed: *Henriot a Geneve.* The case
of three coloured gold, set with
rubies, turquoises and bloodstone.
The fob of three coloured gold.
SWISS: late 18th century.
Watch, 63-1896; fob, M.172-1951

57 WATCH
Signed: *Baillon A Paris.* Enamelled
gold.
FRENCH: mid 18th century.
Casemaker's mark, RC crowned.
Joicey Bequest
M.201-1919

58 NEEDLE-CASE
Coloured gold.
FRENCH: Paris marks for 1797-1809.
M.1048-1910

59 WATCH
Signed: *Froment-Meurice a Paris.*
Silver and gold, with scrolls
inscribed: *Poesie, Musique, Sculp-
ture, Gravure* and the initials of
Thomas Creswick, R.A. (1811-1869),
for whom it was made.
FRENCH (Paris): 1867.
Given by Miss L. Frith
M.8-1922
Other works by Froment-Meurice are
shown in Case 20, Board C, no. 6,
and D, nos. 4, 5, 9, 10, 13.

60 WATCH
Signed: *Dechevaux A Caen.*
Enamelled gold.
FRENCH: second quarter of 19th
century.
M.371-1910

61 WATCH
Signed: *Gregson A Paris.* Enamelled
gold.
FRENCH: late 18th century.
M.197-1919

62 WATCH
Signed: *Lechet A Paris.* Enamelled
gold.
FRENCH: late 18th century.
M.194-1919
Nos. 61 & 62, Joicey Bequest

63 FRAME FOR A MINIATURE
Enamelled gold, set with diamonds
and pearls.
FRENCH: early 19th century.
802 & a-1904

64 WATCH
Enamelled gold, set with pearls. In
the form of a lyre.
FRENCH: about 1820.
235-1876

65 ETUI
Tortoise-shell studded with gold
(piqué decoration).
FRENCH: about 1720.
503-1854

66 BOX
Enamelled gold.
SWISS (Geneva): late 18th century.
Maker's mark, FJ. The maker is
probably a member of the Joanin or
Juanin family, of whom François
Joanin was entered as a master gold
worker in Geneva in 1739 and an F.
Juanin was registered in 1833.
George Mitchell Bequest
261-1878

67 BOX
Coloured gold.
SWISS: late 18th century. Maker's
mark, F.W.
Imitation Paris marks for 1756-62;
genuine marks showing that the
box was imported into Prussia in
the early 19th century.
W.W. Aston Bequest
M.113-1917

68 BOX
Gold, chased and enamelled.
SWISS (Geneva): late 18th century.
Maker's mark, LFT.
Imitation Paris marks for 1768-75
and 1773-74.
264-1878

69 BOX
Gold, chased and enamelled.
SWISS: early 19th century.
Imitation Paris marks for 1762-68;
genuine Paris warranty mark for
1838-47.
263-1878

70 BOX
Gold, with enamelled medallion.
SWISS: late 18th or early 19th
century.
Imitation Paris marks for 1756-62
and 1762-63.
157-1878

71 BOX
Coloured gold, machine-engraved.
SWISS: late 18th century. Maker's
mark, FF crowned.
169-1878
Nos. 68-71, George Mitchell Bequest

25

Case 4 Board J

SWISS BOXES:
late 18th-early 19th century

72 BOX
Coloured gold.
SWISS: late 18th century.
George Mitchell Bequest
176-1878

73 BOX
Enamelled gold, set with a miniature
portrait of a man.
SWISS: late 18th century.
Imitation Paris discharge mark for
1762-68.
George Mitchell Bequest
239-1878

74 BOX
Enamelled gold; the lid set with
crystal chips in silver settings,
in the form of a vase of flowers.
SWISS: early 19th century. Maker's
mark, IGK.
903-1875

75 BOX
Enamelled gold, set with a miniature
of the Duchesse de La Vallière (1644-
1710).
SWISS: about 1820. Maker's mark, M
& P.
George Mitchell Bequest
152-1878

76 BOX
Enamelled gold.
SWISS (Geneva): 1790-1800. Maker's
mark of Georges Rémond & Cie.
Given by Mrs Samuel S. Joseph
M.171-1941

Case 4 Board K

SWISS BOXES:
late 18th century

77 BOX
Coloured gold, set with enamelled
plaques. A watch signed: *Fres Wiss &
Amalric* (Geneva), is inserted in the
lid, and a musical-box in the bottom.
SWISS (Geneva): late 18th century.
Maker's mark, DMC crowned.
Jones Collection
898-1882

78 BOX
Enamelled gold, set with pearls.
SWISS (Geneva): 1780-90. Maker's
mark of Jean Georges Rémond.
444-1873

79 BOX
Gold, the lid decorated with a
mythological scene in brown
camaieu enamel, surrounded by a
border of seed pearls.
SWISS: late 18th century.
Imitation Paris marks for 1758-74
and 1771-72; genuine Paris warranty
marks for 1837-48.
Jodrell Collection
499-1890

80 BOX
Enamelled gold.
SWISS (Geneva): 1780-90. Maker's
mark of Jean Georges Rémond.
253-1878

81 BOX
Gold, enamelled and set with pastes.
SWISS: about 1800.
Imitation Paris marks for 1760-70;
genuine Paris warranty marks for
1837-48.
238-1878
Nos. 80 & 81, George Mitchell
Bequest

Case 4 Board L

SWISS BOXES:
early 19th century

82 BOX
Enamelled gold.
SWISS: early 19th century. Maker's
mark, GW.
257-1878

83 BOX
Siberian onyx, mounted in enamelled
gold.
SWISS: probably early 19th century.
Genuine Paris warranty marks for
1838-47.
178-1878

84 BOX
Enamelled gold, with an enamelled
miniature of Venus.
SWISS: early 19th century.
247-1878

85 BOX
Enamelled gold.
SWISS: about 1800.
Mark of a flower and a crowned
monogram, perhaps in imitation of
pre-Revolutionary French marks.
246-1878
Nos. 82-85, George Mitchell Bequest

86 BOX
Enamelled gold.
SWISS: 1805-1815.
Joicey Bequest
M.210-1919

87 BOX
Enamelled gold.
SWISS: early 19th century.
Imitation Paris marks for 1762-68.
George Mitchell Bequest
251-1878

88 BOX
Enamelled gold.
SWISS: early 19th century.
W.W. Aston Bequest
M.110-1917

89 BOX
Enamelled gold, set with a miniature
portrait of a woman in mid 17th
century costume.
SWISS: about 1800.
Struck with a flower and a crowned
monogram as in no. 85 above.
Given by Mrs. Samuel S. Joseph
M.167-1941

Case 4 Board M

BOXES, all probably SWISS:
about 1800-1830

90 BOX
Coloured gold, set with a miniature.
SWISS: about 1830.
George Mitchell Bequest
158-1878

91 BOX
Coloured gold, with an enamel by
Jean Abraham Lissignol (1749-1819).
SWISS: early 19th century.
Given by Mrs. Carew from the
Farquhar Matheson Collection
M.299-1921

92 BOX
Gold, enamelled in imitation of niello
and set with a Roman mosaic.
SWISS (or ITALIAN): about 1830.
Maker's mark, BO.
Given by Major W.F. St. Clair
M.92-1969

93 BOX
Enamelled gold. An historian
(? Herodotus) with Minerva,
Harpocrates and Mnemosyne.
SWISS (or ITALIAN): about 1800.
Maker's mark, S & D.
W.W. Aston Bequest
M.144-1917

94 BOX
Gold, enamelled in imitation of
niello; monogram *CK*.
SWISS (or ITALIAN): about 1830.
Maker's mark, CCS and a ? fly in a
lozenge.
Henry L. Florence Bequest
M.226-1917

CASE 4
BOARD O
NO. 103

Case 4 Board N

SWISS BOXES:
late 18th and early 19th centuries

95 BOX
Gold, with an enamel plaque.
SWISS: about 1805.
Given by Mrs. Carew from the
Farquhar Matheson Collection
M.275-1921

96 BOX
Enamelled gold, with a miniature of
Cupid and Music.
SWISS: about 1800.
Imitation Paris marks; genuine
Viennese duty mark for 1806-7.
258-1878

97 BOX
Enamelled gold.
SWISS: early 19th century.
252-1878
Nos. 96 & 97, George Mitchell
Bequest

98 BOX
Enamelled gold.
SWISS (Geneva): 1790-1800. Maker's
mark of Georges Rémond et Cie.
Joicey Bequest
M.212-1919

99 BOX
Enamelled gold.
SWISS (Geneva): about 1790-1800.
Maker's mark, possibly that of
Georges Rémond et Cie.
Given by Mrs. Carew from the
Farquhar Matheson Collection
M.298-1921

100 BOX
Enamelled gold, depicting
Geography with two amorini.
SWISS: early 19th century.
Paris warranty marks for 1838-47.
George Mitchell Bequest
256-1878

Case 4 Board O
(Corner of Cases 4 & 5)

VANITY AND VIRTUOSITY:
about 1825-1935

101 NECESSAIRE
Gilt metal, the cover set with
mother-of-pearl and turquoises.
Fitted with twelve chased gold
implements, some decorated with
turquoise enamel. A mechanical
singing bird is concealed beneath an
enamel cover.
FRENCH: about 1825. The gold
implements struck with the mark of
Charles Louis Désir (working in
Paris, 1822-30).
Lent by Mrs A.J. Anson

102 DISH
Silver, with a swirling design of fish
in *plique-à-jour* enamel in relief
(plique-à-jour is a form of *cloisonné* in
which the back, or ground, is
attached temporarily and removed
after firing to create an effect
analogous to stained glass).
FRENCH (Paris): about 1901.
Designed and executed by Eugène
Feuillâtre (1870-1916); signed
FEUILLÂTRE three times on the
underside of the mount.
Shown at the Turin Exhibition, 1902.
Given by Mr Thomas Stainton in
memory of Charles and Lavinia
Handley-Read
M.24-1972

*103 VANITY CASE
Gold and jadeite, the ends of stained
chalcedony (black onyx); the lid set
with rose- and brilliant-cut
diamonds, lapis-lazuli, turquoise,
malachite, rhodochrosite, quartz and
mother-of-pearl.
FRENCH (Paris): about 1926.
Signed: *LACLOCHE FRERES,
PARIS*. Also stamped: LFe, maker's
mark SAM or SMA, a blurred device
and Paris warranty marks for 1847
onwards; London import marks for
18 carat gold, 1926; sponsor's mark,
GF.
The original fitted leather case for
the piece (not shown) stamped with
the Paris address of Lacloche (15 rue
de la Paix) and that of the London
branch (2 New Bond Street)
Bequeathed by Miss J.H.G. Gollan
M.24-1976

104 VANITY CASE
Gilt metal, set with rubies.
FRENCH: about 1935; signed:
BOUCHERON (Paris)
M.44-1980

27

SWISS WATCHES AND OTHER ARTICLES:
about 1760-1850

SWISS BOXES:
about 1790-1830

28

1 WATCH
Signed: *Ls. Duchêne and Fils*
(Geneva). Gold.
SWISS: late 18th century.
57-1898

2 VINAIGRETTE
Enamelled gold, set with pearls.
FRENCH or SWISS: about 1830-40.
Jodrell Collection
507-1890

*3 FRUIT KNIFE
Containing a musical box.
Enamelled gold; pearl border.
SWISS: early 19th century.
Bequeathed by Captain C.O. Gregg-
Carr
M.873-1927

4 WATCH
Signed : *Jn. Ls. Patron Geneva.*
Coloured gold, set with diamond
sparks.
SWISS: late 18th century.
Murray Bequest
M.1051-1910

5 PENDANT
Enamelled gold, pearl border.
SWISS: about 1800.
M.280-1919

**6 CHATELAINE, WITH
WATCH-KEY AND SEAL**
Gold, enamelled and hung with
pearls.
SWISS (Geneva): about 1800.
144-1890

7 WATCH
Enamelled gold, set with pearls.
SWISS: about 1800.
M.191-1919

8 WATCH
Signed: *Truitte et Mourier* (Geneva).
Enamelled gold.
SWISS: about 1760.
M.288-1919
Nos. 7 & 8, Joicey Bequest

9 WATCH
Signed: *Abraham Colomby* (Geneva).
Enamelled gold, set with pastes.
SWISS: late 18th century. Maker's
mark largely obliterated.
Given by Miss G.M. Pratt
M.8-1957

10 SEALING-WAX CASE
Enamelled gold.
SWISS: late 18th century. Maker's
mark, JS crowned.
Imitation Paris marks for 1783-89
and 1784-85.
Given by Mrs. Samuel S. Joseph
M.174-1941

11 MINIATURE CASE
Enamelled gold, set with pearls.
SWISS: about 1800.
M.281-1919

**12 FOB-CHAIN WITH WATCH-
KEY AND SEAL**
Enamelled gold, set with pearls.
SWISS (Geneva): about 1800.
M.291-1919
Nos. 11 & 12, Joicey Bequest

13 WATCH
Signed: *Isaac Soret & Fils* (Geneva).
Coloured gold, set with pastes.
SWISS: late 18th century. Maker's
mark largely obliterated.
Given in accordance with the wishes
of the late Miss M. Bernardine Hall
M.61-1914

14 WATCH
Signed: *Matthey & Compe.*
Enamelled gold.
SWISS: about 1800.
Joicey Bequest
M.283-1919

*15 MUSICAL BOX
In the form of a harp.
Enamelled gold, set with pearls and
rose-cut diamonds in the French
Empire style.
SWISS: perhaps mid 19th century.
Bequeathed by Mr. Percy Victor
Sharman
M.53-1946

16 WATCH
Signed: *Jn. Etne. Piot* (Geneva).
Enamelled gold.
SWISS: about 1820.
Given by Miss G.M. Pratt
M.16-1957

17 WATCH
Enamelled gold, set with pearls.
SWISS: early 19th century.
6922-1860

18 BOX
Enamelled gold, set with an enamel
miniature of de Bailly, Mayor of
Paris in 1793, the first victim of
the Terror.
SWISS: about 1820-30.
The lining of the lid struck with
French marks for 1819-38.
George Mitchell Bequest
153-1878

19 BOX
Enamelled gold.
SWISS (Geneva): early 19th century.
Maker's mark of Rémond, Lamy et
Cie.
Given by Mrs. Carew from the
Farquhar Matheson Collection
M.300-1921

20 BOX
Enamelled gold.
SWISS: ? early 19th century.
Imitation Paris marks for 1756-62
and 1768-75.
165-1878

21 BOX
Enamelled gold.
SWISS: about 1830.
Imitation Paris marks.
255-1878

22 BOX
Enamelled gold.
SWISS: about 1800 (possibly with
the town mark of Vevey).
250-1878
Nos. 20-22, George Mitchell Bequest

23 BOX
Enamelled gold, with a miniature of
Elizabeth Woodville and her children
pleading before Richard III.
SWISS: about 1825.
Jodrell Collection
498-1890

24 BOX
Enamelled gold, set with a miniature
surrounded by pearls.
SWISS (Geneva): 1790-1800. Maker's
mark of Georges Rémond et Cie.
263-1878

SWISS BOXES:
about 1800-1820

SWISS BOXES:
about 1790-1800

25 BOX
Enamelled gold, with a miniature of
Pygmalion.
SWISS: about 1800.
254-1878
Nos. 24 & 25, George Mitchell
Bequest

26 BOX
Enamelled gold, set with pearls.
SWISS: early 19th century. Maker's
mark, B & H.
French import mark introduced in
1864.
Joicey Bequest
M.286-1919

27 BOX
Enamelled gold, with a miniature of
Venus and Hymen lighting the fire of
love.
SWISS: about 1800.
Imitation Paris marks.
George Mitchell Bequest
245-1878

28 BOX
Enamelled gold.
SWISS: ? early 19th century. Maker's
mark, RPC crowned.
Dutch import mark for 1852-1927.
Joicey Bequest
M.236-1919

29 BOX
Enamelled gold, with a miniature of
Hector inciting Paris to fight.
SWISS: about 1810. Maker's mark,
AI.
George Mitchell Bequest
244-1878

30 BOX
Enamelled gold, with a miniature
of Angelica and Medoro.
SWISS: about 1800. Maker's mark,
JS crowned.
Imitation Paris marks for 1774-81,
1778-79 and 1783-89.
Given by Mrs. Samuel S. Joseph
M.163-1941

31 BOX
Enamelled gold.
SWISS (Geneva): about 1800.
Maker's mark, FJ (probably a
member of the Joanin or Juanin
family).
George Mitchell Bequest
248-1878

32 BOX
Enamelled gold, set with pearls.
SWISS: about 1800. Maker's mark,
AI.
Jodrell Collection
497-1890

33 BOX
Enamelled gold.
SWISS (Geneva): late 18th century.
Maker's mark of Jean Georges
Rémond (1746-1820).
Given by Mrs. Carew from the
Farquhar Matheson Collection
M.277-1921

34 BOX
Enamelled gold.
SWISS: about 1800. Maker's mark,
FJ (see no. 31 above).
Paris warranty marks for 1847
onwards.
George Mitchell Bequest
249-1878

35 BOX
Enamelled gold, with a miniature
of an old man reading the Bible to his
family.
SWISS: about 1800.
Imitation Paris marks; genuine
St Petersburg marks, probably for
1818-1864 and a French import mark
introduced in 1864.
Bequeathed by Mr. Henry van den
Bergh
M.4-1960

GERMAN HARDSTONE
BOXES:
about 1770-1800

GERMAN BOXES:
mid – late 18th century

30

36 BOX
A variety of hardstones set in
coloured gold; on the lid, an onyx
cameo of a classical female head.
GERMAN (Dresden): late 18th
century. Signed by J.C. Neuber (1736-
1808).
744-1875

37 BOX
Amethystine quartz, mounted in
gold, with brilliant-cut diamonds
and rubies in silver settings.
GERMAN (Dresden): mid 18th
century.
183-1878

38 BOX
Sixty-seven varieties of hardstone set
in gold.
GERMAN (Dresden): about 1775.
Made by J.C. Neuber; the base of the
box contains Neuber's original
manuscript list of the stones used.
192-1878
Nos. 37 & 38, George Mitchell
Bequest

*39 BOX
Eighty-eight varieties of hardstone
set in gold; on the lid, an enamel
portrait of the philosopher Crates
(c.270 BC).
GERMAN (Dresden): about 1775.
Probably by J.C. Neuber.
W.W. Aston Bequest
M.126-1917

40 BOX
A variety of hardstones set in gold
as floral trails and swags.
GERMAN (Dresden): about 1770.
Probably made by G.C. Stiehl (1708-
92).
George Mitchell Bequest
166-1878

41 BOX
A variety of hardstones set in gold;
on the lid, an agate cameo of
Minerva.
GERMAN (Dresden): about 1770-75.
Probably by J.C. Neuber.
Vienna duty mark for 1806-7.
W.W. Aston Bequest
M.108-1917

42 BOX
Labrador spar, mounted in gold.
GERMAN: about 1800.
George Mitchell Bequest
193-1878

43 BOX
A variety of hardstones set in gold.
GERMAN (Dresden): about 1770.
Probably by J.C. Neuber or G.C.
Stiehl.
W.W. Aston Bequest
M.127-1917

44 BOX
Quartz, mounted in gold and
encrusted with semi-precious stones;
bucolic motifs.
GERMAN (? Dresden): late 18th
century. Possibly made by B.G.
Hoffmann.
George Mitchell Bequest
180-1878

45 BOX
A variety of hardstones set in gold,
with glass and simulated pearls in
enamel; rosette design on lid.
GERMAN (Dresden): about 1775.
Made by J.C. Neuber.
Lent anonymously

46 BOX
Sardonyx, carved and mounted in
gold, with brilliant- and rose-cut
diamonds and emeralds in silver
settings.
GERMAN: mid 18th century.
George Mitchell Bequest
177-1878

47 BOX
A variety of hardstones set in gold;
inside the lid is a portrait miniature
in a frame of simulated pearls.
GERMAN (Dresden): about 1770.
Made by J.C. Neuber.
Lent anonymously

48 BOX
Quartz, mounted in gold and
encrusted with semi-precious stones
in the form of a woman, birds,
flowers and insects.
GERMAN (? Dresden): late 18th
century. Possibly by B.G. Hoffmann.
George Mitchell Bequest
179-1878

Case 5 Board G

GERMAN BOXES:
mid – late 18th century

Case 5 Board H

SWISS WATCHES AND OTHER ARTICLES:
about 1790 – 1850

49 BOX
Gold and mother-of-pearl, set with
hardstones.
GERMAN: mid 18th century.
Baron de Redé Collection
Lent anonymously

50 BOX
Quartz, mounted in gold, set with
brilliant-cut diamonds; designed as a
bale bound with ropes.
GERMAN (Dresden): about 1760.
George Mitchell Bequest
181-1878

51 BOX
A variety of hardstones set in gold,
with enamelled pearls. On the lid, a
miniature of a woman, under glass.
GERMAN (Dresden): about 1775.
Made by J.C. Neuber.
Lent anonymously

52 BOX
Amethystine quartz, mounted in
gold.
GERMAN: mid 18th century.
W.W. Aston Bequest
M.146-1917

53 BOX
Quartz, mounted in gold; the lid
encrusted with coloured stones in the
form of a bouquet.
GERMAN: late 18th century.
George Mitchell Bequest
182-1878

54 ETUI
Enamelled gold and pearls.
SWISS: about 1800. Maker's mark, S
& D.
From the old Geological Museum,
Jermyn Street
4909-1901

55 WATCH
Signed: *Js. Coulin & Amy Bry a
Geneve.* Also signed: *Orazio
Semeraro,* presumably the retailer.
Enamelled gold, set with pearls.
SWISS: late 18th century.
M.187-1919

56 WATCH
Enamelled gold, set with pearls.
SWISS: early 19th century.
M.152-1919

**57 FOB-WATCH WITH WATCH
KEY AND SEAL**
Enamelled gold with gold filigree.
SWISS (Geneva): about 1800.
M.292-1919
Nos. 55-57, Joicey Bequest

58 WATCH
Enamelled gold.
SWISS: about 1835.
Given by Miss A.E. Dell
M.124-1953

59 WATCH
Enamelled and coloured gold, set
with turquoises and pearls.
SWISS: early 19th century.
Evan Roberts Gift
M.163-1915

60 WATCH
Signed: *Moise Constanin* (Geneva).
Enamelled gold.
SWISS: about 1790.
Bernal Collection
2373-1855

61 WATCH
Signed: *Moulinie Geneve.* Enamelled
gold.
SWISS: about 1830.
Given by Miss M. Rathbone
M.13-1943

62 ENGAGEMENT TABLETS
Ivory, with covers of tortoise-shell
mounted in gold and set with
miniatures of King Louis-Philippe
(1773-1850) and Queen Marie-Amélie
of France. Inside are miniatures of
their four younger sons and the
wife of one of them. With gold pencil.
Signed: *Bury Frères A Genève.*
SWISS (Geneva): 1830-40.
Formerly the property of Hélène
Louise Elizabeth, Duchesse
d'Orléans, widow of Louis Philippe's
eldest son, who died in an accident in
1842.
Bequeathed by Sir Bernard Eckstein
M.45-1948

63 WATCH
Signed: *Moulinie Geneve.* Enamelled
gold.
SWISS: about 1830.
Given by Mrs. Denham Parker
M.972-1928

64 FOB-CHAIN
Enamelled gold, hung with three
keys and a vase-shaped pendant.
SWISS: about 1800.
Joicey Bequest
M.290-1919

65 WATCH
Signed *Ls. Reymond, Locle.*
Enamelled gold.
SWISS: about 1850.
Given by Dr. W.L. Hildburgh, F.S.A.
M.171-1951

66 WATCH
Coloured gold.
The Cupids on the dial strike
imitation bells when a repeat
mechanism is pressed.
SWISS: early 19th century.
Given by Miss G.M. Pratt
M.18-1957

67 ETUI
Enamelled gold and pearls.
Probably SWISS: about 1800.
An Italian mark, probably added
later.
Joicey Bequest
M.296-1919

Case 5 Board I

BOXES (mainly GERMAN):
about 1740-1765

68 BOX
Gold, set with panels of steel and
encrusted with gold and silver.
Probably GERMAN: mid 18th
century.
Imitation Paris marks.
8534-1863

69 BOX
Embossed gold.
Possibly GERMAN: mid 18th
century.
173-1878

70 BOX
Enamelled copper with gold mounts.
GERMAN (probably Berlin): 1740-50.
234-1878
Nos. 69 & 70, George Mitchell
Bequest

71 BOX
Bloodstone, set in gold and encrusted
with brilliant-cut diamonds,
emeralds and rubies.
ENGLISH or GERMAN: mid 18th
century.
W.W. Aston Bequest
M.140-1917

72 BOX
Gold and enamel.
GERMAN (Berlin): about 1765.
Maker's mark of D. Baudesson.
Lent anonymously

73 BOX
Amethystine quartz, mounted in
gold, with brilliant-cut diamonds
and rubies in silver settings.
GERMAN: mid 18th century
George Mitchell Bequest
184-1878

Case 5 Board J

GERMAN, AUSTRIAN and SWEDISH BOXES:
about 1780–1830

74 BOX
Twenty varieties of hardstone set in
gold.
AUSTRIAN: Vienna mark for 1796.
Maker's mark, DD.
Given by Colonel F.R. Waldo-
Sibthorp
1962-1898

75 BOX
Bloodstone, mounted in enamelled
gold, set with rose-cut diamonds and
rubies.
GERMAN: about 1820-30.
French import marks for 1838-64.
197-1878

76 BOX
Glass, encrusted with gold and
mother-of-pearl; gold mounts.
Probably decorated by J.M. Heinrici
(1711-1786).
GERMAN: late 18th century.
199-1878
Nos. 75 & 76, George Mitchell
Bequest

77 BOX
Rock-crystal, mounted in gold.
GERMAN: about 1830.
W.W. Aston Bequest
M.121-1917

78 BOX
A variety of hardstones set in gold.
AUSTRIAN: Vienna mark of about
1795. Maker's mark, IGA.
George Mitchell Bequest
190-1878

Case 5 Board K

AUSTRIAN BOXES:
1795- about 1820

79 BOX
Brown aventurine quartz, mounted
in gold.
AUSTRIAN: Vienna marks for 1805.
Maker's mark, I I S.
W.W. Aston Bequest
M.157-1917

80 BOX
Gold, set with miniatures of the
Cascade at Tivoli and another scene,
perhaps after Joseph Vernet (1712-
1789).
AUSTRIAN: about 1820. Maker's
mark, FW.
Vienna mark for ? 1791-1824.
160-1878

81 BOX
Lapis-lazuli, mounted in gold, set
with a miniature of Maximilian I,
King of Bavaria, by Balthasar Speth
(1774-1846), dated 1812.
AUSTRIA (Vienna): about 1812.
189-1878

82 BOX
Smoked quartz, mounted in gold.
AUSTRIAN: Vienna marks for 1795.
196-1878
Nos. 80-82, George Mitchell Bequest

Case 5 Board L

NORTH EUROPEAN BOXES:
about 1750 – 1791

83 BOX
Gold, engraved, enamelled with love scenes *en rose camaieu* and set with panels of *Vernis Martin* in imitation of bloodstone.
AUSTRIAN: about 1760.
Jones Collection
924-1882

84 BOX
Chased steel on gilt ground.
GERMAN: mid 18th century.
Given by Mrs. Carew from the Farquhar Matheson Collection
M.301-1921

*85 BOX
Enamelled gold, set with a miniature of Gustavus III of Sweden (1746-1792), who gave it to Patrick Miller of Dalswinton, whose double-hulled paddle-wheeled ship is depicted on the underside. The sides set with views of Stockholm harbour.
SWEDISH: Stockholm marks for 1791. Maker's mark of Friedrich Fyrwald.
Lent by Mr Macdonald Miller

86 BOX
Lapis-lazuli with silver mounts; on the lid, Diana and Callisto. The underside with the arms of William IV (1711-1751) or William V (1748-1806), the last Stadholder of Orange.
Probably DUTCH: second half of 18th century.
Bequeathed by the Duke of Wellington
M.5-1974

87 BOX
Enamelled gold.
SWEDISH (Stockholm): about 1750.
Maker's mark of Andreas Almgren (1746-1778).
George Mitchell Bequest
162-1878

Case 5 Board M

RUSSIAN BOXES:
late 18th-early 19th century

*88 BOX
Enamelled gold.
RUSSIAN (St Petersburg): about 1820.
St Petersburg marks, probably for 1818-64, and for before 1861.
W.W. Aston Bequest
M.123-1917

*89 PRESENTATION BOX
Gold, decorated with enamels and brilliant-cut diamonds; on the lid, the crowned cipher of Tsar Nicholas II (1868-1918), surrounded by Imperial eagles.
Commissioned from Peter Carl Fabergé (1846-1920).
RUSSIAN: St Petersburg marks for 1896-1907. Mark of Michael Perchin, a Fabergé workmaster.
Bequeathed by Sir William Seeds, K.C.M.G., H.M. Ambassador in Moscow, 1939-40.
M.I-1974

90 BOX
Enamelled gold.
RUSSIAN (St Petersburg): late 18th century.
Maker's mark, IA.
George Mitchell Bequest
260-1878

91 PRESENTATION BOX
Gold and enamel, set with a miniature of Tsar Alexander I of Russia (1777-1825).
RUSSIAN (St Petersburg): early 19th century. Maker's mark of Otto Samuel Keibel. St Petersburg mark for 1795-1826.
This box was presented to Lord Granville Leveson-Gower (1773-1846), 1st Lord Granville, perhaps at the Tsar's coronation in 1801, but more probably when he was ambassador in St Petersburg in 1804-5.
Lent anonymously

92 BOX
Gold, chased and enamelled.
RUSSIAN (St Petersburg): about 1820.
St Petersburg marks for 1818-64.
Maker's mark, WG.
George Mitchell Bequest
164-1878

Case 5 Board N

BOXES (? GERMAN AND POLISH):
about 1730-50

93 BOX
Mother of pearl, mounted and piqué with gold, and set with brilliant-cut diamonds, rubies, emeralds, jacinth and garnets.
Probably GERMAN: about 1730-40.
Vienna duty mark for 1806-07.
W.W. Aston Bequest
M.133-1917

94 SEWING CASE
Moulded and engraved mother of pearl, encrusted with gold. On the lid an allegorical scene. Inside, a shuttle, thimble and other equipment.
GERMAN: (Augsburg) about 1740.
Lent anonymously

95 BOX
Tombac alloy and mother of pearl, with a scene of a stag hunt, probably allegorical; the inside decorated with symbols of love.
Possibly POLISH: mid 18th century.
George Mitchell Bequest
214-1878

34

CASE 5
BOARD E
NO. 39

CASE 5
BOARD M
NO. 88

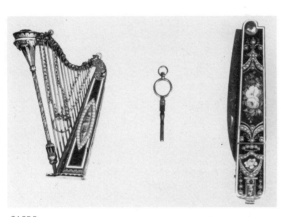

CASE 5
BOARD A
NO. 3

CASE 5
BOARD M
NO. 89

CASE 5
BOARD L
NO. 85

Case 6 Board A

WEST EUROPEAN WATCHES AND OTHER ARTICLES:
18th century

1 ETUI
Gold, chased with medallions of
Jupiter and Juno.
GERMAN: about 1730.
Bond Collection
483-1875

2 WATCH AND PAIR-CASE
Signed: *I:B:Grups Gua: London.*
Silver, the pair-case set with
cornelian. The Royal Arms of Queen
Anne (reigned 1702-1714) engraved
on the inner cover.
DUTCH: early 18th century, made in
imitation of an English watch.
1303-1871

3 WATCH AND PAIR-CASE
Signed: *Benedick Firsten Felder*
(Friedberg). Gilt copper.
GERMAN: early 18th century.
Alfred Williams Hearn Gift
M.130-1923

4 ETUI
Gold-mounted porcelain, decorated in
the manner of J.M. Heinrici.
GERMAN (Dresden): 18th century.
Lent anonymously

5 SCENT-BOTTLE
Gold, chased and enamelled with a
cornelian intaglio.
Probably GERMAN: mid 18th
century.
M.173-1941

6 CHATELAINE
Gold, with gilt metal hook.
Probably GERMAN: first half of
18th century. Maker's mark, WH.
Joicey Bequest
M.307-1919

7 WATCH
Signed: *Georg Albrecht/Zillichau*
(Cylkowa in Silesia). Gold. The Royal
Arms of King George I of England
(reigned 1714-1727) on a roundel at
the back.
POLISH: first half of 18th century.
Bernal Collection
2358-1855

8 CANE TOP
Embossed gold.
GERMAN: second quarter of 18th
century.
522-1868

9 CHATELAINE
Pinchbeck and mother-of-pearl.
?GERMAN: about 1730-35.
Given by Dame Joan Evans, P.P.S.A.
M.271-1975

10 WATCH
Signed: *A Oosterwyk Van Ceulen,
Amsterdam.* Silver.
DUTCH: early 18th century.
Casemaker's mark, PI.
H. Batsford Bequest
M.54-1953

11 WATCH
Signed: *Jos. Machatik, Tabor*
(Bohemia). Coloured and enamelled
gold.
BOHEMIAN: first half of 19th
century.
Joicey Bequest
M.207-1919

12 WATCH AND CHATELAINE
Signed: *Chri. Heinrich Hähnel*
(Fürth). Gold.
GERMAN: first half of 18th century.
Casemaker's mark on pair-case, MD.
3582-1856

13 ETUI
Bloodstone mounted in gold.
WEST EUROPEAN (perhaps
ENGLISH): about 1730.
M.202-1939

14 SCENT-BOTTLE
Gold, chased and enamelled, with a
cornelian intaglio.
Probably GERMAN: mid 18th
century.
182-1864

15 WATCH AND PAIR-CASE
Signed: *Best, London.* Silver, the
pair-case embossed.
DUTCH: an imitation of an English
watch, but with genuine London
hallmarks for 1769-70.
Given by Mrs. F. Rashleigh
253-1891

16 WATCH
Signed: *E. Vredig, London.* Gold,
pierced, engraved and chased.
DUTCH: about 1720, made in
imitation of an English watch.
Given by Miss G.M. Pratt
M.7 & a-1957

17 WRITING TABLETS
Ivory tablets, with silver-gilt cover
chased with Ganymede and the
eagle. Signed: *J.C. Schmidt
Augustea.*
GERMAN (Augsburg): early 18th
century.
299-1854

Case 6 Board B

ITALIAN BOXES:
late 18th–early 19th century

Case 6 Board C

ITALIAN BOXES:
first half of 19th century

Case 6 Board D

SPANISH and ITALIAN BOXES and a SCENT FLASK:·
about 1760-1870

18 BOX
Ischia lava, mounted in gold, and set with a cameo of Angelica and Medoro.
ITALIAN: late 18th century.
Given by Mrs. Carew from the Farquhar Matheson Collection
M.305-1921

19 BOX
Lapis-lazuli, set with Florentine mosaic and mounted in gold.
ITALIAN: early 19th century.
188-1878

20 BOX
Lapis-lazuli, set with a Roman mosaic and mounted in gold.
ITALIAN (Rome): about 1820.
Maker's mark of L. Mascelli (c.1770-1825).
187-1878
Nos. 19 & 20, George Mitchell Bequest

21 BOX
Porphyry, mounted in gold, set with a cameo of Priam kneeling before Achilles.
ITALIAN: late 18th century.
Given by Mrs. Carew from the Farquhar Matheson Collection
M.304-1921

22 BOX
Enamelled gold, set with brilliant-cut diamonds; crowned initials of Victor Emanuel II, King of Italy (1820-1878).
ITALIAN: mid 19th century. Turin marks.
George Mitchell Bequest
154-1878

23 BOX
Lapis-lazuli, set with a Roman mosaic of the Colosseum and mounted in gold.
ITALIAN: (Roman); early 19th century.
Given by Mrs. Carew from the Farquhar Matheson Collection
M.294-1921

24 BOX
Ischia lava, mounted in gold; on the lid a view at Tivoli, in Roman mosaic.
ITALIAN: early 19th century. Rome marks.
Formerly the property of Sir Thomas Lawrence, P.R.A. (1769-1830).
Jones Collection
938-1882

25 BOX
Gold, set with a Roman mosaic.
ITALIAN or SWISS: early 19th century.
George Mitchell Bequest
159-1878

26 BOX
Steel, encrusted with gold and silver.
SPANISH (Madrid): about 1870.
Made by Plácido Zuloaga (1800-1898).
Given by Mrs. Alfred Morrison
M.875-1927

27 BOX
Silver, and parcel-gilt.
ITALIAN (Venice): about 1760-70.
George Mitchell Bequest
218-1878

28 SCENT-FLASK
Bloodstone and gilt metal, with damascened decoration.
SPANISH (Madrid): about 1870.
Made by Plácido Zuloaga and signed with his initials.
M.358-1977

Case 6 Board E

ENGLISH BOXES:
about 1714-1750

29 BOX
Silver-gilt, embossed with a scene of
Hercules choosing between Virtue
and Pleasure.
Probably ENGLISH: mid 18th
century.
Given by Colonel F.R. Waldo-
Sibthorp
1967-1898

30 BOX
Gold, set with an enamel miniature,
perhaps after a composition by
Poussin. Inside, a miniature by
Petitot, perhaps of Louis XIV as a
child.
ENGLISH: about 1745.
From Ham House
H.H. 458-1948

31 BOX
Gold filigree, lined. Inscribed: *The
Gift DG 1714.*
ENGLISH: dated 1714.
Lent anonymously

32 BOX
Gold.
ENGLISH: about 1720-30.
219-1870

33 BOX
Bloodstone, mounted in gold.
ENGLISH: about 1720.
The gift of Sir Robert Walpole (1676-
1745), 1st Earl of Oxford, to Mr
Andrews of Shaw House.
Given by Douglas Eyre, Esq., in
memory of his father and mother,
Henry Richard and Isabella
Catherine Eyre, late of Shaw House,
near Newbury, Berkshire.
M.43-1922

*34 BOX
Gold, the underside chased with the
arms of Carmichael, Earl of
Hyndford (1701-1767); the
decoration adapted from a design for a watch
case by Augustin Heckel (*c.*1690-
1770) and probably chased by him.
Inside, a miniature painting of Diana
and Callisto.
ENGLISH: about 1730-40.
61-1871

Case 6 Board F

ENGLISH BOXES:
about 1720-1760

35 BOX
Agate, mounted in gold.
Possibly ENGLISH: about 1750.
George Mitchell Bequest
185-1878

36 BOX
Gold, with a miniature of Mary,
Queen of Scots, from the portrait
copied by Bernard Lens (1655-1725).
The underside engraved with the
arms of Sir John Hinde Cotton, 3rd
Baronet (d.1752).
ENGLISH: about 1720.
Jones Collection
902-1882

37 BOX
Agate, mounted in embossed gold.
ENGLISH: about 1760.
M.172-1941

38 BOX
Painted glass to simulate agate,
mounted in embossed gold.
ENGLISH: mid 18th century.
Paris marks for 1847 onwards.
M.165-1941
Nos. 37 & 38, given by Mrs Samuel S.
Joseph

Case 6 Board G

ENGLISH BOXES:
about 1750-1760

39 BOX
Red agate-jasper, mounted in gold.
The top appears to be a replacement.
ENGLISH: mid 18th century.
Henry L. Florence Bequest
M.230-1917

40 ETUI
Gold, set with enamel plaques.
One panel signed: *Moser F,* for G.M.
Moser (1706-1783).
ENGLISH: about 1760.
G.M. Moser, born at Schaffhausen,
came to England and worked as a
chaser and enameller. He was elected
the first Keeper of the Royal
Academy.
Lent anonymously

41 BOX
Gold, set with moss-agates, brilliant-
cut diamonds, emeralds, and rubies
in silver settings.
ENGLISH: about 1760. In the
manner of James Cox.
121-1864

37

Case 6 Board H

ENGLISH WATCHES:
18th century

42 WATCH AND PAIR-CASE
Signed: *Ellicot, London.* Gold,
engraved, pierced and chased.
ENGLISH: (inner case), London
hallmarks for 1785-86, casemaker's
mark, VW; (pair-case), first half of
18th century, casemaker's mark, IE.
Given by Colonel F.R. Waldo-
Sibthorp
1923-c-1898

43 WATCH AND PAIR-CASE
Gold, the pair-case embossed and
chased. The movement is associated.
ENGLISH: London hallmarks for
1760-61; casemaker's mark, TC.
Bequeathed by Miss E.A. Evans
442-1902

44 WATCH AND PAIR-CASE
Signed: *Pointer Baker, London.* Gold,
the pair-case embossed and chased.
ENGLISH: London hallmarks for
1766-67; casemaker's mark, HB.
Given by Mr. H.T.G. Watkins
M.43-1948

45 WATCH
By Daniel Delander (*c*.1692-1733),
London. Gold.
ENGLISH: the case bears London
hallmarks for 1768-69.
Lent anonymously

**46 WATCH AND CHATELAINE
AND BROOCH**
Enamelled gold.
Watch signed: *Jams Tregent,
London.*
ENGLISH: second half of 18th
century.
Given by Mrs. C.H. Golding-Bird
M.365-b-1923

47 WATCH AND PAIR-CASE
Signed: *Clarke & Dunster.* Chased
silver.
ENGLISH: first half of 18th century.
138-1907

48 WATCH AND PAIR-CASE
Signed: *Jas Upjohn & Co., London.*
Enamelled gold.
ENGLISH: London hallmarks for
1778-79.
Given by Colonel F.R. Waldo-
Sibthorp
1924-1898

49 PAIR-CASE
Enamelled gold.
ENGLISH: late 18th century.
1065-1855

**50 WATCH (with pair-case and
chatelaine)**
Signed: *Hen King in Lincolns Inn.*
Gold.
ENGLISH: London hallmarks for
1727-28. Casemaker's mark,
IR crowned. (The embossed and
chased pair-case and pinchbeck
chatelaine, about 1760).
Given by Mr. G.R. Brigstocke
M.12 & a-1948

51 WATCH
Signed: *Bushman London.* Chased
silver.
ENGLISH: early 18th century.
Casemaker's mark, IW.
Shoppee Collection
555-1901

52 WATCH
Signed: *To Tompion, London, No.
355.* Gold.
ENGLISH: London hallmarks for
1709-10.
Lent anonymously

53 PAIR-CASE
Enamelled gold.
ENGLISH: late 18th century.
Joicey Bequest
M.209-1919

54 WATCH AND PAIR-CASE
Signed: *J. Paulet Without temple
Bar.* Silver, pierced and engraved.
Engraved with the arms of Onley of
Northamptonshire.
ENGLISH: early 18th century.
M.122-1909

55 WATCH AND CHATELAINE
Enamelled gold.
ENGLISH: London hallmarks for
1779-80.
Joicey Bequest
M.294-1919

56 WATCH AND PAIR-CASE
Signed: *Jn. Curtis, London.* Gold,
embossed and chased with the
Presentation in the Temple, after a
design by Augustin Heckel.
ENGLISH: London hallmarks for
1786-87. Casemaker's mark, IW.
M.6 & a-1957

57 WATCH AND PAIR-CASE
Signed: *George Etherington, London.*
Gold, embossed and chased.
ENGLISH: London hallmarks for
1716-17. Pair-case about 1750.
M.5 & a-1957
Nos. 56 & 57, given by
Miss G.M. Pratt

58 WATCH AND PAIR-CASE
Signed: *Wm. Creak.* Gold, embossed
and chased.
ENGLISH: London hallmarks for
1757-58. Casemaker's mark, ? SC.
Bequeathed by Miss E.A. Taylor
M.394-1926

59 WATCH AND PAIR-CASE
Signed: *Wm. Howard, London.*
Embossed and chased pinch beck
with enamelled face.
ENGLISH: about 1760.
Evan Roberts Gift
M.170-1915

Case 6 Board I

ENGLISH BOXES AND
A CHATELAINE:
about 1760-80

Case 6 Board J

ENGLISH BOXES:
19th century

Case 6 Board K

ENGLISH BOXES:
about 1780 – 1850

60 BOX
Gold, engraved with trophies and
plants in a Neoclassical design.
ENGLISH: London hallmarks for
1776-77. Maker's mark, WH.
Lent by the Earl of Lonsdale

61 BOX
Gold, with translucent enamel.
ENGLISH: 1760-70.
W.W. Aston Bequest
M.116-1917

*62 CHATELAINE
Gold, decorated with translucent
dark blue enamel flowers and riveted
to pinchbeck; the chatelaine fitted
with a pendant watch signed:
Gregson a Paris Hor du Roy; and a
chalcedony seal.
ENGLISH: about 1760-70.
Given by Dame Joan Evans, P.P.S.A.
M.261-b-1975

63 BOX
Chased with enamelled gold.
ENGLISH: 1760-70.
Jones Collection
933-1882

64 BOX
Enamelled gold.
ENGLISH: late 18th century.
Henry van den Bergh Bequest
M.3-1960

65 BOX
Coloured gold, set with red jasper; the
base repaired.
ENGLISH: 19th century.
George Mitchell Bequest
194-1878

67 BOX
Coloured gold, machine-engraved.
ENGLISH: London hallmarks for
1816-17. Maker's mark of James
Lloyd.
Formerly the property of Colonel C.
Waldo-Sibthorp, M.P. for Lincoln.
Given by Colonel F.R. Waldo-
Sibthorp
1963 & a-1898

67 BOX
Gold.
ENGLISH: London hallmarks for
1804-5. Maker's mark of A.J.
Strachan.
Presented in 1814, on the visit of the
allied sovereigns to England, by the
King of Württemberg to William
Gorton, Comptroller to George III
(reigned 1760-1820).
W.J.W. Kerr Bequest
M.33-1957

68 BOX
Ivory, mounted in gold, set with a
miniature portrait of ? Lady
Brudenell by Samuel Shelley
(d.1808).
ENGLISH: late 18th century.
W.W. Aston Bequest
M.153-1917

69 BOX
Silver-gilt, the lid set with a
miniature portrait of a man, a
member of the Maynard family, by
George Romney (1734-1802).
ENGLISH: London hallmarks for
1779-80. Maker's mark, IP.
C.D. Rotch Bequest
M.311-1962 (the miniature P.11-1962)

70 BOX
Tortoise-shell, mounted in gold, set
with a Wedgwood plaque of
Aesculepius and Hygeia in lilac and
sage-green jasper slip.
ENGLISH: late 18th century.
W.W. Aston Bequest
M.152-1917

71 BOX
Ivory, mounted in gold, set with a
miniature of two lovers.
ENGLISH: about 1800.
George Mitchell Bequest
215-1878

72 BOX
Coloured gold, set with a miniature of
King George IV (reigned 1820-1830),
the Royal cipher on the underside.
ENGLISH: about 1821. Maker's
mark of John Northam.
Given by George IV to Richard
Sarell, Treasurer of the Levant
Company in Constantinople.
Lent by Captain R.I.A. Sarell, R.N.

73 BOX
Silver, with a platinum lid decorated
with a scene representing Lucius
Junius Brutus condemning his two
sons to death.
ENGLISH: the silver with
Birmingham hallmarks for 1850-51;
maker's mark of Yapp & Woodward.
The lid of the box made from the first
large platinum ingot produced by
Percival Norton Johnson in 1850.
Lent by Messrs. Johnson Matthey &
Company, Ltd.

Case 6 Board L

CHATELAINES:
first half of 18th century

*74 CHATELAINE
Pinchbeck, with scissors case, needle case, etui, and two thimble cases.
?ENGLISH: about 1730-35.
Given by Dame Joan Evans, P.P.S.A.
M.275-1975

75 CHATELAINE
Pinchbeck, chased with figures of ? Apollo and Minerva.
ENGLISH: 18th century.
Given by Jane Souter Hipkins
M.433-1911

76 CHATELAINE
Pinchbeck, a belt-hook with a pendant etui filled with implements and (later addition) a *breloque* (egg-shaped container) of painted enamel, and a cameo of a woman's head in a diamond border.
Probably GERMAN: about 1740.
Given by Dame Joan Evans, P.P.S.A.
M.276-1975

77 CHATELAINE AND WATCH
Gold and hardstone with mother-of-pearl, table-cut diamonds and rubies.
The watch movement signed: *Arned, London.*
ENGLISH: about 1740.
Lent anonymously

Case 6 Board M

CHATELAINES AND ETUIS:
18th century

78 CHATELAINE
Gilt copper, lattice work and flower design.
ENGLISH: mid 18th century.
M.262-1975

79 CHATELAINE
Pinchbeck and gilt copper set with slivers of agate; hung with a seal and an egg *(breloque)* of caged agate, the rim inscribed on enamel: *JE NE M'ATTACHE QU'A VOUS*
(I only belong to you).
ENGLISH: mid 18th century.
M.269-1975

80 ETUI
Pinchbeck, set with panels of grey agate and a single brilliant-cut diamond as a thumbpiece.
ENGLISH: mid 18th century.
M.270-1975

81 CHATELAINE
Gilt copper, set with two agate panels.
GERMAN: about 1740.
M.259-1975
Nos. 78-81, given by Dame Joan Evans, P.P.S.A.

82 ETUI
Bloodstone, mounted in chased gold.
FRENCH: 18th century.
Jones Bequest
940-1882

83 CHATELAINE
Gilt copper cast openwork with a huntress (? Diana) and other figures.
GERMAN: about 1750.
Given by Dame Joan Evans, P.P.S.A.
M.260-1975

Case 6 Board N

CHATELAINES AND ACCESSORIES:
about 1735-1875

84 ETUI
Gilt copper and pinchbeck, with a relief on one side of Orpheus charming the animals, and on the other of Eurydice appearing to Ceres.
Probably GERMAN: mid 18th century.
M.273-1975

85 CHATELAINE
Gilt copper and pinchbeck, the hook-plate with a relief of Orpheus and the animals.
GERMAN: about 1735.
M.272-1975
Nos. 84 & 85, given by Dame Joan Evans, P.P.S.A.

86 CHATELAINE AND WATCH WITH PAIR-CASE
Embossed gold pair-cased watch and chatelaine.
ENGLISH: the watch: London hall-marks for 1739; the chatelaine about 1750. The watch bears the mark of George Graham, formerly assistant and then partner of Thomas Tompion.
Lent anonymously

87 CHATELAINE
Gilt copper, the hook-plate with a relief of Cleopatra with Caesar and Mark Anthony.
GERMAN: about 1735.
M.265-1975

88 ETUI
Copper-gilt and pinchbeck.
WEST EUROPEAN: mid 18th century.
M.258-1975
Nos. 87 & 88, given by Dame Joan Evans, P.P.S.A.

89 CHATELAINE
Embossed and chased iron; with putti.
Signed: *T. SPALL.INV. & FECIT.*
ENGLISH: about 1875.
Spall studied at the Birmingham School of Art, 1869-1873, probably while apprenticed to Elkington & Company of Birmingham, with whom he subsequently spent his working life.
533-1903

CASE 6
BOARD I
NO. 62

CASE 6
BOARD L
NO. 74

CASE 6
BOARD E
NO. 34

Case 7 Board A

ENGLISH WATCHES AND OTHER ARTICLES:
early – mid 18th century

1 WATCH AND PAIR-CASE
Signed: *Wm. Ackers London*. Silver;
the pair-case pierced and engraved.
ENGLISH: early 18th century.
Casemaker's mark, HR monogram
and LD.
9073-1863

2 WATCH AND PAIR-CASE
Signed: *Tho Johnson Richmond*.
Silver.
ENGLISH: first half of 18th century.
Casemaker's mark, WN.
Brooke Gift
637-1864

3 FRUIT-KNIFE
Gold blade and mother-of-pearl
handle striped with gold. The blade
signed: *Gray*.
ENGLISH: late 18th century.
Formerly belonging to Charles
Mathews, the comedian (1776-1835).
Jones Collection
935-1882

4 WATCH
Signed: *James Reith, Versailles*.
Pierced and engraved gold.
ENGLISH (but made in France):
early 18th century. (Pair-case)
casemaker's mark, IW crowned.
M.127-1909

**5 WATCH AND TWO
PAIR-CASES**
Signed: *Jn. Ellicot, London*. Gold, the
inner-case pierced and engraved, and
the inner pair-case embossed and
chased and signed: *Moser Fecit*.
Outer pair-case of shagreen and
pinchbeck.
ENGLISH: about 1750. (Inner case),
casemaker's mark, J.B.
M.63-1954

6 ETUI
Agate, mounted in gold, set with a
emerald and three brilliant-cut
diamonds, and with gold suspension
chains.
The underside engraved: *Masham
from her Lovin Dux*.
ENGLISH: early 18th century.
Given by Queen Anne to Mrs.
Masham, when the latter supplanted
the Duchess of Marlborough in the
Queen's affection and confidence.
Jones Collection
950-1882

ENGLISH WATCHES
AND OTHER ARTICLES:
*early 18th-early 19th
century*

42

7 WATCH AND PAIR-CASE
Signed: *D. Quare London.* Silver,
pierced and engraved.
ENGLISH: early 18th century.
1362-1904

8 WATCH AND PAIR-CASE
Signed: *Sam Aldworth ye Strand.*
Silver.
ENGLISH: early 18th century.
Given by Mr. Alfred Jones
M.82-1921

9 ETUI
Onyx, mounted in pinchbeck.
ENGLISH: about 1760.
Given by Dame Joan Evans, P.P.S.A.
M.49-1962

10 WATCH
Signed: *Dan Delander London.567.*
Gold. The case engraved with a
version of the arms of Williams of
Cochwillan.
ENGLISH: London hallmarks for
1729-30; casemaker's mark, W.I.
Given by the family of the late
William Macdonald Matthews of
Tunbridge Wells
M.61-1959

11 WATCH AND PAIR-CASE
Gold, embossed and chased.
ENGLISH: about 1760 (the
movement later).
Given by Miss Marie Langton
362-1890

12 CHATELAINE
Steel, with coloured gold decoration.
ENGLISH: about 1770.
M.61-1962

13 CHATELAINE
Steel, with coloured gold decoration.
ENGLISH: about 1760.
M.60-1962
Nos. 12 & 13, given by Dame Joan
Evans, P.P.S.A.

14 BUTT OF A RIDING SWITCH
Gold, embossed and chased.
? ENGLISH: mid 18th century.
M.19-1965

15 WATCH AND PAIR-CASE
Signed: *T. Best, London.* Gilt copper,
pierced and engraved.
ENGLISH: late 18th century.
Probably made for the Turkish
market.
1413-1903

16 WATCH AND PAIR-CASE
Signed: *Geo. Prior, London.*
Engraved pinchbeck; Turkish
numerals. The decoration of the pair-
case, which shows Diogenes and
Alexander, probably Turkish.
ENGLISH: early 19th century.
Made for the Turkish market.
Evan Roberts Gift
M.178 & a-1915

17 WATCH AND PAIR-CASE
Signed: *Jn. Champion, London.*
Gold, embossed and chased.
ENGLISH: dated 1779. Casemaker's
mark, HT.
9018-1863

18 ETUI
Moss agate, mounted in pinchbeck.
ENGLISH: about 1760.
Given by Dame Joan Evans, P.P.S.A.
M.50-1962

19 WATCH AND PAIR-CASE
Signed: *Thos. Mudge, W. Dutton,
London.* Coloured gold, chased.
ENGLISH: about 1780. Casemaker's
mark, IBI.
Given by Miss G.E.A. Fosbery
M.339-1962

ENGLISH WATCHES:
about 1700-1768

**ENGLISH WATCHES
AND OTHER ARTICLES:**
1800-1911

20 WATCH AND PAIR-CASE
Signed: *And. Dickie, Edinburgh.*
Gold, embossed, chased and pierced.
The case ENGLISH: London hall-
marks for 1735-36.
Brooke Gift
632-1864

21 WATCH MOVEMENT
Signed: *Tompion, London No.4413.*
Gilt brass.
ENGLISH: about 1700.
The gold case and dial later.
Lent by Miss I. de B. Lockyer

22 WATCH AND PAIR-CASE
Signed: *Jn. Fladgate, London.* Gold,
embossed and chased.
ENGLISH: London hallmarks for
1766-67. Casemaker's mark, HT.
Given by P.W. Mitchell and Mrs.
Edith Reid in memory of their
brother H.P. Mitchell
M.388-1926

**23 WATCH, PAIR-CASE AND
ITEMS FROM A CHATELAINE**
Repeating watch of gold, the
movement signed: *Marmd. Storr
London 4422.* Inner pair-case, etui
and thimble-case of bloodstone
mounted in gold, brilliant-cut
diamonds and enamel. Outer pair-
case of leather-covered gold.
ENGLISH: about 1750-60. Casemaker's mark, W.W.
Lent by Sir Timothy Harford, Bt.

24 PAIR-CASE FOR A WATCH
Signed: *H. Manley fecit.* Gold,
embossed and chased.
ENGLISH: about 1750.
The case is associated with a
contemporary Dutch watch, the
movement signed: *Gerret Bramer
Amsterdam,* with a pierced and
engraved gold case bearing a
maker's mark, a fish and SG.
654-1872

25 PAIR-CASE FOR A WATCH
Signed: *H. Manly Fec.,* Gold,
embossed and chased.
ENGLISH: about 1750.
288-1854

26 WATCH
Signed: *Geo. Etherington, London.*
Gold, pierced, engraved and chased,
the dial set with table-cut diamonds
and emeralds.
ENGLISH: London hallmarks for
1704-5. Casemaker's mark, ID.
Said to have belonged to the Empress
Elizabeth of Russia.
Given by Mr. Edmund A. Phillips
M.19-1934

27 WATCH
Signed: *Cha: Clay, London.* Gold and
crystal.
ENGLISH: mid 18th century.
4299-1857

28 WATCH AND PAIR-CASE
Signed: *Clay, London.* Gold,
embossed and chased.
ENGLISH: London hallmarks for
1767-68. Casemaker's mark, ID.
Alfred Williams Hearn Gift
M.134-1923

29 WATCH AND PAIR-CASE
Signed: *Ja. Debaufre, London.* Gold.
The pair-case chased and set with
coloured glass.
ENGLISH: London hallmarks for
1723-24. Casemaker's mark, H....
Bernal Collection
2372-1855

30 WATCH AND PAIR-CASE
Signed: *John Thomas St. James's
Street* (London).
Enamelled gold, set with pearls.
ENGLISH: about 1800.
Given by Miss G.M. Pratt
M.13 & a-1957

31 WATCH
Signed: *Litherland Davies,
Liverpool.* Gold, embossed and
chased.
ENGLISH: Chester hallmarks for
1837-38. Casemaker's mark, TH.
Bequeathed by Mr. H.A. Hance
M.IIII-1927

32 HAND
Gold, set with emeralds and garnets.
Possibly from a chatelaine or shawl
pin.
ENGLISH or FRENCH: about 1830.
M.347a-1940

33 SHAWL or CRAVAT PIN
Gold, set with foiled pastes; the head
in the form of a hand.
ENGLISH or FRENCH: about 1830.
Given by Miss M.M. Bennetts
M.16-1968

34 WATCH
Signed: *Smith & Asprey, London.*
Turned and chased gold.
ENGLISH: London hallmarks for
1811-12.
Given by Mrs. Chellini through the
National Art Collections Fund
M.1-1963

**35 CASE FOR A PROPELLING
PENCIL**
Gold, engraved with the inscription:
*W.L.G. Oct. 3 1851 Heb. xiii 7, 8v.
A.L.G.*
ENGLISH: about 1850.
M.9-1972

***36 CASE FOR A PROPELLING
PENCIL**
Gold, enamelled and set with a
turquoise and with medallion
portraits of Queen Victoria (1819-
1901) and Prince Albert (1819-1861).
ENGLISH: about 1850.
Said to have been given by Queen
Victoria to the Emperor
Napoleon III (1808-1873) when he
came to England on a state visit in
1855.
M.74-1967

Case 7 Board E

ENGLISH OBJECTS OF
VERTU:
about 1750-1812

Case 7 Board F
(corner of cases 6 & 7)

MODERN ENGLISH
OBJECTS OF VERTU

44

37 SCENT-BOTTLE
Crystal, mounted in gold, set with
emeralds, rubies and brilliant-cut
diamonds.
? ENGLISH (London): about 1820.
Purchased by the first owner at the
shop of Thomas Hamlet (d.1849), the
natural son of Sir John Dashwood.
Bolckow Bequest
749-1890

*38 VINAIGRETTE
Silver-gilt, set with semi-precious
stones and Scotch pebbles. Signed:
Signed: *G. & M. CRICHTON, 15
PRINCES STREET EDINBURGH.*
SCOTTISH: Edinburgh hallmarks
for 1885-86.
M.117-1966

39 WATCH
Signed: *Rundell & Bridge, London.*
Enamelled gold, set with pearls.
ENGLISH: about 1800.
Bequeathed by Sir Victor Wellesley
M.66-1954

**40 CASE FOR A PROPELLING
PENCIL**
Gold, set with rose-cut diamonds,
rubies, emeralds, sapphires and
an opal. Chased with a rose, a
thistle and a shamrock, emblems
of the United Kingdom.
ENGLISH: about 1821.
Probably a gift from George IV,
perhaps at the time of his coronation
in 1821.
M.25-1975

41 WATCH
Keyless watch in hunting case;
engraved gold.
SWISS: about 1910; with repeating
mechanisms, stop-watch, a calendar
and two-stage chimes. The case
struck with London hallmarks for
1911-12. The inner case signed by the
retailer: *Sir John Bennett, 65
Cheapside, London.*
M.24-1975
Nos. 40 & 41, Hill Bequest

**42 CASE OF IMPLEMENTS
(NECESSAIRE)**
Agate, with gold mounts.
ENGLISH: mid 18th century.
Given by Mrs. Samuel S. Joseph
M.161-1941

43 SCENT FLASK
In the form of a boy holding a lamb.
Agate, with gold mounts set with
diamond sparks and enamelled with
the inscription: JE VOUS L'OFFRE
(I give you this) The figure
possibly carved by an Italian
and mounted in England.
ENGLISH: about 1760.
Murray Bequest
M.1052-1910

44 CASE OF IMPLEMENTS
Agate, mounted with gold openwork.
ENGLISH: third quarter of 18th
century.
961-1882

45 CASE OF IMPLEMENTS
Glass painted to imitate agate; caged
with flowers in gold openwork,
chased and embossed.
ENGLISH: mid 18th century.
960-1882

*46 CASE OF IMPLEMENTS
Glass painted to imitate agate;
mounted in gold, the lid decorated
with precious stones. The contents
include a watch signed: *Williamson,
London,* and other pieces displayed
beside the case.
ENGLISH: mid 18th century.
962-1882
Nos. 44-46, Jones Collection

*47 RATTLE AND WHISTLE
Coloured gold; coral handle.
ENGLISH: London hallmarks for
1811-12. Maker's mark of John Ray &
James Montague.
M.18-1973

48 A JEWELLERY TREE
Gold, set with carved emeralds and
rubies.
ENGLISH: about 1970. Designed by
Gerald Benney and made in his
London workshop, using stones
belonging to his client.
Lent anonymously

49 POWDER COMPACT
Gold, set with emeralds and diamond
sparks.
ENGLISH: about 1970. Designed by
Gerald Benney and made in his
London workshop.
Lent anonymously

50 BOX
18 carat gold, enamelled and set with
rutilated quartz.
ENGLISH: London hallmarks for
1975. Maker's mark of Gerald
Benney.
M.86-1979

51 SCENT FLASK
Crystal mounted in gold.
ENGLISH: London hallmarks for
1978. Maker's mark of Roger Doyle.
Given by Winsor & Newton Ltd.
M.1-1979

52 SCENT FLASK
Crystal mounted in gold; gold bee
finial.
ENGLISH: London hallmarks for
1979. Maker's mark of Roger
Doyle. Designed by the maker for
Penhaligon's Ltd., and shown in the
Gardens Exhibition, V & A, 1979.
Presented by Penhaligon's Ltd.
M.87-1979

53 DRAGONFLY CLOCK
Gold insect with blued steel wings
under a glass dome. Designed and
made by Roger Doyle; the dragonfly
wings executed by Malcom Appleby.
ENGLISH: 1977.
M.126-1978

**54 HEAD OF A EURASIAN
WOMAN**
Carved opal, on a wooden stand.
Designed and made by A.L. Pocock,
who had earlier been employed by
Fabergé, goldsmith to the Imperial
Court of Russia.
ENGLISH: 1951.
M.124-1978

CASE 7
BOARD E
NO. 46

CASE 7
BOARD D
NO. 38

CASE 7
BOARD D
NO. 36

CASE 7
BOARD E
NO. 47

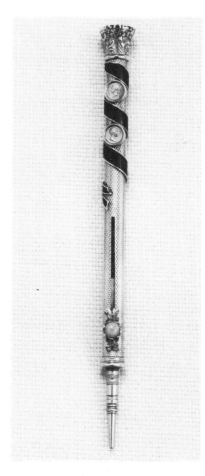

Case 8

SWORDS

1 SMALL-SWORD
The hilt silver-gilt, set with
translucent enamel medallions.
ENGLISH: London hallmarks for
1798-99. Maker's mark of James
Morisset.
Presented to Lieutenant Francis
Douglas by the Marine Society Office
for services during the Mutiny at the
Nore in 1797.
274-1869

2 SMALL-SWORD
The hilt and sheath-mounts
enamelled gold. The shell inscribed:
*Presented to Lt. Colonel James
Hartley in testimony of his brave &
gallant conduct by The Honble East
India Company 1779.* The decoration
of the hilt includes the arms of Lt.
Col. Hartley and of the East India
Company. The sheath signed by
the sword-cutler, *JAMES
SHRAPNELL LONDON.*
ENGLISH: London hallmarks for
1781; maker's mark of James
Morisset.
Lt. Col. James Hartley (1745-1799)
was responsible for saving the
British army from annihilation in
1779 during the Mahratta War.
Carrington-Pierce Collection
M.39-1960

3 SMALL-SWORD
The hilt gold, enamelled with the
arms of the City of London and of
Hill. The shell inscribed to the effect
that the sword was presented to Lt.
General Sir Rowland Hill (1778-1842)
in recognition of his services under
Wellington at the Battle of Vittoria
on 21st June, 1813.
ENGLISH: London hallmarks for
1813-14. Maker's mark of John Ray
and James Montague.
Formerly in the Royal United
Services Museum
M.30-1963

**4 SMALL-SWORD AND
SCABBARD**
The hilt silver-gilt, set with table- and
rose-cut diamonds, rubies and
emeralds.
ENGLISH: about 1757.
Presented to Vice-Admiral Charles
Middleton by the Assembly of
Barbados for capturing a French
privateer.
M.17 & a-1978

45

Case 9

A SELECTION OF WATCHES:
17th – early 19th century

46

5 SMALL-SWORD
Cast, chiselled and pierced gold.
Unmarked.
FRENCH or SWISS: about 1760.
M.40-1973

*6 SMALL-SWORD
The hilt enamelled gold.
DUTCH (Amsterdam); about 1670.
Maker's mark of Joannes Kalkoen,
goldsmith.
F. Mallett Bequest
M.60-1947

CASE 8
NO. 6

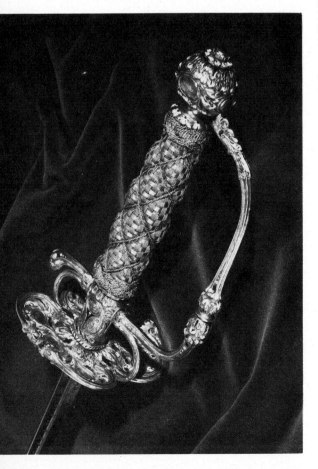

1 WATCH
Signed: *Senebier* (Geneva). Crystal
and gilt-brass.
SWISS: second quarter of 17th
century.
46-1894

2 WATCH
Signed: *Louis Arthaud, A Lyon*
Silver, pierced and engraved.
FRENCH: second half of 17th
century.
Schloss Collection
202-1908

*3 WATCH AND PAIR-CASE
Signed: *Abr. Collomby, London.*
Gold, embossed and chased.
ENGLISH: about 1670. Casemaker's
mark, FA.
Bolckow Bequest
743-1890

4 WATCH
Signed: *Benjamin Hill Londini.*
Crystal and gilt brass with engraved
silver dial.
ENGLISH: mid 17th century.
Schloss Collection
201-1908

5 WATCH
Signed: *Charles Bobinet* (Geneva).
Gilt brass and crystal, with engraved
silver dial.
SWISS: mid 17th century.
Bernal Collection
2355-1855

6 WATCH
Signed: *Charles Bobinet* (Geneva).
Silver, crystal and gilt brass.
SWISS: second quarter of 17th
century.
Lent from the Salting Bequest
M.560-1910

7 WATCH
Gold and enamel.
ENGLISH: mid 17th century.
The (later) movement signed: *Jas
Rousseau,* London.
M.81-1913

8 WATCH
Gold, set with pearls.
FRENCH: about 1830.
Paris warranty marks for 1819-38.
Given by Mr. Alfred Hurst
M.287-1925

9 WATCH
Signed: *J.H. Ester*
Enamelled gold and crystal, set with
almandine garnets and table-cut
diamonds; in the form of a flower
bud.
FRENCH or SWISS: about 1610-20.
785-1901

10 WATCH
Probably by Pierre F. Ingold.
Enamelled gold and crystal.
FRENCH: Paris warranty marks for
1819-38.
Given by Miss Elizabeth A. Mullins
M.98-1916

11 WATCH
Enamelled gold, set with jasper and
onyx. The dial bears the double
monogram *JR* (? Jacobus Rex) with a
royal crown above and orb and
crossed sceptres below.
ENGLISH: second quarter of 17th
century. (The movement and dial
about 1685-90).
According to tradition, this watch
belonged originally to King Charles
II (1630-1685) and was presented by
his brother James II (1633-1701) to a
member of the Pratt family of Cabra
Castle, Co. Cavan, Ireland after
receiving hospitality from him.
M.9-1964

12 WATCH
Signed: *Breguet et Fils* (Paris). Gold.
FRENCH: Paris marks for 1798-1809.
Given by Miss G.M. Pratt
M.19-1957

13 WATCH
Signed: *Senebier* (Geneva). Silver,
gilt brass and crystal; in the
form of a bud.
SWISS: second quarter of 17th
century.
237-1853

*14 WATCH
Enamelled gold, inscribed with the
name of the owner: *E. Shea,* and the
date *1829.*
FRENCH: dated 1829.
328-1897

15 WATCH
Signed: *A. Fremin.* Enamelled gold
and crystal.
FRENCH: about 1600.
Spitzer Collection
Given by Dame Joan Evans, P.P.S.A.
M.238-1975

16 WATCH
Signed: *Jean Rousseau* (Geneva).
Engraved silver, with gilt-brass dial.
SWISS: third quarter of 17th century.
Bernal Collection
2374-1855

17 WATCH
Signed: *J. Bock* (Frankfurt);
Engraved silver and gilt-brass.
GERMAN: first half of 17th century.
Bernal Collection
2368-1855

18 WATCH
Engraved gilt brass and silver.
Signed in Arabic characters: *Jan
Ptru* (? Jean Pattru).
Probably made in Turkey by a
French craftsman.
Mid 17th century.
136-1907

19 WATCH
Signed: *Estienne Hubert A Rouen.*
Engraved and pierced silver.
FRENCH: second half of 17th
century.
Bernal Collection
2367-1855

20 WATCH
Signed: *Nicolas Bernard A Paris.*
Chased and engraved silver, parcel-
gilt.
FRENCH: mid 17th century.
1140-1905

21 WATCH AND PAIR-CASE
Gold, set with rose-cut diamonds.
Tortoise-shell pair-case.
ENGLISH: early 19th century.
Maker's mark of George Prior.
Lent anonymously

22 WATCH AND PAIR-CASE
By Abs. Collomby, London.
Embossed gold; hands in silver set
with brilliants. The watch indicates
the days of the month. Outer case of
shagreen.
ENGLISH: about 1750.
743-b-1890

CASE 9
NO. 3

CASE 9
NO. 14

GREEK:
about 1450 – 600 BC
ETRUSCAN:
7th – 5th century BC

48

The jewellery in these cases, which are in the central room of the gallery, ranges from Egyptian work of the reign of Tuthmosis III (about 1490-1436 BC) to pieces by living artist-craftsmen. The majority is European in origin; it includes a little male jewellery, but most was designed for female use. The chronological sequence is broken by the seven cases in the middle of the gallery. Of these, Cases 24-26, and 28, contain jewels dating from the Renaissance and later which are best viewed in the round. Case 27 is devoted to sentimental and commemorative jewellery, while Cases 29 and 30 are reserved for temporary displays, mainly of recent works lent by the makers.

1 PAIR OF ROSETTES
Gold, decorated with embossed and granulated work.
GREEK: 7th century BC.
8838, 8839-1863

2 CLASP
Gold; with sphinxes in stamped work.
GREEK: 7th century BC.
8857 & a-1863

3 PENDANT
Gold, hung with a lenticular gem of red jasper engraved with two lions.
GREEK: (Mycenaean period): about 1450-1100 BC.
8793-1863
Nos. 1-3 from the John Webb Collection

4 JEWEL
Gold, set with a blue paste.
ETRUSCAN: 7th-5th century BC.
Bequeathed by Mr Bernard H. Webb
M.134-1919

5 EARRING
Gold.
CYPRO-MYCENAEAN: 14th-12th century BC.
Ready Bequest
M22-1959

6 CLASP
Gold; with acorns in stamped work.
GREEK: 7th - 5th century BC.
Webb Collection
8744-1863

7 PAIR OF ROSETTES
Gold, decorated with filigree.
GEEEK: 7th century BC.
3345-1856

8 EARRINGS
'Box' type. Gold, decorated with filigree and granulated work.
ETRUSCAN and GREEK: 7th - 5th century BC.
3347-1856
Webb Collection: 8731 & a, 8750, 8752, 8760-1863
Castellani Collection: 625-1884
250 & a-1891
Ready Bequest: M.17, 18-1959

9 NECKLACE
Gold beads, plain and granulated, and blue glass beads with amber pendants.
GREEK: 7th - 5th century BC.
8851-1863

10 PORTION OF A NECKLACE
Gold, formed of flattened globular beads, plain and minutely granulated.
Probably ETRUSCAN: 7th - 5th century BC.
8847-1863

11 EARRING
'Leech' type. Gold, decorated with filigree.
GREEK: 7th-5th century BC.
8761-1863

12 EARRING
Gold; a siren in stamped work.
GREEK: 7th-5th century BC.
8761-1863

*13 FIBULA
Gold, with winged sphinxes and lion-heads in stamped work.
GREEK: 7th-5th century BC.
8840-1863

14 FIBULA
Gold, with a winged lion in stamped work. On the sheath for the (missing) pin, lions and doves in similar work.
GREEK: 7th-5th century BC.
8841-1863

15 EARRING
Gold, filigree and granulated work.
GREEK: 7th century BC.
8759-1863

16 EARRING
Gold, ending in knots.
GREEK: 7th-5th century BC.
8807-1863

Nos. 9-16, Webb Collection

Case 10 Board B

GREEK AND ETRUSCAN:
7th - 3rd century BC

*1 PENDANT
Gold, with a head of Hera wearing a diadem stamped with anthemion and palmette ornaments.
GREEK: 4th - 3rd century BC.
Found at Kerch in the Crimea.
8487-1863

2 NECKLACE AND PENDANT
Gold, the plaited chain hung with a cylinder seal; chain and bud pendants.
GREEK: 4th - 3rd century BC.
122-1864

3 EARRING
Gold, re-decorated with bosses and beads.
ETRUSCAN: 5th - 3rd century BC.
8749-1863

4 PAIR OF EARRINGS
Gold, chased with palmettes and hung with corded rings; one earring set with a garnet.
ETRUSCAN: 5th - 3rd century BC.
8746, 8758-1863

5 EARRING
Gold, chased with a palmette and lotus flower; hung with a plaited ring.
ETRUSCAN: 5th - 3rd century BC.
8748-1863

6 EARRING
Gold, terminating in a lion's mask.
ETRUSCAN: 5-3rd century BC.
8762-1863
Nos. 1, 3-6, Webb Collection

7 DRESS ORNAMENT
Gold, with filigree decoration.
GREEK: 5th-3rd century BC.
M.25-1959

8 ORNAMENT
Gold, in the form of a hawk.
? GREEK: 7th century BC.
M.19-1959

Nos. 7 & 8, Ready Bequest

9 EARRING
Gold, decorated with wire spirals and applied work.
Originally set with stones (now missing).
ETRUSCAN: 5th-3rd century BC.
8763-1863

10 PAIR OF EARRINGS
Gold, with pendants of bosses and beads.
ETRUSCAN: 5th-3rd century BC.
8732 & a-1863

11 PENDANT
Gold.
ETRUSCAN: 5th-3rd century BC.
Ready Bequest
M.26-1959

12 EARRING
Gold, terminating in a lion-mask.
GREEK: 6th century BC (?).
8754-1863

13 PAIR OF EARRINGS
Gold, stamped with granular ornament.
GREEK: 5th-4th century BC.
8742 & a-1863

*14 ROSETTES, perhaps from a diadem
Gold, with granulated decoration.
GREEK: 7th-5th century BC.
8809, 8810, 8812, 8815, 8817, 8819, 8820, 8821, 8822, 8828, 8835-1863

15 PAIR OF EARRINGS
Gold, chased with palmettes; with plaited rings hanging from applied foliage.
ETRUSCAN: 5th-3rd century BC.
8726 & a-1863

16 PAIR OF EARRINGS
Gold, trumpet-shaped.
ETRUSCAN: 5th-3rd century BC.
8720-1863

17 TWO BRACELET TERMINALS
Gold; bull heads (the original bracelet band has been lost).
GREEK: 7th century BC.
8834, 8835-1863
Nos. 9 & 10, 12-17, Webb Collection

18 PIN, WITH PENDENT RING
Gold; the pin in the form of a bird.
GREEK: 7th century BC.
Given by Dr. W.L. Hildburgh, F.S.A.
M.38-1948

*19 BRACELET
Dark blue glass bands, with gold ram – head terminals.
GREEK: 5th century BC.
8855-1863

20 CHILD'S RING (or part of a larger jewel)
Gold, the head or bezel formed of pellets.
ETRUSCAN: 5th-3rd century BC.
8787-1863

21 PAIR OF EARRINGS
Gold, terminating in lion-masks.
ETRUSCAN: 5th-3rd century BC.
8728 & a-1863
Nos. 19-20, Webb Collection

Case 10 Board C

MEDITERRANEAN:
7th century BC – 1st century AD

1 TWO PENDANTS
Gold. In the form of Ta-urt (Thoeris), a hippopotamus goddess.
EGYPTIAN (Ptolemaic): 4th-1st century BC.
M.32 & a-1963

2 PENDANT
Gold, inlaid with glass. In the form of Bes, a deity of music, war and childbirth.
EGYPTIAN (Ptolemaic): 4th-1st century BC.
M.31-1963
Nos. 1 & 2, Wallis Bequest

3 NECKLACE AND PAIR OF EARRINGS
Gold, strung with beads and ornaments of gold, glass, glazed ware, and ivory; and hung with bronze figures of Harpocrates (Horus), Ceres-Isis, the crowned hawk of Horus, and a griffin.
EGYPTO-ROMAN: about 1st century AD.
From the old Geological Museum, Jermyn Street
4817-b-1901

4 PENDANT
Gold, the lion-headed goddess Sekhmet with sacred eye of Horus.
EGYPTIAN (Ptolemaic): 4th-1st century BC.
Wallis Bequest
M.34-1963

5 CASE FOR AN AMULET
Gold, with the head of Sekhmet.
PHOENICIAN: 7th-6th century BC.
Found at Tharros in Sardinia.
8836-1863

6 CASE FOR AN AMULET (?)
Gold, with the head of Heru (Horus).
PHOENICIAN: 7th-6th century BC.
Found at Tharros in Sardinia.
8837-1863
Nos. 5 & 6, Webb Collection

7 SCARAB
Gold. Inscribed with the name of Tuthmosis III (Pharoah 1490-1436 BC).
EGYPTIAN: (later in date than the inscription).
M.41-1963

8 WEDJET EYE OF HORUS
Gold; a popular amulet.
EGYPTIAN (XXVIth Dynasty or later): 6th-5th century BC.
M.33-1963
Nos. 7 & 8, Wallis Bequest

9 EARRING
Gold, with pierced annular plaque.
ROMAN: 3rd century BC.
6578-1855

10 STUD
Gold, decorated with filigree.
GREEK: 4th-3rd century BC.
Castellani Collection
626-1884

*11 EARRING
Gold.
PHOENICIAN: 7th-6th century BC.
Given by Dame Joan Evans, P.P.S.A.
M.8-1966

12 EARRING
Gold, with a dolphin-head terminal and a stone bead, probably beryl.
EGYPTIAN (Ptolemaic): 2nd century BC.
Wallis Bequest
M.35-1963

13 EARRING
Gold, ending in a goat-head with a garnet set between the horns.
GREEK: 4th-3rd century BC.
Webb Collection
8756-1863

14 EARRING
Gold, with filigree decoration; dove pendant.
GREEK: 4th-3rd century BC.
Ready Bequest
M.20-1959

15 EARRING
Gold; Cupid.
GREEK: 4th-3rd century BC.
Murray Bequest
M.1032-1910

16 NECKLACE
A gold chain strung with garnet beads, the clasp in the form of goat-heads.
GREEK: 3rd century BC.
Montague Taylor Collection
558-1897

Case 10 Board D

HELLENISTIC:
4th – 3rd century BC

*1 ORNAMENT
Gold, with lion-masks.
GREEK: 4th-3rd century BC.
Castellani Collection
624-1884

2 PAIR OF EARRINGS
Gold, each with a pendant in the form of a boat with canopy.
GREEK: 4th-3rd century BC.
Webb Collection
8730-1863

3 NECKLACE
Gold, set with garnets and emeralds.
GREEK: 4th-3rd century BC.
Given by Dame Joan Evans, P.P.S.A.
M.1-1966

4 PAIR OF EARRINGS
Gold, set with garnets; hung with doves decorated with filigree and enamel.
GREEK: 4th-3rd century BC.
Found in the island of Melos
7 & a-1874

5 TWO EARRINGS
Gold, decorated with filigree.
GREEK: 4th-3rd century BC.
One given by Messrs Rollin and Feuardent: 1006-1873
The other from the Webb Collection (incomplete): 8794-1863

6 ANIMAL HEAD (a wild goat)
Gold.
GREEK: 4th-3rd century BC.
Given by Dame Joan Evans, P.P.S.A.
M.17-1966

*7 PAIR OF EARRINGS
Gold, hung with a vase and chains.
GREEK: 4th-3rd century BC.
8729 & a-1863

8 EARRING
Gold; Cupid with Syrinx.
GREEK: 4th-3rd century BC.
8747-1863

9 PAIR OF EARRINGS
Gold, ending in lion-heads.
GREEK: 4th-3rd century BC.
8739 & a-1863
Nos. 7-9, Webb Collection

HELLENISTIC
AND ROMAN:
*3rd century BC - 3rd
century AD*

*10 NECKLACE
Gold chain strung with garnet beads
and two of green glass capped in
gold; the clasp decorated with a head
of a kid.
GREEK: 3rd century BC.
305-1870

11 NECKLACE
Gold, set with garnets.
GREEK: 3rd century BC.
Given by Dame Joan Evans, P.P.S.A.
M.2-1966

12 BRACELET
Plaited gold.
GREEK: 4th-3rd century BC.
Found in the Crimea.
306-1870

13 EARRING
Gold, hung with a pearl and a garnet
bead.
GREEK: 4th-3rd century BC.
M.558-1911

14 PAIR OF EARRINGS
Gold, each set with a glass bead.
GRECO-ROMAN: 4th-3rd century
BC.
Given by Dr W.L. Hildburgh, F.S.A.
M.37 & a-1948

15 PAIR OF EARRINGS
Gold, hollow, each ending in a bull-
head set with a garnet.
GREEK: 4th-3rd century BC.
Joicey Bequest
M.301 & a-1919

16 PAIR OF EARRINGS
Gold, with goat-head terminals.
GREEK: 4th-3rd century BC.
8725 & a-1863

17 PAIR OF EARRINGS
Gold, twisted wire, with lion-head
terminals.
GREEK: 4th-3rd century BC.
8724 & a-1863
Nos. 16 & 17, Webb Collection

**18 RING FOR A LOCK OF
HAIR (?)**
Gold, with lion-head terminals.
GREEK: 4th-3rd century BC.
565-1891

19 PAIR OF EARRINGS
Gold, ending in heads of goats, their
eyes once enamelled.
GREEK: 4th-3rd century BC.
M.1029 & a-1910

20 EARRING
Gold, ending in a horned lion-head
with a rosette between the horns.
GREEK: 4th-3rd century BC.
724-1877

21 EARRING
Gold; a ram-head, with a rosette
above the horns.
GREEK: 4th-3rd century BC.
Given by Dame Joan Evans, P.P.S.A.
M.9-1966

22 HAIRPIN
Gold, with plain knob.
GREEK: 4th-3rd century BC.
Webb Collection
8804-1863

1 EARRING
Gold, hung with a blue glass bead
and an emerald.
GREEK: 3rd century BC.
6577-1855

2 BUTTON
Gold, stamped in relief with the
Three Graces.
GREEK: 3rd century BC.
8831-1863

3 DISC
Gold, stamped in relief with the head
of a Fury.
GREEK: 3rd century BC.
Nos. 2 & 3, Webb Collection
8826-1863

4 EARRING
Gold, the vase-pendant set with
garnets and hung with a pearl.
M.557-1911

5 PAIR OF EARRINGS
Gold, each with a maenad's head
wearing an ivy wreath, and pendent
figure of Cupid.
GREEK: 2nd-1st century BC.
Paris warranty mark for 1847
onwards, in this case used to denote
the gold quality of antique goods.
Webb Collection
8722 & a-1863

6 EARRING
Gold, hung with a garnet and a blue
glass bead.
GREEK: 2nd-1st century BC.
6575-1855

7 NECKLACE
A chain of flat gold links.
GRECO-ROMAN: 2nd-1st century
BC.
Castellani Collection
628-1884

8 COSMETIC CASE
Gold, with corded bands.
GRECO-ROMAN: 2nd-1st century
BC.
Webb Collection
8801-1863

9 PAIR OF EARRINGS
Silver, ending in a demi-lynx.
GREEK: 2nd century BC-2nd century
AD.
211 & a-1892

ETRUSCAN:
5th century BC

52

*10 EARRING
Gold, hung with chains and a figure
of Cupid.
GRECO-ROMAN: 2nd century BC –
2nd century AD.
251-1891

11 EARRING
Gold, hung with a vase, the body of
ivory, and chains ending in pearls
and emerald and garnet beads
GRECO-ROMAN: 2nd century BC –
2nd century AD.
44-1894

12 AMULET
Gold, a figure of Venus standing on a
globe.
ROMAN: 2nd century BC-2nd
century AD.
8799-1863

13 PAIR OF EARRINGS
Gold, strung with lenticular garnet
beads.
ROMAN: 1st-3rd century AD.
8734 & a-1863
Nos. 12 & 13, Webb Collection

14 BRACELET
Gold; in the form of a snake.
ROMAN: 1st century BC – 3rd
century AD.
Given by Dame Joan Evans, P.P.S.A.
M.13-1966

1 BOWL
Gold, lined with a thin sheet of gold
and decorated on the outside with
granulation which, it has been
suggested, may be a nineteenth
century addition.
ÉTRUSCAN: 5th century BC.
Said to have been found in a tomb at
Palestrina.
241-1894

*2 MIRROR
Bronze, engraved with a scene of a
satyr and a maenad.
ETRUSCAN: 5th century BC.
Lent from the Salting Bequest
M.707-1910

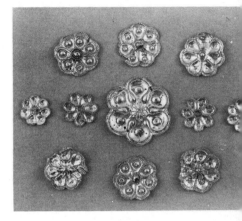

CASE 10
BOARD B
NO. 14

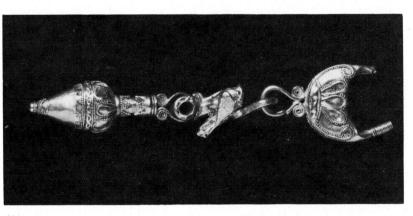

CASE 10
BOARD C
NO. 11

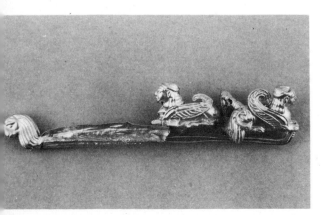

CASE 10
BOARD A
NO. 13

CASE 10
BOARD B
NO. 1

CASE 10
BOARD B
NO. 19

ROMAN:
1st – 4th century AD

*1 PAIR OF EARRINGS   53
Gold, decorated with granules and
hung with porphyry pendants.
1st-4th century AD.
8745 & a-1863

*2 NECKLACE
Amethyst beads united by lyre-
shaped gold links.
2nd century AD.
8844-1863
Nos. 1 & 2, Webb Collection

3 NECKLACE ORNAMENT
Gold, set with a garnet.
2nd-3rd century AD.
Wallis Bequest
M.44-1963

4 PAIR OF EARRINGS
Gold, pierced, with pendants of
emerald matrix.
1st-4th century AD.
6573-6574-1855

5 NECKLACE
A gold chain, strung with malachite
beads.
2nd century AD.
Castellani Collection
629-1884

6 NECKLACE
Gold, with rose quartz and emeralds,
and glass beads.
3rd century AD.
French import mark introduced in
1893 for articles from countries
without customs conventions.
Given by Dame Joan Evans, P.P.S.A.
M.7-1966

7 NECKLACE
A gold chain strung with
chrysoprase and amazon stone
heads.
2nd century AD.
8853-1863

*8 PAIR OF EARRINGS
Gold, strung with pearls; hung with a
bunch of seed pearls.
1st-4th century AD.
8735 & a-1863

Case 11 Board B

ROMAN:
1st – 4th century AD

9 PAIR OF EARRINGS
Gold, set with sapphires and hung
with emeralds and pearls.
1st-4th century AD.
8736 & a-1863
Nos. 7-9, Webb Collection

10 BRACELET
Gold.
3rd century AD.
Given by Dame Joan Evans P.P.S.A.
M.14-1966

11 PAIR OF EARRINGS
Gold, set with garnets and hung with
cornelian and emerald beads.
1st-4th century AD.
Webb Collection
8737 & a-1863

12 PAIR OF EARRINGS
Gold.
2nd century AD.
Given by Dame Joan Evans, P.P.S.A.
M.11 & a-1966

1 NECKLACE
Gold. Pierced clasp and bud
pendant.
ROMAN: 2nd century AD.
M.5-1966

2 PENDANT
Gold, set with plasma cameos of
heads of children and glass beads.
EAST ROMAN: 3rd century AD.
M.16-1966
Nos. 1 & 2, given by Dame Joan
Evans, P.P.S.A.

3 BRACELET
Gold, in the form of a spiral band
with ends in the form of snake-heads.
ROMAN: 1st or 2nd century AD.
Castellani Collection
631-1884

4 PAIR OF EARRINGS
Gold, decorated with filigree
and set with garnets.
ROMAN: 1st-2nd century AD.
Ready Bequest
M.23 & a-1959

5 PENDANT
Oval cabochon quartz, cracked and
stained, with pivoted gold mount.
ROMAN: 1st-2nd century AD.
Castellani Collection
641-1884

6 NECKLACE
Silver-gilt; plaited chains joined by
openwork links. Converts into two
bracelets.
ROMAN: 2nd century AD.
M.8843-1863

**7 TWO RINGS FROM AN
ORNAMENT**
Gold, strung with blue glass beads.
ROMAN: 1st-4th century AD.
8740 & a-1863
Nos. 6 & 7, Webb Collection

8 EARRING
Gold, pierced and set with an
emerald bead.
ROMAN: 1st-4th century AD.
6572-1855

9 PIN
Gold, hung with emeralds.
ROMAN: 1st-4th century AD.
Webb Collection
8802-1863

10 PIN
Gold, in the form of a daisy.
ROMAN: 1st-4th century AD.
6571-1855

11 NECKLACE
Gold. Pierced clasp and bud
pendant.
ROMAN: 2nd century AD.
Given by Dame Joan Evans, P.P.S.A.
M.6-1966

*12 EARRING
Gold, with lapis lazuli bead and
pendant.
ROMAN: 1st-4th century AD.
8800-1863

13 AMULET
Gold; a figure of Ceres.
ROMAN: 1st or 2nd century AD.
8792-1863
Nos. 12 & 13, Webb Collection

14 PAIR OF EARRINGS
Gold, with twisted wires.
SYRIAN: ? 3rd century AD.
207 & a-1872

*15 PAIR OF EARRINGS
Gold, set and hung with pearls,
emeralds and sapphires.
ROMAN: 1st-4th century AD.
8733 & a-1863

*16 EARRING
Gold, pierced, set with a garnet and
hung with pastes and pearls on
wires.
ROMAN: 1st-4th century AD.
8753-1863
Nos. 15 & 16, Webb Collection

17 EARRING
Gold, with a pendant.
GRECO-ROMAN: 1st-2nd century
AD.
Given by Dr. W.L. Hildburgh, F.S.A.
M.18-1943

Case 11 Board C

ROMAN AND GERMANIC:
2nd – 7th century AD

18 BRACELET
Gold.
ROMAN: 2nd-4th century AD.
M.15-1966

19 PAIR OF EARRINGS
Gold, set with pearls.
ROMAN: 1st-2nd century AD.
M.10 & a-1966
Nos. 18 & 19, given by Dame Joan
Evans, P.P.S.A.

20 ORNAMENT (? a child's bracelet)
Gold, with a star-shaped plaque
bearing a cross pattée within a
wreath, in niello.
EARLY CHRISTIAN: ? 3rd century
AD.
806-1893

21 BRACELET
Gold.
ROMAN: 2nd-4th century AD.
Given by Dame Joan Evans, P.P.S.A.
M.78-1969

In general, the jewellers of the
Germanic tribes which overran the
Roman Empire learned their
techniques in Roman workshops.
Admiring polychromic jewellery,
they adopted and developed the use
of foil linings in the settings of
stones, a technique mentioned by
Pliny in the first century AD. The
garnets in the brooch in no. 8 are set
over foil which was first stamped in a
raised grid pattern to ensure the
maximum reflection of light.
Foiled stones and pastes were still
current in the eighteenth century.

1 FASTENING
Bronze, decorated with *champlevé*
enamel.
ROMANO-BRITISH: 2nd or 3rd
century AD.
Found at Hatherop, Gloucestershire.
M16-1920

2 BROOCH
Silver-gilt, set with garnets (two
wanting).
FRANKISH: 6th century AD.
Found at Herpes, Charente.
Transferred from the British
Museum
M.112-1939

3 BROOCH
Bronze, decorated with *champlevé*
enamel.
ROMANO-BRITISH: 3rd century
AD.
Found in 1838 in the foundation of
the old bridge over the Troutbeck at
Kirkby Thore near Appleby.
From the Old Geological Museum,
Jermyn Street
4893-1901

4 BROOCH
Silver-gilt, decorated with niello and
set with garnets over patterned foil.
FRANKISH: 6th century AD.
Found at Herpes, Charente.
Transferred from the British
Museum
M.113-1939

5 BROOCH
Bronze, decorated with *champlevé*
enamel.
PROVINCIAL ROMAN: 2nd or 3rd
century AD.
2828-1855

6 LID OF A SEAL BOX
Gilt bronze, set with a red
composition bead.
PROVINCIAL ROMAN: 2nd or 3rd
century AD.
Given by Dr W.L. Hildburgh, F.S.A
M.178-1930

7 BUTTON
Bronze, decorated with *millefiori*
enamel.
ROMAN-BRITISH: 2nd century AD.
Found near Edenhall, Cumberland.
Given by Sir George Musgrave, Bart.
Transferred from the old Geological
Museum, Jermyn Street
4898-1901

8 BROOCH
Pewter, tinnel and gilt, set with
garnets and decorated with enamels.
JUTISH: 6th century AD.
Found at Faversham.
Transferred from the British Museum
M.116-1939

9 LID OF A SEAL BOX
Bronze decorated with *champlevé*
enamel.
PROVINCIAL ROMAN: 2nd or 3rd
century AD.
Given by Dr W.L. Hildburgh, F.S.A.
M.356-1923

10 PLAQUE
From a hanging bowl. Tinned
bronze decorated with *champlevé*
enamel.
IRISH or BRITISH: 7th century AD.
6926-1860

11 BUTTON
Bronze decorated with *millefiori*
enamel.
PROVINCIAL ROMAN: 2nd century
AD.
4098-1857

12 & 13 TWO PLAQUES
Tinned bronze, decorated with
champlevé enamel.
The plaques (one with its containing
ring) are from the side of a bronze
hanging bowl found at Hitchin in
about 1910.
IRISH or BRITISH: 7th century AD.
M.162 & 163-1923

Case 11 Board D

A. HISPANO-MORESQUE JEWELLERY:
found in an earthen pot in Murcia with coins of the tenth-eleventh century AD, and one of only two known hoards from Moorish Spain.

B. VISIGOTHIC:
7th century

14 PENDANT
Gold bracteate, imitating a coin of Valentinian; obverse, Emperor's head and illegible inscription.
5th-6th century AD.
M.111-1939

15 BUCKLE
Gilt bronze, set with garnets.
? VISIGOTHIC: 6th century AD.
? Found at Albi.
M.118-1939

*16 PENDANT
Gold, imitating a coin of the Justins. Obverse: Emperor's bust, the jowl set with a garnet; inscribed: *DN IVSTINVS PPAV*.
JUTISH: 6th century AD.
Found at Faversham, Kent.
M.115-1939
Nos. 14-16, transferred from the British Museum

1 PART OF A NECKLACE
Coloured glass, coral and silver-gilt beads.
10th — 11th century.
1451-1870

2 PAIR OF EARRINGS
Gold, decorated with filigree rosettes.
10th — 11th century.
1447 & a-1870

3 ORNAMENT
Silver-gilt, formed of rings with filigree sides.
10th— 11th century.
1452a-1870

4 PART OF NECKLACE
Gilt metal beads, decorated with bosses and filigree.
10th — 11th century.
449-1870

5 ORNAMENT
Gold; conjoined triangles with filigree decoration.
10th-11th century.
1543-1870

6 PART OF A NECKLACE
Pearls and silver filigree beads.
10th — 11 century.
1450-1870

7 SEVEN LINKED PLAQUES
Silver-gilt, with filigree decoration, set with pastes (four wanting).
10th-11th century.
1455-1870

8 FOUR LINKED PLAQUES FROM A GIRDLE
Gold, with decoration of applied filigree and bosses.
Probably 10th-early 11th century, and the oldest item in the hoard.
1454-1870

9 TEN SILVER COINS FROM A HEADBAND
The coins of Al Hakem II and Hischem II, Caliphs of Cordova, 961-1009; pierced for attachment to the headband.
10th-11th century.
1448-i-1870

10 ORNAMENT
Silver-gilt; rings with filigree sides, a stone wanting from the centre.
10th-11th century.
1452-1870

11 STRING OF STONES
Seventeen stones (amethyst, emerald, sapphire and balas ruby) and six pearls. Portion of the pendants of the votive crowns of the Visigothic kings, found at Guarrazar, near Toledo, Spain, in 1858.
J.C. Robinson Collection
149-1879

Case 11 Board E

GERMANIC:
5th-8th century AD
MEDIEVAL ISLAMIC
AND HISPANO-
MORESQUE:
11th – 15th century

1 BUCKLE
Iron, inlaid with silver.
MEROVINGIAN: 5th to 8th century.
744b-1898

2 BUCKLE
Iron, inlaid with silver.
MEROVINGIAN: 5th to 8th century.
4510-1858

3 BUCKLE
Iron, inlaid with silver.
MEROVINGIAN: 5th to 8th century.
Given by Dr W L Hildburgh, F.S.A.
M.325-1927

**4 TWO RECTANGULAR
ORNAMENTS**
Iron, inlaid with silver.
MEROVINGIAN: 5th to 8th century.
744c-d-1898

5 EARRING
Gold filigree, set with a pearl;
star-shaped border.
LOMBARDIC: 6th-7th century.
Castellani Collection; transferred
from the British Museum
M.121-1939

6 ROSETTE
With holes for a double string.
Gold, pierced and embossed.
From Cairo.
EGYPTIAN: probably 13th-14th
century.
1558-1871

*7 BRACELET
Gold, embossed and set with stones;
panels of unintelligible Kufic script
on a niello ground, extensively re-
worked.
PERSIAN (Saljuq): 12th century.
M.32-1957

8 PART OF A BRACELET (?)
Gold, embossed with Arabic
inscriptions in Kufic script.
ASIA MINOR (Saljuq): 11th or 12th
century
M.45-1963

9 EARRING
Gold, set with a turquoise (a
replacement).
PERSIAN (found at Bujnurd): 11th-
12th century.
M.21-1971

10 SWORD LOCKET
Copper-gilt, with *cloisonné* enamel.
HISPANO-MORESQUE: 15th
century.
Given by Dame Joan Evans, P.P.S.A.
M.58-1975

57

CASE 11
BOARD A
NO. 8

CASE 11
BOARD A
NO. 1

CASE 11
BOARD B
NO. 12

CASE 11
BOARD B
NO. 15

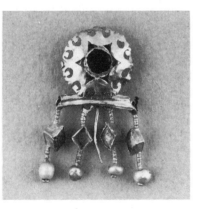

CASE 11
BOARD B
NO. 16

CASE 11
BOARD A
NO. 2

CASE 11
BOARD E
NO. 7

BYZANTINE:
4th – 11th century

MEDIEVAL:
13th – 15th century

58

1 FLASK
Silver, decorated with niello.
11th century.
4512-1858

2 QUATREFOIL
Gold, decorated with niello.
6th or 7th century.
Given by Dame Joan Evans, P.P.S.A.
M.99-1962

3 EARRING
Gold filigree, lacking a stone and
three pendants.
4th-5th century.
Ready Bequest
M.21-1959

4 PLAQUE
Gold, with a dancing-girl in
cloisonné enamel. Similar to one of
the panels of a crown, with the figure
of Constantine Monomachos,
Emperor of the East (1042-1054), in
the National Museum, Budapest.
Doubts have however been cast on
the V & A plaque.
? Mid 11th century.
M.325-1921

5 EARRING
Gold, with filigree decoration; set
with a blue paste, but wanting three
others and three pendants.
4th-5th century.
Webb Collection
8764-1863

6 PENDANT
Gold, set with a garnet.
6th or 7th century.
Given by Dame Joan Evans, P.P.S.A.
M.98-1962

1 SEAL
Silver; St John the Baptist
surrounded by the inscription in
lombardic characters: *S. RICARDI:
DE:LA:BERE*
ENGLISH: late 13th century.
Sir John Evans Collection
M.80-1969

2 RING BROOCH
Gold, inscribed in lombardic
characters: *NON DETVR PETENTI*
(let it not be given up to him who
requests it).
WEST EUROPEAN: 13th century.
M.43-1975
Nos. 1 & 2, given by Dame Joan
Evans, P.P.S.A.

*3 RING BROOCH
Gold, set with rubies and sapphires,
the reverse decorated with a wreath
in niello.
FRENCH: 13th century.
Pichon Collection
547-1897

4 RING BROOCH
Gold, with black letter inscription:
Saunz departir (without division, an
amatory motto).
ENGLISH or FRENCH: early 15th
century.
M.39-1975

5 BEZEL FROM A SEAL
Silver, set with an agate cameo;
inscribed in lombardic characters: *IE
SVI SEL:DE:AMUR:LEL* (I am of
loyal heart).
WEST EUROPEAN: late 13th
century.
Sir John Evans Collection
M.81-1969
Nos. 4 & 5, given by Dame Joan
Evans, P.P.S.A.

6 RING BROOCH
Silver, annular in form; engraved
with magical inscriptions, partly
nielloed.
ITALIAN: 13th century.
Acquired in Florence in 1860.
Waterton Collection
1024-1871

**7 BROOCH WITH CREST OF
PRAYING HANDS**
Gold, with illegible inscription.
WEST EUROPEAN: 14th century.
M.35-1975

***8 BROOCH WITH CREST OF
PRAYING HANDS**
Gold, inscribed: *VI – LIV/IV - VL.*
WEST EUROPEAN: 14th century.
M.48-1975

9 RING BROOCH
Gold, inscribed in lombardic
characters: AVE MARIA GRAC
(Hail Mary, full of grace).
WEST EUROPEAN: 13th century.
M.34-1975
Nos. 7-9, given by Dame Joan Evans,
P.P.S.A.

10 RING BROOCH
Gold, set with rubies and sapphires.
ENGLISH: 14th century.
Found in London.
6808-1860

11 RING BROOCH
Gold, set with rubies and blue
glass.
FRENCH: late 13th century.
Pichon Collection
Lent from the Salting Bequest
M.530-1910

12 RING BROOCH
Gold, set with a ruby and sapphire;
inscribed in lombardic characters:
IEP VAO NEL RLI.
WEST EUROPEAN: 13th century.
M.36-1975

13 RING BROOCH
Gold, inscribed in lombardic
characters: *LE SVI:CI:EN LIV:
DAMI* (I am here in place of a friend).
ENGLISH or FRENCH: 13th
century.
M.49-1975
Nos. 12 & 13, given by Dame Joan
Evans, P.P.S.A.

14 RING BROOCH
Silver-gilt, set with two pastes,
inscribed in lombardic characters:
IOSV IEI ATI VCI (here I am yours).
WEST EUROPEAN: 13th century.
Harman-Oates Collection
M.28-1929

15 RING BROOCH
Gold, inscribed in lombardic
characters: *IES MI CIN VI/DA VI
MN IV.*
WEST EUROPEAN: 14th century.
M.50-1975

16 RING BROOCH
Silver-gilt, with black letter
inscriptions; obverse, + *ihesus
nazerenus Rex Iudeorum* (a
religious/amatory/prophylactic
motto); reverse, *Iohannes Lamb.*
ENGLISH: first half of 15th century.
M.12-1969

*17 PLAQUE
Enamelled gold; the Adoration of the
Magi. Found in the parish
churchyard at Hemel Hempstead,
Hertfordshire.
ENGLISH: 15th century.
M.51-1975

18 ESCUTCHEON
Gold, with black letter inscription:
Abcd cest ma lecon (my lesson is
ABCD).
ENGLISH or FRENCH: 14th century.
M.37-1975
Nos. 15-18, given by Dame Joan
Evans, P.P.S.A.

19 RING BROOCH
Gold, set with rubies (modern
replacements) and an onyx cameo of
a lion and a dog; these two animals in
conjunction were valued in the
Middle Ages as a protection against
dropsy.
The cameo: 1st century BC, set in a
14th century mount. The outer
foliated ring frame probably
FRENCH or BURGUNDIAN: first
half of 15th century.
Bought in Spain by J.C. Robinson
and acquired from his collection
139-1879

*20 HEART-SHAPED BROOCH
Gold, with black letter inscription on
the reverse: *Nostre et tout ditz a vostre
(d)eseir* (ourselves and all things at
your whim).
? FRENCH: 15th century.
Waterton Collection
86-1899

*21 RELIQUARY PENDANT
Silver-gilt, with enamelled
inscription in lombardic characters:
*RELIQUIA. SCI. LEONARDI.
CREMONE* (relic of St. Leonard of
Cremona).
ITALIAN: 14th century.
358-1864

22 RING BROOCH
Silver.
ENGLISH or FRENCH: 14th or 15th
century.
Harman-Oates Collection
M.29-1929

23 RING BROOCH
Gold, with black-letter inscription: +
canc d/epaer/tir (sans departir).
ENGLISH or FRENCH: 15th century.
Given by Dame Joan Evans, P.P.S.A.
M.44-1975

24 RELIQUARY CROSS
Silver-gilt, decorated with
translucent enamel.
ITALIAN: mid-14th century.
M.23-1968

25 RING BROOCH
Gold, with black letter inscriptions: +
*ihesus nazaren rex iudeoru / iaspar:
melchior: baltazar/ M* (the names of
the Three Kings, which do not appear
in the Gospels, were probably
adopted from eastern sources in the
Middle Ages; they were often cited for
prophylactic purposes). The pin
missing.
ENGLISH or FRENCH: late 14th or
early 15th century.
Given by Dame Joan Evans, P.P.S.A.
M.38-1975

*26 BROOCH
Gold; sexfoil, the reverse inscribed in
lombardic characters: *AVE MARIA
GRACIA PLENA DOM.*
WEST EUROPEAN: 13th century.
Rosenheim Collection
M.245-1923

27 RING BROOCH
Silver, inscribed in lombardic
characters: *IHC HOPE VE BEST.*
ENGLISH: 14th century.
Given by Dame Joan Evans, P.P.S.A.
M.47-1975

28 RING BROOCH
Gold, inscribed in lombardic
characters: *PENSEET: DE LI PAR
KI: SUECY* (I think of him by this
token)/*IESUS NAZAREN REX
IUDIORUM:* the pin missing.
ENGLISH or FRENCH: 13th
century.
M.46-1975

29 RING BROOCH
Silver, inscribed in lombardic
characters: *AMI AMET DELI
PENCET* (think of a friend who loves
you) and *IHESVS NAZARENVS
REX IVDEORVM:* the pin missing.
ENGLISH or FRENCH: 14th
century.
M.33-1975
Nos. 28 & 29, given by Dame Joan
Evans, P.P.S.A.

30 PENDENT SEAL
Lead, inscribed: *S. MABIL RELICT
IOH HERMAN* (the seal of Mabil,
widow of Johannes Herman).
WEST EUROPEAN (? German):
13th century.
Begg Bequest
M.324-1975

*31 RING BROOCH
Silver, inscribed in lombardic
characters: *ROBERTI LOVE YAG:
LOVES ME./IHESVS
NAZARENVS REX IVD.*
ENGLISH: late 13th or early 14th
century.
Given by Dame Joan Evans, P.P.S.A.
M.41-1975

MEDIEVAL:
14th-early 16th century

MEDIEVAL:
15th century

*1 GIRDLE
Silver, with medallions bearing the Sacred Monogram and part of the name *MARIA* in lombardic characters.
FRENCH: Paris date letter for 1524-25. Said to have been excavated at St Albans.
13-1899

*2 RING BROOCH
Silver-gilt; lions and eagles raised on foliage.
SCANDINAVIAN: 14th or 15th century.
529-1893

3 HEART-SHAPED BROOCH
Gold, with black letter inscription: *Sanz De Parter.*
? ENGLISH: early 15th century.
Given by Dame Joan Evans, P.P.S.A.
M.40-1975

4 RING BROOCH
Silver, with black letter inscription: *mierchi/vivort* (thanks for life and strength?).
Probably ENGLISH: 15th century.
Found in London.
6809-1860

5 RING BROOCH
Gold; engraved with figures of St George and St Christopher.
ENGLISH: 15th century.
Bernal Collection
2280-1855

6 CAMEO
Onyx: head of a man in profile.
It has been suggested that the cameo is a portrait of René I (1409-1480), Duke of Anjou and (titular) King of Naples.
Lent anonymously

*7 RING BROOCH
Gold, with black letter inscription: *sans de part/ier.*
ENGLISH: early 15th century.
Bernal Collection
2279-1855

8 RING BROOCH
Bronze, inscribed with Roman numerals and fleurs-de-lis.
WEST EUROPEAN: 15th century.
Begg Bequest
M.344-1975

*9 MEDALLION PENDANT
Mother-of-pearl, mounted in silver-gilt. Obverse, the Adoration of the Magi; reverse, the Vernicle.
GERMAN: 15th century.
39-1894

10 POINT (tag for fastening a costume)
Twisted silver wire.
ENGLISH: 15th century.
Recovered from the Thames
M.63-1980

1 PENDANT
Parcel-gilt. Obverse, the Agnus Dei; reverse, the Vernicle.
GERMAN: 15th century.
M.95-1962

2 PENDANT
Silver-gilt. Obverse, the Agnus Dei; reverse, the Sacred Monogram.
GERMAN: 15th century.
St John Hope Collection
M.94-1962
Nos. 1 & 2, given by Dame Joan Evans, P.P.S.A.

3 PENDANT
Silver, parcel-gilt; the Virgin with St Catherine and the Infant Christ, cast in the round.
GERMAN: end of 15th century.
623-1906

*4 THE VIRGIN AND CHILD
Gold, enamelled *en ronde bosse;* probably originally part of a morse (a clasp or fastening of a cope).
FRENCH: about 1400.
829-1891

5 PENDANT
Silver-gilt; St Anne, St James the Great, St Catherine and St Leonard beneath an imbricated canopy; the figures modelled in the round.
GERMAN: late 15th century
808-1891
Nos. 4 & 5, Zouche Collection

6 TRIPTYCH
Silver-gilt. Centre, St George and the Dragon; on the wings, the princess and the king and queen.
ENGLISH: 15th century.
Webb Collection
250-1874

Case 12 Board E

ENAMELS:

*7 ROSARY (the 'Langdale Rosary')
Enamelled gold, consisting of fifty oval AVE beads, six lozenge-shaped PATERNOSTER beads, and a large rounded knop. Each bead is hollow and has on its back or front a subject, either a saint or a scene from the Life of Christ, the title of which is inscribed in black-letter on the rim; two additional beads of later date bear italic inscriptions.
ENGLISH: late 15th century.
There is presumptive evidence that the rosary once belonged to Lord William Howard (1563-1640), the third son of Thomas, Duke of Norfolk (attained and beheaded 1572). The two beads are thought to have been added by Lord William. The rosary passed through the marriage of his great-granddaughter to the Langdales of Houghton Hall, Yorkshire, and old Roman Catholic family, with whom it remained until purchased by the Museum with the aid of funds in the Murray Bequest.
M.30-1934

8 PENDANT
Silver-gilt. Obverse, the Annunciation; reverse, the Nativity.
GERMAN: 15th century.
Lent from the Salting Bequest
M.529-1910

9 CLASP OF A GIRDLE
Silver-gilt; in two parts; in each, a figure of a lady seated in a niche beneath an architectural canopy.
SOUTH GERMAN: late 15th century.
143 & a-1865

The technique of enamelling (fusing coloured glass to a metal base) was known to Mycenaean goldsmiths and was practised in various forms thereafter. In the fourteenth century a new variant, *basse-taille* or translucent enamel, was introduced. The design was chased and engraved in low relief in the metal ground, usually gold or silver, and the vitreous material floated over it to produce a semi-transparent effect which was clearer and lighter where the relief came close to the surface and darker over the hollows.

The objects on this board portray scenes from the New Testament in conveniently portable form for the pious. The technique was later used by Renaissance goldsmiths, often in combination with opaque enamels, to embellish their classicizing designs.

1 DIPTYCH
Silver-gilt, decorated with translucent enamels. Obverse, the Annunciation, the Adoration of the Magi and the Crucifixion; reverse, the Ascension, the Resurrection, the Coronation of the Virgin, St. Christopher and St George.
ENGLISH: first half of 14th century.
Spitzer Collection
M.544-1910

*2 TRIPTYCH
Silver-gilt, decorated with translucent enamels. Obverse, the Resurrection, the Mocking, the Scourging, the Descent from the Cross and the Road to Calvary; reverse, the Crucifixion, the Three Marys, the Descent into Hell, Christ appearing to St Mary Magdalene and the Incredulity of St Thomas.
ENGLISH: first half of 14th century.
M.545-1910
Nos. 1 & 2, lent from the Salting Bequest

3 HALF OF A DIPTYCH
Silver-gilt, decorated with translucent enamels. Obverse, the Annunciation; reverse, the Death of the Virgin.
FRENCH or FLEMISH: second half of 14th century.
Webb Collection
216-1874

4 FOUR PLAQUES
Silver-gilt, decorated with translucent enamels; possibly once part of a girdle preserved amongst the relics of William of Wykeham, Bishop of Winchester (1367-1404) at New College, Oxford.
ENGLISH: late 14th century.
2290-2293-1874

5 TRIPTYCH
Gold, decorated with translucent enamels. Obverse, top rows: St Anne and the Virgin, the Visitation, and St John the Baptist; bottom row: St James the Great, St Edmund and St Giles; above, the Coronation of the Virgin; left wing: St Christopher; right wing: All Saints. Reverse, the stations of the cross and other subjects.
Probably ENGLISH: mid 14th century. An inscription round the edge shows that this piece was given to Claudio Aquaviva, General of the Jesuits (1581-1615), by Elizabeth Vaux, perhaps the well-known Catholic recusant and protector of the Jesuits in England. It is said to have come to her from Mary Queen of Scots.
Given to Father Martin D'Arcy when he was Master of Campion Hall, Oxford (of the English Province of the Society of Jesus).
On loan from Campion Hall, Oxford

6 DIPTYCH
Silver-gilt, decorated with translucent enamel. Obverse, the Annunciation and the Coronation of the Virgin; reverse, St John the Baptist and St John the Evangelist, with quotations from St John: 1,6,14.
FRENCH: late 14th century.
Webb Collection
212-1874

7 PLAQUE
Silver, decorated with translucent enamel; St Paul.
FLEMISH: second half of 14th century.
4508-1858

Case 12 Board F

GERMAN:
15th and 16th centuries

62

*8 DIPTYCH
Silver, parcel-gilt, decorated with
translucent enamel. Obverse, the
Virgin and Child and the Crucifi-
xion; reverse, the Nativity and the
Annunciation, with prayers to Our
Lord and the Virgin Mary inscribed.
FLEMISH: 15th century.
Webb Collection
213-1874

9 THE CRUCIFIXION
Painted enamel on gold.
NETHERLANDISH: early 15th
century.
Magniac Collection
Lent from the Salting Bequest
M.546-1910

The majority of the objects on this
board are devotional pendants which
were sold at places of pilgrimage and
often worn on headgear, or attached
to rosaries. The figures are usually
cast.

**1 PENDANT IN THE FORM OF
A TOURNAMENT SHIELD**
Silver with glass bead pendant; the
Papal arms supported by SS. Peter
and Paul.
GERMAN: early 16th century.
Forrer Collection
496-1903

2 PENDANT
Silver; a cast cross with Pietà group
and the Instruments of the Passion.
GERMAN: about 1500.
45-1872

*3 MEDALLION
Gold, embossed and chased. The
Road to Calvary; probably part of a
morse.
RHENISH or FLEMISH: 15th
century.
1149-1864

*4 PENDANT
Silver with glass pendant; cast
group of the martyrdom of St.
Barbara.
GERMAN: about 1500.
Forrer Collection
501-1903

*5 PENDANT
Crystal and silver-gilt; shield-
shaped. A figure of Christ Crucified
cast and applied to the crystal.
GERMAN: about 1500.
503-1903

6 PENDANT
Silver, parcel-gilt, with ivory and
glass pendant; cast group of the
Virgin and Child with St. John.
GERMAN: 15th century.
Forrer Collection
504-1903

7 DIPTYCH PENDANT
Silver-gilt, with cast figures.
Obverse, St. George and St.
Catherine; reverse, Christ of Pity and
St. James the Great.
GERMAN: 15th century.
Bishop of Hildesheim Collection
14-1873

8 PENDANT
Silver and silver-gilt: a cast Pietà.
GERMAN: late 15th or early 16th
century.
Forrer Collection
495-1903

9 BELT-END
Silver-gilt.
GERMAN: second half of 15th
century.
Given by Dame Joan Evans, P.P.S.A.
M.52-1975.

*10 MEDALLION PENDANT
Silver-gilt and mother of pearl.
Obverse, St. Bartholomew; reverse, a
bishop saint.
GERMAN: about 1500.
Forrer Collection
514-1903

**11 BUCKLE AND END OF A
GIRDLE**
Silver-gilt.
GERMAN: early 16th century.
37 & a-1894

Case 12 Board G

GERMAN DEVOTIONAL:
15th and 16th centuries

1 PENDANT
Silver-gilt; St George.
GERMAN: about 1500.
Forrer Collection
499-1903

2 PENDANT
Silver-gilt; The Crucifixion.
GERMAN: second half of 15th
century.
621-1906

3 PENDANT
Silver-gilt, and hung with a paste
bead; St Sebastian.
GERMAN: about 1500.
500-1903

4 PENDANT
Silver-gilt; St Christopher.
GERMAN: about 1500.
507-1903

5 PENDANT
Silver-gilt; Christ bearing the Cross.
GERMAN: about 1520.
497-1903

*6 PENDANT
Silver; the Adoration of the Magi.
GERMAN: second half of 15th
century.
217-1904
Nos. 3-6, Forrer Collection

7 PENDANT
Silver-gilt; St George and the
Dragon.
GERMAN: late 15th century.
9079-1863

8 PENDANT
Silver-gilt; St George and the
Dragon.
GERMAN: mid 16th century.
513-1903

9 PENDANT
Silver-gilt; the Annunciation.
GERMAN: second half of 15th
century.
510-1903
Nos. 8 & 9, Forrer Collection

10 PENDANT
Silver-gilt; the Coronation of the
Virgin.
GERMAN: late 15th century.
3605-1857

11 ROSARY
Silver, wooden beads and amber,
with the Instruments of the Passion
and pendant of SS Catherine and
Barbara.
GERMAN: late 15th century.
Forrer Collection
517-1903

12 MEDALLION PENDANT
Stag's horn, mounted in silver-gilt.
Obverse, St. George and the Dragon;
reverse, the Vernicle.
GERMAN: 15th century.
4085-1857

13 MEDALLION PENDANT
Silver, engraved. Obverse, Christ in
the sepulchre; reverse. St George and
the Dragon.
GERMAN: about 1500.
104-1865

14 PENDANT
Silver-gilt, hung with a baroque
pearl; the Crucifixion.
GERMAN: second half of 15th
century.
493-1903

15 PENDANT
Silver, parcel-gilt with an onyx bead;
the Adoration of the Magi.
GERMAN: 15th century.
509-1903
Nos. 14 & 15, Forrer Collection

16 MEDALLION PENDANT
Silver-gilt, engraved. Obverse, the
Marriage of St Catherine; reverse,
the Mass of St Gregory.
GERMAN: about 1520.
Tross Collection
68-1867

Case 12 Board H

GERMAN devotional:
15th and 16th centuries

1 CRUCIFIX
Silver-gilt, with a cavity on the
reverse for a relic of the True Cross.
GERMAN: 15th century.
M.303-1912

***2 BUCKLE AND END OF A
GIRDLE**
Copper-gilt, engraved with the
Virgin and Child and St Andrew.
GERMAN: late 15th century.
4526-1858

3 SCENT-CASE
Silver-gilt.
GERMAN: second half of 16th
century.
Given by Dame Joan Evans, P.P.S.A.
M.53-1975

4 PENDANT
Silver-gilt. Obverse, a painting under
glass of the Crucifixion; reverse, an
embossed gold plaque of the
Annunciation.
GERMAN: second half of 16th
century.
Alfred Williams Hearn Gift
M.57-1923

*5 PENDENT CROSS
Silver-gilt, set with a ruby, a
sapphire, garnets and pearls; the
reverse engraved with emblems of
the Passion; there is also a receptacle
for relics.
? GERMAN: 15th century.
4561-1858

6 RELIQUARY PENDANT
Silver, parcel-gilt. Obverse, the
Annunciation; reverse, the Mass of
St Gregory.
SOUTH GERMAN: second half of
15th century.
Debruge-Dumesnil and Soltikoff
Collections
M.168-1906

RENAISSANCE:
16th and early 17th centuries

64

Enamelling was an essential technique of Renaissance gold-smithing. Both opaque and translucent varieties were used by the artist-craftsmen of the sixteenth century. Many of their jewels took the form of miniature sculptures of humans, animals and creatures drawn from classical mythology. One of the best-known examples is the merman pendant known as the Canning Jewel (Case 26, no. 10). By the early seventeenth century a trend towards stones used in formal clusters had already begun to dispossess enamel, which was employed for minor details such as the embellishment of the gold detailing between stones or at the edges of jewels. Though large areas of enamel still appeared on the fronts of some pieces (an important group is shown in Case 14, Board A), in others the technique was mainly used to ornament the backs.

The influence of classical antiquity also ensured the renewed popularity of engraved gems in jewellery. Some were genuine examples (a late classical gem is set in the Gatacre Jewel of about 1560 (Case 26, no. 9). Others were exercises in the classical manner, but even contemporary portraits, such as those of Elizabeth I (1558-1603), demonstrate the effect of a classicising medallic tradition (Case 13, Board D, nos. 3 & 4).

*1 PROPHYLACTIC PENDANT
Gold, enamelled in black and translucent blue, set with a hessonite garnet and a peridot, and hung with a sapphire. The stones are set unbacked to allow their magical properties to reach the skin of the wearer. The back of the setting inscribed: *ANNANISAPTA + DEI* (an invocation to ward off epilepsy) and *DETRAGRAMMATA IHS MARIA* (the first word a reference to the Hebrew name for God, followed by the standard abbreviation of Jesus; these, with the Virgin Mary, are cited with amuletic intention). The pendant, though resembling several drawings by Holbein, seems to have been a common type.
ENGLISH: about 1540-60.
M.242-1975

2 NECKLACE WITH PENDENT CROSS
Gold, enamelled in black and white. Some links in the necklace chain inscribed: *VBI AMOR IBI FIDES* (where is Love, there is also Faith).
ITALIAN: about 1540.
M.117-1975
Nos. 1 & 2, given by Dame Joan Evans, P.P.S.A.

3 CAP BADGE
Gold, with an embossed bust of a Roman emperor in the centre. This was formerly attached to a classical necklace, a marriage almost certainly made by the firm of Castellani of Rome.
? ENGLISH: first half of 16th century.
Alessandro Castellani Collection
630-1884

*4 MEMENTO MORI PENDANT
(the Tor Abbey Jewel)
Enamelled gold, in the form of a skeleton in a coffin, which is inscribed: *THROUGH. THE. RESVRRTION. OF. CHRISTE. WE. BE. ALL. SANCTIFIED.*
ENGLISH: about 1540-50.
Found at Tor Abbey, Devonshire.
3581-1856

5 RELIQUARY CROSS
Gold, with the Instruments of the Passion reserved on black enamel. Compartments inside hold relics, and names of saints are engraved in Italian on the underside of the lid. Probably a prophylactic jewel.
ITALIAN: about 1600.
Given by Miss L.M. Pacy
M.77-1979

6 LOCKET
Agate locket, enclosing a group of St George and the Dragon in enamelled gold.
ENGLISH:early 17th century. There was a court cult of St. George in the early 17th century.
M.70-1975

7 PENDENT CROSS
Gold, set with pearls, rubies and a colourless stone; the reverse enamelled with the Man of Sorrow emerging from the Tomb, and the Evangelists. A pendent jewel missing from the base.
GERMAN: first quarter of 16th century.
M.74-1975

*8 HAT BADGE
Enamelled gold, set with an onyx cameo of a young man in the classical mode, surrounded by spokes set with rubies within a wheel.
ENGLISH: about 1580.
M.69-1975
Nos. 6-8, given by Dame Joan Evans, P.P.S.A.

*9 PENDANT (the Danny Jewel)
Enamelled gold in the form of a ship, mounted with a section of narwhal's tusk ('unicorn's horn'), valued as a detector of poison in the Middle Ages and as an amulet in the 16th century.
ENGLISH: about 1560.
Formerly the property of the Campions of Danny, Sussex.
Bryan Bequest
M.97-1917

10 NECKLACE AND PAIR OF BRACELETS
Gold chains; the clasps decorated with the Sacred Monogram *(IHS)* in enamel and inscribed: *IASMVPL* (the last two letters conjoined).
NORTH EUROPEAN: about 1600.
Given by Dame Joan Evans, P.P.S.A.
M.89-b-1962

*11 PENDANT (the Pasfield Jewel)
Enamelled gold, in the shape of a wheel-lock pistol, forming a whistle, with toilet implements.
ENGLISH: late 16th century.
A family jewel of the Pasfields of Rotherhithe and Barbados; it was damaged in a fire in 1817.
M.160-1922

ENGLISH LIVERY COLLARS:
15th and 16th centuries

12 JEWEL
Onyx cameo of a jester loosely set in an enamelled gold frame with rubies and a rose-cut diamond (another stone wanting).
? ENGLISH: first half of 16th century.
It has been suggested that the cameo represents Henry VIII's jester.
Lent anonymously

1 COLLAR
Silver-gilt, with links in the form of a letter N or V.
ENGLISH: late 15th or early 16th century.
Perhaps the badge of a Town Wait (minstrel).
M.303-1920

*2 COLLAR OF SS
Silver, parcel-gilt.
ENGLISH: 16th century.
Croft Lyons Bequest
M.1022-1926

3 COLLAR OF SS
Silver.
ENGLISH: 16th century.
948-1902

CASE 12
BOARD B
NO. 3

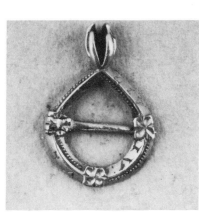

CASE 12
BOARD B
NO. 8

CASE 12
BOARD B
NO. 17

CASE 12
BOARD B
NO. 20

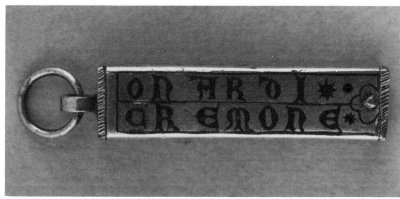

CASE 12
BOARD B
NO. 21

CASE 12
BOARD B
NO. 26

CASE 12
BOARD C
NO. 2

CASE 12
BOARD D
NO. 7

CASE 12
BOARD B
NO. 31

CASE 12
BOARD C
NO. 7

CASE 12
BOARD E
NO. 2

CASE 12
BOARD C
NO. 9

CASE 12
BOARD F
NO. 3

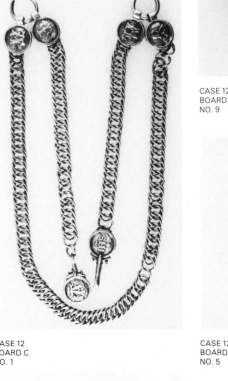

CASE 12
BOARD C
NO. 1

CASE 12
BOARD D
NO. 5

CASE 12
BOARD F
NO. 4

CASE 12
BOARD F
NO. 5

CASE 12
BOARD I
NO. 1

CASE 12
BOARD I
NO. 11

CASE 12
BOARD G
NO. 6

CASE 12
BOARD I
NO. 4

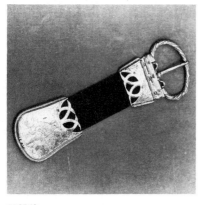

CASE 12
BOARD H
NO. 2

CASE 12
BOARD I
NO. 8

CASE 12
BOARD J
NO. 2

CASE 12
BOARD H
NO. 5

CASE 12
BOARD I
NO. 9

Case 13 Board A

RENAISSANCE:
16th-17th century

1 HAT BADGE
Gold; the Crucifixion in high relief.
SPANISH: mid 16th century.
J.C. Robinson Collection
147-1879

2 MARRIAGE CHAIN
Gold links with enamelled
decoration; clasped hands holding a
heart alternating with shields
bearing the arms of Saxony on one
side and the initials *FWHZS* on the
other.
The initials refer to Friedrich
Wilhelm of Altenburg (1562-1602).
The chain may have been made for
his first marriage in 1583 to Sophie of
Württemberg or his second in 1591 to
Anna Maria of Neuburg.
GERMAN (Saxony): 1583/1591.
Anonymous loan

3 CRUCIFIX
Rock crystal, mounted in silver-gilt.
WEST EUROPEAN: mid 16th
century.
542-1868

4 RELIQUARY PENDANT
Gold, embossed with the arms of the
Mercederians (the Order of St Mary
of Mercy, founded in Barcelona in the
early 13th century).
SPANISH: about 1625.
M.92-1962

5 TOOTHPICK
Enamelled gold, set with two rose-cut
diamonds.
GERMAN: about 1620.
M.68-1975
Nos. 4 & 5, given by Dame Joan
Evans, P.P.S.A.

6 BADGE
Enamelled gold; obverse, the head of
Christ; reverse, the Sacred
Monogram.
NORTH EUROPEAN: about 1630.
Purchased in Norway and presented
by Mr. Walter Child
918-1902

7 PENDANT
Enamelled gold; obverse, the head of
Christ; reverse, the Sacred
Monogram.
NORTH EUROPEAN: early 16th
century.
Given by the Dame Joan Evans,
P.P.S.A.
M.90-1962

8 SIGNET PENDANT
Enamelled gold. Three seals with
scenes from the Passion of Our Lord.
? FRENCH: early 17th century.
543-1868

9 PENDANT
Enamelled gold, set with a sapphire;
hung with a pearl. In the form
of a flask.
WEST EUROPEAN: mid 16th
century.
Given by Dame Joan Evans, P.P.S.A.
M.239-1975

**10 BADGE OF AN ARCHERS'
GUILD**
Above, the Annunciation; below, a
bishop saint and St Sebastian. Silver-
gilt, with stones in gold settings.
Inscribed: *Donavit 1563* and with
initials and dates ranging from 1551
to 1565. At some stage, a leaf was
substituted for a crucifix at the top.
FLEMISH: largely 16th century,
with later alterations and additions.
Bernal Collection
2276-1855

*11 HAT BADGE
Enamelled gold. The head of St John
the Baptist on a charger. Inscribed:
*INTER NATOS MVLIERVM NON
SVREXSIT* (he did not arise among
those born of woman).
FRENCH: early 16th century.
Webb Collection
473-1873

12 NECKLACE
Enamelled gold.
MEDITERRANEAN: early 17th
century.
Given by Dame Joan Evans, P.P.S.A.
M.86-1962

**13 THREE DRESS
ORNAMENTS**
Gold, decorated with translucent
enamel. Two with cherub's heads,
one with fruit.
SOUTH GERMAN: late 16th
century.
Poniatowski and Gurney Collections;
bequeathed by Mr. F. Leverton
Harris
M.422-b-1927

Case 13 Board B

RENAISSANCE:
mid 16th – 17th century

1 PENDANT
Enamelled gold, set with rubies and
hung with pearls; Cupid drawing an
arrow, mounted over a scrolling
openwork plate.
SOUTH GERMAN: about 1600.
M.387-1911

2 TOOTHPICK
Enamelled gold, set with a diamond
and rubies; the figure on the handle
represents Lucretia, wife of
Collatinus. Her rape by Sextus
Tarquinius led to the overthrow of
the last of the Roman kings and the
election of Collatinus and Lucius
Junius Brutus as the first two
consuls in 509 BC.
SOUTH GERMAN: late 16th
century.
294-1854

3 DRESS JEWEL
Enamelled gold, set with an emerald
(the piece has been repaired).
EUROPEAN: about 1600.
Given by Dame Joan Evans, P.P.S.A.
M.71-1975

4 PENDANT
Enamelled gold, set with table-cut
diamonds and rubies and hung with
pearls; the Pelican in its Piety,
mounted over a scrolling openwork
plate.
SOUTH GERMAN: early 17th
century.
4212-1855

*5 PENDANT
Agate cameo of Victory writing on
her shield, a Satyr and a seated
woman, in an enamelled gold mount;
hung with pearls (one wanting).
WEST EUROPEAN: late 16th
century.
Paris warranty mark for 1838
onwards, an indication that the
piece passed through the hands
of a French dealer.
493-1897

*6 PENDANT
Sardonyx cameo of a laureate head
in profile, perhaps an emperor, in an
enamelled gold mount; hung with a
pearl.
GERMAN: late 16th century.
Given by Dame Joan Evans, P.P.S.A.
M.86-1975

*7 PLAQUE
Enamelled gold, set with a ruby;
Moses and the Brazen Serpent.
SOUTH GERMAN: about 1600.
Bequeathed by Mr. E.J. Blaiberg
M.46-1970

***8 MEMORIAL or MEMENTO
MORI LOCKET**
Onyx cameo of two male busts in an
enamelled gold mount set with
rubies; reverse, a painted enamel of a
putto blowing bubbles in a
landscape.
GERMAN: the cameo about 1570, the
setting about 1600.
M.249-1975

*9 PENDANT
Onyx cameo of the Emperor
Augustus Caesar (died 14 AD), in a
narrow gold mount with floral
enamelling; pearl drop.
The cameo ITALIAN: second half of
16th century; the frame a century
later.
M.73-1975
Nos. 8 & 9, given by Dame Joan
Evans, P.P.S.A.

10 PENDANT
Onyx cameo of *putti* and dolphins in
an enamelled gold frame set with
rubies, with figures of Nepture and
Proserpine and other marine motifs.
EUROPEAN: late 16th century, but
the setting has been twice altered
since the late 19th century.
Marlborough Collection
Anonymous loan

*11 PENDANT
Chalcedony cameo of Cleopatra,
based on a classical type of a
Bacchante with snakes, in a
contemporary enamelled gold frame
with ribbon ties.
EUROPEAN: second third of 16th
century.
M.84-1975

12 EAGLE PENDANT
Enamelled gold, set with a baroque
pearl and a ruby; hung with pearls;
representing an eagle and a snake.
EUROPEAN: late 16th century.
Paris warranty mark for 1838
onwards.
M.243-1975
Nos. 11 & 12, given by Dame Joan
Evans, P.P.S.A.

13 SPHINX JEWEL
Enamelled gold, set with rubies and a
diamond. Arms of A. Herzog zu L (?)
painted on the underside of the base;
this and the chain are later
additions.
The sphinx possibly FRENCH:
second half of 16th century.
Anonymous loan

14 LOCKET
Crystal, carved in a shell shape and
mounted in gold.
FRENCH: about 1600.
Given by Dame Joan Evans, P.P.S.A.
M.244-1975

*15 IHS PENDANT
Table-cut diamonds set in gold, a
cross rising from the central letter;
the sides decorated with black
enamel.
NORTH EUROPEAN: about 1550.
M.76-1975
Nos. 14 & 15, given by Dame Joan
Evans, P.P.S.A.

Case 13 Board C

JACOBEAN:
early 17th century

A group of articles from the Cheapside Hoard, found in 1912 when a house was being pulled down between St Paul's Cathedral and the Post Office. Most of the Hoard is in the Museum of London, but the British Museum also has a number of items.

Four fragments of chains in enamelled gold (nos. 1, 4, 5, 7), an enamelled gold pendant with a methyst drops (2), and a further gold pendant with amethyst grapes (6), are lent by the Museum of London. The long enamelled gold chain (3), is owned by the V & A (M.1140-1926).

Case 13 Board D

ENGLISH AND CONTINENTAL:
late 16th and 17th centuries

*1 PENDENT CROSS
Enamelled gold, set with a table-cut diamond and rubies; hung with a pearl.
ENGLISH: second half of 16th century.
French import mark introduced in 1893.
Given by Dame Joan Evans, P.P.S.A.
M.240-1975

*2 LOCKET (the Armada or Heneage Jewel)
Enamelled gold, set with table-cut diamonds and Burmese rubies. Obverse, a bust in gold under rock crystal of Elizabeth I (1558-1603), apparently a version of the Garter Badge of about 1585, surrounded by the inscription: *ELIZABETHA D.G. ANG. FRA. ET. HIB. REGINA* (Elizabeth, by the grace of God Queen of England, France and Ireland). Inside, a miniature of the Queen by Nicholas Hilliard. The hinged back of the locket (shown separately) is enamelled outside with the Ark of the English Church on a stormy sea and the inscription: *SAEVAS. TRANQUILLA. PER. VNDAS* (peaceful on the fierce waves, an allusion to the Queen's function as Defender of the Faith). Inside, an enamelled Tudor rose encircled by leaves and the inscription: *Hei mihi quod tanto virtus perfusa decore non habet eternos inviolata dies* (Alas, that so much virtue suffused with beauty should not last for ever inviolate). This inscription appears on the reverse of the Phoenix medal of 1574. According to tradition, the jewel was given by Elizabeth I to Sir Thomas Heneage (died 1595), a Privy Counsellor and Vice-Chamberlain of the Royal Household. The jewel remained in the possession of the Heneage family until 1902.
ENGLISH: about 1595.
J. Pierpoint Morgan Collection; given by Lord Wakefield through the National Art-Collections Fund
M.81-1935

3 PENDANT (the Wild Jewel)
Enamelled gold, set with a turquoise cameo of Queen Elizabeth I and with diamonds and rubies; hung with pearls.
Said to have been given by Elizabeth I to a god-child, Elizabeth Wild.
ENGLISH: about 1590.
Wild loan

*4 PENDANT (the Barbor Jewel)
Enamelled gold, set with an onyx cameo of Queen Elizabeth I and with table-cut rubies and diamonds; hung with a cluster of pearls. An oak tree enamelled on the back plate.
According to a family tradition, apparently first recorded in 1724, the jewel was made for William Barbor (died 1586), to commemorate his delivery from the stake by the death of Queen Mary in 1558. Neither the cameo nor the setting can however be dated before the late 16th century.
ENGLISH: about 1590-1600.
Given by Miss M. Blencowe
889-1894

*5 LOCKET
Enamelled gold, enclosing miniatures on vellum of King James I (1603-1625) and an ark on a stormy sea, with the inscription: *STET SALVA PER VNDAS* (may it go safely through the waves). From the workshop of Nicholas Hilliard, the portrait of James I derives from a miniature of about 1605 in Windsor Castle.
ENGLISH: about 1610.
Given by Dame Joan Evans, P.P.S.A.
M.92-1975

6 SEAL AND CASE
Sapphire seal engraved with the arms of Knyvett and mounted in enamelled gold, with a gold case, also enamelled. Probably the personal seal of Sir Thomas Knyvett (1539-1618).
ENGLISH: about 1580.
M.52-1980

*7 MINIATURE CASE
Gold, enamelled with flowers around a central red rose.
NORTH EUROPEAN: last quarter of 16th century.
Given by Dame Joan Evans, P.P.S.A.
M.67-1975

SPANISH devotional:
16th-early 17th century

8 BADGE OF THE ORDER OF THE GARTER
Enamelled gold; the Lesser George, worn from a ribbon at the side of the body. (St. George's lance missing). Said to have belonged to Thomas. Wentworth, Earl of Strafford (died 1641).
ENGLISH: about 1640.
273-1869

9 TOOTHPICK
Enamelled gold, set with a ruby; representing the Hand of Time, with a death's head finial.
ENGLISH: about 1620.
Frank Ward Bequest
M.32-1960

10 MOURNING SLIDE
Pierced gold, with enamelled skulls, cross-bones, a winged heart, flowers and leaves.
? ENGLISH: mid 17th century.
Given by Dame Joan Evans, P.P.S.A.
M.75-1975

11 IHS PENDANT
Gold, set with hog-back diamonds, a cross rising from the central letter; the reverse enamelled with the Instruments of the Passion. The old-fashioned cut of the diamonds probably indicates re-use.
Said to have belonged to William Howard, Viscount Stafford, beheaded 1680 for alleged complicity in the Titus Oates plot.
NORTH EUROPEAN: late 16th century.
M.248-1923

1 RELIQUARY CROSS
Enamelled gold; obverse, (inset), the Crucifixion and other subjects in *verre eglomisé,* a technique of executing paintings behind glass and then backing them with gold foil. Reverse (shown), applied Instruments of the Passion.
SPANISH: early 17th century.
Given by Dame Joan Evans, P.P.S.A.
M.242-1975

2 RELIQUARY CROSS
Enamelled gold, set with hog-back and table-cut diamonds.
SPANISH: early 17th century.
299-1866

3 HEART PENDANT
Rock crystal enclosing the Sacred Monogram, a cross, and a heart pierced by three nails, in an aureole, all in enamelled gold; outer frame also in enamelled gold.
SPANISH: first half of 17th century. From the Treasury of the Cathedral of the Virgin of the Pillar, Saragossa. One of a group of jewels purchased by the Museum in 1870, when the Cathedral authorities sold off treasures presented to the shrine of the Virgin in order to complete their building programme. The cult of the Virgin of the Pillar derived from the legend that the Virgin Mary was miraculously transported to the banks of the river Ebro in AD 40 to assist St James the Greater.
346-1870

4 PENDANT WITH MONOGRAM OF THE VIRGIN
Enamelled gold and lapis-lazuli; the crown above the monogram set with pastes.
SPANISH: first third of 17th century.
Given by Dame Joan Evans, P.P.S.A.
M.251-1975

5 PENDANT
Rock crystal mounted in enamelled gold; hung with pearls. Set with panels of *verre egomisé* representing St John the Baptist and St James.
SPANISH: late 16th century.
Spitzer Collection
M.538-1910

6 PLAQUE
Rock crystal mounted in enamelled brass; set with a panel of *verre eglomisé* representing the Adoration of the Magi.
The setting SPANISH: early 17th century.
M.542-1910

7 PENDANT
Rock crystal mounted in enamelled gold; hung with a pearl. Obverse, a panel of *verre eglomisé* representing the Road to Calvary and (inset), the Risen Christ appearing to St Mary Magdalene.
ITALIAN: early 17th century.
Spitzer Collection
M.540-1910
Nos. 5-7, lent from the Salting Bequest

8 VIRGIN OF THE PILLAR PENDANT
Cast figure, decorated with enamel; stars and sickle moon reserved on the Virgin's cloak.
SPANISH: second quarter of 17th century.
From the Treasury of the Cathedral of the Virgin of the Pillar, Saragossa
343-1870

9 PENDANT
Cast and enamelled gold figure of the Virgin of the Immaculate Conception mounted on gold openwork, enamelled and set with crystals; hung with pearls.
SPANISH: about 1625.
French import mark introduced in 1893.
Given by Dame Joan Evans, P.P.S.A.
M.241-1975

*10 PENDANT
Table-cut crystals mounted in enamelled gold. The suspension loop missing.
SPANISH: early 17th century.
Given by Dr. W.L. Hildburgh, F.S.A.
M.145-1937

72

11 PENDANT
Rock crystal mounted in enamelled
gold, enclosing a miniature on
vellum of the head and shoulders of
the Virgin Mary; relics of St Tranquil
set in the back.
SPANISH: about 1600.
French import mark introduced in
1864.
Given by Dame Joan Evans, P.P.S.A.
M.250-1975

12 PENDANT
Rock crystal, mounted in enamelled
gold set with emeralds, enclosing
painted reliefs of the Crucifixion and
a head of Christ; inscription from St
Matthew, XVI, 24.
SPANISH: late 16th century.
Later inscribed with the initials: *FM*.
Lent from the Salting Bequest
M.458-1910

13 PENDANT
Rock crystal, mounted in enamelled
gold, enclosing miniatures on paper
of the head of Christ and the Virgin
Mary; inside, a phylactery with the
words of the Last Gospel in Latin
(John, 1-14) and a prayer in Spanish.
SPANISH: about 1600.
From the Treasury of the Cathedral
of the Virgin of the Pillar, Saragossa
333-1870

1 CHAIN AND PENDANT
Silver. The pendant with a cast
winged archer; rock crystal and
silver drops.
GERMAN: early 17th century.
279-1903

2 CRUCIFIX
Silver-gilt; reverse, the Virgin and
Child, cast.
GERMAN: early 16th century.
4399-1857

3 PENDANT
Red coral; set with, obverse, an
enamelled gold plaque of the Crucifixion; reverse, the Resurrection.
ITALIAN: late 16th century.
105-1865

4 GNADENPFENNIG
Silver-gilt; medal of Johann Philip
von Gebsattel, Bishop of Bamberg.
GERMAN: the medal dated 1601.
Tross Collection, Paris
66-1867

5 PENDANT
Enamelled gold; obverse, the head of
St. John the Baptist; reverse, the
Virgin and Child.
SPANISH or ITALIAN: mid 17th
century.
Dutch standard mark, 1893-1906.
Given by Dame Joan Evans, P.P.S.A.
M.87-1975

6 LOCKET
Rock crystal mounted in enamelled
gold, decorated with filigree.
MEDITERRANEAN: early 17th
century.
34-1894

7 CORONET
Enamelled gold, set with emeralds,
rubies and pearls.
SOUTH GERMAN: about 1600.
French import mark introduced in
1864.
747-1893

8 EARRING
Enamelled gold openwork, set with
rubies.
ITALIAN or HUNGARIAN: about
1625.
169-1872

9 FLOWER SPRAY
Enamelled gold openwork, set with
pearls.
SOUTH GERMAN: early 17th
century. Applied maker's symbol (? a
hand).
610-1872

10 LINK OF A CHAIN
Enamelled gold openwork, with a
cast figure of Temperance.
SOUTH GERMAN: early 17th
century.
9038-1863

*11 BRACELET
Gold chain: enamelled clasp.
NORTH EUROPEAN: early 17th
century.
36-1894

1 PENDANT
Gold, decorated with *champlevé* enamel and set with table- and faceted point-cut diamonds.
SOUTH GERMAN: (perhaps from an Imperial workshop in Prague or Austria): about 1615.
Found in the Castle of Ambras, near Innsbruck, in the Tirol (see also no. 2 below).
696b-1868

2 CHAIN
Enamelled gold, set with pearls.
SOUTH GERMAN: about 1615. On the back of each link, an applied plaque bearing the maker's initials R.V in monogram.
Found in the Castle of Ambras (see no. 1).
696-1868

*3 JEWEL
Probably a converted buckle.
Enamelled gold, set with table- and faceted point-cut diamonds.
HUNGARIAN: about 1630.
Purchased under the terms of the Francis Reubell Bryan Bequest
M.447-1927

4 JEWEL
Enamelled gold, set with a topaz and garnets; hung with pearls.
GERMAN: early 17th century.
M.61-1975

5 BROOCH
Enamelled gold, set with a table-cut diamond and two pearls.
GERMAN: about 1600.
M.59-1975

6 JEWEL
Enamelled gold, set with table-cut diamonds; hung with a pearl. In the form of a heart under a crown.
SOUTH GERMAN: about 1615.
M.105-1975

*7 DRESS ORNAMENT
Enamelled gold, set with rubies and emeralds, a table-cut diamond and a ruby; also set and hung with pearls.
Central openwork heart with a skull and cross-bones, two arrows and other devices.
? GERMAN: early 17th century.
M.66-1975

8 NECKLACE
Enamelled gold, set with green glass.
? SPANISH: 17th century.
M.65-1975
Nos. 4-8, given by Dame Joan Evans, P.P.S.A.

*9 CHAIN
Enamelled gold, set with rubies.
GERMAN: about 1620.
The four small links set with octagonal garnets are later additions.
34-1894

10 PENDANT
Jacinth cameo of the Virgin, set in enamelled gold.
WEST EUROPEAN: about 1610.
M.62-1975

11 PENDANT
Gold, set with garnets and hung with a pearl; the back enamelled.
? GERMAN: about 1650.
M.256-1975

12 MEMENTO MORI PENDANT
Enamelled gold, in the form of a coffin, with cross-bones on the suspension chains and a skull pendant. The coffin opens to disclose an enamelled skeleton, the initials *I.G.S.* above its head and the inscription: *HIE. LIEG. ICH. VND. WARTH. AVF. DIH* (Here I lie and wait for you).
GERMAN: first half of 17th century.
M.74-1975
Nos. 10-12, given by Dame Joan Evans, P.P.S.A.

1 SLIDE PENDANT
A cornelian intaglio of a Bacchante in a gold mount, set with turquoises; floral enamelling on reverse. The intaglio 1st century B.C., but repolished.
The setting ?GERMAN: second third of 17th century.
Marlborough Collection
Given by Dame Joan Evans, P.P.S.A.
M.255-1975

2 ENCOLPION (reliquary cross)
Enamelled copper-gilt.
EAST EUROPEAN: 17th century.
99-1866

3 AMULET FOR A BABY
Coral, mounted in enamelled gold filigree.
?ITALIAN: about 1600.
Given by Dr. W.L. Hildburgh, F.S.A.
M.53-1952

4 PENDANT
Onyx cameo of a Roman head crowned with a laurel wreath in an enamelled gold mount, set with crystals and garnets.
Probably HUNGARIAN: 17th century.
Given by Dame Joan Evans, P.P.S.A.
M.85-1975

5 BADGE
Enamelled gold. Obverse, the Holy Family; reverse, a Maltese cross in white enamel; in the style of Giuseppe Bruno of Messina.
SICILIAN: mid 17th century.
French warranty mark for 1838 onwards.
1285-1871

6 PENDANT
Enamelled gold, set with pearls and garnets; cast figure of the Infant Christ standing in a niche.
ITALIAN or HUNGARIAN: 17th century.
Murray Bequest
M.997-1910

7 PENDANT
Enamelled gold; cast group of the Virgin and two angels with the Holy Shroud under crystal.
Possibly FRENCH (Besançon): mid 17th century.
M.79-1975

Mainly 17th century

*8 PENDANT
Enamelled gold, set with an onyx cameo of the Devotion of Curtius; hung with a pearl.
The cameo, inspired by the work of Francesco Tortorino, probably ITALIAN (Milanese): late 16th or early 17th century; the mount about 1630.
M.89-1975

*9 LOCKET
Enamelled gold. The Holy Shroud, held by St. Charles Borromeo and attendant angels.
ITALIAN: (probably Turin): first quarter of 17th century.
M.77-1975

10 DECADE ROSARY CHAIN WITH CRUCIFIX
Perhaps intended as a bracelet. Crystal, with enamelled gold and pearls; the crucifix hung with pearls.
ITALIAN: 17th century.
French import mark for 1864 onwards.
M.82-1975

*11 PENDANT
Gold, set with an amethyst cameo of a boy/Cupid. A double monogram pounced on the reverse; hung with pearls.
WEST EUROPEAN: mid 17th century. The suspension loop dated 1658.
M.83-1975
Nos.7-11, given by Dame Joan Evans, P.P.S.A.

*1 JEWEL
Enamelled gold, set with table-cut diamonds, rubies and emeralds. In the centre, a ruby set as a heart, pierced by two arrows. In the back a locket containing a miniature of a man.
Probably PRAGUE Court workshop in the Hungarian manner: about 1610-20.
Said to have belonged to Francis Rákóczy, Prince of Transylvania, perhaps the champion of the Protestants who was concerned in a plot to separate Hungary from the house of Habsburg, which failed in 1671.
Harley Teleki Collection
M.461-1936

*2 BREAST ORNAMENT
Gold openwork leaf and scroll design, set with table- and faceted point-cut diamonds and decorated with enamel; five pendants. Constructed in three stages, a back plate, enamelled black, a front plate set with diamonds and decorated with white enamelled pellets; the topmost layer is formed of a central rosette.
? DUTCH: about 1630.
Rubens's portrait of his second wife, Hélène Fourment (Alte Pinakothek, Munich) shows her wearing a similar ornament.
Given by Dame Joan Evans, P.P.S.A.
M.143-1975

3 PAIR OF BRACELETS
Composed of units in gold, decorated with enamel and set with garnets and pearls in the 17th century manner.
HUNGARIAN: perhaps 18th or early 19th century.
M.466, 468-1936

4 PAIR OF EARRINGS
Silver-gilt, each enamelled and set with an emerald, garnets and pearls.
HUNGARIAN: about 1700.
M.469 & a-1936

*5 JEWEL
Gold, enamelled and set with a ruby (possibly re-set in the 19th century) and faceted point-cut diamonds.
HUNGARIAN: late 17th century.
M.467-1936
Nos. 3-5, Harley Teleki Collection

6 RELIQUARY CROSS
Gold, decorated with filigree and enamel.
HUNGARIAN: early 17th century.
1652-1856

7 CROSS
Enamelled gold, hung with pearls and garnets.
? HUNGARIAN: 17th century.
M.1004-1910

8 JEWEL
Enamelled gold, set with pearls.
HUNGARIAN: 17th century.
Later brooch-fitting.
Harley Teleki Collection
M.464-1936

9 SCENT-CASE
Gold, decorated with filigree and enamel.
HUNGARIAN: 17th century
235-1853

10 PENDANT
Enamelled gold, set with amethysts, emeralds and a baroque pearl; hung with pearls. The Pelican in its Piety.
HUNGARIAN: early 17th century.
M.458-1936

11 PENDANT
Enamelled gold, set with an emerald and garnets; hung with pearls. A stork killing a snake.
HUNGARIAN: about 1600.
M.457-1936
Nos. 10 & 11, Harley Teleki Collection

Case 13 Board J

16th and 17th centuries

1 ORNAMENT FOR A NOBLEMAN'S COSTUME
Silver, parcel-gilt, decorated with enamel and set with an amethyst, table-cut crystals and semi-precious stones and pearls.
TRANSYLVANIAN-SAXON: late 17th century.
Given by Dame Joan Evans, P.P.S.A.
M.54-1975

*2 PAX
Enamelled gold; a relief representing the miraculous appearance of St James at the Battle of Clavijo; the frame a later addition by Reinhold Vasters, master goldsmith of Aachen (working 1853-90).
SPANISH: about 1530.
The frame, with an alternative setting, was designed by Vasters while the pax was in the Spitzer Collection.
Lent from the Salting Bequest
M.551-1910

*3 PART OF A PAX
Enamelled gold; a relief, representing the Adoration of the Magi.
SOUTH GERMAN: about 1530.
Formerly owned by the Collegiate Church at Hall, near Innsbruck.
Lent from the Salting Bequest
M.551-1910

4 BOOK-COVER
Gold, embossed and enamelled; obverse, a panel representing the Creation of Eve, surrounded by figures, flowers, scrolls and other devices; reverse, the Fountain of Youth.
SOUTH GERMAN: about 1570.
Formerly attributed to Benvenuto Cellini (1500-1571), and said to have belonged to Queen Henrietta Maria (1609-1669), consort of Charles I.
736-1864

*5 LID OF A TANKARD
Gold, decorated with translucent enamel. Shown separately, the medallion from the inside, bearing the arms of Nicholas, Count of Esterhazy, Galantha and Frakno (died 1645), inscribed round the border: *1642 c:NICO:EZTERHAZI-REG:VNG:PALATINVS.EQVES. AUR·VEL:S:C:R:M:INT:CON:ET. PERHVN: LOCVMTEN.*
HUNGARIAN: dated 1642.
M.10-1932

*6 BOOK-COVER
Copper-gilt, set with plaques enamelled in relief.
DUTCH: about 1670.
Given by Dame Joan Evans, P.P.S.A.
M.99-1975

7 MORSE
Silver-gilt, set with turquoises, pearls, garnets and pastes; cast figures of the Virgin and Child with attendant saints in gabled settings, with animals and figures on the borders.
HUNGARIAN: 17th century.
Maker's mark, FS with a comet in a shaped escutcheon.
M.63-1943

8 BREAST ORNAMENT
Silver-gilt, set with pastes and crystals in clawed collets.
(The middle stone a later addition.)
TRANSYLVANIAN-SAXON: 17th or 18th century. Maker's mark, MHG.
Given by Mr. Louis C.G. Clarke, F.S.A.
M.34-1922

*9 BELT BUCKLE
Gilt and silvered brass with tracery, figures, dolphins and other devices.
HUNGARIAN: engraved *I.K.* and dated 1698.
Given by Dame Joan Evans, P.P.S.A.
M.97-1975

CASE 13
BOARD B
NO. 6

CASE 13
BOARD B
NO. 8

CASE 13
BOARD B
NO. 9

CASE 13
BOARD B
NO. 11

CASE 13
BOARD B
NO. 15

CASE 13
BOARD A
NO. 11

CASE 13
BOARD D
NO. 1

CASE 13
BOARD D
NO. 5
2 Views

CASE 13
BOARD D
NO. 4

CASE 13
BOARD D
NO. 2
3 Views

CASE 13
BOARD E
NO. 10

CASE 13
BOARD D
NO. 7

CASE 13
BOARD F
NO. 11

CASE 13
BOARD G
NO. 3

CASE 13
BOARD G
NO. 7

CASE 13
BOARD G
NO. 9

CASE 13
BOARD J
NO. 2

CASE 13
BOARD J
NO. 9

CASE 13
BOARD J
NO. 6

CASE 13
BOARD H
NO. 9

CASE 13
BOARD H
NO. 11

CASE 13
BOARD H
NO. 8

CASE 13
BOARD I
NO. 5

CASE 13
BOARD J
NO. 3

CASE 13
BOARD J
NO. 5

CASE 13
BOARD I
NO. 1

CASE 13
BOARD I
NO. 2

ENAMELLED WORK:
17th century

78

Most of the pieces on this board are enamelled in opaque blue and white, often heightened with other colours. The bow, one of the most characteristic Baroque devices, appears in nos. 2, 4 & 5. This motif persisted in Rococo and Neoclassical jewellery.

1 PENDANT
Gold medallion, enamelled in colours with the Visitation, after an engraving of Raphael's Visitation (Prado, Madrid); pyramidal diamonds set in the border. Reverse, the engraved monogram *AM* below a coronet.
FRENCH: late 17th century.
1195-1864

*2 BODICE ORNAMENT
Gold, enamelled in blue and white and set with table-cut diamonds; in the form of a bow and jabot, the latter pierced in imitation of lace.
? FRENCH: mid 17th century.
From the Treasury of the Cathedral of the Virgon of the Pillar, Saragossa, to which it was presented in 1679 by the Marquis de Navarens
322-1870

*3 BACK OF A MINIATURE CASE
Gold, enamelled in blue, white, black and pink; interlaced L's below a French royal crown, the monogram of Louis XIII (1610-1643) or his successor, Louis XIV.
FRENCH: mid 17th century.
Given by Dame Joan Evans, P.P.S.A.
M.120-1975

*4 LOCKET
Gold, enamelled in blue and white, touched with black, set with table-cut diamonds and hung with seven pendants. Surmounted by a true lovers' knot, the emblem of the Trinity and with esclavos (S with a line through = s = clavo, i.e., slave), a common punning symbol of devotion.
FRENCH or SPANISH: about 1675.
From the Treasury of the Cathedral of the Virgin of the Pillar, Saragossa
326-1870

*5 NECKLACE WITH PENDANT
Gold, enamelled in blue, white and black, set with table-cut diamonds and hung with a pearl and a large sapphire drop; the necklace composed of bows alternating with knots, the centre a large bow with two flowers.
? FRENCH: about 1660.
Bequeathed by Lady Alma Tadema
M.95-1909

6 MINIATURE CASE
Silver-gilt, enamelled, in relief in blue, white, pink and black with floral and foliated decoration.
? FRENCH: mid 17th century.
622-1906

*7 MINIATURE CASE
Gold, enamelled in black and white with flowers and pea-pods closely related to a design by Jean Toutin I (1578-1644) engraved in 1619.
? FRENCH: about 1620.
M.246-1975

8 BACK OF A MINIATURE CASE
Gold, enamelled in blue, white and black, partly in relief; crown-shaped front to the suspension loop and on the case, the monogram *EDICB* below a coronet within laurel branches.
FRENCH: mid 17th century.
M.112-1975

9 RELIQUARY CROSS
Gold, enamelled in blue, white, green and black; hung with pearls. The reverse set with turquoises.
FRENCH: early 17th century.
M.127-1975

*10 MINIATURE CASE
Gold, enamelled in blue and black with a scene of Bacchus and Ariadne copied from an engraving by Michael Dorigny after Simon Vouet. Reverse, Venus and Adonis after a painting by Vouet in the J. Paul Getty Museum, Malibu, California.
FRENCH: about 1650.
M.114-1975

11 MINIATURE CASE
Gold, enamelled in relief in blue and white, black, pink and green; inside, a miniature of a young man.
NORTH EUROPEAN: about 1680.
M.115-1975
Nos. 7-11, given by Dame Joan Evans, P.P.S.A.

Case 14 Board B

PAINTED ENAMEL-WORK:
16th-18th century

1 LOCKET
Painted enamel on silver-gilt.
Obverse, a man and woman in
classical dress clasping hands by a
flaming altar, inscribed: *Mon Coeur
L'adresse;* reverse, *L'Amour S'exerce.*
FRENCH: second half of 17th
century.
1310-1871

2 MINIATURE-CASE
Gold with painted enamel flowers;
set with a crystal and table-cut
diamonds.
NORTH EUROPEAN: about 1680.
Inside, an enamel miniature of St.
Philip Neri signed: *Kutze p(inxit):*
GERMAN: dated 1750.
Given by Dame Joan Evans, P.P.S.A.
M.80-a-1975

3 CRUCIFIX
Gold rusticated cross, the figure of
Christ partly enamelled; the Sacred
Monogram a later addition.
NORTH EUROPEAN: 16th century.
260-1869

4 PENDANT
Enamelled gold openwork, set with
rubies and hung with pearls. The
pendent drop is formed of clasped
hands beneath a crown, with a dove
below.
FRENCH: second half of 17th
century.
611-1872

5 LOCKET
Gold; obverse, the Virgin and Child
in painted enamel; reverse, the Holy
Shroud of Besançon.
FRENCH: 18th century.
M.8-1959

6 LOCKET
Gold; obverse, St. Barbara in painted
enamel; reverse, the Holy Shroud of
Besançon.
FRENCH: 18th century.
Nos. 5 & 6, Ready Bequest
M.7-1959

*7 PENDANT
Gold, with a white enamelled
suspension loop; obverse, a portrait
of a woman in a border of emeralds;
reverse, a cornelian.
NORTH EUROPEAN: about 1610.
M.247-1975

8 PENDANT
Enamelled gold, set with table-cut
diamonds. The reverse engraved
with the initials *CB* on each side of a
heart pierced by arrows. The sides
inscribed: *FIDEL.IUSQ.A.LA.
MORT.LE.PAREIL.DE VOUS.A.
MON.CONFORT* (Faithful unto
death, the likeness of you is my
comfort).
FRENCH: about 1610-20.
M.110-1975
Nos. 7 & 8, given by Dame Joan
Evans, P.P.S.A.

9 NECKLACE
Enamelled gold scrolling openwork
set with emeralds and hung with
pearls.
NORTH EUROPEAN: early 17th
century.
M.291-1910

10 NECKLACE
Enamelled gold scrolling openwork,
set with table-cut crystals, hung
with pearls under a series of crowns
with fleurs-de-lis between.
? ITALIAN: early 17th century;
struck four times with the French
import mark for 1864-91.
2821-1856

11 PAIR OF EARRINGS
Enamelled gold, scrolling openwork,
set with garnets, hung with pearls.
NORTH EUROPEAN: early 17th
century.
58 & a-1898

*12 NECKLACE
Gold, enamelled in opaque and
translucent colours, and hung with
pearls on red enamel stars.
NORTH EUROPEAN: early 17th
century.
M.108-1975

13 LOCKET PENDANT
Gold, decorated with black enamel on
front and back, the front set with
emeralds.
NORTH EUROPEAN: about 1650.
M.252-1975
Nos. 12 & 13, given by Dame Joan
Evans, P.P.S.A.

14 FRAGMENT OF A CHAIN
Enamelled gold, set with medallions
bearing a cipher alternating with
true lover's knots.
FRENCH: second half of 17th
century.
4228-1857

*15 JEWEL
Amethystine chalcedony head of
Augustus in the style of Alessandro
Cesati (working in Italy about 1538-
1564). Originally set as a slide in
enamelled gold but converted into a
pendant in the 19th century.
The setting ITALIAN: about 1630.
Arundel and Marlborough
Collections
Given by Colonel Sir C. Wyndham
Murray, K.C.B.
M.133-1922

16 PENDANT
Enamelled gold; a relief of angels
adoring the Exposed Host, set
under glass.
FRENCH: mid 17th century.
Bernal Collection
2281-1855

17 PENDANT
Enamelled gold; a border of table-cut
rubies framing a relief under glass of
Christ bearing the Cross.
FRENCH: about 1660.
Webb Collection
220-1874

18 MIRROR PENDANT
Laurel wreath frame of gold, with
opaque enamelled decoration; the
mirror glass a replacement.
FRENCH: about 1660.
Given by Dame Joan Evans, P.P.S.A.
M.83-1962

EMAIL EN RESILLE SUR VERRE:
early 17th century

80

The technique of enamelling on gold leaf let into designs engraved on glass was practised on the Continent in the late sixteenth and early seventeenth century. Surviving examples, which are rare, indicate that the method was in use in France in the late sixteenth century spreading from there to central Europe.

1 PLAQUE
Email en résille; rabbits and scrolls.
FRENCH: early 17th century.
8.5-1892

2 PLAQUE
Email en résille on dark blue glass, representing Samson defeating the Philistines.
CENTRAL EUROPEAN: early 17th century.
491-1897

*3 LOCKET
Email en résille on transparent brown glass; flowers and a scroll inscribed: *VT: VIDI: VT: PERII* (Virgil, Ecl. viii.41)
FRENCH: about 1600.
It was stated by the former owner that the enamelled gold frame was a replacement.
Lent from the Salting Bequest
M.543-1910

4 PENDENT PLAQUE
Email en résille on brown glass, mounted in silver-gilt; vase and bird design.
CENTRAL EUROPEAN: early 17th century
490-1897

5 LOCKET
Email en résille on blue glass, mounted in enamelled gold. Hung with a baroque pearl.
FRENCH: about 1620.
Given by Dame Joan Evans, P.P.S.A.
M.65-1952

6 PENDENT PLAQUE
Email en résille on blue glass, mounted in silver-gilt. The Adoration of the Shepherds, from a design by Valentin Sezenius, dated 1623.
CENTRAL EUROPEAN.
Another enamel from this design is in the Museo Civico, Pavia.
6996-1860

7 MINIATURE CASE
Enamelled gold frame with a portrait miniature of Henri III (1551-1589), after the equestrian miniature of the King by Jean Clouet. The reverse set with a plaque of *émail en résille* on a blue ground (the back of the case is shown here).
FRENCH: early 17th century.
Given by Dame Joan Evans, P.P.S.A.
M.66-1952

8 GIRDLE
Plaques of *émail en résille* on alternately transparent and bright blue glass; silver-gilt links and enamel clasp.
CENTRAL EUROPEAN: early 17th century.
The plaques may have been made separately and later made into a belt, though there is another girdle with similar plaques in the Wallace Collection, London.
Webb Collection
484-1873

1 JEWEL
Enamelled gold openwork, set with rose- and table-cut crystals, and garnets.
WEST EUROPEAN: mid 17th century.
M.129-1975

2 CROSS
Silver, set with rose-cut crystals; the back gold, with pink tulips in painted enamel.
WEST EUROPEAN: second half of 17th century.
M.74-1962

3 PENDENT
Enamelled gold openwork lozenge, set with sapphires, rubies, emeralds and rose-cut diamonds, the back with a bowl of fruit in painted enamel.
WEST EUROPEAN: second half of 17th century.
M.84-1962

*4 LINKS OF A CHAIN
Enamelled gold, set with rose-cut diamonds, rubies and emeralds.
? FRENCH: about 1650; the end links probably VIENNESE: about 1840.
M.106-1975

5 PENDENT CROSS
Emeralds set in gold, formerly enamelled; the back with scroll and foliated decoration in painted enamel.
WEST EUROPEAN: second half of 17th century.
M.102-1975

*6 BOW
Enamelled gold, set with rubies and hung with a pearl; the back with flowers in painted enamel.
WEST EUROPEAN: second third of 17th century.
The bow is probably a unit from a necklace or bracelet.
M.94-1975

7 PENDANT
Silver-gilt, set with emeralds, rubies and table-cut diamonds; the back engraved.
? GERMAN: about 1700.
M.57-1962
Nos. 1-7, given by Dame Joan Evans, P.P.S.A.

A. MODELS FOR GOLDSMITH'S WORK:
16th-18th century

8 PENDANT
Enamelled gold, set with table-cut diamonds and rubies; in the form of a vessel with handle.
WEST EUROPEAN: late 17th century
339-1864

9 NECKLACE
Rose-cut diamonds, set in gold; the backs of the settings enamelled; the clasp enamelled with Apollo and Daphne.
WEST EUROPEAN: second half of 17th century.
M.88-1975

*10 BROOCH
Gold, chased, with a painted relief of Rebecca at the well; rock crystal face.
ENGLISH or DUTCH: mid 17th century.
M.90-1975
Nos. 9 & 10, given by Dame Joan Evans, P.P.S.A.

11 ORNAMENT
Table- and rose-cut crystals, set in gold ? lined with mirror glass, with enamelled pellets; the back enamelled with flowers.
WEST EUROPEAN: second half of 17th century
Croft Lyons Bequest
M.972-1926

12 TWO BUTTONS
Rose-cut crystals set in gold with enamelled decoration; the backs with black sprigs on white painted enamel.
WEST EUROPEAN: mid 17th century.
Given by Dame Joan Evans, P.P.S.A.
M.93 & a-1975

13 PART OF AN ORNAMENT
Rose-cut pastes set in silver; the back enamelled in blue.
WEST EUROPEAN: second half of 17th century.
830, 831-b-1864

14 CRUCIFIX
Silver.
WEST EUROPEAN: late 17th century.
832-1864
Nos. 13 & 14, Brooke Gift

*15 NECKLACE
Gold, decorated with enamel and set with pastes and pearls; enamelled on the back. Shell clasp.
WEST EUROPEAN: mid 17th century.
Given by Dame Joan Evans, P.P.S.A.
M.118-1975

16 BUTTON
Rose-cut crystals set in silver, ? lined with mirror glass; the back enamelled in black and white. Converted into a brooch.
WEST EUROPEAN: second half of 17th century.
Croft Lyons Bequest
M.973-1926

17 SLIDE AND TWO BUTTONS
Rose-cut crystals set in silver, ? lined with mirror glass; the back enamelled with sprigs.
WEST EUROPEAN: second third of 17th century.
These were not originally a set.
Given by Dame Joan Evans, P.P.S.A.
M.78-b-1975

18 PART OF A NECKLACE
Faceted crystals set in silver; the backs enamelled with flowers.
WEST EUROPEAN: late 17th century.
Croft Lyons Bequest
M.974-1926

1 RING MODEL
Cast brass; the ring still has the sprue and part of another ring attached.
ENGLISH: 16th or 17th century.
Found in the Thames.
M.66-1980

*2 MODEL FOR A PENDENT JEWEL
A *cire-perdue* (lost wax) casting in gilt bronze, set with garnets.
ITALIAN: 2nd half of 16th century.
M.459-1911

3 MODEL FOR THE LID OF A BOX
Brass, with a medallion depicting William III (1650-1702); signed by Domaine Dassier (1641-1714) of Geneva.
WEST EUROPEAN: about 1700.
Given by Mr Murray Marks
M.45-1914

4 PLAQUETTE
Modelled in wax on a slate ground; signed *MARCVS GVNTER FE. 1730*.
Presumably a goldsmith's model, as Gunter worked for the trade in England and on the Continent.
? ENGLISH: 1730.
128-1906

5 JEWELLERY PATTERN
Lead.
GERMAN: 16th century.
M.43h-1967

6 JEWELLERY PATTERN
Lead.
GERMAN: late 16th century.
M.43d-1967

7, 8 & 9 JEWELLERY PATTERNS
Lead.
GERMAN: 16th century.
M.43k, m, o-1967

10 JEWELLERY PATTERN
Lead; two hands clasping a heart in token of eternal fidelity.
GERMAN: 16th century.
M.43g-1967

81

B. BADGES:
18th – 20th century

11 JEWELLERY PATTERN
Lead.
GERMAN: 16th century.
M.43n-1967

12 MODEL FOR A MEDAL
Copper, embossed with a scene
representing Minerva directing a
youth to the Temple of Fame at the
summit of a steep and rugged hill.
Above is scratched the inscription:
*HAUD FACILEM ESSE VIAM
VOLVIT*. Signed: *G.M. Moser fecit
1767*.
ENGLISH: 1767.
George Michael Moser (1706-83), the
most distinguished chaser of his
time, was born in Switzerland but
worked in London from 1726 until his
death. This model was probably
an unused design submitted by
Moser for the gold medal of the Royal
Academy.
596-1869

**13 PENDENT BADGE OF
JOHN ANSTIS the Elder,
Garter King at Arms,** with
chain.
Enamelled with the cross of St
George impaling the Royal Arms,
1714-1801, within the Garter.
ENGLISH: 1730.

**14 & 15 TWO PENDENT
BADGES OF THE ORDER OF
THE BATH**
Gold, with enamel decoration, one
with the reverse side uppermost,
showing the white horse of Hanover;
the other with two interlocked G's
between three crowns. Made for John
Anstis the younger as Blanc Coursier
Herald and Genealogist of the Order
of the Bath, 1725.
ENGLISH: 1725.
See also Case 15, Board G,
nos. 2 & 3
Nos. 13-15, M.5-8-1937

**16 BADGE OF THE ORDER OF
CARLOS III OF SPAIN (1716-
1788)**
Enamelled gold and faceted silver.
SPANISH: perhaps late 18th
century.
249-1864

**17 FRAME OF THE BADGE OF
A MAID OF HONOUR TO THE
TSARINA MARIE
FEODOROVNA OF RUSSIA**
The frame silver, backed with
engraved gold; in the form of an
initial M surmounted by the Russian
imperial crown, its finial a Maltese
cross in gold. Formerly set with
precious stones. Attached to a blue
ribbon of watered silk; pinned to this
ribbon, a red ribbon from which
depends a silver medal commemorating Tsar Alexander III
(reigned 1881-1894).
RUSSIAN: about 1890.
Presented by the Marquise de
Mérindol in memory of her mother,
the Comtesse Elisabeth Olsoufieff,
born Princess Abamalek-Lazarew,
who wore the badge at the lying-in-
state of Tsar Alexander III
M.33-1981

***18 BADGE OF A GRAND
MASTER OF THE SOCIETY OF
FREEMASONS**
Silver, parcel-gilt, set with red, green
and white pastes.
ENGLISH: about 1880.
M.33-1971

**19 BADGE OF THE
HABERDASHERS' COMPANY**
Enamelled gold plaque of a past
Master of the Company and the
motto: *SERVE AND OBEY*. The
reverse inscribed: *Colonel Henry L.
Florence, V.D.*
ENGLISH (London): dated 1915-16.
Maker's mark of Carrington &
Company Ltd.
Bequeathed by Colonel Florence
M.225-1917

Case 14 Board F

ENAMEL-WORK:
17th century

*1 LOCKET
Enamelled gold, set with table-cut
crystals. Obverse, an enamelled bust
of Pope Gregory XIII (1572-85), after
a medal by Gianfederigo Bonzagna;
reverse, arms of Carl Caspar Van
Leyen, Elector of Trier, 1652-76.
GERMAN: third quarter of 17th
century.
Given by Dame Joan Evans, P.P.S.A.
M.60-1975

2 PENDANT
In the form of a bowl with fruit, in
relief. Enamelled gold, set with
point-cut diamonds.
? GERMAN: late 17th century.
504-1854

3 PAIR OF BUCKLES
Enamelled gold, decorated with
scallop shells.
WEST EUROPEAN: last third of
17th century.
Given by Dame Joan Evans, P.P.S.A.
M.96-a-1975

4 JEWEL
In the form of a bust of a woman.
Enamelled gold.
DUTCH: second half of 17th century.
Given by Colonel Sir C. Wyndham
Murray, K.C.B.
M.131-1922

**5 RELIGIOUS MINIATURE
CASE**
Enamelled gold, set with table-cut
pastes on the front and with painted
enamel flowers on the back,
surrounding the letters *MAR* for the
Virgin Mary; miniature wanting.
NORTH EUROPEAN: second half of
17th century.
Given by Dame Joan Evans, P.P.S.A.
M.72-1975

6 ORNAMENT
Enamelled gold flower, set with a
table-cut diamond; adapted to make a
pin later.
WEST EUROPEAN: second half of
17th century.
340-1864

*7 PENDANT
Enamelled gold, set with an onyx
cameo, a portrait of Livia, (*c*.56 BC -
29 AD), wife of Augustus.
The cameo 1st century BC, in the
manner of Dioscorides, the official
gem-carver to the Julian-Claudian
House.
The setting NORTH EUROPEAN:
mid 17th century.
Marlborough Collection
Given by Dame Joan Evans, P.P.S.A.
M.119-1975

8 PIN
Enamelled gold bow, set with rubies;
hung with a small bow and two
scrolling devices. Perhaps a hair
ornament.
WEST EUROPEAN: second half of
17th century.
Later Rome mark.
2824-1856

9 LOCKET
Enamelled gold; obverse, the
Nativity; inside and reverse, the
Adoration of the Magi, the Flight
into Egypt and the Massacre of the
Innocents.
GERMAN: late 17th century.
French import marks introduced in
1864.
Joicey Bequest
M.213-1919

***10 NECKLACE AND PAIR OF
EARRINGS.**
Gold, decorated with painted enamel
and set with table-cut emeralds and
pearls; the units in the form of
flowers, with a butterfly pendant;
hung with a cabochon emerald.
? ITALIAN: last third of 17th
century.
M.254-b-1975

11 MINIATURE CASE
Gold, decorated with painted enamel
flowers; inside, an enamelled
landscape.
WEST EUROPEAN: second third of
17th century.
M.95-1975
Nos. 10 & 11, given by Dame Joan
Evans, P.P.S.A.

12 PENDANT
In the form of birds and a basket of
fruit, in relief. Silver-gilt, enamelled,
set with rubies and garnets; hung
with pearls.
? GERMAN: late 17th century.
296-1854

MAINLY SPANISH:
about 1620-1720

COMMEMORATIVE, SENTIMENTAL AND RELIGIOUS:
about 1650-1730

84

1 PENDANT
Emeralds set in gold openwork, the reverse engraved.
SPANISH: late 17th century.
M.138-1975

2 PAIR OF BRACELET CLASPS
Topazes set in silver openwork.
SPANISH: about 1680.
M.77 & a-1962

*3 PENDANT
Amethysts set in gold openwork with enamelled decoration on a pierced plate behind the stones; three pendants.
SPANISH: second quarter of 17th century.
M.141-1975

*4 BODICE ORNAMENT AND PAIR OF EARRINGS
Rose-cut diamonds and topazes set in silver and gold scrolling and foliated openwork; the settings engraved on the reverse.
? DUTCH: second half of 17th century.
M.98-b-1975
Nos. 1-4, given by Dame Joan Evans, P.P.S.A.

5 PENDENT BADGE OF THE ORDER OF SANTIAGO
Amethysts and topazes set in gold, the reverse partly enamelled; in two parts, the lower with an applied sword/cross.
SPANISH: first half of 17th century.
See no. 7 below and Board I following, nos. 8, 13 & 14.
M.5-1912

6 PENDENT BADGE OF THE HOLY INQUISITION
An emerald encased in enamelled gold. Obverse, the black-and-white cross of St Dominic (the Dominicans were prominent in the inquisition of heretics). Reverse, a green cross symbolising the hope of repentance before punishment, and salvation; an olive branch signifying the mercy afforded the repentant; and a sword, the punishment of the obdurate.
SPANISH: about 1620-30.
Probably worn by a woman to show her support for the policies of the Church.
M.308-1910

7 PENDENT BADGE OF THE ORDER OF SANTIAGO
Rock crystal and enamelled gold; a red enamel sword/cross applied to the front.
SPANISH: early 17th century.
This pendant is so small that it is suggested that it was made for a child.
226-1864

8 PENDANT
Crystals set in enamelled silver openwork; pendent rosette.
WEST EUROPEAN (possibly SPANISH): second half of 17th century.
Given by Dame Joan Evans, P.P.S.A.
M.100-1975

9 RELIQUARY PENDANT
An onyx cameo of the Virgin and Child, set in silver-gilt openwork.
SPANISH: early 17th century.
4055-1856

10 PENDANT
Gold openwork, set with garnets and rose-cut crystals. Obverse, a painting under crystal of St. Joseph with the Infant Christ; reverse, Christ.
SPANISH: about 1700.
Given by Mr Walter Child
1413-1904

11 PENDANT
Enamelled gold. Obverse, a painting under crystal of the Infant Christ with St John the Baptist; reverse, the Presentation in the Temple.
SPANISH: about 1720.
Alfred Williams Hearn Gift
M.58-1923

Some of the English pieces on the board demonstrate the persistence during the Commonwealth of loyalist feeling towards Charles I, executed in 1649, and his son Charles II, who was restored to the throne in 1660.

1 PENDANT
In the centre, a silver-gilt medal with, obverse, Charles I (1600-1649); and, reverse, Queen Henrietta Maria by Thomas Rawlins (? 1620-1670); border of brilliant-cut diamonds.
ENGLISH: mid 17th century; the diamond mount late 18th or early 19th century.
Lent by Lord O'Hagan

2 LOCKET
Silver, heart-shaped, with an embossed Cupid.
Inscribed: *NOE HEART MORE TRUE THEN* (sic) *MINE TO YOU.*
ENGLISH: second half of 17th century. Maker's mark, RA.
S.H.J. Johnson Bequest
M.3-1958

*3 SLIDE PENDANT
Gold frame enamelled on the back, set with a painted miniature of Charles I and Charles II (1630-1685).
ENGLISH: about 1650-60.
Given by Dame Joan Evans, P.P.S.A.
M.251-1975

4 LOCKET
Silver-gilt, heart-shaped. Obverse, an engraved eye and tears; inside, a medallion of Charles I.
ENGLISH: after 1649.
Brooke Gift
827 & a-1864

5 MINIATURE CASE
Gold.
ENGLISH: about 1680; the engraving attributed to the watch-case engraver Abraham Martin of London.
Lent by Mrs. C.E. Radford

6 PENDENT CROSS
Table-cut crystals set in gold, with enamel decoration.
From the same workshop as the cross shown as no. 9 on this board.
SPANISH: first quarter of 17th century.
French import mark for 1864-93.
Given by Dame Joan Evans P.P.S.A.
M.123-1975

7 SILVER MEDAL OF CHARLES I
By Thomas Rawlins, with contemporary cast and gilt copy.
ENGLISH: mid 17th century.
92-1866, 813-1891

8 PENDANT
Plum-stone, carved with the heads of Charles I (obverse) and the future Charles II (reverse).
ENGLISH: about 1643.
Frank Ward Bequest
M.10-1960

9 PENDENT CROSS
Table-cut crystals set in gold with enamel decoration.
See also no. 6 on this board.
SPANISH: first quarter of 17th century.
M.128-1975

10 LOCKET
Silver, heart-shaped. Obverse stamped with a head of Charles II; reverse, Queen Catherine of Braganza (1638-1705).
ENGLISH: 1662.
M.104-1962
Nos. 9 & 10, given by Dame Joan Evans, P.P.S.A.

11 LOCKET
Silver, heart-shaped. Inscribed: *LOVE GOD IN HART.*
ENGLISH: 17th century.
Brooke Gift
827-b-1864

12 LOCKET
Silver, heart-shaped. Obverse inscribed: *Prepared Be To Follow Me/CR;* reverse: *Live and Dy in Loyalty;* inside: *I Morne for Monerchie,* with a medallion of Charles I.
ENGLISH: after 1649.
Croft Lyons Bequest
M.811-1926

13 LOCKET
Silver, heart-shaped. Obverse, an applied bust of Charles II; inside, a medallion of Charles I.
ENGLISH: second half of 17th century.
Brooke Gift
827-1864

14 PENDENT CROSS
Table-cut crystals set in gold with enamel decoration; hung with a pearl.
SPANISH: early 17th century.
M.122-1975

15 MOURNING BUCKLE
Gold, set with crystals over: *Eliz Harman/Obt 11 Ap/98 Ata 27,* worked in gold thread on hair; the reverse engraved.
ENGLISH: dated 1698.
M.91-1975
Nos. 14 & 15, given by Dame Joan Evans, P.P.S.A.

*16 LOCKET (shown in two parts)
Copper-gilt, containing a miniature of Major William Carlos (d. 1689). The reverse engraved with Charles II and Carlos hiding in an oak tree at Boscobel House after the battle of Worcester, and the obverse with the arms and motto granted to the latter in commemoration of the event.
Inside inscribed:
Renewned Carlos! Thow hast won the day (Loyalty Lost) by helping Charles away, From Kings-Blood-Thirsty-Rebels in a Night, made black with Rage, of theives, & Hells dispight Live! King-Loved Sowle thy fame by Euer Spoke
By all whilst England Beares a Royalle Oake.
ENGLISH: second half of 17th century
Charles II, crowned at Scone, marched southwards with his followers in 1651 but was routed by Cromwell's army at Worcester. Eluding his pursuers, he was eventually conveyed by his supporters to France.
898-1904

17 MOURNING BUCKLE
Gold, set with crystal over: *Ann Harford 1728,* worked in gold thread on hair.
ENGLISH: dated 1728.
M.136-1975

18 PENDENT CROSS
Rose-cut crystals set in gold and silver with enamel decoration.
WEST EUROPEAN: second half of 17th century.
M.109-1975
Nos. 17 & 18, given by Dame Joan Evans P.P.S.A.

19 MOURNING BUCKLE
Gold, set with crystal over: *Hannah Kell/dyed 6th April 1725 aged 8 years,* worked in gold thread on hair.
ENGLISH: dated 1725.
M.22-1960

Case 14 Board I

MAINLY IBERIAN:
late 17th-18th century

1 SLIDE AND PENDANT
Table-cut emeralds set in gold openwork. The slide in the form of a bow with two foliated units below, the lowest a cross.
SPANISH: probably mid 18th century. Struck with an unidentified mark.
M.84-1913

*2 BODICE ORNAMENT
Table-cut emeralds and diamonds set in foliated gold openwork radiating from a central rosette, with the addition of enamelled flowers and insects mounted on springs ('tremblers'). One large and six small pendants; a hook at the back for fastening to a bodice.
SPANISH: about 1700.
From the Treasury of the Cathedral of the Virgin of the Pillar, Saragossa
325-1870

3 SLIDE AND PENDANT
Table- and rose-cut diamonds set in gold openwork; the slide a bow with two foliated units below, the lowest a cross.
Probably SPANISH: mid 18th century.
M.83-1913

4 BADGE
Silver-gilt, set with garnets and emeralds and enamelled with the arms of the Mercedarians.
SPANISH (Aragon): early 18th century.
Given by Dame Joan Evans, P.P.S.A.
M.91-1962

5 PENDANT
Rose-cut diamonds set in gold scrolling openwork; in two parts.
SPANISH: early 18th century.
From the Treasury of the Cathedral of the Virgin of the Pillar, Saragossa
408-1873

6 BODICE ORNAMENT
Rose-cut diamonds set in gold scrolling openwork, surmounted by a shell; bow pendant and five drops (another is missing). Two hooks at the back for fastening to the bodice.
SPANISH: late 17th century.
From the Treasury of the Cathedral of the Virgin of the Pillar, Saragossa, to which it was presented by the Marquesa de la Puebla, mentioned by Madame d'Aulnoy (1650-1705) as one of the beauties of the Spanish Court
320-1870

7 PAIR OF EARRINGS
Table-cut diamonds set in gold openwork, with drops.
SPANISH: late 17th century.
From Arica in Chile.
417-1869

8 PENDENT BADGE OF THE ORDER OF SANTIAGO
White topaz spokes set in gold; pendent sword/cross of garnets and white topaz.
SPANISH: late 18th century.
The order is the senior of the four Spanish military orders.
Given by Dame Joan Evans, P.P.S.A.
M.79-1962

*9 BADGE OF THE HOLY INQUISITION
Enamelled gold. Obverse, the black-and-white cross of St Dominic. Reverse, symbols of repentance and salvation, mercy, and punishment.
SPANISH: about 1630. Mark, GD.
See also Board G preceding, no. 6.
232-1864

10 PENDANT
Gold openwork, set with emeralds and a blue paste; a pin is a later addition.
SPANISH: 18th century.
238-1864

11 PENDANT
Table- and rose-cut diamonds set in scrolling gold openwork; in two parts.
SPANISH: late 17th century.
324-1870

12 PENDANT
Table- and rose-cut diamonds set in scrolling gold openwork; in two parts.
SPANISH: late 17th century.
407-1873
Nos. 11 & 12, from the Treasury of the Cathedral of the Virgin of the Pillar, Saragossa

13 PENDENT BADGE OF THE ORDER OF SANTIAGO
Garnets in the form of a sword/cross set in silver; white topaz borders.
SPANISH: about 1630.
Given by Dame Joan Evans, P.P.S.A.
M.80-1962

14 MINIATURE PENDENT BADGE OF THE ORDER OF SANTIAGO
Gold, set with emeralds and diamond sparks, with pendent ruby sword/cross.
SPANISH: late 18th century.
22-1866

15 PENDANT
Rose-cut diamonds and topazes set in silver; in two parts.
PORTUGUESE: probably mid 18th century.
Given by Sir Walter Child, who acquired it in the Azores
M.590-1911

16 PENDANT OR BREAST ORNAMENT
Table-cut diamonds set in scrolling gold foliated openwork; in three parts.
IBERIAN: late 17th century. The middle section appears to be earlier.
From the Treasury of the Cathedral of the Virgin of the Pillar, Saragossa
406-1873

17 BUCKLE
Silver, set with rose-cut diamonds; in three parts.
? PORTUGUESE: about 1710.
Lisbon mark for old silver, 1886 and French import mark introduced in 1893.
M.132-1975

Case 14 Board J

ROSARIES:
17th century

18 SLIDE
In the form of a vase of flowers. One hog-back, and table-cut diamonds, set in gold and silver; hung with a pearl.
WEST EUROPEAN: late 17th or early 18th century. French import mark as in no. 17 above.
M.150-1975
Nos. 17 & 18, given by Dame Joan Evans, P.P.S.A.

1 Glass and silver-gilt filigree; mounted with the emblems of the Passion and with a pendent cross of St Walburga.
BOHEMIAN: third quarter of 17th century.
174-1866

2 Gold.
FRENCH: late 17th century.
Lent by Messrs. Walter Bull & Son

CASE 14
BOARD A
NO. 4

CASE 14
BOARD A
NO. 7

CASE 14
BOARD A
NO. 10
2 Views

CASE 14
BOARD A
NO. 2

CASE 14
BOARD A
NO. 5

CASE 14
BOARD B
NO. 7

CASE 14
BOARD B
NO. 12

CASE 14
BOARD B
NO. 15

CASE 14
BOARD D
NO. 4

CASE 14
BOARD C
NO. 3

CASE 14
BOARD D
NO. 10

CASE 14
BOARD D
NO. 15

CASE 14
BOARD F
NO. 7

CASE 14
BOARD F
NO. 1

CASE 14
BOARD G
NO. 3

CASE 14
BOARD D
NO. 6

CASE 14
BOARD E
NO. 2

CASE 14
BOARD F
NO. 10

CASE 14
BOARD E
NO. 18

CASE 14
BOARD H
NO. 3

CASE 14
BOARD I
NO. 9

Case 15 Board A

Late 17th and early 18th centuries

1 BODICE ORNAMENT OR STOMACHER
Rose-cut pastes set in silver; in the form of a bow, two intermediate units, and a cross. The lower of the two middle units perhaps a replacement.
Probably ENGLISH: about 1720.
Given by Dame Joan Evans, P.P.S.A.
M.134-1975

2 PENDANT
Gold, set with an enamelled group of a tea-party, modelled in relief.
ENGLISH: mid 18th century.
M.33-1960

3 PAIR OF BUTTONS
Silver, set with stamped gold foil heads under crystal of George, Prince of Wales, later George III (1738-1820), and his brother Edward, Duke of York (1739-1767).
ENGLISH: about 1758.
M.31 & a-1960
Nos. 2 & 3, Frank Ward Bequest

4 RELIQUARY CROSS
Peridots and rose-cut diamonds set in silver-gilt; the back engraved with *Régence* ornament and furnished with a compartment for a relic.
GERMAN: about 1730.
M.54-1962

5 PENDANT
Gold, set with a cameo under crystal of George I (reigned 1714-1727).
ENGLISH: about 1715.
M.111-1962
Nos. 4 & 5, given by Dame Joan Evans, P.P.S.A.

6 PAIR OF SLEEVE-LINKS
Gold, set with a cipher in gold wire under crystal.
ENGLISH: early 18th century.
Frank Ward Bequest
M.30 & a-1960

7 BODICE ORNAMENT OR STOMACHER
Emeralds and pearls set in silver-gilt; in fifteen stages, with loops at the back for attachment to clothing.
GERMAN: early 18th century.
4560-1858

CASE 14
BOARD H
NO. 16

CASE 14
BOARD I
NO. 2

CASE 14
BOARD G
NO. 4

Case 15 Board B

17th and 18th centuries

8 PAIR OF EARRINGS
Silver and gold, set with rose-cut
diamonds.
IBERIAN: about 1740.
Murray Bequest
M.1027 & a-1910

*9 PENDENT CROSS
Rose-cut diamonds and rubies set in
silver and gold openwork.
? GERMAN: early 18th century.
397-1864

10 EARRING
Rubies and brilliant- and rose-cut
diamonds set in silver, parcel-gilt.
GERMAN (Ulm): about 1740.
Alfred Williams Hearn Gift
968a-1872

11 PENDANT
Emeralds, brilliant-cut diamonds
and seed pearls set in silver.
EUROPEAN: about 1740-60.
237-1894

12 NECKLACE
Table- and rose-cut rock crystal and
emeralds set in gold.
SPANISH or ITALIAN: late 17th
century. Mark of a bell on the clasp
and the letter *B* (probably later).
Lent by Messrs Walter Bull & Son

13 PENDANT
Enamelled gold; in the centre, Ecce
Homo, surrounded by scenes from
the Passion; the reverse with painted
enamel flowers; pendent pearl.
SPANISH: early 18th century.
Alfred Williams Hearn Gift
M.65-1923

**1 PENDENT CROSS, EARRING
AND PIN**
Rose-cut diamonds and rubies set in
silver, backed with gold.
NORTH EUROPEAN: 18th
century. Maker's mark, JA, on the
earring loop.
1156-1158-1864

2 NECKLACE
Amethysts and brilliant-cut crystals
set in gold.
Probably ENGLISH: early 18th
century.
Given by Dame Joan Evans, P.P.S.A.
M.130-1975

3 SLIDE AND PENDANT
Rose-cut diamonds and brilliant-cut
rubies set in silver, parcel-gilt.
NORTH EUROPEAN: early 18th
century.
M.113-1909

4 RING
Enamelled gold, set with rubies.
GERMAN: early 17th century.
The enamelled figure 3 on the head of
the ring relates to the pendent badge
shown as no.6, the design of which
also incorporates a 3, as well as an
anchor and a cluster of forget-me-
nots, which in turn relates it to the
badge shown as no.5. All three pieces
were probably German court
decorations.
213-1870

5 BADGE
Enamelled gold; an anchor, a bird
with a heart and a forget-me-not
depending from an Electoral bonnet.
GERMAN: about 1700.
9081-1863

6 BADGE
Enamelled gold; crossed palm leaves,
a skull, three forget-me-nots, two
hearts and the initials *PWC BVM*
below a coronet; pearl drop.
GERMAN: about 1700.
451-1873

7 MEDALLION
Silver; St Anthony of Padua with the
Infant Christ; inscribed: *ANT. D.P.*
and dated 1785.
SWISS (St. Gall and Thurgau): 1785.
192-1870

*8 MEDALLION
Silver-gilt; the reverse (shown here)
commemorates St Martin and other
early Christian martyrs. Obverse,
Max Gandolf von Künburg,
Archbishop of Salzburg.
AUSTRIAN: dated 1682.
Tross Collection, Paris
67-1867

*9 PENDANT
Diamond sparks and rubies set in
gold and silver openwork; a bow
applied to the front of the suspension
loop.
Probably PORTUGUESE: 18th
century.
M.85-1913

10 PENDANT
Gold; probably struck to commemo-
rate the elevation of Prince William
Charles Henry Friso (died 1751) to
the dignity of Stadholder of the
Netherlands under the title of
William IV.
DUTCH: 1747.
Given by Dame Joan Evans, P.P.S.A.
M.97-1962

**11 PAIR OF HEAD-DRESS
ORNAMENTS**
Enamelled gold, set with pearls.
? SPANISH: about 1730. Struck with
two unidentified marks.
165 & a-1894

12 NECKLACE
Table- and rose-cut diamonds and
pearls set in gold.
SPANISH: early 18th century.
Given by Dame Joan Evans, P.P.S.A.
M.126-1975

13 FRAME FOR A MINIATURE
Table-cut diamonds and rubies set in
silver.
ENGLISH: early 18th century.
M.349-1910

*14 PAIR OF EARRINGS
Gold ribbon and floral tops, painted
porcelain drops; incomplete.
? GERMAN: mid 18th century.
Circ.319, 320-1910

SPANISH and GERMAN: *18th century*

Second half of the 18th century

92

*15 CROSS
Gold rococo scrolls, overlaid with a crystal cross mounted in silver; the back engraved.
FLEMISH or GERMAN: about 1740.
M.55-1962

16 PAIR OF SLEEVE BUTTONS
Gold, set with porcelain plaques, painted with half-length figures of peasant women.
Probably GERMAN: 18th century.
M.58 & a-1962
Nos. 15 & 16, given by Dame Joan Evans, P.P.S.A.

1 NECKLACE AND TWO PENDANTS
Brilliant- and rose-cut diamonds and topazes set in silver; an emerald in one pendant.
SPANISH: mid 18th century.
M.139-b-1975

2 PENDENT CROSS AND PAIR OF EARRINGS
Cornelians and rose-cut diamonds set in silver gilt.
GERMAN: the cross about 1720 and the earrings slightly later.
M.81-b-1962

3 PENDANT
Topazes set in silver.
SPANISH: first half of 18th century.
M.140-1975

4 NECKLACE AND PAIR OF EARRINGS
Topazes and rose-cut diamonds set in silver.
SPANISH: mid 18th century.
M.142-b-1975
Nos. 1-4, given by Dame Joan Evans, P.P.S.A.

*5 CAMEO PENDANT
Onyx head of Dionysus in a gold surround set with amber, turquoises and rubies; the back engraved.
The cameo 1st century AD; the setting probably GERMAN: about 1730.
M.132-1922

6 NECKLET
Cornelians set in silver; pendant. Designed to be tied with a ribbon.
Probably GERMAN: about 1740.
M.82-1962

7 PENDANT
Amber bust of a woman with a jewelled plume, set in gold.
GERMAN: mid 18th century.
M.131-1975
Nos. 6 & 7, given by Dame Joan Evans, P.P.S.A.

1 SPRAY ORNAMENT
Probably originally a hair ornament; later converted into a brooch.
Rubies and brilliant-cut diamonds set in gold and silver, decorated with enamel.
RUSSIAN: about 1750-70. Probably executed by immigrant craftsmen.
From the Russian Crown Jewels.
Cory Bequest
M.85-1951

*2 PARURE
Comprising a bodice ornament in two parts, in the form of a bow from which is suspended a scrolling unit and pendants; a flower spray, probably to be worn in the hair; a slide button and a pair of girandole earrings (complex earrings, often with bows or ribbons but always having two or more pear-shaped pendants). The spray has been altered. Blue and white sapphires set in gold.
? FRENCH: about 1760.
Given by Dame Joan Evans, P.P.S.A.
M.163-d-1975

*3 BOUQUET
Gold, enamelled and set with rose- and brilliant-cut diamonds, the flowers tied with a bow. The back fitted with a detachable hook for fastening to the bodice (not shown).
SPANISH: late 18th century.
From the Treasury of the Cathedral of the Virgin of the Pillar, Saragossa, to which it was presented by Dona Juana Rabasa, wife of the Minister of Finance to Charles IV of Spain (1788-1808).
319-1870

4 FLOWER BROOCH
Brilliant-cut diamonds and pastes set in silver.
NORTH EUROPEAN: about 1770.
M.47-1962

5 FLOWER BROOCH
Crystals set in silver.
WEST EUROPEAN: late 18th century.
M.65-1962
Nos. 4 & 5, given by Dame Joan Evans, P.P.S.A.

Case 15 Board E

POMANDERS, SCENT CASES AND FLASKS:
14th-17th century

6 PAIR OF EARRINGS
Foiled colourless crystals (described as *minas novas* when the earrings were acquired by the Museum), set in silver openwork; incomplete.
? PORTUGUESE: late 18th century.
806 & a-1902

7 NECKLACE
Table- and rose-cut diamonds set in silver; pendant.
NORTH EUROPEAN: late 18th century.
Given by Dame Joan Evans, P.P.S.A.
M.169-1975

8 EARRING
Table- and rose-cut diamonds set in silver openwork, with a gold loop at the back; flower and ribbon motifs, with three pendants.
SPANISH: late 18th century.
From the Treasury of the Cathedral of the Virgin of the Pillar, Saragossa
323-1870

Many of these articles were carried on a chain suspended from the waist

1 POMANDER
Silver, parcel-gilt, decorated with niello. Inside, inscriptions relating to the Judgment of Paris.
ITALIAN: 14th century.
Londesborough and Wyndham Cook Collections; Francis Reubell Bryan Bequest
M.205-1925

2 COMBINED ROSARY BEAD AND POMANDER
Silver-gilt, with pierced gothic tracery.
FLEMISH or GERMAN: about 1500.
918-1853

3 POMANDER
Silver-gilt.
SPANISH (Toledo): end of 16th century.
1226-1871

*4 SCENT FLASK
Silver-gilt, set with *champlevé* enamel bosses.
SPANISH: about 1620.
M.799-1926

*5 SCENT FLASK
Silver-gilt, decorated with niello.
? SPANISH: 17th century.
M.1018-1926
Nos. 4 & 5, Croft Lyons Bequest

6 COMBINED POMANDER AND VINAIGRETTE
Silver, decorated with moresques in niello in the style of Michel Le Blon (1587-1656) and others.
WEST EUROPEAN: early 17th century.
Alfred Williams Hearn Gift
M.105-1923

7 POMANDER
Silver; engraved design filled with mastic.
WEST EUROPEAN: first half of 17th century.
Given by Miss Mabel M. Boore
M.105-1939

8 COMBINED POMANDER AND VINAIGRETTE
Silver, parcel-gilt.
WEST EUROPEAN: first half of 17th century.
Given by the Misses Dagmar and Gladys Farrant in memory of Arthur and Maud Loscombe Wallis
M.84-1933

9 SCENT CASE
Silver, decorated with translucent enamel.
? ENGLISH: about 1620.
Given by Dr W.L. Hildburgh, F.S.A.
M.9-1948

10 SCENT CASE
Crystal, mounted in silver-gilt.
? GERMAN: early 17th century.
Given by Miss Mabel M. Boore
M.106-1939

11 COMBINED POMANDER AND VINAIGRETTE
Silver, parcel-gilt; engraved with the symbols of the Evangelists.
? GERMAN: 17th century
37-1876

12 SCENT CASE
Silver; in the form of a skull.
? GERMAN: 17th century.
Croft Lyons Bequest
M.804-1926

13 SCENT CASE
Silver-gilt; in the form of a skull and a woman's head.
Probably GERMAN: 17th century.
Forrer Collection
516-1903

14 SWEETMEAT BOX
Silver; the engraved design filled with mastic.
In the lid, a compartment with a sliding cover engraved with a shrouded figure and the inscription:
Let this suffize where loue supplize.
ENGLISH: first half of 17th century.
M.186-1922

15 SWEETMEAT BOX
Engraved silver.
DUTCH: second quarter of 17th century.
1132-1864

BUCKLES:
18th and 19th centuries

16 SCENT CASE
Silver; fitted with a squirt and a
vinaigrette.
NORTH EUROPEAN: 17th century.
345-1908

17 POMANDER
Silver-gilt filigree.
? WEST EUROPEAN: 17th century.
328-1864

18 POMANDER
Gold filigree, enclosing a ball of
ambergris.
? WEST EUROPEAN: 17th century.
Given by Miss E. Mackworth Dolben
849-1892

19 POMANDER
Silver-gilt.
DUTCH: 17th century; maker's
mark, a crowned D over TF in
monogram.
Croft Lyons Bequest
M.771-1926

*20 POMANDER
Silver.
DUTCH: second half of 17th century.
794-1891

21 SCENT CASE
Silver, parcel-gilt, with a pierced
figure composition.
GERMAN: second half of 17th
century.
Bernal Collection
2284-1855

22 SCENT FLASK
Silver-gilt.
GERMAN: 17th century.
Croft Lyons Bequest
M.800-1926

23 SCENT CASE
Silver-gilt; in the form of a snail.
GERMAN: 17th century.
107-1872

*24 SCENT CASE
Silver-gilt; in the form of a snail.
GERMAN: 17th century.
Given by Miss L.F.M. Preston
M.128-1929

25 SCENT CASE
Silver-gilt; in the form of a snail.
GERMAN: 17th century.
M.805-1926

26 SCENT CASE
Silver-gilt; in the form of a snail.
GERMAN: 17th century.
M.805-1926

27 SCENT CASE
Silver-gilt, in the form of a frog on a
leaf.
GERMAN: 17th century.
M.807-1926
Nos. 25-27, Croft Lyons Bequest

*28 SCENT FLASK
Silver-gilt; engraved with Lucretia, a
cherub and foliage.
WEST EUROPEAN: late 17th
century.
Given by Miss Mabel M. Boore
M.108-1939

29 VINAIGRETTE
Silver-gilt.
? DUTCH: about 1680.
Bequeathed by Miss Ethel Gurney
M.187-1939

30 POMANDER
Silver-gilt.
? ENGLISH: late 17th century.
1446-1870

31 SCENT FLASK
Silver-gilt; in the form of a woven
covered basket.
WEST EUROPEAN: 17th century.
W.T. Johnson Bequest
M.1782-1944

32 SCENT FLASK
Gold; in the form of a double gourd.
WEST EUROPEAN: second half of
17th century.
Given by Dame Joan-Evans, P.P.S.A.
M.113-1875

Buckles were used to fasten stocks (at
the back or side back of the neck),
knee breeches and other articles of
men's clothing and at certain periods
appeared on women's bodices; but
most surviving specimens are shoe
buckles, which were favoured by both
sexes. Shoe buckles went out of
fashion in the early nineteenth
century, except for use with
ceremonial dress. They reappeared in
female (and some male) fashions
in the 1870s.

Buckles were usually made with steel
chapes, which comprised a spindle
with prongs and pinder or loop.

1 MOURNING BUCKLE
Black japanned brass; inscribed:
*CAROLINA D.G./MAG. BR. ET/
HIB.REG.OB.20/NOV 1737 AE.55.*
ENGLISH: 1737.
Queen Caroline (1683-1737), consort
of George II, was the daughter of
John Frederick, Margrave of
Brandenberg-Anspach.
M.8-1973

2 KNEE BUCKLE
Silver; reeded and foliated ribbon
rim; anchor-shaped steel pinder or
loop.
FRENCH: Paris marks for 1765-66.
Maker's mark, F.D.L.P. with star.
M.35-1909

3 KNEE BUCKLE
Gold; ribbon and rosette design;
anchor-shaped pinder.
ENGLISH: about 1780. Maker's
mark, IR in script.
954-1864

4 KNEE BUCKLE
Silver, set with pastes; anchor-
shaped pinder.
ENGLISH: about 1770-80.
950-1864

5 STOCK BUCKLE
Silver, set with pastes.
ENGLISH: about 1770.
951-1864
Nos. 3-5, Brooke Gift

6 STOCK BUCKLE
Silver, with faceted pellets on rim.
ENGLISH: about 1780. Maker's
mark, RR.
Given by Mr Francis Buckley
M.1-1934

7 SHOE BUCKLE
Silver, in the form of a bow; set with
pastes.
ENGLISH: about 1760.
Given by Mr Robert Holland
899-1877

8 SHOE BUCKLE
Silver, set with pastes.
ENGLISH: about 1760-70.
903-1900

9 ? SHOE BUCKLE
Silver; ribbon and floral trail rim, set
with marcasites.
WEST EUROPEAN: about 1770.
Given by Dame Joan Evans, P.P.S.A.
M.168-1975

10 SHOE BUCKLE
Silver; rosette and ribbon rim, set
with pastes.
ENGLISH: about 1770.
947-1864

11 SHOE BUCKLE
Silver, set with pastes.
ENGLISH: about 1770.
945-1864

12 SHOE BUCKLE
Silver, with rosettes; set with pastes.
ENGLISH: about 1780-90.
946-1864
Nos. 10-12, Brooke Gift

13 ? SHOE BUCKLE
Silver; openwork floral trail; set with
green cabochon pastes and
marcasites. The chape missing.
Probably ENGLISH: about 1780-90.
224-1864

14 SHOE BUCKLE
Silver; interlaced ribbon rim, set with
marcasites.
ENGLISH: about 1780-90.
Pfungst Reavil Bequest
M.51-1969

15 SHOE BUCKLE
Silver; ribbon and rosette rim, set
with pastes.
ENGLISH: about 1780-90.
M.40-1909

16 PAIR OF SHOE BUCKLES
Gold and silver rim, with rosettes; set
with pastes.
ENGLISH: about 1780-90.
Worn by Admiral Sir Rupert George
(1749-1823).
M.9 & a-1973

17 SHOE BUCKLE
Cut steel, mounted with jasper
plaques by Wedgwood.
ENGLISH: about 1776-90.
Pfungst Reavil Bequest
M.2-1969

18 SHOE BUCKLE
Stamped gold on brass; foliated
ribbon and rosette design.
ENGLISH: about 1770-80.
M.37-1909

19 PAIR OF SHOE BUCKLES
Cut steel, with faceted beaded rim
and leather-covered centre; the
fastening stamped: *BOULTON &
SMITHS PATENT.*
ENGLISH (Birmingham): about
1792-1806.
The patent was granted to James
Smith in 1792 and operated in
conjunction with Matthew Boulton of
the Soho Manufactory.
Given by Mr René de l'Hôpital
M.187 & a-1926

20 SHOE BUCKLE
Silver; ribbon and rosette rim.
ENGLISH: about 1780-90. Maker's
mark of Thomas Wallis, London.
M.33-1909

21 SHOE BUCKLE
Silver; ribbon and rosette rim.
ENGLISH: about 1780-90. Maker's
mark, IP (perhaps for Jonathan
Perkins, London).
M.36a-1909

22 SHOE BUCKLE
Silver; openwork rim with rosettes.
ENGLISH: about 1785-95. Maker's
mark IC (perhaps for J.B. Cole,
London).
M.39-1909

23 SHOE BUCKLE
Silver; openwork rim with rosettes.
ENGLISH: London hallmark for
1794-95. Maker's mark IC (see 22
above).
M.38-1909

24 SHOE BUCKLE
Silver; openwork flower and leaf
design.
? ENGLISH: about 1790. Maker's
mark IF in script (perhaps for John
Faux, London).
M.32-1909

25 SHOE BUCKLE
Silver; openwork trail and faceted
pellet rim.
ENGLISH: about 1795. Maker's
mark TK (perhaps for Thomas
Kirkham, London).
M.30-1909

26 SHOE BUCKLE
Silver; running husk frieze on rim.
ENGLISH: about 1790. Maker's
mark GS in script (perhaps for
George Smith II, London).
M.34a-1909

27 SHOE BUCKLE
Silver; openwork rim of reeded ovals.
ENGLISH: late 18th century.
Maker's mark SC (perhaps for
Samuel Cooke, London).
M.31-1909

28 SHOE BUCKLE
Silver; stylised anthemion rim.
Fitted with a spring clip chape of a
type patented by William Eley in
1784.
ENGLISH: London hallmark for
1811-12. Maker's mark, JA (probably
for James Atkins, London).
Given by Miss Jane Souter Hipkins
M.418-1911

29 PAIR OF SMALL BUCKLES
Fitted with loops at the back and
entirely for ornamental use. Silver,
set with pastes.
Probably FRENCH: late 19th
century.
Lent anonymously

96

1 CROWN FOR AN EFFIGY
Silver-gilt, set with crystals and
pearls.
SPANISH: late 17th century.
Given by Dame Joan Evans, P.P.S.A.
M.172-1975

***2 CORONET**
Silver-gilt; the circlet inscribed:
MISERERE. MEI. DEUS.
SECUNDUM. MAGNAM.
MISERICORDIAM. TUAM. (Pity
me, Lord, according to thy great
mercy). The crest damaged.
ENGLISH: early 18th century.
M.4-1937

**3 SCEPTRE OF GARTER KING
AT ARMS**
Silver, parcel-gilt, the head of gold,
enamelled alternately with the
cross of St George impaling the arms
of George I (1714-1727) and the cross
of St George within the Garter.
ENGLISH: London hallmarks for
1714-16. Maker's mark of Francis
Garthorne.
M.9-1937
Nos. 2 & 3, formerly owned by the
Anstis family. See also Case 14,
Board E, nos. 13-15.

CASE 15
BOARD A
NO. 9

CASE 15
BOARD B
NO. 15

CASE 15
BOARD C
NO. 5

CASE 15
BOARD D
NO. 2

CASE 15
BOARD B
NO. 9

CASE 15
BOARD B
NO. 14

CASE 15
BOARD E
NO. 4

CASE 15
BOARD E
NO. 5

CASE 15
BOARD E
NO. 20

CASE 15
BOARD E
NO. 24

CASE 15
BOARD E
NO. 28

CASE 15
BOARD D
NO. 3

CASE 15
BOARD G
NO. 2

Case 16 Board A

PASTE:
about 1760-1800

Pastes, like precious stones, were traditionally set in mounts with closed backs, lined with foils. In the late eighteenth century precious stones began to be mounted in unbacked settings, but most paste jewellery continued to be set in the old manner.

1 NECKLACE
Opaline (a variety of paste imitating opal) and white pastes set in silver. Rosettes alternating with leaf devices; pendant with bow and drop.
? FRENCH: about 1760.
M.154-1975

2 PAIR OF EARRINGS
Opaline and white pastes set in silver; girandole type.
? FRENCH: about 1760.
M.154a & b-1975

*3 NECKLET
Opaline and white pastes set in silver openwork; bow pendant. Two loops for a ribbon tie.
? FRENCH: about 1760.
M.159-1975

*4 NECKLACE
Faceted opaline and white pastes set in silver.
WEST EUROPEAN: about 1790-1800.
M.158-1975
Nos. 1-4, given by Dame Joan Evans, P.P.S.A.

5 BROOCH
Opaline and white pastes set in silver.
WEST EUROPEAN: about 1760.
Given by Mr. Cecil Crofton
M.325-1922

6 FIVE BUTTONS
Three large, two small.
Opaline and white pastes set in silver.
WEST EUROPEAN: last quarter of 18th century.
M.154 i-m-1975

7 SET OF SIX BUTTONS
Opaline and white pastes set in silver.
WEST EUROPEAN: about 1770.
M.154 c-h-1975

*8 BODICE ORNAMENT
Opaline and white pastes set in silver; a bow with drop.
WEST EUROPEAN: about 1770.
M.160-1975

*9 JEWEL
Opaline and white pastes set in silver; flowers held by a bow.
? ENGLISH: about 1790.
M.161-1975

10 PENDANT
Opaline and white pastes set in silver; a bow with pendant.
WEST EUROPEAN: last quarter of 18th century.
M.157-1975

11 BRACELET CLASP
Opaline and white pastes set in silver.
WEST EUROPEAN: about 1790-1800.
French import mark for 1864-93.
M.156-1975

12 PENDANT
Opaline pastes set in silver; girandole form, altered into a brooch.
WEST EUROPEAN: about 1760-80.
M.155-1975
Nos. 6-12, given by Dame Joan Evans, P.P.S.A.

Case 16 Board B

RUSSIAN AND FRENCH:
about 1750-1800

*1 FORTY-SIX DRESS ORNAMENTS
Brilliant-cut diamonds set in silver; shuttle-shaped. The backs of some pieces inscribed with the Russian royal inventory numbers for 1764, and one with a monogram.
RUSSIAN: about 1770.
Perhaps made by Louis Duval of St. Petersburg, goldsmith to the Crown.
M.95, 95/1-45-1951

*2, 3 & 4 THREE BOW-SHAPED BODICE ORNAMENTS
Brilliant-cut diamonds set in silver.
RUSSIAN: about 1760. Perhaps made by Duval of St. Petersburg. With nos. 1 & 8, among the Crown Jewels sold after the Russian Revolution by the Bolshevik government.
M.93, 94 & a-1951
Nos. 1-4, Cory Bequest

5 DOVE BROOCH
Brilliant-cut diamonds, emeralds and a ruby set in silver; the back shows signs of alterations.
FRENCH: about 1755.
M.56-1962

*6 PAIR OF BRACELET CLASPS
Gold with brilliant-cut diamonds ornamenting central plaques of blue paste, one of which bears the initials of Marie Antoinette (1755-1793), and the other the turtle doves and hymeneal torches used as a device at the time of her marriage to Louis XVI. Both have the wreath of Trianon, symbolising the splendours of the French Crown.
FRENCH: about 1770.
M.51 & a-1962

7 BROOCH
Rock crystal and quartz set in gold and silver.
FRENCH: about 1800.
French import marks for 1864-93 and for 1893 onwards.
M.64-1962

Case 16 Board C

DIAMONDS, PASTES AND MARCASTLES:
about 1720-1780

*8 PAIR OF SHOE BUCKLES
Brilliant-cut diamonds and sapphires set in silver; shaped pinder.
RUSSIAN (St. Petersburg): about 1750.The pinder struck with an indecipherable name in Cyrillic letters.
M.48 & a-1962
Nos. 5-8, given by Dame Joan Evans, P.P.S.A.

1 NECKLACE WITH BROOCH-PENDANT AND BRACELET CLASP
Gilt openwork designs under glass, with borders of marcasites (faceted crystals of iron pyrites) set in silver.
FRENCH or SWISS: late 18th century.
M.170-b-1975

*2 NECKLET
Blue and white pastes set in silver floral openwork; pendent dove. Fitted with loops for ribbon ties.
FRENCH: about 1760.
M.69-1962

3 BUCKLE
Blue and white pastes set in silver.
WEST EUROPEAN: about 1770.
M.70-1962

*4 NECKLACE WITH TWO ALTERNATIVE PENDANTS
Mainly rose-cut diamonds and topazes set in silver openwork in a ribbon and flower pattern. The pendants with drops.
? FRENCH: about 1760.
M.165 & a-1975

5 PENDENT CROSS
Probably a bodice ornament.
Crystals set in silver openwork; in two parts.
WEST EUROPEAN: about 1720.
M.166-1975

6 PENDANT
Crystals set in silver; an openwork bow with flowers; pendent dove.
? FRENCH: second third of 18th century.
Portuguese mark for antique work after 1886.
M.68-1962

7 PAIR OF EARRINGS
Pastes set in silver-gilt.
? ENGLISH: about 1760.
M.72 & a-1962

*8 BROOCH AND PENDANT
Pastes set in silver-gilt; shell-shaped, the pendant with a suspension loop in the form of a bow.
WEST EUROPEAN: late 18th century.
French import mark introduced in 1893.
M.171 & a-1975

*9 PART OF A NECKLET
Marcasites and topazes set in silver openwork in a floral design.
? FRENCH: about 1760-1770.
M.162-1975
Nos. 1-9, given by Dame Joan Evans, P.P.S.A.

About 1750-1800

A. VINAIGRETTES, SCENT CASES AND SCENT FLASKS:
18th-19th century

100

1 BROOCH AND PAIR OF EARRINGS
Chrysoberyls set in silver openwork; the brooch a bouquet, the earrings with bow tops and long drops.
Probably PORTUGUESE: late 18th century.
French import mark introduced in 1893.
Given by Dame Joan Evans, P.P.S.A.
M.125-1975

*2 NECKLET WITH TWO ALTERNATIVE PENDANTS AND PAIR OF EARRINGS
White topaz and pastes set in silver openwork, the necklace with a long pendant depending from a complex bow. The earrings with similar drops.
FRENCH: late 18th century.
Bequeathed by Mrs. A.E. Stuart
M.104-1930

3 AIGRETTE
Chrysoberyls set in silver; a spray with a single flower; feathered scrolling stem.
Probably PORTUGUESE: about 1760. Struck twice with an unidentified mark.
M.66-1962

*4 PENDANT AND BRACELET CLASP
Crystals set in silver; decorated with enamelled gold enclosing sheaves in gold wire. The pendant has a suspension loop in the form of a bow.
SWISS: about 1800.
342-1864 and M.67-1962
No. 3 and the clasp in no.4 given by Dame Joan Evans, P.P.S.A.

*5 PAIR OF EARRINGS
Crystals set in silver; complex tops and elongated drops.
SPANISH: late 18th century.
306 & a-1897

6 BODICE ORNAMENT AND PAIR OF EARRINGS
Chrysoberyls set in silver. The bodice ornament with stylised flowers and leaves; five pendants. Girandole earrings.
Probably PORTUGUESE: about 1760.
Given by the Rt. Honble Sir C.W. Dilke, in fulfilment of the wishes of Lady Dilke
1538-b-1904

7 JEWEL
Chrysoberyls set in silver openwork; a flower spray in the centre.
IBERIAN: mid 18th century.
Bequeathed by Mr. Cecil Crofton
M.5-1936

*8 PENDANT AND PAIR OF EARRINGS
Pastes set in silver openwork; flower sprays with pendants; girandole earrings.
? FRENCH: mid 18th century.
French import mark introduced in 1893.
Given by Dame Joan Evans, P.P.S.A.
M.78-b-1962

9 NECKLACE
A single row of pastes set in silver, backed with gold.
ENGLISH: about 1800.
M.66-1925

10 PAIR OF EARRINGS
Chrysoberyls set in gold and silver; open drops with stars and crescents in the centre.
IBERIAN: about 1795.
18 & a-1866

1 COMBINED SCENT-CASE AND SEAL
Silver.
DUTCH: early 18th century.
M.796-1926

2 VINAIGRETTE
Silver.
? GERMAN: 18th century.
M.797-1926
Nos. 1 & 2, Croft Lyons Bequest

3 SCENT CASE
Silver-gilt, in the form of a crowned heart.
GERMAN: 18th century.
9076-1863

4 SCENT CASE
Silver-gilt, in the form of a snail shell.
? GERMAN: 18th century.
9077-1863

5 CASE (for Oil of St. Walburga)
GERMAN: 18th century.
Croft Lyons Bequest
M.802-1926

6 SCENT FLASK
Silver-gilt, with reliefs of musicians.
? FRENCH: first quarter of 18th century.
J.A. Tulk Bequest
M.20-1956

7 VINAIGRETTE
Silver.
GERMAN: 18th century.
M.801-1926

8 SCENT FLASK
With cornelian and onyx intaglios, including one of Henri IV (1589-1610).
FRENCH: second half of 18th century.
M.780-1926
Nos. 7&8, Croft Lyons Bequest

9 SCENT CASE
Silver-gilt, with *cloisonné* enamel.
? HUNGARIAN: 18th century.
Magniac Collection
667-1892

B. SCOTTISH ORNAMENTS
17th-18th century

10 VINAIGRETTE
Enamelled gold; in the form of a chestnut.
? FRENCH: about 1840.
Given by Dame Joan Evans, P.P.S.A.
M.85-1969

11 VINAIGRETTE
Silver.
WEST EUROPEAN: early 19th century.
Croft Lyons Bequest
M.791-1926

12 VINAIGRETTE
Enamelled gold; in the form of a chestnut.
FRENCH: about 1840.
Paris warranty mark for 1838 onwards.
Given by Dame Joan Evans, P.P.S.A.
M.103-1975

13 PLAID BROOCH
Silver, decorated with niello.
SCOTTISH: dated 1769 on the back.
M.13-1972

14 BROOCH
Gold; a crowned heart, pierced by arrows. The initials *W.M.* engraved on the reverse.
SCOTTISH: 17th century.
Given by Dame Joan Evans, P.P.S.A.
M.45-1975

***15 LUCKENBOOTH BROOCH**
Silver; a crowned heart.
SCOTTISH: 18th century.
Maker's mark: J.J.
Croft Lyons Bequest
M.809-1926

16 BROOCH
Silver; a heart set with pastes.
SCOTTISH: 18th century.
M.76-1962

17 PLAID BROOCH
Silver.
SCOTTISH: mid 17th century.
M.93-1962
Nos. 16 & 17, given by Dame Joan Evans, P.P.S.A.

CASE 16
BOARD A
NO. 4

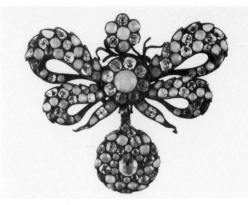

CASE 16
BOARD A
NO. 8

CASE 16
BOARD A
NO. 9

CASE 16
BOARD A
NO. 3

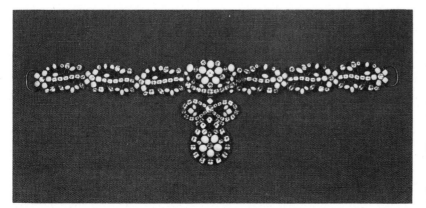

CASE 16
BOARD B
NO. 1

102

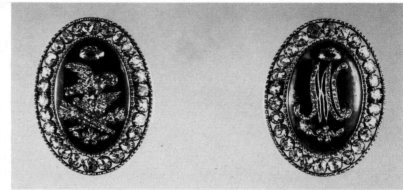

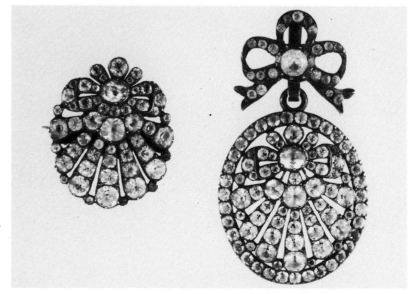

CASE 16
BOARD B
NO. 6

CASE 16
BOARD B
NOs. 2, 3 & 4

CASE 16
BOARD B
NO. 8

CASE 16
BOARD C
NO. 2

CASE 16
BOARD C
NO. 4

CASE 1
BOARD
NO. 9

CASE 16
BOARD D
NO. 2

CASE 16
BOARD C
NO. 8

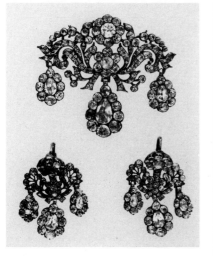

CASE 16
BOARD D
NO. 8

CASE 16
BOARD E
NO. 15

CASE 16
BOARD D
NO. 5

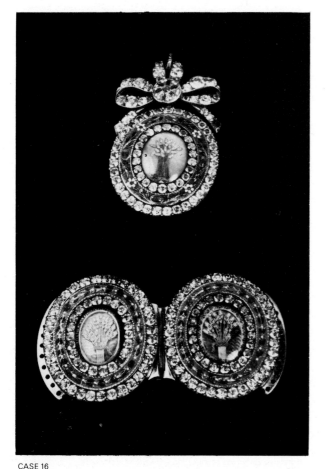

CASE 16
BOARD D
NO. 4

ENGLISH:
late 18th-early 19th century

1 PENDENT CROSS
Garnets set in gold; a variant of the
Maltese cross; later converted into a
brooch.
ENGLISH: late 18th century.
M.359-1910

2 PAIR OF EARRINGS
Rubies and table-cut diamonds set in
silver and gold; girandole type. The
hooks are replacements.
ENGLISH: mid 18th century.
Mayrick Collection
207 & a-1900

*3 NECKLET WITH PENDANT
Garnets set in silver-gilt floral
openwork; pendant in two stages.
ENGLISH: mid 18th century.
Given by Captain A. Heywood-
Lonsdale
M.2692-1931

4 PENDANT
Gold, set with an enamel miniature
of Queen Charlotte (1744-1818) after
Mary Moser (d.1819), in a pearl and
garnet frame.
ENGLISH: about 1795.
695-1868

5 PENDENT CROSS
Garnets, set in gold; a variant of the
Maltese cross; later converted into a
brooch.
ENGLISH: early 19th century.
M.361-1910

6 PAIR OF KNEE BUCKLES
Pastes set in silver.
ENGLISH: 18th century.
57-1865

7 PENDENT CROSS
Garnets and rose-cut diamonds set in
gold; the diamonds in a lobed cross,
tear-shaped garnets radiating from
the intersection.
ENGLISH: late 18th century.
57-1865

**8 NECKLACE AND PAIR OF
EARRINGS**
Garnets set in gold; stylised flower
units.
ENGLISH: late 18th century.
Lent by Mrs L.M. Bosanquet (1&2)

104

9 SCARF-RING
Gold, set with an enamel portrait of Prince Charles Edward, the Young Pretender (1720-1788).
ENGLISH: third quarter of 18th century.
Given by Miss P.D. Stanbridge
M.45-1967

10 BROOCH
A peridot surrounded by eight coloured stones and small diamond sparks set in gold.
ENGLISH: about 1760.
56-1865

11 PAIR OF KNEE BUCKLES
Pastes set in silver.
Worn by William Shield (1748-1829), the composer.
ENGLISH: early 19th century.
Hipkins Gift
M.419 & a-1911

12 BROOCH
Garnets set in gold; possibly once part of a corsage ornament.
ENGLISH: late 18th century.
Lent by Mrs L.M. Bosanquet (3)

13 PENDANT
Gold, set with a bloodstone cameo of William Augustus, Duke of Cumberland (1721-1765), third son of King George II.
ENGLISH: about 1750.
The Duke of Cumberland defeated the Jacobite supporters of Prince Charles Edward at Culloden in 1746 and hunted down the surviving rebels with great severity.
Given by Dame Joan Evans, P.P.S.A.
M.113-1962

14 PENDANT
Enamelled gold, commemorating the restoration to health of George III (1760-1820), after an attack of madness; the King's cipher below a crown. Inscribed: *REGI. AMATO. REDVCI/MART/MDCCLXXXIX.*
ENGLISH: dated 1789.
A similar pendant is in the Hull Grundy Collection, British Museum
W.J.W. Kerr Bequest
M.34-1957

15 MOURNING PENDANT
Enamelled gold in the form of an urn, set with amethysts and inscribed with the names: *Charles/ Yeatman/ Charles/Foot.*
ENGLISH: about 1790.
M.187-1975

16 BRACELET
Copper plaques, with painted enamels representing Jupiter, Bacchus, Cupid and Psyche and two goddesses.
ENGLISH or SWISS: last quarter of 18th century.
M.41-1962

17 PAIR OF BRACELET CLASPS
Gold, set with painted enamel plaques of a male and a female profile in garnet surrounds.
ENGLISH: about 1790-1800.
M.42 & a-1962
Nos. 15-17, given by Dame Joan Evans, P.P.S.A.

1 NECKLACE, PENDENT CROSS AND BRACELET
Brilliant-cut pastes set in silver, backed with gold; the bracelet clasp a replacement. The set once included earrings.
ENGLISH: about 1810.
Given by Mrs B.M. Nichols
M.32-b-1972

2 PIN
Urn-shaped enamelled gold head, set with brilliant-cut diamonds.
ENGLISH: last quarter of 18th century.
Bequeathed by Mr Arthur Penryn Milstead
M.167-1951

3 PIN
The head a porcelain mask, surrounded by gold foliage set with rose-cut diamonds, rubies and emeralds.
WEST EUROPEAN: mid 18th century.
338-1864

4 PIN
The head the bust of a blackamoor in enamelled gold, set with a ruby and brilliant-cut diamonds.
WEST EUROPEAN: mid 18th century.
Bequeathed by Mr Arthur Penryn Milsted
M.166-1951

5 PIN
The head a sapphire bordered by rose-cut diamonds, set in silver, backed with gold.
ENGLISH: early 19th century.
Pfungst Reavil Bequest
M.48-1969

6 NECKLACE
Brilliant-cut pastes set in silver, backed with gold. Stylised paired buds or leaves linking four rosettes; pendant missing.
? ENGLISH: about 1800.
M.62-1962

Case 17 Board C

CUT STEEL AND MARCASITE:
about 1760-1840

7 NECKLACE WITH PENDANT
Amethysts and pastes set in silver
openwork; long pendant with pear-
shaped drop.
WEST EUROPEAN: about 1800.
French import mark introduced in
1893.
M.135-1975

*8 NECKLACE
Brilliant-cut crystals set in silver,
backed with gold. Leaf and bud
pendants; central pendant missing.
ENGLISH: about 1810.
M.63-1962
Nos. 6-8, given by Dame Joan Evans,
P.P.S.A.

**9 NECKLET AND PENDENT
CROSS**
Brilliant-cut crystals set in silver and
coloured gold.
FRENCH: about 1825. Paris
warranty mark for 1819-1838.
99-1864

10 BUTTON
Brilliant- and rose-cut crystals set
in silver.
ENGLISH: about 1760.
M.4-1932

11 PAIR OF SLEEVE-LINKS
Brilliant-cut pastes set in silver.
? ENGLISH: 18th century.
Brooke Gift
958, 959-1864

12 FRAME FOR A MINIATURE
Rose-cut diamonds set in silver,
backed with gold.
WEST EUROPEAN: about 1800.
19-1865

13 FLOWER JEWEL
Brilliant-cut pastes set in silver and
coloured gold. Perhaps once the head
of a pin.
? ENGLISH: about 1810-20.
Given by Mr Cecil Crofton
M.227-1930

The manufacture of cut steel in
England is said to go back to the
sixteenth century and beyond. In the
eighteenth century, Woodstock in
Oxfordshire was renowned for its cut
steel, but towards the end of the
century the lead had been taken by
Wolverhampton, closely followed by
Birmingham. Matthew Boulton was
among the Birmingham manufac-
turers to set Wedgwood plaques in cut
steel. British production greatly
decreased in the nineteenth century
owing to growing French
competition.
Marcasites (faceted crystals of iron
pyrites) were particularly popular in
France and Switzerland in the mid
eighteenth century, remaining in
demand on a somewhat lower level
thereafter.

1 PAIR OF BRACELETS
Bands of cut steel sequins; oval
clasps decorated with circular and
shuttle-shaped faceted studs.
ENGLISH: late 18th century.
Pfungst Reavil Bequest
M.53 & a-1969

2 NECKLACE WITH PENDANT
Blue pastes and marcasites set in
silvered copper. Pendant with bow.
? FRENCH: about 1810-40; silver
loops at each end (later additions)
with an unidentified maker's mark
and the Paris warranty mark for
1838 onwards.
M.164-1975

3 BROOCH
Marcasites set in silver, with a glass
bead.
? FRENCH or SWISS: about 1810.
M.149-1975

4 NECKLACE
Marcasites set in silver openwork in
a floral design. Pendant missing.
? FRENCH or SWISS: about 1760-70.
M.144-1975
Nos. 2-4, given by Dame Joan Evans,
P.P.S.A.

5 BROOCH
Light blue opaque glass plaque,
mounted with a trophy in marcasites
and framed with marcasites set in
silver; converted from a pendant.
? FRENCH or SWISS: about 1780-90.
M.58-1969

6 HOOK FOR A CHATELAINE
Dark blue glass plaque mounted with
marcasites and framed with
marcasites set in silver.
Probably SWISS: struck with the
Paris import mark for 1768-74.
M.59-1969

*7 PENDANT
Dark blue opaque glass plaque,
mounted with a trophy of marcasites
and set in a silvered copper frame
with marcasites.
FRENCH or SWISS: about 1780-90.
M.57a-1969
Nos. 5-7, Pfungst Reavil Bequest

8 BROOCH
Marcasites set in silver, in the form
of a basket of flowers.
? FRENCH or SWISS: about 1770.
Given by Dame Joan Evans, P.P.S.A.
M.147-1975

9 NECKLET
Marcasites set in silver openwork
similar to that of no.4.
? FRENCH or SWISS: about 1760-70.
Pfungst Reavil Bequest
M.27-1969

Case 17 Board D

CUT STEEL,
MARCASITES AND
CAMEOS:
about 1770-1820

1 FOB
Cut steel, set with a jasper medallion
and hung with a jasper vinaigrette
by Wedgwood with, obverse, a profile
portrait of George, Prince of Wales
(later George IV, 1820-1830). Reverse,
the Prince of Wales's feathers.
Modelled by John Lochée (worked
Wedgwood's, 1774-1788).
ENGLISH: about 1787-88.
Lochee's model was also reproduced
by Tassie in paste.
M.23-1969

2 PENDANT
Gold, enamelled and set with a jasper
plaque by Wedgwood of Hercules and
the Cretan bull; border of half pearls.
ENGLISH: about 1780-90.
M.5-1969
Nos. 1 & 2, Pfungst Reavil Bequest

3 PLAQUE
Cut steel, mounted with a jasper
plaque by Wedgwood of Libra, a sign
of the Zodiac.
ENGLISH: about 1775. The setting
perhaps executed in Matthew
Boulton's Soho Manufactory,
Birmingham.
1089-1868

4 BUTTON
Cut steel frame, set with a jasper
plaque by Wedgwood of the signs of
the Zodiac.
ENGLISH: about 1780-90.
Pfungst Reavil Bequest
M.4-1969

5 WATCH AND CHATELAINE
Watch: gold, set with marcasites.
Signed: *J.L. Reynaud & Compe a
Ferney/3357.*
Chatelaine: silver and gold, set with
red pastes and marcasites.
SWISS: about 1780. The case
stamped GA below a fleur-de-lis (a
Swiss maker's mark).
French import marks for 1864
onwards.
Given by Dame Joan Evans, P.P.S.A.
M.268 & a-1975

6 BROOCH
Cut steel frame, set with a jasper
plaque by Wedgwood of Hercules and
the Arcadian stag, from a model
probably supplied by John Flaxman,
junior.
ENGLISH: about 1780-90.
Pfungst Reavil Bequest
M.6-1969

7 CLASP
Cut steel frame, mounted with a
jasper plaque of Iris by Wedgwood.
ENGLISH: about 1770-80. The
setting perhaps by the Soho
Manufactory.
1088-1868

8 SLEEVE-LINK
Agates set in silver.
WEST EUROPEAN: second third of
18th century.
Brooke Gift
962-1864

9 PENDANT
A hardstone cameo of a classical
male head surrounded by marcasites
set in silver openwork and hung
with pearls; a locket fitting at the
back.
? SWISS: about 1810-20.
M.145-1975

**10 NECKLACE WITH
PENDANT**
Mother-of-pearl centres and paste
borders set in silver; pendant
with bow.
Possibly ENGLISH: late 18th
century.
M.151-1975

**11 NECKLACE WITH
PENDANT
AND BUCKLE**
Enamelled plaques in imitation of
turquoises with marcasite borders set
in silver.
Possibly ENGLISH: late 18th
century.
M.133-b-1975
Nos.9-11, given by Dame Joan
Evans, P.P.S.A.

12 NECKLACE
Shell cameos set in gold slips,
connected by chains; scenes of Wine
and Love.
ITALIAN: about 1800.
Given by Mary Houghton of Florence
Circ. 182-1948

Early 19th century

1 PAIR OF BROOCHES
Gold frame enclosing silhouettes by
John Miers (1787-1872): one has a
locket fitting at the back containing
hair.
ENGLISH: early 19th century.
Given by Mr J.A. Pollak in memory
of his mother
M.13 & a-1970

2 BRACELET
Coloured gold clasp with enamel
decoration; chain band strung with
wooden beads.
? ENGLISH: about 1805.
M.65-1935

*3 BROOCH
Coloured gold, set with a shell cameo
of a classical male head.
? FRENCH: about 1810-20.
Given by Dame Joan Evans, P.P.S.A.
M.38-1962

4 BRACELET
Gold, set with coloured glass plaques.
? ENGLISH: about 1815.
Given by Mr Spencer G. Perceval
209-1904

*5 COMB
Silver, cast in imitation of cut steel.
ENGLISH: Birmingham hallmarks
for 1809-10. Maker's mark of Henry
Adcock.
Croft Lyons Bequest
M.820-1926

6 BROOCH
Silver-gilt filigree, set with a Roman
mosaic of a bird.
The Roman mosaics used in
jewellery are miniature versions of
a traditional technique employed on
a large scale in church decoration;
they are composed of minute tesserae
of coloured glass or ceramic.
ITALIAN: about 1815.
Given by Dame Joan Evans, P.P.S.A.
M.35-1962

7 PENDANT
A bloodstone cameo head of Christ;
reverse, the Virgin Mary; set in gold
frame with *cannetille* ornament
(see no. 11 below).
FRENCH (Paris): about 1840. The
gold mount with the Paris warranty
mark for 1838 onwards.
Bolckow Bequest
738-1890

8 BUST OF GEORGE IV
Gold, set with diamonds.
ENGLISH: 1820-30.
Bequeathed by Mrs H.F. Mosscockle
M.1815-1944

9 GOLDSMITH'S TYPE-MODEL FOR CASTING BUSTS OF GEORGE IV.
Bronze.
ENGLISH: 1820-30.
Given by Miss A.P. Lested
M.22-1962

*10 PENDANT WITH PORTRAIT MEDALLION OF GEORGE IV
Gold, the portrait mounted on a blue
paste ground. Signed: *Rundell,
Bridge et Rundell, J. Barber F*(ecit).
ENGLISH (London): about 1821.
Probably a coronation gift from the
King, who was crowned in 1821. The
recipient was George Purefoy
Jervaise (d.1847) of Herriard Park,
Basingstoke. Jervaise served George
IV in the Privy Purse office.
J. Barber, a medallist, was
occasionally associated with
Rundell, Bridge & Rundell, the Royal
Goldsmiths, of Ludgate Hill in the
City of London.
M.104-1966

11 BRACELET
Band of plaited hair; gold mounts
and clasp with *grainti* (tiny applied
pellets), and *cannetille* (wire spiral)
ornament, and applied stamped
decoration; set with a shell cameo
possibly representing Alexander,
Roxana and a genius with torch and
arrow.
? SWISS in the French manner:
about 1825.
Cory Bequest
M.64-1951

FRENCH IMPERIAL JEWELLERY:
early 19th century

1 SPRAY OF LAUREL
Brilliant-cut diamonds and rubies,
open-set in silver and gold; an
ornament to be worn in the hair or on
the bodice.
With its original case stamped in
gold on the lid with the crowned·
initial of the Empress Josephine
(1763-1814), the first wife of the
Emperor Napoleon I.
FRENCH: about 1805.
Lent through Messrs Wartski

*2 NECKLACE AND PAIR OF EARRINGS
Faceted table-cut emeralds in borders
of brilliant-cut diamonds; briolette
emerald drops; open-set in gold and
silver. Extra drops were added to the
back of the necklace in the 1820s.
Part of a parure presented by
Napoleon to his adopted daughter
Stéphanie de Beauharnais (1789-
1860), a connection of the Empress
Josephine, on her marriage to the
Grand Duke of Baden's heir in 1806.
FRENCH (Paris): 1806. Probably
made by Nitot.
The marriage was arranged to
consolidate the Confederacy of the
Rhine. A photograph of Gerard's
portrait of the bride wearing the
complete parure is shown with the
necklace and earrings. The painting
belongs to the Grand Duke of Baden.
Given by Countess Margharita
Tagliavia
M.3-b-1979

3 TWO PARURES OF CAMEOS
Mounted in gold with enamel
decoration.
The cameos ITALIAN: 18th and
early 19th century; the settings
FRENCH: about 1808. One piece
struck with Parisian marks for 1798-
1809.
The parures are traditionally said to
have formed part of the Neapolitan
Crown Jewels, subsequently passing
to the Empress Josephine,
presumably through the agency of
Napoleon's sister Caroline, whose
husband Joachim Murat was created
King of Naples in 1808. The gift
probably, however, comprised the
engraved gems alone, which were
mounted for Josephine in Paris.
On loan from a Private Collection

CASE 17
BOARD A
NO. 3

CASE 17
BOARD E
NO. 11

CASE 17
BOARD B
NO. 8

CASE 17
BOARD C
NO. 7

CASE 17
BOARD E
NO. 5

CASE 17
BOARD E
NO. 10

About 1795-1819

DIAMONDS AND PRECIOUS STONES:
about 1810-1830

NEOCLASSICAL:
about 1805-1830

109

1 PAIR OF EARRINGS
Gold openwork, with enamel and pearl decoration; hung with pearls and emeralds.
Probably FRENCH: about 1798.
M.44 & a-1962

2 BROOCH (a trophy of love)
Enamelled gold, set with cornelians, pearls and emeralds.
FRENCH: about 1800.
M.37-1962
Nos. 1 & 2, given by Dame Joan Evans, P.P.S.A.

3 NECKLACE
Enamelled gold filigree, set with pearls; floral motifs.
FRENCH: about 1810.
205-1864

4 PAIR OF EARRINGS
Gold, set with pearls and rose-cut diamonds.
FRENCH: late 18th century.
Given by Dame Joan Evans, P.P.S.A.
M.45 & a-1962

5 EIGHT SYMBOLS OF THE AGES OF MAN
Gold; the majority of the symbols correspond with Shakespeare's Seven Ages of Man (*As You Like It,* Act 2, 7).
FRENCH: about 1815. Paris warranty mark for 1809-19.
Given by Miss A.M. Lees
M.103-g-1945

6 SAUTOIR
Gold, enamelled and set with rose-cut diamonds and pearls. A long neck-lace worn in the 1790s and early 1800s over one shoulder and under the other, inspired by military dress.
Probably FRENCH: about 1795.
French import marks for 1864-93.
Given by Dame Joan Evans, P.P.S.A.
M.43-1962

1 NECKLACE AND PAIR OF EARRINGS
Peridots in brilliant-cut diamond borders, open-set in silver, backed with gold.
WEST EUROPEAN: the three large central units of the necklace probably date from about 1810, and may originally have formed part of a tiara or another necklace.
The rest of the units, and probably also the earrings, are of a later date.
M.118-b-1951

2 FUSCHIA SPRAY ORNAMENT
Brilliant-cut diamonds open-set in silver, backed with gold.
? RUSSIAN: about 1815.
M.116-1951

*3 PENDANT AND PAIR OF EARRINGS
Brilliant-cut diamonds open-set in silver in a rosette design. The backs show signs of having been altered.
ENGLISH: about 1820-30.
M.78-b-1951

4 FLOWER BROOCH
Brilliant-cut diamonds, rubies and emeralds set in gold and silver.
FRENCH: about 1810.
M.84-1951

5 AIGRETTE
Brilliant-cut diamonds, turquoises, an emerald and other coloured stones; some added subsequently (probably between 1820 and 1835) to increase the polychromatic effect of the piece.
? FRENCH: mainly about 1810.
M.127-1951

*6 NECKLACE AND PAIR OF EARRINGS
Table-cut sapphires in brilliant-cut diamond borders, open-set in silver, backed with gold; the necklace in two rows, graduated.
ENGLISH: about 1810.
M.89-b-1951
Nos. 1-6, Cory Bequest

*1 WREATH
Enamelled gold, set with diamonds, pearls and a paste cameo; in hinged sections rising to a peak in the centre (shown flat).
WEST EUROPEAN: about 1815.
Joicey Bequest
M.293-1919

*2 PENDANT
Cornelian intaglio of Jupiter and Venus with Cupid, set in enamelled gold. The intaglio probably engraved by Luigi Pichler (1773-1854), a professor at the Vienna Academy, in the first decade of the 19th century.
WEST EUROPEAN: about 1807.
The intaglio acquired by Prince Stanislas Poniatowski (1754-1833) for his collection of antique gems. It was discovered after the Prince's death that the majority of his gems were of recent date, but there is no proof that he himself was party to the deception.
Poniatowski and Wyndham Cook Collections
M.36-1940

3 NECKLACE
Gold, set with hardstone mosaics (*pietre dure* or Florentine mosaics) representing butterflies. The units connected by chains.
FRENCH: about 1805.
Given by the Rt. Honble Sir George R. Lowndes, P.C., K.C.S.I., K.C.
M.176-1941

4 NECKLACE, BROOCH AND EARRINGS
Shell cameos of *putti,* mounted in gold; a pendant missing from the necklace.
ITALIAN: about 1810.
1314-c-1871

5 BROOCH
Agate cameo of a panther, in gold 'Roman' setting.
? ITALIAN: about 1830.
Bolckow Bequest
739-1890

Case 18 Board D

BERLIN IRON JEWELLERY:
about 1804-1855

The iron foundries set up in Prussia between the seventeenth and early nineteenth centuries were celebrated for the fineness and precision of their castings. Large and small objects were produced. Napoleon, entering Berlin with his victorious French troops in 1806, was so interested in the work of the foundries that he removed some of the models to France. Berlin iron jewellery, the earliest examples of which date from about 1804, came into prominence during the Prussian War of Liberation of 1812-14. To help finance the struggle, patriotic German ladies exchanged their gold wedding rings and other jewellery for iron equivalents inscribed, for example, Gold gab ich für Eisen (I gave gold for iron). After the Napoleonic wars were over, iron trinkets, often produced by craftsmen trained in the jewellery trade, were exported from Prussia all over the world. A few Parisian firms also manufactured iron jewellery and it is sometimes difficult to distinguish between the French and German work, especially as the Devaranne firm, for instance (see nos. 8 & 12) is among those known to have supplied wares to retailers in Paris and elsewhere. Austrian factories also producing ironwork obtained models from Prussia, and similar work was turned out in Bohemia.

1 NECKLACE
With polished steel mounts.
About 1820-30.
From the old Geological Museum, Jermyn Street
5371-1901

*2 PAIR OF EARRINGS
About 1830.
778 & a-1904

3 COMB
With a cameo of Iris set in the gallery.
About 1820.
546-1899
Nos. 2 & 3 given by Mr. Sydney Vacher

4 NECKLACE AND PAIR OF EARRINGS
In the gothic style; the necklace has polished steel mounts.
About 1820-30.
96-c-1906

5 BROOCH
Vine leaf motifs, with a central rosette.
About 1820, probably by Johann Conrad Geiss.
Given by Mrs. Lintorn-Orman
M.40-1921

6 PIN
With a design of vines.
The design about 1820, perhaps by Geiss.
This example may have been shown at the Great Exhibition of 1851.
934-1852

7 IRON CROSS
Obverse, the head of Frederick William III of Prussia; the reverse inscribed: *Unvergeslich 1813.*
The original Iron Cross was designed by K.F. Schinkel, 1813; this one is a variant, perhaps worn by loyal female supporters of the Prussian War of Liberation.
Given by Mr. A. Woodhouse
M.278-1928

8 PIN
The design dating from about 1833; this example probably shown at the Great Exhibition of 1851 by S.P. Devaranne of Berlin.
Siméon Pierre Devaranne, goldsmith and manufacturer of cast iron, was, like Geiss, recognised as an artist-craftsmen by the Berlin Royal Academy.
935-1852

9 PAIR OF EARRINGS
In the gothic style, similar to those in no.4 above, but with different tops.
About 1820-30.
Given by Mrs. Lintorn-Orman
M.36-1921

10 BELT ORNAMENT
The design about 1820. Signed: *A.F. Lehmann a Berlin.*
From the old Geological Museum, Jermyn Street
5370-1901

*11 NECKLACE
Openwork plaques of classical subjects alternating with flowers, set in gold; intermediate links with gold griffins' heads.
About 1815-20
454-1898

12 PAIR OF EARRINGS
Openwork butterflies; drops set over polished steel. The design about 1815-20; this example probably shown at the Great Exhibition of 1851 by S.P. Devaranne of Berlin.
922 & a-1852

13 BRACELET
Gothic tracery and classical acanthus foliage.
About 1820-30.
96b-1906

BERLIN IRONWORK:
about 1815-62

*1 NECKLACE
Iron cameos on polished steel mounts set in gold; steel mesh ribbon.
About 1815-20.
Joicey Bequest
M.308-1919

2 NECKLACE
Plaquettes of flowers set in gold; steel mesh ribbon.
About 1815-20.
Given by Miss Joan Hassall
M.5-1972

3 NECKLACE
With classical figures in silhouette, alternating with vine leaves in an acanthus frame.
About 1820.
Given by Miss Little
M.46-1925

4 BUCKLE
About 1820. Signed: *Devaranne Ac. Kunstl a Berlin.*
54-1866

5 BRACELET
About 1815-20, probably by S.P. Devaranne of Berlin.
50-1866
Nos. 4 & 5, given by Mr. W. Bemrose

6 NECKCHAIN
? FRENCH: about 1825.
M.75-1909

*7 CROSS
? FRENCH: about 1825.
M.39-1921

8 BRACELET
The clasp signed: *A.F. Lehmann/ Berlin.*
About 1820-30.
M.35-1921
Nos. 7 & 8, given by Mrs. Lintorn-Orman

9 BRACELET
The design about 1820-30; this specimen probably shown at the Great Exhibition of 1851.
936-1852

10 LOCKET BROOCH
The centre matches the units of the bracelet above.
938-1852

11 BRACELET
The design about 1820-30; this specimen similar to a bracelet shown at the Great Exhibition of 1851 by S.P. Devaranne of Berlin.
937-1852

12 FAN
One of a pair made under the direction of Edward Schott at Ilsenburg-am-Harz to demonstrate the fineness which could be achieved in iron castings. It was shown at the International Exhibition of 1862. The other fan was presented to Princess Frederick William (later the Empress Frederick William) of Prussia (1840-1901), Queen Victoria's eldest daughter.
From the old Geological Museum, Jermyn Street
5369-1901

CHATELAINE
Cut steel, the hook-plate formed as a crowned monogram.
Probably FRENCH: early 19th century, with later additions.
Pfungst Reavil Bequest
M.32-1969

CASE 18
BOARD B
NO. 6

CASE 18
BOARD B
NO. 3

112

CASE 18
BOARD C
NO. 1

CASE 18
BOARD D
NO. 2

CASE 18
BOARD C
NO. 2

CASE 18
BOARD E
NO. 1

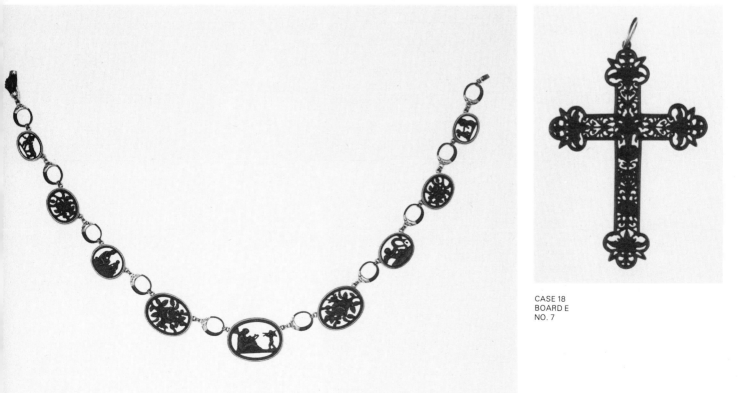

CASE 18
BOARD E
NO. 7

CASE 18
BOARD D
NO. 11

Case 19 Board A

NEOCLASSICAL:
1810-1840

1 NECKLACE, BROOCH AND PAIR OF EARRINGS
Gold filigree, set with garnets; the brooch in the form of a cross.
FRENCH: about 1835.
The earrings, which have additional *cannetille* decoration, are from a different set.
Cory Bequest
M.68-c-1951

2 TIARA (a 'Spartan diadem', shown in two parts)
Gilt metal, set with agate and onyx cameos of classical heads.
FRENCH: about 1810.
Formerly the property of the 1st Baroness Cowley, 2nd wife of Sir Henry Wellesley (1773-1846), created 1st Lord Cowley in 1828.
Given by Lady Bertie of Thame
M.10-1955

*3 PENDENT CROSS
Amethysts set in simple gold wire filigree; the pendant loop an addition, possibly taken from an earring.
ENGLISH: about 1825. Probably made by Rundell & Bridge of Ludgate Hill.
Joicey Bequest
M.269-1919

4 BROOCH AND PAIR OF EARRINGS
Gold filigree, with *cannetille* and *grainti* decoration, set with turquoises and pearls. The brooch in the form of a tasselled bow.
WEST EUROPEAN: about 1835-40.
Cory Bequest
M.77-b-1951

5 NECKLACE AND PAIR OF EARRINGS
Gold mesh and filigree, with enamelled decoration, set with chrysoprases. Necklace centre with three pendants.
FRENCH: about 1825. Paris warranty marks for 1819-38.
Given by Dame Joan Evans, P.P.S.A.
M.32 & a-1962

Case 19 Board B

NEOCLASSICAL:
1820-1830

1 BRACELET
Coloured gold, decorated with enamel and set with an amethyst and pearls.
FRENCH: about 1825. Paris warranty mark for 1819-38.
M.91-1951

2 NECKLACE WITH PENDANT AND TWO PAIRS OF EARRINGS
Amethysts set in gold filigree with *cannetille* decoration; each unit of necklace connected by chains.
? FRENCH: about 1820.
M.137-d-1951
Nos. 1 & 2, Cory Bequest

*3 TIARA FRONT
Stamped copper-gilt, set with chrysoprase.
ENGLISH: about 1835.
Given by Dame Joan Evans, P.P.S.A.
M.146-1975

4 NECKLACE
Openwork links with *cannetille* decoration.
Probably ENGLISH: about 1830.
Given by Mrs. C.M. Harper
M.20-1972

5 PAIR OF EARRINGS
Gold filigree with *cannetille* decoration, set with turquoises. Long drops.
Probably FRENCH: about 1830.
M.14 & a-1962
Given by Dame Joan Evans, P.P.S.A.

6 NECKLACE AND PAIR OF EARRINGS
Gold filigree with *cannetille* and *grainti* decoration, set with emeralds, citrines, sapphires, garnets, rubies, aquamarines, peridots and pearls.
FRENCH: about 1820.
Cory Bequest
M.124-b-1951

Case 19 Board C

1815-1835

*1 CROSS
Gold; the front set with pearls and emeralds, the reverse decorated with enamelled rosettes on lobed terminals.
? FRENCH: about 1830-40.
Given by Dame Joan Evans, P.P.S.A.
M.39-1962

2 WREATH/NECKLACE
Brilliant-cut diamond flowers and foliage set in silver, with ruby stamens set in gold; gold frame. For wearing on the head or around the neck; shown here as a necklace. The fitting to convert the piece into a necklace is a replacement for an earlier one.
WEST EUROPEAN: about 1835.
M.45-1980

3 BROOCH
A topaz surrounded by pearls and tiny emeralds set in gold.
ENGLISH: about 1815.
Bequeathed by Mrs Ethel V. Dollman
M.87-1957

114

1 NECKLACE WITH PENDANT AND PAIR OF EARRINGS
Gold filigree with *cannetille* and *grainti* decoration, set with amethysts and pearls.
? FRENCH: about 1820-30.
M.138-b-1951

2 NECKLACE AND PAIR OF EARRINGS
Gold filigree with *cannetille* and *grainti* decoration, set with jade, chrysoprases and rubies; the earrings were probably not made to match the necklace.
? FRENCH: about 1825.
M.139-b-1951

*3 BRACELET WITH LOCKET CLASP
Coloured gold, set with brilliant-cut diamonds and rubies.
? ENGLISH: about 1830.
M.119-1951

4 LOCKET BRACELET
Coloured gold openwork, with *cannetille* and *grainti* decoration, set with semi-precious foiled stones and pastes; each link has a locket fitting at the back.
? FRENCH: about 1825.
M.88-1951
Nos. 1-4, Cory Bequest

5 BROOCH
Gold, set with an emerald, turquoises and topazes; in the form of a basket of flowers.
FRENCH (Paris): about 1830.
Unidentified maker's mark. Paris warranty mark for 1819-38.
Given by the Contessa Gautier
M.642-1911

6 NECKLACE WITH PENDANT AND BRACELET
Gold mesh and filigree with *cannetille* and *grainti* decoration, set with chrysoprases, brilliant-cut diamonds and rubies.
? FRENCH: about 1825.
Given by Dame Joan Evans, P.P.S.A.
M.31 & a-1962

1 NECKLACE
Stamped gold units mounted on flexible links; the piece apparently made from a shorter necklace and a matching bracelet.
? FRENCH: about 1825.
Said to have been given from her personal jewellery by Lady Aberdeen (1792-1833) to Lady Louisa Russell (1812-1904), 2nd daughter of the 6th Duke of Bedford, as a wedding gift. Lady Louisa married in 1832 the 2nd Marquess of Hamilton, later 1st Duke of Abercorn.
Given by the Hon. Margaret Ishbel Sinclair
M.17-1970

2 PENDANT
Onyx intaglio of Bacchus surrounded by cameo *putti* and Bacchantes, set in an openwork gold frame.
? ITALIAN: about 1830.
Ready Bequest
M.28-1959

3 PAIR OF EARRINGS
Enamelled gold filigree, set with small stones.
WEST EUROPEAN: about 1825.
Maker's mark, J.M.
Given by Dame Joan Evans, P.P.S.A.
M.40 & a-1962

4 PENDANT-BROOCH
Gold, with *grainti* decoration; set with pastes.
WEST EUROPEAN: about 1830.
Joicey Bequest
M.272-1919

5 BROOCH
Shell cameo of the Three Graces set on a swivel; gold frame in the form of leaves and flowers, set with garnets.
? FRENCH: about 1840.
Given by Miss Edith M. Dunne
Circ. 91-1952

6 SPRAY
Seed pearls mounted on a mother-of-pearl frame; an ornament for the hair or the bodice.
ENGLISH: about 1820.
Given by Mrs Mary Blanche Dick
M.349-1975

7 NECKLACE, PENDANT, BROOCH and HAIR PIN
Seed pearls mounted on mother-of-pearl; the pendant decorated with moonstones and peridots set in gold.
ENGLISH: about 1815.
Given by Miss M.C. Sandys-Wünsch
M.290-c-1976

8 COMET BROOCH
Pastes set in silver and gold.
ENGLISH: about 1835.
Bequeathed by Mrs. B.M. Nicholls
M.32c-1972

9 NECKLACE
Seed pearls mounted on mother-of-pearl; one unit has been repaired.
ENGLISH: about 1815.
Presented by the Sandeman family
M.32-1974

10 MEMENTO MORI STOCK PIN
The head enamelled gold and a baroque pearl, forming a skull.
WEST EUROPEAN: possibly early 19th century.
Said to have belonged to Napoleon I.
Given by Colonel D.H. Colnaghi
M.279-1920

11 BROOCH
Biscuit porcelain plaque encrusted with flowers, set in a plain gold slip.
ENGLISH (Derby): about 1845.
The plaque signed on the reverse: *S.S./DERBY*, perhaps the signature of Susanna Stephan (*c*.1811-1861).
M.16-1973

Case 19 Board F

1835-1845

Case 19 Board G

1825-1850

1 BROOCH
A citrine set in stamped gold.
ENGLISH: about 1835-40.
M.216-1929

2 BROOCH
Shell cameo of Ariel on a bat's back;
gold scrolling frame.
The cameo probably ITALIAN:
about 1840. The treatment of the
subject, taken from Shakespeare's
The Tempest (5, 1), closely resembles
a painting by Joseph Severn (1793-
1869) in the V & A (no.1410-1869).
Severn, Keats's friend, spent many
years in Rome.
Given by Mrs L.M. Festing
M.274-1921

3 SPRAY BROOCH
Coloured gold, set with rose- and
brilliant-cut diamonds.
WEST EUROPEAN: about 1830.
Given by Dame Joan Evans, P.P.S.A.
M.34-1962

***4 NECKLACE AND PAIR OF
EARRINGS**
Coloured gold and pearls in the form
of vine leaves and grapes.
Probably ENGLISH: about 1835-45.
M.134-1951

5 NECKLACE
Coloured gold and pearls in the form
of vine leaves and grapes.
Probably ENGLISH: about 1835-45.
M.133-1951
Nos. 4 & 5, Cory Bequest

6 BROOCH
Stamped openwork set with foiled
crystals; a pendant attached to the
brooch and another suspended from
a chain.
ENGLISH: about 1835.
Given by Dame Joan Evans, P.P.S.A.
M.33-1962

**7 BROOCH AND PAIR OF
EARRINGS**
Stamped gold, set with carbuncles
(almandine garnets, cut *en
cabochon*).
ENGLISH: about 1835.
Joicey Bequest
M.265-b-1919

*1 TRAIL OF FLOWERS
Amethysts, topazes, pearls,
turquoises and garnets set in gold; in
three pieces, connected by rings.
Probably from a head ornament.
WEST EUROPEAN: about 1835-45.
M.143-1951

**2 PART OF A HEAD
ORNAMENT**
Crystals, rubies, amethysts, topazes
and rose-quartz set in enamelled
gold; later brooch fitting.
WEST EUROPEAN: about 1835-45.
M.83-1951
Nos. 1 & 2, Cory Bequest

*3 PAIR OF EARRINGS
Gold openwork, set with chryso-
prases.
WEST EUROPEAN: about 1845.
M.266 & a-1919

4 BRACELET
Stamped gold, set with malachite.
? FRENCH: about 1835.
M.276-1919

**5 BROOCH AND PAIR OF
EARRINGS**
Stamped gold, set with peridots.
The brooch with pendants.
ENGLISH: about 1835.
M.264-b-1919
Nos. 3-5, Joicey Bequest

**6 BRACELET WITH HEART
LOCKET**
Large gold chain links; the locket
stamped: *GRATITUDE*.
ENGLISH: about 1830.
Said to have been given to Queen
Adelaide (1792-1849) by William IV
(1765-1837) after his recovery from an
illness.
Given by Mrs A. Rolt
M.308-1975

*7 BADGE
Gold, inscribed: *Arden*. Awarded to
one of the Archers of Meriden in
1826.
ENGLISH: about 1825.
Archery was a popular pastime in the
first half of the 19th century.
Given by Miss Helen Legge
M.1129-1926

8 PARURE
Comprising a necklace, pendant-
brooch and pair of earrings. Stamped
and enamelled gold, set with pink
foiled crystals.
? SWISS: about 1835-40; struck with
two unidentified marks.
Given by Dame Joan Evans, P.P.S.A.
M.36-c-1962

9 BRACELET
Gold, with foliated decoration.
Centre, a miniature of a child.
Inscribed inside the band: *Elizabeth,
/daughter of Edward Long/married
Lord Henry Howard./died 1834.*
Locket fitting at the back for hair.
English: about 1834.
Lent anonymously

*10 BRACELET
Gold, with foliated scrolls, set with
brilliant-cut diamonds, pearls and
turquoises. Centre, an enamel
miniature by William Essex of Queen
Adelaide (1792-1844).
ENGLISH: signed on the back by the
artist and dated 1834. The original
box (not shown) bears the label of the
Royal Goldsmiths, Rundell & Bridge
of Ludgate Hill.
William Essex (1784-1869) was
miniature painter to William IV and
Queen Adelaide.
Lent anonymously

1830-1885

NATURALISM IN
DIAMONDS:
about 1820-1870

1825-1880

116

***1 BRACELET WITH
ALTERNATIVE CENTRES**
Enamelled gold, set with rose- and
brilliant-cut diamonds; one centre
has a miniature portrait of Mr.
Pandeli Ralli, the other of his wife.
FRENCH (Paris): about 1850.
Maker's mark, JC with a bird. Paris
warranty mark for 1847 onwards.
Bequeathed by Mrs. H. Digby Neave,
granddaughter of Mr and Mrs Ralli
M.12, 13-1955

*2 SPRAY BROOCH
Silver, set with brilliant-cut pastes
and with articulated pendants *à
pampilles*. A bodice ornament, hung
with rains of stones, a fashion
introduced in France in the 1840s.
FRENCH: about 1850.
Given by Mr. Frederick D. Meller
M.4-e-1971

3 BROOCH WITH PENDANT
Silver, set with pearls and brilliant-
cut diamonds, in a bow shape;
pendent drop with a baroque pearl.
WEST EUROPEAN: about 1885.
M.96-1951

4 BROOCH
Silver and gold, set with brilliant-cut
diamonds, emeralds, a ruby and
pearls; in the form of a jewelled and
tasselled pearl bow, with a mother-of-
pearl backing.
WEST EUROPEAN: about 1830.
M.128-1951

5 NECKLACE
Enamelled gold, set with rose- and
brilliant-cut diamonds, rubies,
emeralds, pearls and a sapphire.
WEST EUROPEAN: about 1870; the
clasp of earlier date, probably about
1840.
M.136-1951

6 PAIR OF EARRINGS
Enamelled gold, set with brilliant-cut
diamonds, rubies and pearls;
probably adapted from pendants to
match the necklace, no.5 above.
WEST EUROPEAN: about 1860.
M.136a & b-1951
Nos. 3-6, Cory Bequest

**1 SIX SPRAYS AND A
BUTTERFLY ORNAMENT**
Brilliant-cut diamonds, with a few
rose-cut specimens, set in silver,
backed with gold.
FRENCH and ENGLISH: about
1830-70.
M.140 a-g - 1951

*2 WREATH
Brilliant-cut diamonds, with a few
rose-cut specimens, set in silver, lined
with gold.
Probably ENGLISH: the basic
structure a wreath of Neoclassical
design, about 1820-30. The blossoms
may have been added later.
M.117-1951

***3 SPRAY OF ROSES,
CARNATIONS AND OTHER
FLOWERS**
A bodice ornament.
Brilliant-cut diamonds, with a few
rose-cut specimens, set in silver,
backed with gold. Some flowers
mounted on springs to form
'tremblers'.
Probably ENGLISH: about 1850; the
three leaf and bud sprays added
from a piece of about 1830. The
design is similar to French work
of about 1820-30, but a bodice
ornament of this type was
shown by Hunt & Roskell of London
at the Great Exhibition of 1851.
M.115-1951

4 SPRAY
Brilliant-cut diamonds, with a few
rose-cut specimens, in three attached
units, with two 'tremblers', set in
silver; a bodice and head ornament.
WEST EUROPEAN: about 1860.
M.140-1951
Nos. 1-4, Cory Bequest

*1 PARURE
Comprising necklace with pendant,
brooch, pair of earrings and an
unmounted plaque. Gold, set with
semi-precious stones and enclosing
enamelled miniatures of peasants in
the costumes of the Swiss cantons.
The names of the cantons are
inscribed on the reverse of the
plaques.
SWISS: about 1825.
Cory Bequest
M.79-c-1951

2 SCARF-RING
Enamelled gold, set with a crystal.
SWISS: mid 19th century.
9078-1863

*3 BROOCH
Painted ceramic plaque depicting a
chapel in a mountain landscape, set
in a lacquered frame.
GERMAN or AUSTRIAN: about
1860.
Circ.68-1950

4 BROOCH
Lava cameo of Flora, set in gold.
ITALIAN: about 1850-80.
Given in memory of Captain N.S.
Williamson by Gladys M. Bawden
Circ. 411-1960

5 PAIR OF EARRINGS
Carved malachite cameos, set in
gold.
ITALIAN: about 1840.
Given by Mrs K.E. Sargent
M.39 & a-1961

6 BRACELET
Enamelled gold, set with pearls, in
the form of a branch of vine.
FRENCH (Paris): about 1850. Paris
warranty marks for 1847 onwards.
Cory Bequest
M.102-1951

*7 BROOCH
Malachite cameo of a Cupid,
mounted in gold.
ITALIAN: about 1850.
Pfungst Reavil Bequest
M.34-1969

8 BROOCH
Enamelled gold and coral; in the
form of a sprig of holly.
? FRENCH: about 1850-1865.
M.70-1951

**9 NECKLACE AND PAIR OF
EARRINGS**
Enamelled gold mounted with
amethysts; in the form of vines.
FRENCH: about 1840-50.
M.135-b-1951
Nos. 8 & 9, Cory Bequest

*PIQUE (mainly tortoise-shell,
inlaid with gold and silver); one
example (no.1) set with pastes: about
1830-1900.
No. 1 lent; M. 49, 55-b, 58, 62, 65 & a,
66 & a, 69 & a, 70 & a, 102 - 1911;
M.102a, 206-1960.

CHATELAINE   117
Cut steel. The hook-plate
inscribed on the reverse;
*Durham/Cutler to H.R.H. Prince
Albert/456 Oxford Street.*
ENGLISH: about 1851.
Shown by Joseph Banks Durham at
the Great Exhibition of 1851; the
piece was described in the official
catalogue as 'Highly polished and
richly cut steel chatelaine, with
improved scissors and tablet'.
Given by Mrs Gilbert Russell
M.10-1971[1]

CASE 19
BOARD C
NO. 1
2 Views

CASE 19
BOARD A
NO. 3

CASE 19
BOARD B
NO. 3

CASE 19
BOARD D
NO. 3

CASE 19
BOARD F
NO. 4

CASE 19
BOARD G
NO. 1

CASE 19
BOARD G
NO. 3

CASE 19
BOARD G
NO. 7

CASE 19
BOARD G
NO. 10

CASE 19
BOARD H
NO. 1

CASE 19
BOARD H
NO. 2

CASE 19
BOARD I
NO. 3

CASE 19
BOARD I
NO. 2

CASE 19
BOARD J
NO. 1

CASE 19
BOARD J
NO. 3

CASE 19
BOARD J
NO. 7

CASE 19
BOARD K

Case 20 Board A

About 1825–1860

1 BROOCH
Enamelled gold, in the form of a bow
interlaced with brilliant-cut
diamonds and ruby sprays. Pendent
heart locket.
ENGLISH: about 1845.
M.60-1951

2 RUSTICATED BRACELET
Enamelled gold, set with pearls; in
the form of an entwining branch.
WEST EUROPEAN: about 1850.
M.107-1951

3 BROOCH
Enamelled gold, set with pearls and a
brilliant-cut diamond in the form of a
bow with a chain fringe; fitted with a
locket back.
ENGLISH: about 1845-55.
M.141-1951

4 BRACELET
Enamelled gold rings, set with rose-
cut diamonds.
ENGLISH: about 1840-50.
M.59-1951

5 PAIR OF EARRINGS
Enamelled gold, set with rose-cut
diamonds.
ENGLISH: about 1850-60.
M.61 & a-1951

6 PADLOCK LOCKET
Enamelled gold, set with rose-cut
diamonds; probably a pendant for a
bracelet.
ENGLISH: about 1840-50.
M.74-1951

7 BRACELET
Enamelled gold segments, set with
pearls; hinged to form a flexible
band. The clasp of patent design,
inscribed: *Registered 28 Novr 1850*
(probably as a 'Useful Design').
ENGLISH: about 1850-53.
M.87-1951

8 JEWEL
Enamelled gold, set with brilliant-cut
diamonds; probably once a slide,
adapted into a brooch.
? ENGLISH: about 1880.
M.123b-1951

9 PENDANT
Enamelled gold and silver, set with
brilliant-cut diamonds; fitted with a
locket back.
? ENGLISH: about 1860.
M.123a-1951

10 BROOCH
Enamelled gold and silver, set with
brilliant-cut diamonds.
Probably copied from M.123a-1951
(no. 9 above), in order to make a set.
? ENGLISH: about 1885.
M.123-1951

11 BODICE ORNAMENT
Comprising two brooches linked by a
chain.
Enamelled gold, set with rose-cut
diamonds and one brilliant; one
brooch, set with a diamond star,
contains a Swiss watch signed by
David Soret of Geneva (d.1780),
presumably re-cased when this
ornament was made.
ENGLISH: about 1825-40.
Ornaments of this kind, fashionable
in the late 1820s and the 30s, were
worn with one brooch pinned to the
centre front and the other to the
shoulder of the bodice.
M.59a-c-1951

12 BROOCH
Enamelled gold, set with pearls and
diamond sparks; three enamelled
bosses set with diamond stars,
mounted on a pin.
ENGLISH: about 1860-90.
M.75-1951
Nos. 1-12, Cory Bequest

***13 BROOCH AND PAIR OF
EARRINGS**
Gold plaques decorated with
compositions of a bird, a nest with
eggs, and forget-me-nots; the brooch
fitted with a locket back.
ENGLISH: about 1860-75. Possibly
made by Harry Emanuel of London.
Given by Miss Dorothy Simmons
M.2-b-1965

14 PENDANT
Tortoise-shell, decorated with an
applied bird composition similar to
no.13 on this board; set with
pearls.
ENGLISH: about 1860-75.
M.62-1951

15 BRACELET
Engraved and enamelled gold
links, pierced with trefoils;
each link set with a pearl.
ENGLISH: about 1825.
M.101-1951
Nos. 14 & 15, Cory Bequest

Case 20 Board B

VARIATIONS ON TURQUOISE:
about 1830-1860

*1 SERPENT NECKLACE AND ARMLET
Silver and gold, *pavé*-set (close-set) with turquoises; with pearls, rubies and brilliant-cut diamonds.
Probably ENGLISH: about 1835-1840.
M.58-1851

2 PAIR OF EARRINGS
Gold, *pavé*-set with turquoises, rubies and pearls; in the form of twisted peacock feathers.
? ENGLISH: about 1835-40.
M.131 & a-1951

3 BRACELET
Flexible band of gold, with clasp and central motif of gold filigree with *cannetille* and *grainti* decoration, set with pearls and turquoises. The filigree pieces were taken from another bracelet and re-mounted with a new slide and band.
WEST EUROPEAN: about 1830-50.
M.110-1951

*4 IVY LEAF NECKLACE WITH PENDANT AND PAIR OF EARRINGS
Gold, enamelled in turquoise, set with brilliant-cut diamonds. The necklace has a flexible chain.
? ENGLISH: about 1845-55.
M.125-b-1951

5 NECKLACE AND PAIR OF EARRINGS
Gold, *pavé*-set with turquoises and with rose and brilliant-cut diamonds.
ENGLISH: about 1845-55.
M.126-1951

6 NECKLACE, PAIR OF EARRINGS AND BROOCH
Gold, the necklace with *pavé*-set turquoises and half-pearls, the units linked by gold chains. The earrings set only with turquoises, and the brooch with a brilliant-cut diamond and turquoises.
Probably ENGLISH: about 1860. These pieces are unlikely to have been made as a set.
M.92-1951

7 CENTRE ORNAMENT FROM A BRACELET
Gold, *pavé*-set with turquoises, rubies, emeralds and pearls; in the form of a Tudor rose, altered into a brooch.
Fitted with a locket back.
Probably ENGLISH: mid 19th century.
M.129-1951

8 BRACELET
Pavé-set turquoises and brilliant-cut diamonds; flexible gold chains.
Probably ENGLISH: about 1860.
M.100-1951

9 CONVOLVOLUS BROOCH
Gold, with *pavé*-set turquoises and with pearls.
? ENGLISH: about 1835-1850.
M.82-1951
Nos. 1-9, Cory Bequest

Case 20 Board C

MAINLY CORAL AND CAMEOS:
about 1840-1865

*1 PENDANT
Enamelled gold, set with a carbuncle.
ENGLISH: about 1860.
Given by Dame Joan Evans, P.P.S.A.
M.101-1962

2 PAIR OF EARRINGS
Enamelled gold, set with paste cameos of classical female heads.
Probably ENGLISH: about 1865.
Given by Mrs. Jessica G. Turner
M.187 & a-1937

3 PAIR OF SLEEVE LINKS
Coral cameos; half-figures of Bacchantes set in gold.
ITALIAN: about 1840.
Given by Mrs. K.E. Sargent
M.38 & a-1961

*4 TIARA
Branch coral, mounted on a gilt brass frame.
ITALIAN: about 1850-60.
Circ.382-1960

5 PAIR OF EARRINGS
Carved coral and gold. Long drops.
ITALIAN: mid 19th century.
Given by Miss G.M. Robertson
M.4 & a-1962

*6 PENDANT AND PAIR OF BROOCHES
Coral cameos of Bacchus, Apollo and Venus set in gold and hung with pearls; the drop on the pendant also set with diamond sparks. All three items originally convertible, the pendant into a brooch and the brooches into pendants. The fittings now incomplete.
FRENCH (Paris): about 1854. The pendant has an illegible maker's mark; the two brooches stamped: *F. MEURICE*, with Paris warranty marks for 1838 onwards.
The set came to the Museum in its original case with the label of F.-D. Froment-Meurice. Probably one of the last sets of jewellery to be sold by François-Désiré Froment-Meurice (1802-1855) before his death, and similar to an item shown by his widow at the Paris Universal Exhibition, 1855.
Given by Dame Joan Evans, P.P.S.A.
M.30-b-1962

ANTIQUARIAN, including GOTHIC REVIVAL:
about 1820-1855

7 FLORAL BROOCH
Coral flowers; gold pin.
ITALIAN: mid 19th century.
Given by Miss G.M. Robertson
M.3-1962

8 BROOCH
Coral cameo of a Bacchante,
mounted in gold.
ITALIAN: about 1850-60.
M.34-1961

9 BROOCH
Coral cameo of a head of Bacchus,
mounted in gold.
ITALIAN: about 1850.
M.35-1961

10 CLASP
Coral cameo of a Medusa head
wreathed in gold snakes; flanked by
coral hands mounted with turquoise
and furnished with gold bracelets.
ITALIAN: about 1840.
M.36-1961
Nos. 8-10, given by Mrs K.E. Sargent

*1 HEADBAND
Enamelled gold, set with a ruby,
brilliant-cut diamonds, turquoises
and pearls; inscribed; *CHRISTI
CRUX EST MEA LUX* (Christ's
cross is my [guiding] light).
Designed by A.W.N. Pugin (1812-
1852) as part of a gothic parure for
the lady whom he proposed to make
his third wife. Jilted in 1848, he met
and married Jane Knill in the same
year, giving her the parure.
ENGLISH (Birmingham): 1848.
Made by John Hardman &
Company.
The complete parure was shown at
the Great Exhibition of 1851. The
Museum owns three items from it
(nos 1, 6 & 7 on this board).
M.10-1962

*2 *COMMESSO* OF QUEEN VICTORIA
Shell cameo (Bull's mouth or *Cassis
rufa*), mounted with gold, enamelled
and set with table-cut and cabochon
emeralds and rose-cut diamonds;
gold frame with enamelled roses of
Lancaster and York.
The cameo is a free adaptation
(reversed) of Thomas Sully's portrait
of Queen Victoria in Garter Robes,
dated 1838 (a version of the painting
in the Wallace Collection was
engraved by Wagstaff and published
in 1839). The reverse of the shell
signed: *Paul Lebas/Graveur/1851/
Paris.*
FRENCH (Paris): 1851. The gold
mounts struck with the maker's mark
of Félix Dafrique and a French
export mark in use from 1840
onwards.
Dafrique was probably responsible
for reviving the Renaissance vogue
for *commessi,* small works of art
made from a combination of stones
(in this case, shell is substituted for
hardstone). The jeweller was
awarded a Prize Medal at the Great
Exhibition of 1851 for 'polychromic
cameos', which probably included
this example.
M.340-1977

3 SCARF-PIN
Gold; the head set with an enamel
portrait of Queen Victoria (1819-1837)
by William Essex (1784-1869), after
Winterhalter's painting of 1843 in the
Royal Collections.
ENGLISH: about 1850.
Bolckow Bequest
750-1890

4 ST GEORGE AND THE DRAGON BROOCH-PIN
Cast and enamelled gold.
FRENCH (Paris): about 1855. Made
in the workshops of F-D Froment-
Meurice.
Purchased by the Museum from the
Paris Universal Exhibition of 1855;
stolen during or immediately after
the 1939-45 war, when the collections
were dispersed. Recovered, minus its
fittings, in 1953.
2659-1836

*5 AMAZON PIN
Cast and enamelled gold; the
Amazon, on horseback, attacking a
panther.
FRENCH (Paris): about 1855. Made
in the workshops of F.-D. Froment-
Meurice; his signature, largely
obliterated, on the stem.
Purchased by the Museum from the
Paris 1855 exhibition; stolen, and
recovered in 1953, with no. 4 above.
2660-1856

*6 NECKLACE WITH PENDENT CROSS
Enamelled gold, set with cabochon
garnets and pearls.
Designed by A.W.N. Pugin as part of
the parure cited in no. 1 above.
M.21-1962

*7 BROOCH
Enamelled gold, set with a ruby,
cabochon garnets, turquoises and
pearls.
Designed by A.W.N. Pugin as part of
the parure cited in no.1 above.
M.20-1962
Nos. 6 & 7, given in memory of Mrs
C.E. Gladstone by Lady Alford and
Miss Eileen Riddell

8 FIRST CLASS BADGE OF THE ROYAL ORDER OF VICTORIA AND ALBERT
Double cameo portrait of Queen Victoria and the Prince Consort engraved in onyx in the workshop of Tommaso Saulini (1793-1864) after the obverse of the Great Exhibition medals, by William Wyon; signed: *T. SAULINI.* Mounted in a frame with projecting panels in the Elizabethan manner (see Case 13, Board D, no. 2); the frame surmounted by the imperial crown, set with diamonds, rubies and emeralds. The brilliant-cut diamonds in the frame replaced by pastes, probably about 1880-1900. The cameo ITALIAN (Rome): about 1862-64; the setting ENGLISH (London): about 1864, executed by R. & S. Garrard, the Crown Jewellers. The Royal Order of Victoria and Albert was instituted by the Queen on 10 February 1862, after the Prince Consort's death. Membership of the First Class was confined to female members of the English and Continental royal families.
M.180-1976

9 PENDANT-BROOCH
Enamelled gold, set with a brilliant-cut diamond, garnets, emeralds, rubies and an amethyst drop; hung with green glass beads and pearls.
FRENCH (Paris): 1855. Maker's mark, A & A ... (?). Paris warranty mark for 1847 onwards.
Presumably the unknown maker was an outworker employed by the Froment-Meurice firm.
Shown by Froment-Meurice's widow at the Paris Universal Exhibition, 1855, where it was purchased by the Museum.
2657-1856

10 BRACELET
Silver, parcel-gilt, with enamel decoration; cast figures of cherubs alternating with openwork panels of foliage.
FRENCH (Paris): about 1850. Made in the workshops of F.-D. Froment-Meurice.
Purchased by the Museum from the Great Exhibition of 1851
167-1854

11 PENDANT-BROOCH (The Virgin Immaculata)
Enamelled gold, set with rose- and brilliant-cut diamonds, sapphires and a large carbuncle: the Virgin on a sickle moon above the carbuncle, symbolising the world.
WEST EUROPEAN: about 1850.
Bequeathed by Mrs H.F. Mosscockle
M.1814-1944

*12 CROSS
Gold, enamelled and decorated with applied gothic devices in stamped gold; set with pearls and rubies.
ENGLISH: about 1820-25.
Traditionally said to have been a wedding gift on the marriage of a member of the Bowes-Lyon family. Possibly the recipient was the bride of Thomas George Lyon-Bowes, Lord Glamis, who was married in December 1820.
Bequeathed by Miss M.G. Last
M.169-1978

13 BROOCH
Enamelled silver; cast figure of an angel with a viol. Perhaps formerly part of a larger piece of jewellery.
FRENCH (Paris): about 1844. Made in the workshops of F.-D. Froment-Meurice and signed with the name of the firm. The small cast figures used by Froment-Meurice and other French goldsmiths were employed in a variety of settings.
Acquired under the Harrap Bequest
M.12-1964

14 BROOCH
Cast silver figure of an angel with a scroll, probably once oxidised.
FRENCH (Paris): about 1844.
Ascribed to F.J. Rudolphi.
M.341-1962

15 BROOCH
Silver, parcel-gilt; cast figures of two angels flanking a stone (treated quartz).
FRENCH (Paris): about 1845.
Probably an inexpensive pastiche of the work of Froment-Meurice and Rudolphi.
M.27-1981
For a further example of Rudolphi's work, see Board E, no. 15 below.

1 THREE SPECIMENS OF GEM-SETTING (under a glass dome)
A scarf pin in the form of a bust of St George with a plumed helmet; a miniature coronet; and the Prince of Wales's feathers. The bust of St George set with a rose-cut diamonds, rubies, pearls and pavé-set turquoises.
ENGLISH (London): 1864. Made by John Whenman of Clerkenwell. Shown by the maker at the North London Working Classes Industrial Exhibition, 1864, at which he was awarded a first prize certificate.
Given by Mr J.H. Whenman
785-1902

2 BRACELET
Gold, with turquoise and pearl decoration.
Probably ENGLISH: about 1860. The French fashion for cuff *(manchette)* bracelets spread over much of Europe, including England.
Cory Bequest
M.103-1951

3 PAIR OF EARRINGS
Gold, with plaited fringes and ovoid drops.
ENGLISH (London): a Registry mark for 2nd March 1857 shows that the design was registered by Sparrow Brothers, London.
Given by Miss Edith J. Hipkins
M.257 & a-1925

4 BROOCH
Gold, decorated with an enamelled cross; set with half-pearls.
ENGLISH (? Birmingham); about 1862. Probably made by T & J Bragg of Birmingham.
7994-1863

*5 PENDANT (in the 'Holbein style')
Enamelled gold, set with a carbuncle and chrysoberyls.
ENGLISH (London): about 1860. Pendants of this kind were shown by several London firms, including Howell & James and London & Ryder, at the London International Exhibition of 1862. None is directly based on a design by Holbein.
Circ. 95-1961

123

124

6 BRACELET
Gold, with enamelled interlaced
ornament, with rose- and
brilliant-cut diamonds in the
middle of pavé-set turquoises
surrounded by half-pearls.
ENGLISH (Birmingham): about
1862. Made by T. & J. Bragg.
7992-1863

7 BRACELET
Gold, with enamelled decoration;
set with a carbuncle and pearls.
ENGLISH (Birmingham): about
1862. Made by T & J Bragg.
Nos. 6 & 7 were probably shown by
the Bragg firm at the International
Exhibition of 1862, where they were
purchased for the Museum.
7993-1863

8 BROOCH-PENDANT
A ruby, rose-cut diamonds, emeralds
and river pearls, set in gold; carved
emerald drop, detachable.
Probably INDIAN in the English
manner: about 1860-70.
M.21-1979

9 BROOCH
An onyx and half-pearls set in gold.
FRENCH (Paris): about 1860-70. An
unidentified maker's mark (? FA).
Paris warranty mark for 1847
onwards.
Cory Bequest
M.106-1951

10 NECKLACE
Silver-gilt; a mesh chain with five
electrotyped medallion pendants, the
fronts set with imitation lapis-lazuli
and the backs with intaglios of
classical heads.
FRENCH (Paris): about 1862. Made
by Gueyton.
8008-1862

11 BROOCH
Painted porcelain plaque with the
bust of a woman, inscribed:
CONSTANCE; open silver mount
with enamel decoration, set with
garnets.
French (Paris): about 1862. Made by
Gueyton.
Nos. 10 & 11 were shown by the
maker at the International
Exhibition of 1862, where they were
purchased by the Museum.
8006-1862

12 BROOCH-PENDANT
Cornelian cameo of a Bacchante in a
recessed gold frame edged by
brilliant-cut diamonds; signed by
Georges Bissinger (working in Paris
in the second half of the 19th
century). Scratch-lettered: *? 8.W.*
FRENCH (Paris): about 1870.
M.3-1980

13 BROOCH
Gold, decorated with enamel and set
with emeralds and rose-cut
diamonds.
FRENCH (Paris): about 1875.
Illegible maker's mark, perhaps that
of Marret frères et Jarry.
Bequeathed by Captain Walter
Dasent, R.N.
M.348-1940

14 PIN AND TWO SOLITAIRES
Steel, with false damascening in the
manner of Tissot (1815-1887),
mounted in gold. The pin head with
Bellerophon on Pegasus, the
solitaires with different versions of
St George and the Dragon, one of
which may be based on the reverse of
the pattern crown for George III,
1820, by Benedetto Pistrucci (1784-
1855).
FRENCH (Paris): about 1875.
Illegible maker's marks on all three
items (possibly AL). The pin and one
solitaire with Paris warranty marks
for 1847 onwards.
M.23-b-1981

15 BRACELET
Cast and oxidised silver, set with
cabochon emeralds in gold. In the
centre, an openwork quatrefoil with
an emerald surmounted by two putti,
surrounded by vine and rococo foam
ornament.
FRENCH (Paris): about 1840.
Maker's mark of F.J. Rudolphi. Paris
warranty marks for 1838 onwards.
In sharkskin case; the lining
stamped: *RUDOLPHI./BT des
CAPUCINES, 23/Paris.*
M.50-1981

The Antiquarian movement, which
inspired designers and manufac-
turers to emulate historic styles and
collectors to acquire original
specimens, inevitably also
encouraged the activities of fakers
who were only too willing to
compensate for the scarcity of
genuine work on the market. Not all
the objects on this board were
produced with intent to deceive. The
parure (no.4) was openly exhibited as
an exercise in historicism at Paris in
1855, and the necklace and earrings
(no.3) are examples of traditionalist
work. The darkest suspicious may,
however, be harboured of the rest.
No. 7 is by Reinhold Vasters of
Aachen (working about 1853-1890),
one of the most accomplished fakers
of the second half of the nineteenth
century.

1 NECKLACE
In the manner of about 1700.
Burmese rubies set in silver-gilt.
WEST EUROPEAN: about 1820-30.
M.101-1975

2 PENDANT
In the Italian Renaissance style.
Enamelled gold, set with table-cut
rubies and emeralds, and hung with
pearls.
Probably ITALIAN (Rome): about
1865.
Compare this with the signed
Castellani pendant shown below
(Board G, no.4). The overall
construction of this piece, and most
of the detailing, is strikingly similar
to that of the signed pendant, the
chief difference being that two rubies
set proud in individual scalloped
frames are substituted for a single
sapphire intaglio. There is a growing
body of evidence that the Castellani
firm supplemented its acknowledged
historicist productions with more
dubious objects, either old pieces
improved by additions or (as in this
instance) with works which might be
passed off as antique by dealers.
M.64-1975
Nos. 1 & 2, given by Dame Joan
Evans, P.P.S.A.

CASTELLANI OF ROME AND NAPLES

3 NECKLACE AND PAIR OF EARRINGS
In the manner of about 1740.
Enamelled gold, set with pearls.
HUNGARIAN: mid 19th century.
Harley Teleki Collection
M.455-b-1936

4 PARURE (necklace, bracelet, brooch and earrings)
In the manner of the 17th century.
Silver-gilt, painted in imitation of enamel and set with almandine garnets, emeralds, emerald pastes, and (mainly imitation) pearls.
AUSTRIAN (Vienna): about 1855.
Made by Schlichtegroll.
Shown by the maker at the Paris Universal Exhibition of 1855 and purchased there by the Museum as an example of the excellence of cheap production.
2664-d-1856

5 PENDANT
A double-tailed mermaid, in the manner of the 16th century.
Enamelled gold, set with faceted point-cut diamonds and rubies and hung with pearls; the body is a bead.
Based on a piece in the Green Vaults, Dresden.
Probably AUSTRO-HUNGARIAN: second half of 19th century.
Struck with a French mark (Nancy) for gold and silver wares imported from countries without Customs Conventions, 1864-1893.
M.57-1975

6 BELT-TAG
In the manner of the late 15th century.
Silver, parcel-gilt, decorated with niello. Inscribed: *AMOR/E.VOLE* (Love flies).
WEST EUROPEAN: about 1830-40.
M.57-1975
Nos. 5 & 6, given by Dame Joan Evans, P.P.S.A.

7 PENDANT
In the Italian Renaissance style.
Enamelled gold, set with rubies, table-cut diamonds and pearls; the figure group, Charity between Temperance and Prudence.
GERMAN (Reinhold Vasters of Aachen): about 1870-80.
Spitzer Collection
Lent from the Salting Bequest
M.534-1910

*8 PART OF A CAP BADGE
A man and a woman, in the manner of a mid 15th century brooch in the Kunsthistoriches Museum, Vienna.
Enamelled gold.
? AUSTRO-HUNGARIAN: 2nd half of 19th century.
The original is illustrated in Joan Evans, A *History of Jewellery, 1100-1870* col. pl. 1.
Given by Dame Joan Evans, P.P.S.A.
M.42-1975

The archeological jewellery made by the Castellani firm, which was closely based on extant Greek, Etruscan and Roman work, was widely admired and imitated, especially between about 1850 and 1880. The firm was founded in Rome in 1814 by Fortunato Pio Castellani (1793-1865). His eldest son Alessandro (1824-1883), an ardent patriot who was imprisoned in Rome for his political activities, escaped in 1858 and set up a workshop in Naples, probably in the early 1860s. Earlier in the century, a Neapolitan jeweller named Sarno had produced jewellery in the antique classical manner, and it is possible that Alessandro Castellani was able to recruit some of his surviving workmen. Alessandro continued at Naples his firm's hitherto unsuccessful experiments in reviving the lost classical art of granulation (the decoration of gold surfaces with patterns formed of minute grains of gold, individually so small as to be virtually invisible to the naked eye). He claimed a large measure of success in the early 1860's, though he never achieved the fineness of classical work. Carlo Giuliano (see Boards H and J) and Giacinto Melillo (see no.6 on this board), both worked for Alessandro Castellani, whose brother, Augusto, ran the firm in Rome after their father's retirement.

*1 THREE PENDENT MASKS
Gold, with coarse granulated decoration.
ITALIAN (Naples): about 1830-60.
Perhaps by a former workman of Sarno or another Neapolitan jeweller who experimented in the reproduction of classical jewellery.
Webb Collection
8864-c-1863

2 TWO SCARABS
One amber, the other bloodstone, set in gold as pendants; incomplete.
ITALIAN (Rome): about 1858.
Probably made by Castellani of Rome.
Purchased in Rome in 1858 by Henry Cole, the first Director of the South Kensington Museum, later the Victoria & Albert Museum.
5595, 5596-1859

FOLLOWERS OF
CASTELLANI:
about 1865-1890

126

3 NECKLACE, WREATH AND PAIR OF EARRINGS
Gold, set with pearls; the gold leaves of the myrtle wreath mounted on velvet, the pearls re-used from family jewels of the donor.
ITALIAN (Rome): 1869. Made by Castellani; the earrings only signed with the firm's monogram, two addorsed Cs on a shaped and applied plaque.
Executed as a wedding gift in 1869 for Emily Bootle-Wilbrahim (1848-1934), wife of James, Lord Lindsay (1847-1913), later the 26th Earl of Crawford. Suggestions for the design were made by Michelangelo Caetani, Duke of Sermoneta (1804-1883), patron and collaborator of the Castellani family. The necklace was apparently inspired by a reconstructed piece of classical date which was sold by Alessandro Castellani to the British Museum; the earrings are Byzantine in type.
Given by the Dowager Countess of Crawford
M.62-64a-1921

*4 PENDANT
Enamelled gold, set with rubies, a pearl, a bevelled diamond and a large sapphire intaglio of a battle scene (a cast of the intaglio is also displayed); hung with pearls.
ITALIAN (Rome): about 1865.
Applied plaque with the Castellani monogram.
Compare this piece with the pendant on Board F (no.2).
Henry L. Florence Bequest
M.222-1917

*5 NECKLACE AND PAIR OF PENDANTS
Gold; the pendants perhaps from a diadem. The medallions of the pendants represent Thetis riding a sea-monster and carrying the armour of Achilles; hung with rosettes and bud-like drops.
ITALIAN (Rome): about 1870.
Applied plaque with the Castellani monogram.
Made after Greek originals of about 360 BC excavated at Kul Oba in South Russia in 1864 and acquired for the Hermitage Museum, St Petersburg (Leningrad).
The pendants (or similar specimens) shown by Castellani at the Paris Exhibition of 1878.
638-b-1884

*6 NECKLACE
Gold; a plaited band with pendants decorated with filigree and enamel.
ITALIAN (Naples): about 1870.
Made by Giacinto Melillo (1846-1915) for Castellani, after a Greek original of the 3rd century BC found at Melos and sold by Alessandro Castellani to the British Museum (72.6.660).
Signed with Melillo's mark, the initials GM. A similar necklace is in the Castellani Collection, the Villa Giulia, Rome.
637-1884
Nos. 5 & 6, purchased from the sale of Alessandro Castellani's effects Rome, 1884

*7 BRACELET
Gold, set with agate scarabs.
ITALIAN (Rome): about 1860.
Unsigned, but said by the donor to have been purchased from Castellani.
Bolckow Bequest
736-1890

*8 PAIR OF BRACELETS
Gold, with hinged panels with applied wire and granulated decoration.
ITALIAN (Naples): about 1870.
Signed with the monogram AC in applied wire, for Alessandro Castellani.
The bracelets were probably made for exhibition purposes; the design of the panels is adapted from Etruscan baule-type earrings, 7th-5th century BC, probably from examples in the Campana Collection, Louvre.
Purchased from the sale of Castellani's effects, 1884
634, 635-1884

1 CASE
Gold; obverse, a plaque with enamelled borders flanked by cherubs, with an inscription describing the manufacture of a necklace made by Carlo Giuliano in London and bequeathed by him to the Museum in 1895. The necklace (except for the pendant, no.2 below) was stolen in 1898. The 157,580 gold grains in the case represent the number of grains used to ornament the necklace.
ENGLISH (London): about 1865-70.
Carlo Giuliano (d. 1895), a Neapolitan by birth, worked for the Castellani firm in Italy and is thought to have been set up in business in London by Alessandro Castellani. His early work in London closely resembles Castellani's productions in the classical manner. He later evolved a distinctive style of his own, using stones and enamel to create rich polychromatic effects.
Given by Messrs C & A Giuliano to accompany the necklace bequeathed by their father
26-1896

2 PENDANT
From the stolen necklace (see no.1 above)
Granulated gold rosette; amphora drop.
ENGLISH (London): about 1865.
Applied shaped plaque with Carlo Giuliano's first mark, CG in monogram, which was based on the monogram of the Castellani firm (see Board G).
Bequeathed by Carlo Giuliano
3a-1896

*3 NECKLACE WITH PENDENT MASK OF ACHELOUS
Granulated gold beads and mask.
ENGLISH (London): about 1865.
Applied plaques with Carlo Giuliano's first mark in conjunction with his second, C.G. in Roman capitals.
163-1900

4 STUD
Granulated gold openwork.
ENGLISH (London): about 1865-70.
Plaque with Carlo Giuliano's second mark.
1a-1896

GIULIANO AND OTHERS:
about 1865-1900

5 SCARF PIN
Gold, with a granulated head.
ENGLISH (London): about 1865-70.
Made by Carlo Giuliano.
14-1896
Nos. 4 & 5, bequeathed by Carlo Giuliano

6 BRACELET
Gold, with lion-mask terminals and filigree decoration; the design inspired by Greek earrings.
Probably GERMAN or AUSTRIAN: about 1870-90. This bracelet has no connection with Giuliano, but demonstrates the widespread influence of the Castellani firm.
M.19-1972

7 PAIR OF EARRINGS
Gold openwork of stylised floral trellis, with applied pellets; articulated fringe.
ENGLISH (London): about 1865-70.
Plaque with Giuliano's first mark.
Given by Messrs. C & A Giuliano
169 & a-1900

*8 PAIR OF STUDS
Gold, in the form of stylised flowers, the centres and alternating petals granulated; filigree ornament.
ENGLISH (London): about 1865.
Plaque with Giuliano's first mark.
Bequeathed by Carlo Giuliano
15 & a-1896

9 PAIR OF ROSETTE EARRINGS
Gold openwork; the central bosses granulated; filigree ornament.
ENGLISH (London): about 1865.
Plaque with Giuliano's first mark.
167 & a-1900

10 PAIR OF EARRINGS
Gold and fresh water pearls, based on a Roman design; articulated pendants with plaques of simulated granulation.
ENGLISH (London): about 1870.
Plaque with Giuliano's second mark.
170 & a-1900
Nos. 9 & 10, given by Messrs. C & A Giuliano

11 BROOCH
A white cornelian intaglio engraved with a sacrifice, mounted in gold. Originally set with its chased gold slip in an early 19th century gold box and subsequently mounted with an outer frame as a brooch.
The new setting ENGLISH (London): about 1870. Plaque with the plumed monogram (addorsed Ps, surmounted by stylised Prince of Wales's feathers) of Phillips Brothers of Cockspur Street.
The firm held a royal warrant as jewellers to Albert Edward, Prince of Wales, later Edward VII (1841-1910).
Bolckow Bequest
740-1890

12 BROOCH
Gold, openwork, decorated with filigree.
Designed by Pasquale Novissimo (d.1914), who worked for Carlo Giuliano.
ENGLISH (London): about 1880.
Given by the artist's daughter, Miss Linda Novissimo
M.26-1925

13 BROOCH
Gold, decorated with filigree and cast lioness-heads and lion-masks, and set with mother-of-pearl.
ENGLISH (London): about 1865.
Plaque with Giuliano's first and second marks.
Given by Messrs. C & A Giuliano
166-1900

*14 BRACELET
Gold, with filigree decoration.
? ENGLISH: about 1865.
Given by Messrs. J.R. Ogden & Sons
M.438-1936

*15 BRACELET
Gold, with filigree decoration and a ram-head terminal.
ITALIAN or ENGLISH: about 1860-70.
Given by Miss H.M. Jenkins, a friend of the Novissimo family, who ascribed it to Pasquale Novissimo
M.13-1956

1 NECKLACE WITH PENDANT
Gold, decorated with enamel and set with brilliant-cut diamonds, rubies and pearls.
ENGLISH (London): about 1890.
Applied plaque with Carlo Giuliano's second mark.
Lent by arrangement with Messrs. Wartski

2 PENDANT
Enamelled gold, set with an amethyst and pearls; amethyst and pearl drop.
Designed by Pasquale Novissimo for Carlo Giuliano.
ENGLISH (London): about 1880.
Given by Miss Linda Novissimo
M.36-1928

3 PENDANT
Enamelled gold, set with rubies, sapphires and pearls, enclosing an onyx cameo portrait of Marie de Medicis, Queen of France (1573-1642), after a cameo in the Cabinet des Médailles, Paris. The cameo signed: *G. Bissinger* and numbered: *3204*.
Locket fitting at the back; drop with two pearls.
The setting ENGLISH (London): about 1865. The gold work bears Carlo Giuliano's first mark.
165-1900

4 PENDANT
Enamelled gold, decorated with rubies; three pendent drops set with diamond chips and hung with river pearls. Locket fitting at the back.
ENGLISH (London): about 1867.
Applied plaque with Carlo Giuliano's second mark.
This vase-shaped pendant, with three enamelled cherub terms, is similar to one shown by Harry Emanuel of New Bond Street at the Paris Universal Exhibition of 1867.
164-1900
Nos. 3 & 4, given by Messrs. C & A Giuliano

5 NECKLACE
Gold openwork, decorated with enamel and with brilliant-cut diamonds and pearls.
ENGLISH (London): about 1902.
Made by Carlo Giuliano's sons and successors, Carlo junior and Arthur Giuliano.
M.31-1970

128

6 PENDANT-BROOCH
Gold openwork, set with a brilliant-cut diamond and rubies; hung with diamonds and chrysoprase on chains.
ENGLISH (London): about 1900.
Made by C & A Giuliano.
Given by Mrs E.M. Costello
M.34-1960

7 NECKLACE
Gold, decorated with enamels, pearls and lapis lazuli.
ENGLISH (London): about 1880.
Applied plaque with Carlo Giuliano's second mark.
Lent by arrangement with Messrs. Wartski

8 BRACELET
Gold, addorsed honeysuckle units, alternating with sapphires.
ENGLISH (London): about 1900.
Applied plaque with C & A Giuliano's mark, C & A G, in Roman capitals.
M.30-1970

9 BROOCH
Silver and gold openwork, enamelled and set with rose- and brilliant-cut diamonds; hung with a pearl.
ENGLISH (London): about 1900.
Made by C & A Giuliano.
M.28-1970
Nos. 8 & 9, given by Mrs. E.M. Costello

10 LOCKET
Enamelled gold, bearing the Egyptian hieroglyph *nefer* (beautiful).
ENGLISH (London): about 1900.
Sold by C & A Giuliano.
Given by Mr Cecil F. Crofton
M.6-1923

11 CADUCEUS BROOCH
Enamelled gold, set with a pearl.
ENGLISH (London): about 1900.
Applied plaque with the mark of C & A Giuliano.
Given by Mrs E.M. Costello
M.29-1970

12 VULTURE NECKLACE
Gold, hung with garnets.
ENGLISH (London): about 1870.
Plumed mark of Phillips Brothers of Cockspur Street.
Bequeathed by Dr Rose Graham, D.Litt., F.S.A.
M.1-1964

13 MUFF CHAIN
Enamelled gold and pearls.
ENGLISH (London): about 1900.
Rubbed mark of C & A Giuliano.
Given by Mrs E.M. Costello
M.96-1969

14 NECKLACE AND PAIR OF EARRINGS
Enamelled gold, hung with cameos of classical masks in chalcedony and onyx; in the late 18th century Neoclassical manner.
ENGLISH (London): 1867. Applied plaque with the mark of John Brogden of Henrietta Street, Covent Garden, JB in Roman capitals.
Shown by Brogden at the Paris Universal Exhibition of 1867.
Bolckow Bequest
734-b-1890

*1 BRACELET
Gold; hinged with applied stylised floral decoration in a generalised classical manner.
ENGLISH (London): about 1860.
Made by C.F. Hancock & Company of Bruton Street.
737-1890

2 BRACELET
Gold, with applied decoration representing Ashurbanipal (668-627 BC), King of Assyria, sacrificing on his return from a lion hunt, after a relief in the British Museum. On the clasp, a Babylonian cylinder in steatite.
ENGLISH (London): about 1860.
Maker's mark of John Brogden.
The Assyrian sculptures in the British Museum excavated by Sir A.H. Layard were a source of inspiration to many designers.
Layard published *Nineveh and its Remains* (1848-9) and *Nineveh and Babylon* (1853).
735-1890
Nos 1&2, Bolckow Bequest

3 NECKLACE
Gold tubular links.
ENGLISH: about 1860.
Given by Miss Victoria Leveson-Gower
M.41-1969

4 COMB
Tortoiseshell; hinged copper-gilt gallery decorated with an applied lyre, wreath and scrolling foliage outlined in filigree.
FRENCH: about 1875.
Formerly belonging to Madame Adelina Patti (1843-1919).
Given by Mrs Natalie Tingey
M.29-1942

5 BRACELET AND PENDANT
Gold, set with Roman mosaics and decorated with filigree.
ITALIAN: about 1870.
Bequeathed by Mrs. Noel Laetitia Kelby
M.224-225-1976

CELTIC REVIVAL:
about 1849-1900

6 GIRDLE
Steel panels, damascened and set
with enamels, lapis-lazuli, Roman
mosaics and onyx cameos; the
cameos signed: *L. Rosi.*
ITALIAN (Vicenza): the steel signed
by Antonio Cortellazzo.
Probably shown at the International
Exhibition, London, 1871.
Given by Mr. W.D. Clark
Circ. 336-1958

7 BROOCH
Gold, set with a reverse intaglio
crystal representing the head of a
terrier, polychromed.
ENGLISH: about 1875-90.
Cory Bequest
M.65-1951

8 PENDANT-BROOCH
Gold, set with a Roman mosaic figure
of Vesta; locket fitting on the reverse.
ITALIAN: about 1875-85.
Given by Mrs. Burkinyoung
844-1907

9 PENDANT
Silver frame with niello decoration;
in the centre, a panel of Florentine
mosaic representing a butterfly, a fly
and a beetle; locket fitting on the
reverse.
Probably GERMAN: about 1880.
Given by Mrs D.R. Bridgman
M.13-1974

10 PENDENT CHARM
In the form of a book, with engraved
and enamelled covers; inside, four
receptacles for photographs.
WEST EUROPEAN: about 1890.
Given by Dr. W.L. Hildburgh
M.109-1953

11 PAIR OF EARRINGS
Gold, set with glass and aventurine
paste mosaic.
ITALIAN (probably Venice): about
1865.
Given by Mr George A.H. Tucker
774-a-1902

12 BROOCH
Gold, set with a brilliant-cut
diamond; locket fitting on the
reverse.
Probably ENGLISH: about 1865.
Given by Miss C. Dickson
M.27-1972

13 BANGLE
Gold, in the archeological taste, set
with a star sapphire and a ruby.
RUSSIAN (St. Petersburg): 1908.
Mark of August Fredrik Hollming
(1854-1915), workmaster to Peter
Carl Fabergé.
Given by the National Art
Collections Fund
M.170-1976

14 BRACELET
Silver, in narrow panels so that it can
be rolled up to fit into a barrel-shaped
case.
ENGLISH (London): about 1870. The
bracelet bears the plumed mark of
Phillips Brothers of Cockspur Street;
the firm's name stamped on the
inside lining of the case (shown).
The classical design is a development
of a panelled bracelet shown by the
firm at the Paris Universal
Exhibition of 1867.
M.111-1978

15 CROSS AND CHAIN
Gold, the cross with alternative
crystal, jadeite and lapis lazuli
insets.
RUSSIAN (St. Petersburg): about
1900. Russian warranty mark; mark
of Gabriel Niukkanen, workmaster
to Peter Carl Fabergé.
Given by Dame Joan Evans, P.P.S.A.
M.92-1962

Scottish and Irish jewellery based on
archeological designs and made of
local materials enjoyed widespread
popularity in the nineteenth century.
Scottish jewellers were working with
native stones in the eighteenth
century. It was not however until the
second half of the nineteenth century
that the rage for their wares spread
outside Scotland. The scale of the
demand led to the mass-production of
pebble jewellery, mainly executed in
Birmingham and passed off as
Scottish.
Irish bog-oak jewellery was popular
but not as highly-regarded as the
scaled-down reproductions of eighth
century jewellery which were made
and sold as shawl-pins and brooches
in Dublin and elsewhere in Ireland
from the 1840s onwards. The most
celebrated of the originals to be used
in this way was the so-called 'Royal
Tara' brooch (now in the National
Museum, Dublin), which was found
in August 1850. The titles of the other
pieces listed below were all in use in
the nineteenth century.

1 SHAWL BROOCH (after the
'Moor' brooch)
Parcel-gilt metal, partly oxidised.
IRISH (Dublin): about 1853. Made by
G & S Waterhouse of Dublin.
Purchased by the Museum from the
Irish Industrial Exhibition of 1853
231-1854

2 SHAWL BROOCH (after the
'Arbutus berry' brooch)
Parcel-gilt metal, pennanular,
decorated with three modelled
berries.
IRISH (Dublin): about 1851. Made by
G. & S. Waterhouse of Dublin.
Examples of this pattern were shown
at the Great Exhibition of 1851 and
the Irish Industrial Exhibition of
1853
2747-1853

129

130

*3 SHAWL BROOCH (after the
'Ogham' or 'Clarendon' brooch)
Gilt metal, pennanular, decorated
with enamel; the reverse engraved
with an Ogham inscription. A
Registry mark shows that the design
was registered on 24 July 1849.
IRISH (Dublin): about 1850. Made by
G. & S. Waterhouse.
Examples of this design were shown
at the Great Exhibition of 1851 and
the Irish Industrial Exhibition of
1853
2749-1853

4 SHAWL BROOCH (after the
'Royal Tara' brooch)
Parcel-gilt metal, pennanular, set
with pearls, 'Irish diamonds' and
amethysts.
IRISH (Dublin): about 1851. Made by
G. & S. Waterhouse.
Purchased by the Museum from the
Great Exhibition of 1851
920-1852

5 SHAWL BROOCH
Silver, pennanular, set with a yellow
smoky-quartz ('Cairngorm'),
'Scottish pebbles' and pastes; *JLM* in
monogram engraved on the back.
In the SCOTTISH manner: late 19th
century.
Given by Mrs. W.S. Merriman
M.22-1965

**6 DOUBLE SCARF or SHAWL
PIN**
'Scottish pebbles' (mainly agates) set
in silver; in the form of two pins
linked by a chain.
Probably SCOTTISH: about 1845.
Given by Mr. F.D. Fletcher
M.136-1978

**7 BROOCH AND TWO
SOLITAIRES**
'Scottish pebbles' set in gold.
? SCOTTISH: about 1860.
Acquired with the original case (not
shown) bearing the stamp of G & M
Crichton, Jewellers, of Edinburgh.
M.55-b-1980

8 BROOCH
'Scottish pebbles' set in silver; a
Registry mark on the back shows
that the design was registered on 14
October 1865 by James Fenton, a
Birmingham manufacturer.
ENGLISH (Birmingham): about
1865.
Circ. 278-1961

9 BRACELET
Smoky-quartz and 'Scottish pebbles'
(grey agate) set in silver.
? SCOTTISH: about 1855.
Given by Miss R.E.P.L. Sherratt
M.311-1975

The increasing rigidity of mourning
conventions during the reign of
Queen Victoria gave great
encouragement to the manufacture
of black jewellery. Expensive work in
black-enamelled gold (see Case 21,
Board B, nos. 3, 7-10, 13 & 16) was
made by hand. Jet was much in
demand, and the workshops in
Whitby, Yorkshire near the main
source of the material, produced
articles which often comprised hand-
carved details applied to mass-
produced bodies turned on lathes.
Mass-production methods, and the
use of substitute materials, brought
mourning jewellery within reach of
all but the poorest. No. 2 was
moulded in vulcanite (a preparation
of indiarubber and sulpher hardened
under intense heat); nos. 1 & 3 are
'French jet', executed in cast glass
mounted on metal; the rest are jet.
No. 1 lent anonymously; no. 2 given
by Miss A.L. Wyatt, no. 3 by Miss
Marguerite Hirst, no. 4 & 5 by
Mrs C. Ball, no. 6 by Mrs B.M.
Dickens, no. 7 by Miss B.L.
Edmundson.
M.17-1971; M.40, 62, 63, 64,
65-1974

CASE 20
BOARD A
NO. 13

CASE 20
BOARD B
NO. 1

131

CASE 20
BOARD B
NO. 4

CASE 20
BOARD C
NO. 1

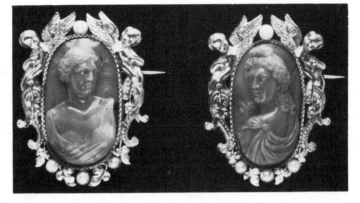

CASE 20
BOARD C
NO. 4

CASE 20
BOARD C
NO. 6

CASE 20
BOARD D
NO. 1

CASE 20
BOARD D
NO. 2

CASE 20
BOARD D
NO. 5

132

CASE 20
BOARD D
NOS. 6 & 7

CASE 20
BOARD D
NO. 12 2 Views

CASE 20
BOARD E
NO. 5

CASE 20
BOARD G
NO. 1

CASE 20
BOARD G
NO. 4

CASE 20
BOARD F
NO. 8

CASE 20
BOARD G
NO. 5

CASE 20
BOARD G
NO. 8

133

CASE 20
BOARD G
NO. 6

CASE 20
BOARD G
NO. 7

CASE 20
BOARD H
NO. 15

CASE 20
BOARD H
NO. 3

CASE 20
BOARD H
NO. 8

CASE 20
BOARD H
NO. 14

CASE 20
BOARD K
NO. 3
(reverse)

CASE 20
BOARD J
NO. 1

1875-1890

About 1860-1900

134

1 BRACELET
Translucent and *plique-à-jour* enamel in gold openwork, set with pearls and brilliant-cut diamonds.
FRENCH (Paris): about 1875; acquired by the donor from Frédéric Boucheron (1830-1902).
Boucheron acquired the rights to a patent for *plique-à-jour* from the French enamelist Riffault, who had worked on its revival.
747-1890

*2 CROSS
Translucent enamel on gold, set with pearls and diamonds; sold as a pair with the bracelet (no.1) above, but it lacks the *plique-à-jour* of the bracelet.
FRENCH (Paris): about 1875; purchased from Boucheron.
748-1890
Nos. 1 & 2, Bolckow Bequest

3 SPRAY
Turquoises in brilliant-cut diamond borders mounted in gold and silver.
WEST EUROPEAN: about 1880.
Cory Bequest
M.97-1951

4 FAN BROOCH
Gold, set with a miniature painting of an allegorical love scene signed by Fernand Paillet (1850-1918); gold tassels and cords suspended from a brilliant-cut diamond.
FRENCH (Paris): about 1890. Signed on the reverse: *Boucheron*.
The original fitted case (not shown) stamped with the addresses of Boucheron in London, St. Petersburg, New York and Paris.
Given by the National Art-Collections Fund (Miss J.H.G. Gollan Bequest)
M.171-1976

5 LOCKET AND PAIR OF EARRINGS
Gold, set with enamelled plaques and pearls.
WEST EUROPEAN: about 1880.
Given by Dr. W.L. Hildburgh, F.S.A.
M.173-b-1951

6 NECKLACE WITH PENDANT AND PAIR OF EARRINGS
Gold, set with turquoises, pearls and rose-cut diamonds and painted enamel plaques of cherubs. The pendant has a locket fitting at the back.
GERMAN or AUSTRO-HUNGARIAN: about 1880.
Given by Mrs. Hannah Blum
M.26-b-1975

*7 CROSS WITH CHAIN
The cross gold, set with pearls and lapis lazuli; flexible gold chain.
Probably ENGLISH: about 1875.
Given by Miss Victoria Leveson-Gower
M.15 & a-1962

8 BRACELET
Gold, set with half-pearls and rose- and brilliant-cut diamonds. The centre pierced with scrolls and bordered by pellets.
WEST EUROPEAN: about 1880.
M.14-1956

1 NECKLACE AND PAIR OF EARRINGS
Cabochon and faceted garnets; the necklace with pendants in the front. The earrings, though of the same date, do not match.
? BOHEMIAN: about 1875.
Given by Dr. W.L. Hildburgh F.S.A.
M.175-b-1951

2 CRESCENT BROOCH
Brilliant-cut diamonds set in gold.
ENGLISH: about 1890-1900.
Bequeathed by Miss D.B. Simpson
M.98-1978

3 BRACELET
Gold, enamelled in black and set with pearls and brilliant-cut diamonds, the pendants decorated with the letter A, a cross (Faith), an anchor (Hope), a heart and a star. Perhaps inspired by work in the Moroccan manner produced by Crouzet senior of Paris (c.1816-c. 1895).
? FRENCH: about 1860.
Black enamelled jewellery was fashionable mourning wear.
Cory Bequest
M.104-1951

*4 MAN IN THE MOON BROOCH
Carved moonstone in a crescent-shaped frame of brilliant-cut diamonds, with a shooting star.
ENGLISH: about 1888.
M.269-1977

5 NECKLACE
Graduated opal beads spaced by small crystal beads; gold clasp.
ENGLISH: about 1900.
M.96-1978

6 HEART PENDANT
An opal set in gold, surrounded by diamonds.
ENGLISH: about 1890-1900.
M.97-1978
Nos. 5 & 6, bequeathed by Miss D.B. Simpson

AESTHETIC
NOVELTIES AND
EXOTICA:
1867-about 1900

7 BROOCH AND PAIR OF EARRINGS
Gold openwork, enamelled in black and set with rose- and brilliant-cut diamonds and pearls, with pearl and diamond pendants; in the Moroccan manner of Crouzet.
FRENCH (Paris): about 1860-70. Paris warranty mark for 1847 onwards.
M.120-1951

8 FOUR UNITS
(? From a bodice ornament)
Gold, enamelled in black and set with pearls and brilliant-cut diamonds inthe Moroccan manner of Crouzet; the Arabic inscription is a nonsense.
? FRENCH: about 1860-70.
M.146-1951

9 LOCKET
Gold, enamelled in black and set with pearls.
FRENCH or ENGLISH: about 1860-70.
M.148-1951

10 NECKLACE
Gold, enamelled in black, the links set with pearls. Pearl tassels, possibly inspired by Indian jewellery.
FRENCH or ENGLISH: about 1855-70.
M.111-1951
Nos. 7-10, Cory Bequest

11 BEE BROOCH
The bee gold, set with rose-cut diamonds and a pearl, mounted on a gold bar brooch.
ENGLISH: about 1890-1900.
Bequeathed by Miss D.B. Simpson
M.99-1978

12 BROOCH
Reverse crystal intaglio of a sailor's hat, the ribbon inscribed: *HMS MINOTAUR;* set on a gold bar brooch.
? ENGLISH: about 1900. The donor's family lived for some time in Hong Kong, so that the brooch might have been executed there.
Given by Miss J. Crawford
M.71-1979

13 BRACELET
Brilliant-cut diamonds and pearls set in gold with black enamel fillet.
Probably ENGLISH: about 1875.
M.109-1951

14 BRACELET
Pearls and brilliant-cut diamonds set in gold.
ENGLISH: about 1880; maker's mark, A & G.
M.108-1951

15 PAIR OF EARRINGS
Gold filigree, set with pearls, possibly inspired by Indian jewellery.
ENGLISH: second half of 19th century.
M.122 & a-1951
Nos. 13-15, Cory Bequest

16 LOCKET
Gold; obverse, an applied initial *L* in brilliant-cut diamonds edged with black enamel; reverse, a commemorative inscription dated October 7, 1871.
ENGLISH: 1871-72.
Given by Mrs. O.C. Leveson-Gower
M.11-1972

17 PENDANT
Gold, decorated with translucent blue enamel; brilliant-cut diamond border and inner ring. Reverse, an inscription dated 8 March, 1883.
ENGLISH: about 1883.
Lent anonymously

1 NECKLACE
Gold, strung with ancient Egyptian beads.
The mounting ENGLISH: late 19th century, possibly by Phillips Brothers.
Given by Sir John Aird to the novelist Marie Corelli (1855-1924). Bequeathed by Miss Marie Corelli
M.384-1924

2 NECKLACE
Cloisonné enamels of birds, flowers and insects in the Japanese taste, mounted in gold.
FRENCH (Paris): about 1867-70.
Maker's mark of Alexis Falize (1811-1898). Similar work was perhaps shown by Falize at the Paris Universal Exhibition of 1867.
1043-1871

*3 BROOCH AND PAIR OF EARRINGS
Gold, the decoration stamped and applied, in the Japanese taste.
ENGLISH: about 1880.
M.299-b-1975

*4 NECKLACE
Enamelled gold, with pearl pendants, in the Indian taste.
ENGLISH (London); about 1867.
Maker's mark, RP in Roman capitals for Robert Phillips of Phillips Brothers, Cockspur Street. This was Phillip's own mark, as against the plumed P monogram of the firm, used elsewhere (see Case 20, Board H, no. 11).
Shown by Robert Phillips at the Paris Universal Exhibition, 1867.
549-1868

5 LOCKET
Gold, decorated with *cloisonné* enamel in the Chinese taste.
FRENCH (Paris): about 1867-70.
Maker's mark of Alexis Falize.
Acquired under the Harrap Bequest
M.22-1963

6 LOCKET
Gold, decorated with *cloisonné* enamel in the Indian taste.
FRENCH (Paris): about 1870.
Maker's mark of Alexis Falize.
1045-1871
Nos. 2 & 6, purchased by the Museum from the International Exhibition, London, 1871

THE MORRIS CIRCLE

136

7 BROOCH
Gold, in the form of a Japanese fan.
ENGLISH: about 1880.
M.182-1976

8 BROOCH
Coloured gold, engraved and
decorated with applied birds and
foliage in gold and copper, in
imitation of Japanese encrusted
work.
? ENGLISH: about 1880-90.
Stamped: *15 carat.*
Circ. 346-1963

9 BRACELET
Gold, and shakudo panels from two
and a half Japanese purse mounts.
The panels JAPANESE: first half of
19th century. Probably assembled in
FRANCE: about 1880.
Lent anonymously

10 BROOCH
A panel of shakudo work, set in a
gold frame. The panel JAPANESE:
about 1870-1880. The frame WEST
EUROPEAN: 1880.
M.300-1975

11 PAIR OF EARRINGS
Gold, with modelled and painted
birds on a swing.
Sold by Leroy of Paris and Regent
Street, London.
FRENCH: about 1875. Paris
warranty mark for gold from 1847
onwards.
Lent anonymously

The majority of pieces on this board
comprise the greater part of the
bequest of Miss May Morris (1862-
1938), designer, embroideress and
jeweller. The rest were given shortly
after May Morris's death by her
friend and companion Miss Vivien
Lobb, who believed that all the jewels
she presented were the work of May
herself. Some of them are, but others
are not (including a ring by Charles
Ricketts which is shown elsewhere,
in Case 34, Board K, no. 9).

May (Mary) Morris was the younger
daughter of William Morris (1834-
1896) and his wife Janey (Jane).
Some of the pieces in her bequest
were probably family jewels. Others
came originally from the collection of
Dante Gabriel Rossetti (1828-1882),
as they appear in several of his
paintings, for some of which Mrs
Morris was the model. Rossetti, who
was an avid collector of properties for
his paintings, was in love with Janey
Morris and must have given her the
jewellery. No. 21 is in a different
category: it is a case made to contain
William Morris's hair after his death.

No. 7, lent from a private collection,
was designed by Morris's friend, the
painter Sir Edward Burne-Jones
(1833-1898).

1 BROOCH
A topaz set in a filigree frame.
WEST EUROPEAN: about 1825.
Formerly in the possession of
Mrs William Morris.
M.45-1939

2 BROOCH
A citrine set in a gold frame with
cannetille decoration.
WEST EUROPEAN: about 1820-30.
Formerly in the possession of Mrs
William Morris
M.44-1939

3 PENDANT WITH CHAIN
The pendant: rock crystal, cut *en
cabochon,* set in a gilt metal
surround with small pieces of rock
crystal.
ENGLISH: about 1870-80.
The plaited gold chain FRENCH:
about 1880.
French export mark for 1879
onwards.
M.38 & a-1939

*4 NECKCHAIN
Stamped gold links; Janey Morris's
wedding ring has been slipped on to
the chain, probably by her daughter
May.
The chain ENGLISH: about 1830-40.
The ring, of 22 carat gold, bears
London hallmarks for 1858 (the year
of her marriage); maker's mark, JO.
The chain was worn by Janey Morris
when she sat to Rossetti for *Mariana*
(1870), from Shakespeare's *Measure
for Measure.* The painting is in the
Aberdeen Museum and Art Gallery.
M.37 & a-1939

5 BRACELET
Gold, set with rubies. The clasp
formed of two dragon heads flanking
a water pot.
SOUTH INDIAN or BURMESE:
perhaps mid 19th century.
The bracelet is worn by the Bride in
Rossetti's painting, *The Bride* or *The
Beloved,* for which a professional
model posed. The painting, executed
in 1865-66, and retouched in 1873, is
in the Tate Gallery.
M.39-1939
Nos. 1-5, May Morris Bequest

6 PIN
Gold, set with a milky opal, pearls
and topazes.
ENGLISH: about 1903. Probably
designed and made by May Morris in
the manner of Georgie Gaskin (Mrs
Arthur Gaskin). The Gaskins were
family friends (see Case 21, Board I).
Given by Miss Vivien Lobb
M.21-1939

7 BIRD BROOCH
Gold, the bird set with cornelians and
turquoises; ruby eye; the surrounding
leaves and berries enamelled.
Designed by Sir Edward Burne-
Jones.
ENGLISH (London): about 1890.
Signed by the maker, Carlo Giuliano,
with his second mark.
Lent anonymously

8 BROOCH
Gold, with *cannetille* and *grainti*
decoration, set with rubies and
emeralds.
WEST EUROPEAN: about 1820-30.
Formerly in the possession of Mrs.
William Morris.
May Morris Bequest
M.43-1939

9 PAIR OF EARRINGS
Enamelled gold, hung with pearls.
? ENGLISH: about 1900. Possibly
made by May Morris after a
traditional design.
Given by Miss Vivien Lobb
M.22 & a-1939

10 HEART-SHAPED BROOCH
Silver, with applied rosettes; set with
three large pastes.
? WEST EUROPEAN: mid 19th
century.
The brooch was worn as a pendant by
Rossetti's housekeeper and model,
Fanny Cornforth, in *The Blue Bower*
(1865), in the Barber Institute of Fine
Arts, University of Birmingham.
Formerly in the possession of
Mrs William Morris.
May Morris Bequest
M.40-1939

11 RING
Gold, set with a cabochon spinel.
ENGLISH: about 1903. Probably
designed and made by May Morris.
Given by Miss Vivien Lobb
M.19a-1939

12 RING
Gold, set with a cabochon emerald.
ENGLISH: about 1850.
The ring appears on the tray held by
a winged attendant (for which May
Morris was the model) in Rossetti's
La Bella Mano (1875), in the Dela-
ware Art Museum, Wilmington,
Delaware.
May Morris Bequest
M.36-1939

13 RING
Gold, set with a cabochon ruby.
ENGLISH: about 1900. Probably
designed and made by May Morris.
M.19-1939

14 PIN
Gold, set with an agate, emeralds and
pearls.
ENGLISH: about 1903. Probably
designed and made by May Morris in
the manner of Georgie Gaskin.
M.20-1939

15 PAIR OF EARRINGS
Gold, set with sapphires and pearls.
ENGLISH: about 1901. Probably
designed and made by May Morris.
M.23 & a-1939

16 COMB
Ivory teeth; the head silver, set with
mother-of-pearl, a fire opal matrix,
sapphires and green stained
chalcedony.
ENGLISH (London): about 1905.
Designed and made by Joseph Hodel;
signed by the artist.
Shown by Hodel at the Arts and
Crafts Exhibition, 1906, where it was
presumably acquired by May Morris.
M.18-1939
Nos. 13-16, given by Miss Vivien
Lobb

17 BUCKLE
Gold, set with emeralds.
? INDIAN: mid 19th century.
Formerly in the possession of Mrs
William Morris.
M.42-1939

18 BUCKLE
Gold, with *cannetille* and *grainti*
decoration; with two applied snakes.
WEST EUROPEAN: about 1825.
Formerly in the possession of Mrs
William Morris.
M.41-1939
Nos. 17 & 18, May Morris Bequest

19 GIRDLE
Silver roundels, set with river pearls,
garnets and chrysoprase, connected
by chains.
ENGLISH: about 1905. Designed and
made by May Morris.
Shown by May Morris at the Arts
and Crafts Exhibition, 1906.
M.17-1939

20 HEART-SHAPED PENDANT
Silver, with applied rosettes; set with
amazonite, a turquoise, pearls and
lapis-lazuli.
ENGLISH: about 1903. Designed and
made by May Morris after Rossetti's
brooch (see no. 10 above).
M.24-1939
Nos. 19 & 20, given by Miss Vivien
Lobb

**21 CASE CONTAINING
WILLIAM MORRIS'S HAIR**
Gold plates on a wooden carcass;
locket fitting at the back for Morris's
hair.
Designed by Robert Catterson Smith.
ENGLISH: London hallmarks for
1896-97; maker's mark partly illegible
(? C.J.). A plaque on the back
inscribed with a verse by F.S. Ellis,
Morris's friend and publisher:
*For folk unborn this shrine doth hold
Thy silvered lock, Oh! heart of gold
Should time's hand mar it, yet thy
mind
Shall live, in deathless words
enshrined.*
M.33-1939 .

22 BELT AND HANGER
Silver, the links of cast floral
ornament.
Probably GERMAN: 17th century.
A slightly more elaborate version of
this type is shown in Case 38, Board
B, no. 1.
This belt worn by Janey Morris when
she posed for Rossetti's *Astarte
Syriaca* (1877), in the Manchester
City Art Gallery.
Formerly in the possession of Mrs
William Morris.
M.34-1939
Nos. 21 & 22, May Morris Bequest

138

1 WAIST CLASP
Silver, set with an opal; in two parts. Probably designed by Oliver Baker (*c.*1856-1939) for the Cymric range of jewellery and silver launched by Liberty & Company of Regent Street in 1898/99.
ENGLISH: Birmingham hallmarks for 1899-1900. Maker's mark of Liberty & Co. (Cymric) Ltd. (a mark registered by the makers, W.H. Haseler & Company of Birmingham). Made for Mrs John Llewellyn, the wife of the director of Liberty & Company who administered the Cymric scheme.
M.306-1975

2 PENDANT
Silver frame, set with pearls, with a mother-of-pearl plaque; profile head of a girl in ivory, silver and silver-gilt; baroque pearl pendant.
ENGLISH: about 1900-01. Designed and made by A.C.C. Jahn, Principal of Wolverhampton School of Art.
M.85-1947

*3 BROOCH
In the form of an angel.
Silver, parcel-gilt, set with an opal and pearls; ivory head.
ENGLISH: 1900-01. Designed and made by A.C.C. Jahn.
M.84-1947
Nos. 2 & 3, Jahn Bequest

4 THE WAGNER GIRDLE
In several parts.
Steel, set with enamelled plaques depicting Tristan and Isolde. The hook inscribed: *E.J.H., L.I.H/1896 MADE BY ALEX. FISHER.*
ENGLISH (London): dated 1896. Designed and made by Alexander Fisher (1864-1936) for Mrs Emslie J. Horniman.
Exhibited in an unfinished state at the Royal Academy in 1895.
Given by Mrs. O.E. Bostock and Mr Ivan Horniman
M.20-1943

5 PLAQUE FOR A BUCKLE
Beaten aluminium set with a yellow paste.
SCOTTISH (Glasgow): about 1900. Designed and executed by Talwin Morris.
Circ. 68-1959

6 PAIR OF BUCKLES
Bronzed copper set with green pastes; in the form of stylised butterflies.
SCOTTISH (Glasgow): about 1900. Designed and executed by Talwin Morris.
Circ. 57 & a-1959
Nos. 5 & 6 are illustrated in *Modern Design in Jewellery and Fans, Studio* magazine, 1901-02.

1 PEACOCK PENDANT-BROOCH
Silver and gold, set with pearls and diamonds; a ruby in the peacock's eye, the body a baroque pearl, the spreading tail mounted with blister pearls and diamond sparks. The bird perches on a spherical pearl, above a brilliant-cut diamond and blister pearl drop.
ENGLISH (London): about 1899-1900.
Designed by C.R. Ashbee (1863-1942) for his wife Janet, whom he married in 1898, and made by the Guild of Handicraft Ltd. at Essex House, Mile End Road, London.
Anonymous loan

2 NECKLACE
Gold units in the form of flowers, set with peridots.
ENGLISH (Chipping Campden): about 1903. Designed by C.R. Ashbee and made by the Guild of Handicraft Ltd. in Chipping Campden, Gloucestershire, to where it had removed from the East End of London in 1902.
M.165-1978

*3 CHAIN NECKLACE WITH PEACOCK PENDANT
Silver and gold, in the form of a peacock, set with blister pearls, diamond sparks and a demantoid garnet for the eye; three pearl pendants.
ENGLISH (London): 1901. Designed by C.R. Ashbee and made by the Guild of Handicraft Ltd. at Essex House. Dutch import marks.
M.23-1965

4 PEACOCK PENDANT WITH CHAIN
Enamelled gold peacock, curved around turquoise matrix; three turquoises set in the chain.
ENGLISH (London): about 1902. Designed by C.R. Ashbee and made by the Guild of Handicraft Ltd. The piece has been altered; when published in 1902 the chain was bridged by an elaborate trellis.
Circ. 330-1959

5 SHIP PENDANT (the 'Craft of the Guild')
Enamelled gold, set with an Australian opal and diamond sparks; hung with three tourmalines.
ENGLISH (Chipping Campden): about 1903. Designed by C.R. Ashbee and made by the Guild of Handicraft Ltd.
Bequeathed by Miss M.C. Annesley
M.4-1964

6 PENDANT
Gold, with a double-sided enamelled representation of the Virgin and Child against a cross.
SCOTTISH (Edinburgh): 1906. Designed and made by Phoebe Anna Traquair (1852-1936). Signed on the reverse of the enamel with the artist's initials, *PAT*, and dated 1906.
Given by Mrs. H.V. Bartholomew
M.193-1976

7 PENDANT
Enamelled gold.
Designed by Archibald Knox (1864-1933) for the Cymric jewellery range of Liberty & Company, Regent Street.
ENGLISH (Birmingham): about 1900. Made by W.H. Haseler & Company for Liberty & Company. for Liberty & Company.
Acquired under the terms of the Harrap Bequest
M.64-1964

8 PENDANT ('Cupid the Earth Upholder')
Gold, enamelled and set with coloured foiled glass.
SCOTTISH (Edinburgh): 1902. Designed and made by Phoebe Traquair; signed by the artist, titled and dated 1902 on the reverse.
Given by Mrs Crompton
Circ. 210-1953

9 BROOCH
Enamelled gold frame, set with an opal.
ENGLISH: 1928. Designed and made for his daughter Joan's twenty-first birthday by Fred Partridge, who had formerly worked for Ashbee's Guild of Handicraft.
Engraved on the back with her birth-sign of Virgo.
M.14-1976

10 PENDANT
Silver, decorated with *plique-à-jour* enamel to represent intertwined birds and set with a cabochon amethyst.
ENGLISH: about 1912.
Designed and made by May Hart Partridge (d.1917), wife of Fred Partridge.
M.32-1968
Nos. 9 & 10, given by Miss Joan Partridge

*1 NECKLACE
Gold, set with blister pearls and opals, the open units connected by chains.
Designed by Archibald Knox for the Cymric jewellery range.
ENGLISH (Birmingham): about 1902. Made by W.H. Haseler & Company for Liberty & Company.
Circ. 208-1961

2 PENDANT ('The Love Cup')
A painted enamel set in gold.
SCOTTISH (Edinburgh): 1902. Designed and made by Phoebe Traquair; signed by the artist, titled and dated 1902 on the reverse.
Given by Mrs. H.V. Bartholomew
M.192-1976

3 PENDANT
Gold and silver, set with cabochon rubies, chrysoprases, sapphires, aquamarines and opals; in the form of an open ring hung with a niche with a Madonna and Child; a pendant below. A dove, symbol of the Holy Ghost, suspended from the loop above.
ENGLISH (Birmingham): 1906. Designed and made by John Paul Cooper (1869-1933).
J. Paul Cooper was head of the metalwork department at Birmingham School of Art, 1904-07.
Handley-Read Collection
M.30-1972

*4 PENDANT ('The Love Cup': second version)
A painted enamel set in gold.
SCOTTISH (Edinburgh): 1907. Designed and made by Phoebe Traquair; signed by the artist, titled and dated 1907 on the reverse.
Given by Mrs H.V. Bartholomew
M.194-1976

5 NECKLACE
Enamelled plaques in gold mounts, connected by chains.
SCOTTISH (Edinburgh): about 1908. Designed and made by Phoebe Traquair (the centre plaque the same subject as in Board F, no.8 above; signed and titled by the artist, *Eros Atlas*).
Given by Mrs H.V. Bartholomew
M.404-1977

139

ART NOUVEAU: *about about 1897-1906*

140

6 BROOCH
Cloisonné enamel plaque set in a
gold frame decorated with enamel.
ENGLISH (London): about 1914.
Designed and made by Harold
Stabler (1872-1954). Signed on the
reverse: *STABLER*.
Given by Miss M. McLeish in
memory of Harold and Phoebe
Stabler
Circ.503-1956

**7 CHAIN NECKLACE WITH
PENDANT**
Gold, the pendant surmounted by a
cast cherub and set with a painted
enamel plaque with lilies-of-the-
valley surrounded by pearls in
openwork; the drop set with a
sapphire; sapphires and pearls on the
chain.
Probably designed and made by
Nelson Dawson (1864-1939); the
enamel by his wife Edith.
M.20-1979

8 FLOWER BROOCH
Gold, set with an opal.
ENGLISH (Wolverhampton): about
1900-01. Designed and made by
A.C.C. Jahn.
Jahn Bequest
M.83-1947

9 NECKLACE WITH PENDANT
Silver and gold, decorated with niello
and set with semi-precious stones,
with small pendants in the form of
angels, and a large pendant of the
Madonna and Child.
ENGLISH (London): about 1906.
Designed and made by Harold
Stabler.
Given by Miss M. McLeish in
memory of Harold and Phoebe
Stabler
Circl. 502-1956

10 BROOCH
Silver openwork, set with an
enamelled floral plaque and with
amethysts.
ENGLISH (London): about 1900.
Designed and made by Nelson
Dawson; the enamel by his wife
Edith.
Circ. 264-1955

*11 PENDANT AND CHAIN
Gold and silver-gilt, set with an
enamel plaque of a cluster of irises,
and with drops of opal and amethyst.
ENGLISH (London): dated 1900.
Designed and made by Nelson
Dawson; the enamel, probably by
his wife Edith, signed with the
initial *D* enclosed by a leaf.
Circ. 263-1955
Nos. 11 & 12, given by Mrs Rhoda
Bickerdike and Miss Mary Dawson

12 BRACELET
Gold, the front cast with a female
nude; set with pearls and opals.
ENGLISH: about 1900-01. Designed
and made by A.C.C. Jahn.
Jahn Bequest
M.81-1947

13 BRACELET AND PENDANT
Enamelled plaques set in gold,
connected by gold chains.
SCOTTISH (Edinburgh): 1905.
Designed and made by Phoebe
Traquair; the central plaque signed
by the artist and dated 1905 on the
reverse.
Given by Mrs Crompton
Circ. 211-1953

1 HORNET BROOCH
Gold, with *plique-à-jour* and
translucent enamel.
Designed by C. Desroziers.
FRENCH (Paris): about 1900.
Maker's mark of Georges Fouquet
(1862-1957); signed: *G. FOUQUET*.
Paris warranty mark for 1847
onwards.
Acquired by the Museum from the
Paris 1900 Exhibition
957-1900

***2 TIARA COMB AND BODICE
ORNAMENT** ('Sweet Peas')
Bleached tortoise-shell comb; gold
hinge; the head or gallery of horn,
rough-carved into an arcade and
overlaid with sweet pea blossoms in
cast glass; enamelled gold stems. Set
with three topazes. The bodice
ornament has translucent and
plique-à-jour enamel wings, a topaz
with glass sweet peas in the centre.
FRENCH (Paris): about 1903-4.
Designed by René Lalique (1860-
1945) and made in his workshops.
The tiara comb signed (twice) and the
bodice ornament (once): *LALIQUE*.
M.116 & a-1966

*3 LABURNUM PLAQUE
Probably the front of a 'dog-collar'
(worn with rows of beads, pearls or
black ribbon round the neck), but
perhaps also used to conceal the
fastenings of a high collar. Gold
openwork, set with rose- and
brilliant-cut diamonds and decorated
with *plique-à-jour* enamel.
FRENCH: about 1900.
Given by Dame Joan Evans, P.P.S.A.
M.27-1962

4 BROOCH
Gold, with two translucent enamelled
goldfish; set with two fire opals.
FRENCH (Paris): 1904-06. Designed
by René Lalique and made in his
workshops. Signed: *LALIQUE*.
Bequeathed by Sir Claude Phillips
M.520-1924

5 BROOCH
Matted and burnished gold, with enamel, pearls and rose- and brilliant-cut diamonds; a relief of female heads, overlaid with mistletoe.
FRENCH (Paris): about 1903. Made in Georges Fouquet's workshops. Signed: *G. FOUQUET*. Paris warranty mark for 1847 onwards.
M.19-1979

*6 ORCHID HAIR ORNAMENT
Gold, with *plique-à-jour* enamel, brilliant-cut diamonds and rubies.
BELGIUM (Brussels): 1902. Designed and made by Philippe Wolfers (1858-1929). Signed with his monogram, *PW*, and inscribed: *EX. UNIQUE,* signifying that the design is the only one of its kind.
M.11-1962

7 WINGED COMB HEAD
Originally a tiara comb
Bleached tortoise-shell, set with rose- and brilliant-cut diamonds and pearls; the comb teeth are missing.
Probably FRENCH: about 1900.
M.16-1978

8 BROOCH
Enamelled copper, set with opals and pearls.
FRENCH: 1900. Designed and made by Annie Noufflard.
Acquired by the Museum from the Paris 1900 Exhibition
963-1901

9 PENDANT
Enamelled gold, set with brilliant-cut diamonds, emeralds and a ruby; hung with a pearl.
Probably GERMAN: about 1903.
Circ. 221-1960

10 PLAQUE
Translucent enamel on copper embossed with figures of a mother and child.
FRENCH (Paris): about 1905. Designed by René Lalique and made in his workshops. Signed: *LALIQUE.*
M.519-1924

11·PENDANT (Medusa head)
Gold, decorated with encrusted enamel.
FRENCH: about 1899. Attributed to René Lalique.
This is a variation of a brooch by Lalique in the form of a female head with flowers and waving corn.
M.521-1924
Nos. 10 & 11, bequeathed by Sir Claude Phillips

*12 BUCKLE
Cast silver, parcel-gilt.
FRENCH (Paris): about 1897. Designed by René Lalique and made in his workshops. Signed: *LALIQUE.*
French import mark introduced in 1893.
M.111-1966

*1 PENDANT-BROOCH
Enamelled gold and silver, set with rubies and an emerald. In the centre, an embossed relief of Christ on the cross in the form of a tree, after a medieval tradition, with the Heavenly City in the background.
ENGLISH: about 1906. Designed by Henry Wilson (1864-1934) and probably made in his Kent workshop. Formerly in the collection of Charles and Lavinia Handley-Read; acquired in their memory with the aid of Mr Thomas Stainton
M.73-1979

2 WINGED TIARA
Crystal and chalcedony set in gold decorated with enamelling; surmounted by an oxidised silver figure of Cupid in a shell.
ENGLISH: about 1908. Designed by Henry Wilson and probably made in his Kent workshop.
Circ. 362-1958

3 NECKLACE
Enamelled gold, set with emeralds.
ENGLISH: about 1905. Designed by Henry Wilson and probably made in his London workshop.
Lent by Miss Orrea Pernel
O.P.1.

4 NECKLACE
Gold, set with star rubies, emeralds and moonstones and decorated with an enamelled gold plaque of a running stag, seed pearls and baroque pearl drops.
ENGLISH: about 1910. Designed by Henry Wilson and made in his Kent workshop.
Circ. 364-1958

5 COMB
Silver, the head decorated with a pierced medallion of a crab, the symbol of the zodiacal sign Cancer; set with cabochon garnets.
ENGLISH: about 1900. Designed by Henry Wilson and probably made in his London workshop.
Circ. 214-1960

141

142

6 NECKLACE AND PENDANT
Silver wire openwork with gold
details, set with opals and emerald
pastes.
ENGLISH (Birmingham): about
1922. Designed by Georgie Cave
Gaskin (1866-1934) and made in the
Edgbaston workshop run in
association with her husband,
Arthur Gaskin (1862-1928).
Circ. 355-1923

7 PENDANT
Silver wire framework, set with opals
and emerald pastes.
ENGLISH (Birmingham): about
1920. Designed by Georgie Cave
Gaskin and possibly made in the
Gaskins' workshop in Edgbaston.
The reverse signed with the initial *G*.
A re-working of a theme first used by
Mrs Gaskin in about 1910.
Circ. 222-1921

8 NECKLACE WITH PENDANT
('Love-in-a-Mist')
Enamelled silver with framework set
with pearls; pearl drops, turquoise
clasp; silver guard chains.
ENGLISH (Olton, Warwickshire):
about 1910. Designed by Georgie
Cave Gaskin and made in the
Gaskins' workshop in Olton.
Made for Mrs Emmeline H. Cadbury;
presented by her to the Museum
Circ. 359-1958

9 BROOCH
Silver wire framework, set with opals
and emerald pastes.
ENGLISH (Birmingham): about
1922. Designed by Georgie Cave
Gaskin and made in the Gaskins'
workshop in Edgbaston; the reverse
signed with the initial *G*.
Circ. 896-1923

10 PENDANT
Silver wire framework, set with opals,
tourmalines and emerald pastes.
ENGLISH (Birmingham): about
1920. Designed by Georgie Cave
Gaskin and probably made in the
Gaskins' workshop in Edgbaston.
Circ. 223-1921

**11 NECKLACE WITH
PENDANT** ('Clover')
Silver wire framework with gold
details, set with opals and topaz.
ENGLISH (Birmingham): about
1920. Designed by Georgie Cave
Gaskin and probably made in the
Gaskins' workshop in Edgbaston.
A re-working of a theme first used by
Mrs Gaskin in about 1910.
Circ. 226-1921
Nos. 6, 7, 9, 10, 11, purchased from
the Gaskins

1 NECKLACE
Silver openwork, decorated with
enamelled flowers and set with
cabochon moonstones in gold collets.
ENGLISH (? Birmingham): about
1902. Inspired by the work of Arthur
and Georgie Gaskin.
Circ. 348-1963

2 BROOCH
Silver and gold openwork, set with
amethysts and pearl blisters,
with a baroque peal pendant.
ENGLISH (Birmingham): about
1905. Designed and made by Carrie
Copson, a pupil of Arthur Gaskin at
the Vittoria Street School for
Silversmiths and Jewellers.
Circ. 619-1954

3 CLOAK CLASP
Silver, set with roundels of *plique-à-
jour* enamel representing the infant
Cupid, and flowers; the ends of
crystal, mounted with silver,
decorated with enamel and set with
pearls.
ENGLISH: about 1903. Designed by
Henry Wilson and probably made in
his London workshop.
Circ. 361-1958

4 BELT CLASP
Silver, set with amethysts, garnets,
heavily-flawed emeralds and other
stones; a large openwork boss in the
centre ornamented with sprays.
ENGLISH: about 1905. Designed by
Henry Wilson and probably made in
his London workshop.
Handley-Read Collection
M.29-1972

5 BUCKLE AND BELT-TAG
Silver, decorated with enamel and set
with moonstones, amethysts and
other stones; cast roundels of stags
and birds.
ENGLISH: about 1905. Designed by
Henry Wilson and probably made in
his London workshop.
Lent anonymously

*6 MORSE (the 'Tree of Life')
Gold frame, backed with silver and set with emeralds, enclosing a translucent enamel of the Crucifixion.
ENGLISH (LONDON): about 1906. Designed by Alexander Fisher and made by Fisher and J. Davis.
Shown London, 1907; Ghent, 1913; Paris (Louvre), 1914.
M.39-1968

7 BUCKLE
Silver.
FRENCH (Paris): about 1900.
Maker's mark of Ferdinand Erhart.
M.49-1970

8 JASMINE BROOCH
Enamelled gold.
Probably GERMAN: about 1903.
Circ. 480-1963

9 STICK-PIN
Gold, the head enamelled in red and set with rose- and brilliant-cut diamonds in the form of a Russian imperial crown above the monogram *E*.
AUSTRO-HUNGARIAN (Vienna): about 1890. Maker's mark (? AN). Vienna standard mark for 1865-1922 and an indecipherable mark.
Possibly made for Elizabeth Feodorovna (1864-1918), daughter of Louis IV, Grand Duke of Hesse and the Rhine, who married the Grand Duke Serge of Russia (1857-1905) in 1884.
M.29-1981

10 PARASOL HANDLE
Carved and bleached horn, the head a floral trellis, set with pearls and small rubies. With it are eight tortoise-shell covers for rib-ends.
FRENCH (Paris): about 1900.
Signed: *L. GAILLARD.*
M.5-1980

11 PARASOL HANDLE
Wood, the head rock crystal, engraved with flowers and set with amethysts; enamelled gold collar. With it, eight gilt covers for rib-ends.
The original case stamped: *J.C. VICKERY/179, 181 & 183 REGENT ST. W.*
Given by Mrs Antony Acton
M.32-h-1970

CASE 21
BOARD A
NO. 2

CASE 21
BOARD D
NO. 4

CASE 21
BOARD A
NO. 7

CASE 21
BOARD C
NO. 3

CASE 21
BOARD C
NO. 4

CASE 21
BOARD E
NO. 3

CASE 21
BOARD F
NO. 3

CASE 21
BOARD G
NO. 1

CASE 21
BOARD G
NO. 4

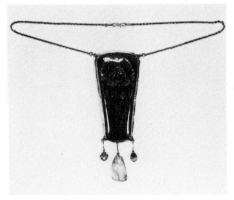

CASE 21
BOARD G
NO. 11

CASE 21
BOARD H
NO. 2

CASE 21
BOARD H
NO. 3

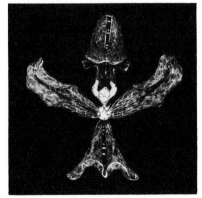

CASE 21
BOARD H
NO. 6

CASE 21
BOARD H
NO. 13

CASE 21
BOARD I
NO. 1

CASE 21
BOARD J
NO. 6

Case 22 Board A

ARTS AND CRAFTS:
1896-1906

1 NECKLACE
Silver wire openwork with gold
pellets; mounted with turquoises.
Incomplete: see no. 2 below.
ENGLISH (Chipping Campden):
about 1903. Designed by C.R. Ashbee
(1863-1942) and made by the Guild of
Handicraft.
Given by Mrs G. Tekvar
M.37-1982

2 BROOCH
Silver-gilt and gold, enamelled and
set with turquoises; a framed plaque
of a ship in full sail, representing
the 'Craft of the Guild'. Formerly
the centre of an elaborate pendent
front to the necklace above; two
turquoises were added to the
corners of the frame when the piece,
removed from the necklace, was
converted into a brooch.
ENGLISH (Chipping Campden):
about 1903. Designed by C.R. Ashbee
and made by the Guild of Handicraft.
The complete necklace was shown at
the second annual exhibition of the
Guild of Handicraft, Dering Yard,
1903.
Given by Mrs J.C. O'G. Anderson
Circ. 118-1959

3 BROOCH
Circular enamelled copper plaque set
in a silver frame; decorated with
looping silver wires, set with blister
pearls and hung with baroque pearls.
To judge by a contemporary
photograph of the brooch, the
baroque pearl in the centre is a
replacement for a stone.
ENGLISH (London): about 1896.
Designed by C.R. Ashbee and made
by the Guild of Handicraft.
A brooch of similar design was
shown by Ashbee at the Arts and
Crafts Exhibition, 1896.
M.43-1980

4 PENDANT AND CHAIN
Silver-gilt, set with cabochon
amethysts, moonstones and garnets.
ENGLISH: about 1905. This piece,
characteristic of the Artificers'
Guild (originally founded by Nelson
Dawson and transferred to
Montogue Fordham in 1903), is
perhaps the work of J. Paul Cooper or
of Edward Spencer (1872-1938), two
of its principal artists.
M.17-1981

5 PENDANT AND CHAIN
Silver, set with labradorites and an
opal.
DANISH (Copenhagen): about 1906.
Made in the workshop of Georg
Jensen and signed with his full
name, his initials, and numbered:
5826 and *G.18*.
Given by Mrs G. Tekvar
M.4-1982

Case 22 Board B

ART DECO:
1913-about 1950

1 BASKET PENDANT
Gold wire basket, filled with flowers
formed of pearls, rubies, emeralds
and brilliant-cut and pear-shaped
diamonds.
WEST EUROPEAN: ? about 1920.
Cory Bequest
M.80-1951

2 BASKET BROOCH
Small brilliant-cut diamonds set in
gold; hardstone flowers.
? GERMAN: about 1925. Maker's
mark: BS. Mark *750*, for 18 carat
gold.
M.359-1977

3 PAIR OF EARRINGS
Brilliant-cut diamonds set in white
gold, each long drop with black-
stained chalcedony cut *en cabochon*.
FRENCH (Paris): about 1925.
Maker's mark illegible. Signed:
JANESICH.
Paris warranty marks for 1847
onwards and other illegible marks.
M.24 & a-1982

*4 PENDANT
With suspension ribbon and pin.
Brilliant-cut diamonds, carved
sapphires, black chalcedony and
jade, set in a platinum and gold
frame in the Chinese taste.
FRENCH (Paris): about 1925.
Maker's mark, AJ. Signed:
JANESICH. Paris warranty marks
for platinum and gold.
M.74-1979

5 BROOCH
Brilliant-cut diamonds and black-
stained chalcedony set in a lozenge-
shaped platinum frame.
FRENCH (Paris): about 1912.
Purchased in the New York branch of
Cartier by the donor's father as a
present for her mother, Christmas
1913.
Given by Lady Reigate
M.212-1976

146

*6 CYPRESS TREE PIN
Emeralds, brilliant-cut diamonds
and black-stained chalcedony set in
white gold and platinum.
WEST EUROPEAN: about 1928.
Struck with the French warranty
mark introduced in December 1927
for foreign wares in mixed gold and
platinum. Sold by Lacloche frères at
their London branch. The original
case (not shown) stamped:
*LACLOCHE FRERES 15 RUE DE
LA PAIX/ PARIS/ & 2 BOND
STREET/ LONDON.*
Bequeathed by Miss J.H.G. Gollan
M.25-1976

7 BROOCH-CLIP ('Reflection')
White gold shell, set with sapphires,
brilliant-cut diamonds and
moonstones.
FRENCH (Paris): about 1935.
Signed: *TRABERT & HOEFFER,*
and *MAUBOUSSIN:* struck with the
pattern number *4378.*
M.168-1978

*8 BROOCH
Yellow and white brilliant-cut and
baguette diamonds, carved rubies,
emeralds and sapphires set in
platinum and gold, with two large
star sapphire drops. In the form of a
vase of flowers over a looped
pendant.
FRENCH (Paris): about 1930.
Maker's mark illegible. Paris
warranty marks for gold and
platinum.
M.142-1978

9 BROOCH-PENDANT
Turquoise matrix cut *en cabochon,* in
a black-stained chalcedony frame
decorated with brilliant-cut
diamonds in white gold.
FRENCH (Paris): about 1930.
Signed: *G. FOUQUET.* French
import mark introduced in 1893 for
gold articles; pattern number *11427.*
M.167-1978

10 BROOCH
Lapis lazuli cut *en cabochon* and blue
glass set in white gold.
FRENCH (Paris): 1934. Signed:
RAYMOND TEMPLIER; pattern
number *16290.* A related drawing in
the Templier record books survives in
private possession in France.
M.18-1979

11 WATCH-BRACELET
The band of flexible gold links; in the
centre, a watch signed:
*VACHERON-CONSTANTIN/
GENEVE/ SWISS,* concealed by a
hinged cover set with brilliant-cut
diamonds and sapphires.
WEST EUROPEAN: about 1950.
Maker's mark. *IR.* Indecipherable
? animal stamp.
M.25-1982

12 NECKLACE
Two tubes of flexible white and
yellow gold, one ending in a band of
rubies and the other with sapphires;
pointed gold drops; detachable scroll
clip centre, set with brilliants banded
by baguette rubies and sapphires.
ENGLISH: London hallmarks for
1947-48, for 18 carat gold. Maker's
mark, E.P. Acquired in a case (not
shown) bearing the stamp of
Wartski, of London and Llandudno.
M.29-1982

1 BRACELET
Chromium-plated brass, set with
hematite.
Designed by Naum Slutzky (1898-
1965) of the Bauhaus, 1929. The
design GERMAN (Dessau): 1929. Re-
made by the artist in England, 1960.
Circ. 1235-1967

2 NECKLACE WITH PENDANT
Chromium-plated brass tubes; the
pendant panelled.
Designed by Naum Slutzky.
The design GERMAN (Dessau):
1929. Re-made by the artist, 1960.
Circ. 1234-1967

3 NECKLACE
Chromium-plated brass tubes.
Designed by Naum Slutzky.
The design GERMAN (Dessau): 1929.
Re-made by the artist, 1960.
Circ. 1233-1967

**4 TELESCOPIC CIGARETTE
HOLDER**
Stained wood, inlaid with silver wire.
WEST EUROPEAN: about 1925.
Circ. 40-1972

5 BROOCH ('Sheba Regina')
Gold and silver, set with a carved
ivory head of Sheba, mother-of-pearl,
pearls, opals, tourmalines, crystals
and other stones; enamelled leaves.
ENGLISH (Birmingham): about
1936. Designed and made by George
Hunt. Mark, GH in a shield.
Exhibited Paris, 1937; Royal Society
of Miniaturists, 1938.
Circ. 657-1969

6 PEACOCK BROOCH
Silver-gilt openwork, enamelled and
set with opals, moonstones, garnets,
peridots and pink zircon.
ENGLISH (Birmingham): 1936.
Designed and made by George Hunt.
Maker's mark, GH.
M.41-1971

7 BROOCH
Silver and silver-gilt openwork, set
with moonstones and sapphires.
ENGLISH (Birmingham): 1935.
Designed and made by George Hunt.
M.44-1971

Case 22 Board D

LOAN COLLECTION OF JEWELLERY FROM A RUSSIAN FAMILY

*8 BROOCH
Carved Chinese jade set in silver and gold, with mother-of-pearl, an almandine garnet and an opal.
ENGLISH (Birmingham): about 1930. Maker's mark, GH.
M.42-1971
Nos. 6-8, bequeathed by Mrs E.D. Amphlett

The jewellery is lent by Baron von Düsterlohe *gennant* von Distler, whose family settled in the Baltic territories of the Russian Empire in the sixteenth century. The family fortunes were greatly advanced through a connection with the descendants of Plato Zoubov, a Moslem from the Crimea who joined the Russian army and became the last lover of Catherine the Great (reigned 1762-1796). Catherine made Zoubov a Prince.

1 SERPENT BRACELET
Enamelled gold, set with rose- and brilliant-cut diamonds and emeralds.
ENGLISH: about 1835.
Reputedly once owned by Mrs FitzHerbert, who in 1785 made a morganatic marriage with George, Prince of Wales (1762-1830), later George IV. Outliving the King, Mrs FitzHerbert died in 1837.

2 PAIR OF EARRINGS
Emeralds and brilliant-cut diamonds set in gold; the screw fittings are a replacement for the original hooks.
RUSSIAN: about 1805, in the French manner.

3 BRACELET
Gold; the clasp set with brilliant-cut diamonds and a large cabochon emerald which came from the treasury of the Shah of Persia and was sold to Catherine the Great shortly before her death. Passing through an intermediary to her lover, Prince Zoubov, the stone had a varied history until it came into the hands of the present owner's great-grandfather in about 1865. By this time it had already been set in the bracelet.
The bracelet RUSSIAN: about 1830.

4 SPRAY FROM A TIARA
Brilliant-cut diamonds in an open-backed gold setting.
Formerly owned by Prince Plato Zoubov.
RUSSIAN: early 19th century.

5 FOUR DRESS RINGS
Gold, set variously with brilliant-cut diamonds, emeralds, sapphires and rubies.
RUSSIAN: late 19th century.
For use in Town or Country.

6 SIX 'MORNING RINGS'
Gold, set with brilliant-cut diamonds.
RUSSIAN: about 1860.
Worn in combination by noblemen to harmonise with their clothes.

7 BROOCH
Brilliant-cut diamonds and rubies set in gold.
RUSSIAN: about 1914-20.

8 BROOCH-CLIP
Rock crystal embellished with two navette diamonds springing from clusters.
RUSSIAN: about 1914-17.
Given to the lender's mother as a wedding present by Madame Naryshkin, Mistress of the Robes to the Tsarina, Alexandra Feodorovna (1872-1918).

9 BROOCH
Opal, originally belonging to Prince Plato Zoubov, re-mounted with a brilliant-cut diamond surround.
? RUSSIAN: about 1914-16.

10 BROOCH
Gold, decorated with enamel and set with rose-and brilliant-cut diamonds.
RUSSIAN (St. Petersburg): about 1914-17.
Purchased from Fabergé by the lender's grandmother (the original Fabergé case has survived).

11 SPRAY
Ruby and brilliant-cut diamond flowers, set in gold and silver; enamelled leaves and pendent briolette diamond.
Probably VIENNESE: about 1880.

12 BROOCH
A Baroque pearl, said to have come from an Indian temple and formerly owned by Prince Plato Zoubov; re-mounted in Paris with rose-cut diamonds and rubies.
FRENCH (Paris): about 1895.

13 RING
The Zoubov ruby, given to Lieutenant Zoubov by Catherine the Great; re-set as a ring with a brilliant-cut diamond surround.
? FRENCH (Paris): about 1935-50.

About 1870-1958

148

14 RING
An emerald set in a brilliant-cut
diamond surround.
RUSSIAN (St. Petersburg): early
20th century.

15 CORONET BROOCH (a hair
ornament)
Brilliant-cut diamonds and emeralds
set in gold; the stones taken from a
long brooch/pin presented to the
lender's grandmother in 1865,
probably by Tsar Alexander II (1818-
1881).
RUSSIAN: early 20th century.

16 PAIR OF SLEEVE-LINKS
Gold, set with brilliant-cut diamonds
and emeralds.
RUSSIAN: won in a yachting event
by the lender's father, 1913-14.
Damaged in the Revolution, re-set
1920/1923.

1 CROSS WITH CHAIN
The cross gold, set with half-pearls
and a sapphire; blue enamelled
border. Twisted gold rope chain.
Designed by Thomas Connold.
ENGLISH: about 1870. Executed by
an unknown maker.
Bequeathed by Miss F.E. Connold
M.19-1981

**2 NECKLACE, PAIR OF
EARRINGS AND TWO
BROOCHES**
Opals, rubies (including star rubies)
and stained chalcedony set in silver.
Designed by Sybil Dunlop.
ENGLISH (London): about 1934.
Made under the direction of W.W.
Nathanson in Sybil Dunlop's
workshop in Kensington Church
Street. Signed on the reverse of the
settings: *S. Dunlop/London W.8.*
Acquired in a box with the label of
Sybil Dunlop (not shown)
M.27-d-1979

3 BROOCH
Silver, set with a polished pebble.
Made after a design by Jean (Hans)
Arp (1887-1966).
The design FRENCH: 1960. Made by
Johanan Peter at Ein Hod, Israel.
Stamped on the reverse: *MADE IN
ISRAEL/ST 925.* Peter's label is also
applied to the back.
Circ. 395-1962

4 BROOCH
Silver.
Designed by Henning Koppel for
Georg Jensen.
DANISH (Copenhagen): about 1950.
Stamped *GEORG JENSEN/
STERLING/DENMARK/327.*
London import marks for 1958 and
maker's mark of Georg Jensen Ltd.
Circ.136-1959

5 NECKLACE
Brilliant-cut diamonds in gold claw
settings in knife-edge gold mounts.
Detachable lozenge-shaped pendant
with drops, hooked on to the necklace
with diamond festoons.
RUSSIAN (St Petersburg): late 19th
century. Said to have been made by
the Fabergé workmaster August
Holmström (1829-1903). St.
Petersburg mark in use until 1899. In
wooden case with velvet lining,
stamped with the name and Moscow
address of the Fabergé firm.
Given by the lender's father to his
mother as a wedding present in
December 1916 or January 1917.
Lent by Baron von Düsterlohe

6 PENDANT AND CHAIN
Silver, set with three pieces of smoky
quartz.
Designed by Jan Salakari.
FINNISH: about 1955-60. Made by
the firm of Kaunis Koru.
Circ. 62-1962

7 BROOCH
Gold and silver.
ITALIAN: 1958. Designed and made
by Arnaldo Pomodoro; signed by the
artist and dated 1958.
Circ. 63-1960

8 BROOCH
Silver-gilt, set with a brilliant-cut
diamond.
Designed and modelled by Bernard
Meadows.
ENGLISH: London hallmarks for
1961-62. Made by H.J. Company from
the artist's wax model. The original
gold version of this design was
awarded a third prize in the De Beers
competition for British jewellery,
1961.
Circ. 15-1962

*9 BROOCH
Oxidised silver.
Designed by John Donald.
ENGLISH: London hallmarks for
1960-61. Maker's mark of John
Donald. One of a pair originally
acquired from the artist by the
Worshipful Company of Goldsmiths
at the International Exhibition of
Modern Jewellery held at
Goldsmiths' Hall in 1961.
Purchased from the Company.
M.346-1977

10 BROOCH
Silver-gilt, set with cabochon rubies.
Designed and modelled by Robert
Adams.
ENGLISH: 1961. Made by H.J.
Company from the artist's plaster
model.
The original version of this design, in
gold and diamonds, was awarded a
third prize in the De Beers
competition for British jewellery,
1961.
Circ. 12-1962
Nos. 8 & 10 are part of a collection of
jewellery modelled by painters and
sculptors at the joint suggestion
of the Goldsmiths' Company and the
Victoria & Albert Museum. The
complete collection, not shown here
for reasons of space, includes works
by William Scott, Elisabeth Frink
and Terry Frost.

1 NECKLACE
Brass spirals.
FRENCH (Paris): about 1938.
Designed and made by Alexander
Calder (1898-   ).
Shown at the Mayor Gallery,
London, 1938 and at the
International Exhibition of Modern
Jewellery, Goldsmiths' Hall,
London, 1961.
Circ. 19-1962

2 COLLAR
Silver-gilt, cast and mounted as
overlapping units.
ENGLISH: London hallmarks for
1968. Maker's mark of Anthony
Hawkesley. Signed: *Anthony
Hawkesley* and numbered: *6/50*.
Given by the artist
M.25-1973

3 NECKLET
Gold wire twisted into irregular
panels as a dog-collar.
GERMAN: 1957. Designed and made
by E.R. Nele.
Acquired from the Milan Triennale,
1957, and shown at the International
Exhibition of Modern Jewellery,
Goldsmiths' Hall, 1961.
Circ. 475-1960

4 COLLAR
Silver-gilt; inspired by a wing collar.
Designed by Richard Smith.
ITALIAN (Milan): 1968. Made by
Gem Montebello of Milan and signed
by the makers. Stamped: *800,*
signifying the silver standard.
Artist's proof for the numbered
edition of two made in gold.
Given by the artist
Circ. 489-1972

5 PLAQUE ('Legende 3')
Silver and acrylic; part of a series
which included two brooches, the
designs for which are in the V&A
Print Room.
GERMAN: 1975. Designed and made
by Rüdiger Lorenzen.
Acquired from the Scottish Arts
Council touring exhibition, Jewellery
in Europe, 1976.
M.183-1976

Group of pieces in iron wire with
traces of silver (probably indicating
that the metal was formerly plated),
set with pastes and fragments of
shell; designed and executed by Sir
Alfred Gilbert (1854-1934). The
jewellery probably dates from the
late 1890s and early 1900s, though it
is perhaps slightly later than a
documented necklet in a private
collection which was made by the
artist for Miss Dorothy Quick in
1897/98, using strips of metal and
wire in combination.
From the artist's studio; exhibited at
the Royal Academy, 1934 (catalogue
no. 1512).
Presented by Mr Sigismund Goetze
in the name of the artist.
The complete collection (not all
shown here):
M.74-85-1934

CASE 22
BOARD B
NO. 4

CASE 22
BOARD B
NO. 6

150

CASE 22
BOARD B
NO. 8

CASE 22
BOARD C
NO. 8

CASE 22
BOARD E
NO. 9

Case 23 Boards A-E

WORK BY MODERN ARTIST-CRAFTSMEN

The objects on these boards will be changed periodically to enable the Museum's expanding collection of contemporary work to be shown by turns. The artists' names are placed at the side of the board together with the accession numbers. Further pieces, including jewellery in titanium and resin, are displayed in Case 42. These last will also be changed from time to time. Two necklaces (by Wendy Ramshaw and Georgina Follett) are included in the permanent display in Case 24. Artists, designers and craftsmen represented in the modern collection include the following:

Vicki Ambery-Smith
Robert Adams
Muriel Ainger
Malcolm Appleby
Martin Baker
Frances Bendixson
Ingeborg Bratman
Michael Burton
Sophie Chell
Kevin Coates
Ros Conway
David Courts
Marilyn Davidson
Alan Davie
Edward de Large
Thomas Dobbie
John Donald
Roger Doyle
Nichola Fletcher
Gerda Flöckinger
Georgina Follett
Bertel Gardberg
Brian Glassar
Martha Gumn
Bill Hackett
Anthony Hawkesley
Susanna Heron
Barbara Jardine-Otway
Michael Kane
Mary Lloyd
Rüdiger Lorenzen
Alistair Mc Callum
Catherine Mannheim
Julia Manheim
Bernard Meadows
Jacqueline Mina
Clarissa (Mitchell)
Roger Morris
E.R. Nele
Celia Over
Martin Page
Beverley Phillips
Diego Piazza
Mario Pinton
Arnaldo Pomadoro

Case 24

PENDANTS AND NECKLACES:
about 1870-1977

David Poston
Sara Pothecary
Wendy Ramshaw
Jan Salakari
Herman Schafran
Richard Smith
Gunilla Treen
Karen Wagstaff
David Watkins

1 PENDENT CROSS
Silver-gilt openwork, decorated with *plique-à-jour* enamel in relief and set with diamonds.
FRENCH: about 1905. Signed *CTE DU SUAU DE LA CROIX*. Paris warranty mark for 1838 onwards.
553-1905

2 NECKLACE, EARRINGS AND PENDANT
From a parure which also includes a pair of bracelets and a brooch.
Late 18th century Wedgwood medallions set in gold.
ENGLISH: the setting about 1870.
Pfungst Reavil Bequest
M.24-b-1969

3 MOTH PENDANT WITH CHAIN
Enamelled gold, set with rose- and brilliant-cut diamonds.
FRENCH (Paris): about 1900. Made by Lucien Gaillard (b.1861). Signed by the artist.
M.24-1960

4 PEACOCK PENDANT
Gold, decorated with *plique-à-jour* enamel and set with rose- and brilliant-cut diamonds, opals and emeralds. Opal drop.
FRENCH (Paris): about 1900. Made by L. Gautrait. Signed with the maker's initials. Other versions of this jewel are known to exist.
Acquired by the Museum from the Paris 1900 Exhibition
965-1901

*5 PENDANT
Enamelled gold, set with rubies; obverse, a bust of a woman against irises; pearl drop wanting.
FRENCH (Paris): 1900. Made by Emile Froment-Meurice (1837-1913); signed by the artist.
Bequeathed by Captain Walter Dasent, R.N.
M.347-1940

6 PENDANT
Gold, decorated with *plique-à-jour* enamel and set with a peridot and brilliant-cut diamonds; representing a woman in a woodland; drop wanting.
FRENCH (Paris): about 1900; ? mark of Joé Descomps (b.1872).
M.L. Horn Bequest
M.40-1961

7 NECKLACE WITH PENDANT
Gold, set with opals, pearls and chrysoprases and decorated with enamel; the pendant medallion has a kneeling figure of a girl.
ENGLISH (London): about 1905. Designed by Henry Wilson (1864-1934) and made in his London workshop.
Cir. 363-1958

8 PENDANT
Gold, set with a ruby, sapphire, emeralds, pearls, peridots and moonstones and decorated with enamel.
ENGLISH: about 1908. Designed by Henry Wilson and probably made in his Kent workshop.
Anonymous loan

9 PENDANT
Gold openwork, with baroque pearls, sapphires, emeralds and semi-precious stones. At the back, hidden by the baroque pearls, a pendant relief of the Virgin and Child with the legend: *MATER CHRISTI*.
ENGLISH (London): about 1900. Designed by Henry Wilson and made in his London workshop. Maker's mark, HW in monogram.
Circ. 331-1960

10 PENDANT
Gold, set with smoky quartz.
FINNISH: about 1958. Designed by Bertel Gardberg and made by the Westerbrook Company.
Circ. 24-1962

*11 NECKLACE
Gold, turned and decorated with enamel.
ENGLISH (London): 1971. Designed and made by Wendy Ramshaw. First shown in the exhibition of British design held in the Louvre, 1971, and part of a group of jewellery (see also Case 34, Board M, nos.1 & 3) which gained the artist a Council of Industrial Design award in 1972.
M.169-1976

PENDANTS:
late 16th and early 17th centuries

152

12 NECKLACE
Gold, hung with opal beads and with flower pendants in gold and *plique-à-jour* enamel.
ENGLISH: 1977. Designed and made by Georgina Follett.
M.149-1978

CASE 24
NO. 5

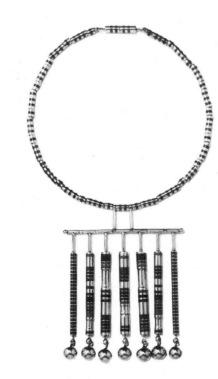

CASE 24
NO. 11

1 VASE PENDANT
Crystal, mounted in silver-gilt, with paintings of the Crucifixion and St. Francis receiving the Stigmata.
SPANISH: 17th century.
Alfred Williams Hearn Gift
M.61-1923

2 PENDANT (The Virgin of the Immaculate Conception)
Enamelled gold, set with table-cut crystals; hung with pearls.
SPANISH (Saragossa): about 1600-1620.
Jewels of the Virgin of the Immaculate Conception, who was portrayed standing on a sickle moon, were common in Spain in the first half of the 17th century. They were a manifestation of the movement to have the Immaculate Conception promulgated as dogma.
From the Treasury of the Cathedral of the Virgin of the Pillar, Saragossa
340-1870

3 PENDANT (The Virgin of the Pillar with attendant angels).
Enamelled gold, set with table- and rose-cut crystals.
SPANISH (Saragossa): early 17th century.
From the Treasury of the Cathedral of the Virgin of the Pillar, Saragossa
342-1870

4 PENDANT (The Virgin of the Pillar with adoring angels)
Enamelled gold, set with table- and rose-cut crystals; hung with pearls.
SPANISH (Saragossa): about 1610-20.
From the Treasury of the Cathedral of the Virgin of the Pillar, Saragossa
341-1870

5 VASE PENDANT
Rock crystal, mounted in enamelled gold; the suspension loop hung with a pearl.
WEST EUROPEAN: late 16th century.
Lent from the Salting Bequest
M.531-1910

6 PENDANT
Enamelled gold openwork, set with rubies and hung with pearls; surmounted by a Muse. The suspension loop and plaque a replacement in silver, set with a garnet and hung with a pearl.
GERMAN: early 17th century.
2756-1855

7 POMANDER
Enamelled gold openwork, decorated and hung with pearls; worn at the end of a girdle.
Probably GERMAN: early 17th century.
298-1854

8 RELIQUARY CROSS
Rock crystal and enamelled gold, with cavities containing relics.
MEDITERRANEAN: early 17th century.
330-1864

9 PENDENT CROSS
Rock crystal and enamelled gold, containing a relic of the True Cross. Painted on one side with the Crucifixion and on the other with the Instruments of the Passion and the initials *LSC* (SANCTAE LIGNUM CRUCIS).
SPANISH: late 16th century.
Lent from the Salting Bequest
M.538-1910

10 PENDANT
Enamelled gold frame, set with an onyx cameo head of Jupiter, under crystal; the cameo a replacement.
The setting ITALIAN: second half of 16th century, the cameo 18th century.
323-1891

11 PENDANT
Enamelled gold openwork, set with a table-cut diamond, emeralds, rubies; architectural setting with Diana, stag and hound; hung with pearls.
SOUTH GERMAN: ? about 1580.
Lent from the Salting Bequest
M.533-1910

PENDANTS:
late 16th-18th century

12 PENDANT
Jacinth bust of a woman, mounted in gold, hung with pearls; the reverse engraved with the Virgin of the Assumption.
The jacinth bust HELLENISTIC: 1st century BC; the setting early 17th century.
Purchased in Madrid
294-1866

13 PENDENT CROSS
Rock crystal, mounted in enamelled gold; perhaps from a religious vessel, though fitted with a suspension loop.
SPANISH: early 17th century.
469-1869

14 PENDANT
Enamelled gold, hung with a pearl; obverse, the Vernicle; reverse, the Agnus Dei and Instruments of the Passion.
WEST EUROPEAN: late 16th century.
Lent from the Salting Bequest
M.532-1910

*15 PENDANT
Onyx cameo head of Hercules set in enamelled gold; the sapphire drop and emeralds set in silver-gilt are modern additions.
GERMAN: last third of 16th century.
297-1854

16 PENDANT
Enamelled gold, set with rubies and point- and table-cut diamonds; architectural setting with the Adoration of the Magi; hung with a pearl.
SOUTH GERMAN: about 1580.
Anonymous loan

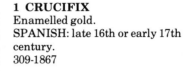

CASE 25
NO. 15

1 CRUCIFIX   153
Enamelled gold.
SPANISH: late 16th or early 17th century.
309-1867

2 PENDENT CROSS
Table-cut amethysts, set in enamelled gold, with three fleurs-de-lis terminals.
SPANISH: about 1600-1620.
From the Treasury of the Cathedral of the Virgin of the Pillar, Saragossa
344-1870

*3 PENDANT (the Agnus Dei)
Enamelled gold, set with a table-cut diamond and garnets; hung with pearls.
HUNGARIAN: late 16th century.
Harley Teleki Collection
M.456-1936

4 PENDENT SCENT FLASK
(a cat on a cushion)
A baroque pearl in the form of a cat's body set in enamelled gold with an emerald, rubies and pearls.
WEST EUROPEAN: about 1575.
Lent from the Salting Bequest
M.535-1910

*5 PENDANT (a lizard)
Enamelled gold, set with pearls and an emerald.
WEST EUROPEAN: late 16th century.
Lent from the Salting Bequest
M.537-1910

6 CRUCIFIX
Gold, decorated with filigree and enamel; hung with pearls.
ADRIATIC: late 16th century.
M.115-1909

7 CRUCIFIX
Purple glass, mounted in enamelled gold; pearl drop.
MEDITERRANEAN: late 17th century.
Murray Bequest
M.998-1910

8 PENDANT (a dragon)
Enamelled gold, set with emeralds
and rubies; pearl drops.
? COLONIAL SPANISH: early 17th
century.
Lent from the Salting Bequest
M.536-1910

*9 PENDANT (the 'Gatacre Jewel')
An amethyst cameo of Medusa in a
ribbon and cornucopia frame; the
pearl drops a replacement and the
enamelled plate at the back removed
and reinstated upside down at some
stage.
The cameo probably late ROMAN;
the setting ?ENGLISH: about
1550-60. Similar ribbon frames
appear in engravings by Virgil
Solis (1514-1562).
The jewel belonged to the Gatacre
family of Shropshire and was
romantically known as the 'Fair
Maid of Gatacre' after Joan (b.1509),
daughter of Robert Gatacre.
M.7-1982

*10 THE CANNING JEWEL
(a Merman)
A baroque pearl mounted in
enamelled gold set with pearls, table-
cut diamonds and carved Indian
rubies, the latter added when the
jewel was in India. Various parts
were re-backed, probably in India;
the blister pearl pendant also a
replacement.
The design probably FLEMISH, the
execution ITALIAN: about 1570.
Traditionally said to have been given
by a Medici prince to a Moghul
emperor.
Acquired in India by Charles John,
2nd Viscount Canning, Governor-
general of India, 1856-62.
Given by Mrs Edward S. Harkness
M.2697-1931

11 PENDANT (the Pelican in its
Piety)
Enamelled gold, set with a foiled red
paste and hung with pearls; the
bird's back decorated with black-and-
white moresques.
SPANISH: about 1550-75.
335-1870

12 PENDANT (a parrot on a perch)
Enamelled gold, set with a table-cut
foiled crystal and hung with pearls.
SPANISH: about 1600.
337-1870

13 PENDENT SCENT FLASK
A pine cone mounted in enamelled
gold.
SPANISH: about 1600.
339-1870
Nos. 11-13, from the Treasury of the
Cathedral of the Virgin of the Pillar,
Saragossa

14 GNADENPFENNING
Enamelled gold, set with a medal of
Maximilian III (1557-1618),
Archduke of Austria, by Alessandro
Abondio (c. 1570- after 1645), dated
1612; enamelled with the Archduke's
arms.
SOUTH GERMAN: early 17th
century.
Lent from the Salting Bequest
M.547-1910

*15 PENDANT (a hound on a
cornucopia)
Enamelled gold, set with rubies,
table-cut diamonds and an emerald;
hung with pearls.
SPANISH: about 1603. In the
manner of the Barcelona goldsmith
Gabriel Ramon.
From the Treasury of the Cathedral
of the Virgin of the Pillar, Saragossa
336-1870

16 GNADENPFENNIG
Enamelled gold, set with an
enamelled medal of Wilhelm, Count
Palatine of the Rhine (1548-1626),
dated 1572; hung with pearls.
Spitzer Collection
Lent from the Salting Bequest
M.548-1910

17 PENDANT (a hound on a
cornucopia)
Enamelled gold, set with spinels,
crystals and an emerald; hung with
pearls.
SPANISH: about 1603. In the
manner of Gabriel Ramon.
From the Treasury of the Cathedral
of the Virgin of the Pillar, Saragossa
334-1870

18 GNADENPFENNIG
Enamelled gold, set with a medal of
Alberecht VI of Bavaria (1584-1666),
after a wax portrait of 1618 by
Alessandro Abondio; hung with
pearls.
GERMAN (Munich): about 1620. The
medal, as well as the setting,
probably executed by Christian
Ulrich Eberl (active 1600-1634).
Tross Collection, Paris
69-1867

*19 PENDANT (a three-masted
ship)
Enamelled gold, hung with pearls.
GREEK ISLANDS: probably 18th
century.
Formerly described as Venetian, 16th
century.
Spitzer Collection
696-1893

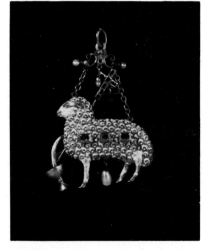

CASE 26
NO. 3

Case 27 Side A

Commemorative and Sentimental Jewellery: *17th – 19th century*

155

1 PENDANT
Gold, with the royal cipher of
Charles I (1625-1649) in gold wire
mounted over his hair.
At the back, the inscription: *CR REX
MARTYR.*
ENGLISH: about 1750.
M.103-1962

2 PENDANT
Gold, set with a miniature of Mary of
Modena, consort of James II
(1685-1688).
ENGLISH: about 1685.
M.105-1962
Nos. 1 & 2, given by Dame Joan
Evans, P.P.S.A.

3 PENDANT
Gold, set with a miniature of Charles
II (1660-1685).
ENGLISH: about 1680.
M.9-1960

4 PENDANT
Gold, set with the crowned cipher of
Mary II of England (1689-1694)
over hair and with an enamelled
skull at the back.
ENGLISH: 1694.
M.7-1960
Nos. 3 & 4, Frank Ward Bequest

5 SLIDE
Silver, with a coloured engraving of
William III (1689-1702). The back
enamelled.
ENGLISH: about 1700.
M.106-1962

6 SLIDE
Gold, with a miniature of Mary II of
England.
ENGLISH: 1694.
M.109-1962
Nos. 5 & 6, given by Dame Joan
Evans, P.P.S.A.

7 BROOCH
Probably once a slide.
Gold, with a miniature of William
III & Mary II and the royal ciphers.
ENGLISH: about 1690.
Frank Ward Bequest
M.80-1960

8 SLIDE
Converted into a pendant.
Gold, with gold wire and enamel decoration representing the royal cipher of Mary II above a skull and bones.
Inscribed: *MEMENTO MARIA REGINA OBIT, 28 DECEMBRIS 94.*
Given in memory of Mary Julia Hunnybun of Godmanchester, by her nephew Martin Travers
M.10-1948

9 PENDANT
Gold, with the cipher of William III against an enamelled pavilion with angels above and inscribed: *OB. MAR. 1702.*
ENGLISH: 1702.
M.289-1962

10 BROOCH
Possibly adapted from a slide or pendant.
Gold, enclosing the inscription: *On ye death of K. William III. Mourn Justice Liberty Religion Peace Lament on Royal Patron's sad Decease. Your brave Protector Peace, is now no more, whose greatness was all good and kind his power, whilst widow'd Europe fills the Air with Cries . . . defenceless nations wept . . . obsequies . . . Ob. Mar . . .*
ENGLISH: 1702.
M.108-1962

11 SLIDE
Enamelled silver, set with pearls and with the crowned cipher of Mary II, with skull and bones mounted on hair and the inscription: *MEMENTO MARIA REGINA OBIT 28 DECEMBER 1694.*
ENGLISH: 1694.
M.107-1962

12 MEDALET
Gold, with a portrait medallion of George III (1760-1820), signed by Thomas Wyon (d.1830). The back engraved with the crown, the royal monogram and the inscription: *Obt. 29th Jan 1820 Aet. 81.*
ENGLISH: 1820.
M.110-1962

13 BADGE OF THE PITT CLUB
Silver-gilt, with a glass medallion portrait of William Pitt, encircled by the inscription: *NON SIBI SED PATRIAE VIXIT.* The back with a commemorative inscription and the name of Samuel Clay, a member of the Pitt Club.
ENGLISH: about 1806.
M.116-1962

*14 PENDANT·
Gold, set with a miniature portrait of Princess Charlotte (1796-1817), the only child of the Prince of Wales, later George IV, and Caroline of Brunswick. Charlotte married in 1816 Leopold of Saxe-Coburg, afterwards King Leopold of the Belgians, and died in childbirth the following year. Reverse, the Royal Arms in enamel and pendant inscribed: *PC/1817.* The miniature is by or after Charlotte Jones, miniature painter to the Princess. The artist painted a portrait of the same composition in 1814.
ENGLISH: 1817-18.
M.82-1969
Nos. 9-14, given by Dame Joan Evans, P.P.S.A.

15 LOCKET
Gold, in the form of an urn, set with pearls and rubies, enclosing plaited hair.
ENGLISH: about 1780.
M.58-1950

16 LOCKET
Gold, with an openwork bow, set with pearls and emeralds, enclosing plaited hair. Reverse, a painted coronet above the cipher *FE.*
ENGLISH: third quarter of 18th century.
M.59-1950

17 LOCKET
Enamelled gold, enclosing a painted monogram: *MCC,* decorated with hair and the motto: *FIDELLE ET SECRET.* The back set with hair.
ENGLISH: about 1780.
M.57-1950

18 PENDANT
Enamelled gold, with a painted flower decorated with hair and the motto: *RICORDATI DE ME.* The back set with plaited hair.
ENGLISH: about 1780.
M.56-1950
Nos. 15-18, bequeathed by Mrs Isobel Baynes

19 BROOCH
Silver openwork bow, set with rose- and brilliant-cut diamonds and rubies, and enamelled gold ribbon, also gem-set, inscribed: *ELIZ EYTON OBIT FEB 1754 AET 81.* surrounding a hair locket.
ENGLISH: 1754.
M.121-1962

20 CLASP
Gold, set with a portrait of a woman, a spaniel at her elbow. A plait of hair inserted at the back.
ENGLISH: late 18th century.
M.97-1969
Nos. 19 & 20, given by Dame Joan Evans, P.P.S.A.

21 LOCKET OR PIN
Engraved gold frame enclosing a miniature of an urn with the initials *WWL* surmounted by the inscription: *A Pledge of Eternal Affection.*
ENGLISH: late 18th century.
941-1888

22 LOCKET
Gold frame enclosing a miniature of a woman seated by a tomb bearing the initials *IG* and inscribed: *Not lost but gone before.* A cherub above bears a scroll inscribed: *To Bliss.*
ENGLISH: late 18th century.
920-1888

23 BROOCH OR PIN
Gold frame enclosing a painted miniature of two women standing by an altar, one of them holding a heart. Inscribed on the back: *M.C. died 7th dec. 18 (II ?) Aged 63.*
ENGLISH: about 1811.
977-1888

24 LOCKET
Engraved gold frame enclosing a
miniature of Britannia with a ship in
the distance. At the back, plaited hair
and a label inscribed: *Jackson*.
ENGLISH: late 18th century.
943-1888

25 PENDANT OR BROOCH
Engraved gold frame enclosing a
paste cameo of John Wesley (1703-
1791) with the inscription: *He Rests
From His Labours*, and *Revd John
Wesley A.M. ob 2 March, 1791 Aet 88*.
ENGLISH: 1791.
Given by Dr. Joan Evans, P.P.S.A.
M.126-1962

26 BROOCH
Gold, set with pearls and with a
painted ivory plaque representing
doves on a basin of applied gold foil,
under the inscription: *Lamour*.
FRENCH or ENGLISH: late 18th
century.
970-1888

27 LOCKET OR BROOCH
Engraved gold frame enclosing a
miniature of a woman standing by a
tomb inscribed: *Not lost but gone
before*. Above, a cherub with a label
inscribed: *To bliss*.
ENGLISH: late 18th century.
934-1888

28 LOCKET
Engraved gold frame set with hair
enclosing a miniature, embellished
with hair and pearls, of a woman by
a tomb bearing the initials *BEC*
beneath the inscription: *I Mourn for
them I Loved*. At the back, knots of
plaited hair.
ENGLISH: late 18th century.
945-1888

29 CLASP
Gold, decorated with seed pearls and
set with a miniature of a woman in a
turban.
ENGLISH: late 18th century.
Given by Dr. Joan Evans, P.P.S.A.
M.83-1969

30 PAIR OF CLASPS
Enamelled gold with ivory plaques
painted with trophies, set with hair
and diamond sparks.
ENGLISH: late 18th century.
2196 & a-1899

31 CLASP
Enamelled gold, set with a miniature.
ENGLISH: late 18th century.
Given by Dr. Joan Evans, P.P.S.A.
M.84-1969

32 LOCKET
Gold frame with openwork bow set
with garnets and enclosing a
painting adorned with pieces of hair,
of a man fishing.
ENGLISH: mid 18th century.
930-1888

33 SLIDE
Gold, with an enamelled skull and
the initials *HB* and *WB* in gold wire
mounted on hair.
ENGLISH: early 18th century.
1127-1864

34 NECKLACE
Crystals, over blue foil painted with
devices in white, on silver backings,
with contemporary ribbons. The
devices are: a skull and crossbones;
the initials *EJ* beneath a coronet; a
putto holding leaves; a cornucopia;
two cherubs with a flaming heart; a
skeleton on a tomb inscribed: *At
Rest;* a dolphin; an angel with two
crosses; a crowned lion; a winged
skull; a bull; the sun, moon and stars;
a lyre and butterfly; *EJ* as above;
flowers; clasped hands with a heart;
a skull above a crown with
inscriptions: *GLORIA* and
VANITAS: a *putto* with a lance; an
elephant's head and trident; a sea
animal in a shell.
ENGLISH: third quarter of 17th
century.
M.50-1967

35 BROOCH OR PIN
Enamelled gold frame enclosing a
painted miniature, embellished with
ivory, gold foil and hair, of a woman
seated by a broken column, with an
angel pointing to a label inscribed:
Weep not, it falls to rise again.
ENGLISH: about 1800.
965-1888

36 PIN OR LOCKET
Engraved gold, enclosing a miniature of a woman in a landscape.
ENGLISH: late 18th century.
969-1888

37 PENDENT LOCKET
Gold frame enclosing a composition
in hair, metal and seed pearls on
opaline paste of an urn with the
initials *FW* beneath a willow.
ENGLISH: late 18th century.
956-1888

38 LOCKET
Engraved gold frame enclosing a
miniature of a woman seated
beneath a tree, a dog at her feet,
pointing to a locket or plaque.
ENGLISH: late 18th century.
922-1888

39 PENDANT
Gold, the border set with half-pearls
surrounding an embroidery of two
birds under faceted crystal.
ENGLISH: about 1700.
Frank Ward Bequest
M.22-1960

40 PENDANT
Enamelled gold, set with an emerald
and garnets, enclosing hair under
glass, inscribed: *Prudence Fixes Me
Octr 15th*, the back engraved: *Have
My Friendship for Ever Aug 16 1746*.
ENGLISH: 1746.
Given by Dr. Joan Evans, P.P.S.A.
M.120-1962

*41 PENDANT
Gold frame with plaited hairwork
enclosing a hair wheatsheaf (the
Vasa crest), bound with a diamond
band, on blue glass. At the back, an
inscription in seed pearls: *Sir
William Chambers died March 1796,
Aged 74*.
ENGLISH: 1796.
Part of a collection of relics of the
architect Sir William Chambers
(1726-1796) bequeathed to the
National Portrait Gallery. This piece
transferred to the Victoria & Albert
Museum.
M.7-1958

42 BROOCH
Gold frame, set with seed pearls and
enclosing plaited hair.
ENGLISH: late 18th century.
972-1888

COMMEMORATIVE AND SENTIMENTAL JEWELLERY:
17th – 19th century

158

43 BROOCH OR LOCKET
Engraved gold frame enclosing a miniature of a woman standing by a tomb inscribed: *MARY WEEPS-HEAVEN REJOICES,* beneath a willow.
ENGLISH: late 18th century.
953-1888

44 LOCKET
Engraved gold frame enclosing a miniature of a woman handing a heart pierced by an arrow to a figure of Death, surmounted by an inscription: *I ALONE CAN HEAL.*
ENGLISH: late 18th century.
950-1888

*45 LOCKET OR PIN
Engraved gold frame decorated with enamel, enclosing a miniature, embellished with gold wire and pearls, of a standing figure by a tomb bearing the initials *MM,* beneath a willow.
ENGLISH: late 18th century.
942-1888

46 LOCKET
Gold, set with a miniature portrait of a man in military uniform, signed (unidentifiable). On the reverse, the initials *F.G.B.* in seed pearls on a hair ground.
Possibly GERMAN: about 1800.
946-1888

47 BROOCH OR LOCKET
Gilt copper frame enclosing a miniature of a woman by a tomb beneath the inscription: *Sacred to the Memory of Dear Parents.*
ENGLISH: about 1800.
938-1888

*48 PAIR OF CLASPS
Coloured gold, set with miniature paintings in grisaille of Faith and Hope, after a window by Sir Joshua Reynolds (1723-1792) at New College, Oxford.
ENGLISH: late 18th century.
Acquired in Stockholm, allegedly having come from Russia.
Given by Dame Joan Evans, P.P.S.A.
M.79 & a-1962

1 SLIDE
Silver, set with a coloured engraving of John Lake (1624-1689), Bishop of Chichester.
ENGLISH: 1688.
Lake was a royalist who in 1688 refused to take the oath of allegiance to William and Mary.
M.114-1962

2 SLIDE
Silver, set with a coloured engraving of Thomas White (1628-1698), Bishop of Peterborough. The back enamelled.
ENGLISH: 1688.
White, like Lake, refused to take the oath of allegiance to William and Mary and was deprived of his see in consequence.
M.115-1962
Nos. 1 & 2, given by Dame Joan Evans, P.P.S.A.

3 and 4 LOCKET (in two parts)
Agate mounted in enamelled gold, painted with miniature portraits of a man and his wife.
ENGLISH: first half of 17th century.
7003-1860

5 SLIDE
Gold, with an enamelled skeleton on a coffin inscribed: *I Rest,* and two angels supporting a cartouche with the initials *MT* embroidered in gold thread on a background of hair.
ENGLISH: about 1700.
M.14-1960

6 SLIDE
Gold, with a skull on a winged hour-glass and two cherubs on an enamelled coffin, inscribed: *MEM. MORI* with the initials *EB,* on a background of hair. Engraved on the back *obt 6 Feb 1697.*
ENGLISH: 1697.
M.12-1960
Nos. 5 & 6, Frank Ward Bequest

7 SLIDE
Converted into a brooch.
Gold, with two enamelled angels bearing a celestial crown and a cipher embroidered in gold thread on a background of hair. The back inscribed: *Sr An: Leake Kil'd by ye French off of Malaga Augt 13th 1764.*
Sir Andrew Leake, R.N., served in the Mediterranean during the war of the Spanish Succession.
ENGLISH: 1764.
Given by Dame Joan Evans, P.P.S.A.
M.124-1962

8 SLIDE
Gold, with four enamelled gold cherubs and a cipher on a background of hair.
ENGLISH: about 1690.
Given by Miss Jessie Turtle
M.31-1951

9 SLIDE
Silver, parcel gilt, set with blue pastes and pearls and with an enamelled Cupid shooting an arrow at a flaming heart upon an altar. The back enamelled.
ENGLISH: about 1690.
Given by Dame Joan Evans, P.P.S.A.
M.125-1962

10 PENDANT
Gold, set with crystals with an enamelled Cupid against a roundel of plaited hair and inscribed: *JE ME MEURS MA MERE,* a translation of a line in Anacreon Ode XL, probably from a version by Mathurin Regniers.
Probably ENGLISH: late 17th century.
Frank Ward Bequest
M.21-1960

11 SLIDE
Gold and silver, set with pearls enclosing an enamelled device of clasped hands and a flaming heart mounted on hair.
ENGLISH: early 18th century.
1634-1903

12 PENDANT
Brass, in the shape of a coffin enclosing woven hair. Inscribed: *PB obit ye 17 Marc 1703 Aged 54 years.*
ENGLISH: 1703.
Given by Dame Joan Evans, P.P.S.A.
M.119-1962

13 SLIDE-CLASP
Gold, with a pair of enamelled Cupids holding flaming hearts with a gold wire cipher between, above the motto: *Mine For Yours*.
ENGLISH: about 1700.
M.24-1960

14 SLIDE
Gold, with two gold angels holding an enamelled skull, with the cipher *GL* (?) in gold thread on a background of hair.
ENGLISH: about 1700.
M.15-1960

15 SLIDE
Gold, with an enamelled gold skeleton flanked by angels above a coffin inscribed: *Come Ye Bless(ed)*; on a background of hair.
ENGLISH: about 1700.
M.13-1960

16 SLIDE
Gold, with an enamelled skeleton holding an arrow with the initials *IC*, on a background of hair. Engraved on the back: *IC OBT 6 JUL AETA 3 YE 8 MO*.
ENGLISH: about 1700.
M.11-1960
Nos. 13-16, Frank Ward Bequest

17 BROOCH
Gold frame, set with seed pearls and enclosing a representation of an urn in pearls on a glass ground.
? FRENCH: late 18th century.
960-1888

18 LOCKET
Engraved gold frame, with enamel decoration, enclosing a composition of an urn in gold, seed pearls and mother-of-pearl on glass.
? FRENCH: late 18th century.
926-1888

19 BROOCH
Gold, set with a basket of flowers in seed pearls and gold mounted on blue glass.
Probably FRENCH: late 18th century.
1726-1869

20 LOCKET
Gold frame enclosing a composition in mother-of-pearl on glass, of an altar inscribed: *A Vous Dedié*, with flaming hearts above and a basket of flowers.
FRENCH: late 18th century.
931-1888

21 BRACELET CLASP
Converted into a locket.
Gold frame, set with seed pearls, enclosing a miniature of a woman with a dove and a crane mounted on an enamelled blue ground embellished with seed pearls.
Possibly ENGLISH: late 18th century.
923-1888

22 LOCKET
Engraved gold frame with enamel decoration, enclosing the initials *EC* under a coronet executed in gold and seed pearls on a ground of hair. The back inscribed: *Countess Dowager of Home died 15 Jany 1784*.
ENGLISH: 1784.
929-1888

23 LOCKET
Gold frame, set with pearls enclosing a miniature of a girl; the back has a receptacle for hair.
ENGLISH: about 1790.
Given by Dame Joan Evans, P.P.S.A.
M.132-1962

24 PENDANT
Gold, set with pearls enclosing hair. The back inscribed: *Frances Fisher obt 4 Nov 1802 Aet 53*.
ENGLISH: 1802.
927-1888

25 LOCKET
Gold openwork frame, set with seed pearls, enclosing a heart-shaped receptacle for hair.
ENGLISH: late 18th century.
933-1888

26 LOCKET
Gold frame, set with pearls, enclosing a silk ground for the insertion of hair.
ENGLISH: late 18th century.
951-1888

27 BROOCH
Gold frame in the form of a serpent, set with seed pearls and a ruby, enclosing a glass-fronted locket for hair.
ENGLISH: about 1800.
957-1888

28 LOCKET
Gold frame and loop in the form of a padlock, set with seed pearls, and with a gold key on a chain. The glass centre also set with pearls.
ENGLISH: about 1800.
928-1888

29 PENDANT
In the form of a padlock.
Gold, set with garnets, enclosing hair.
ENGLISH: about 1800.
Given by Dame Joan Evans, P.P.S.A.
M.127-1962

30 BROOCH
Gold frame, set with amethysts and seed pearls, enclosing plaited hair.
Probably ENGLISH: early 19th century.
982-1888

31 BROOCH
Gold frame, set with seed pearls and jet, enclosing plaited hair. Inscribed on the back: *S.R. OBT 29 JUNE 1818, AET 61*.
ENGLISH: 1818.
961-1888

32 BROOCH OR PIN
Gold frame, enamelled and set with seed pearls, enclosing plaited hair. Engraved on the back: *Henry Crewe Moseley, born 3d of Jany 1779; died 18th of July . . .*
ENGLISH: about 1800.
958-1888

33 EYE LOCKET
Gold, set with pearls and enclosing an eye painted on ivory. The back set with hair and pearls.
ENGLISH: about 1800.
935-1888

34 LOCKET
Enamelled gold frame inscribed: *LOUISA BOHUN: OB:14: APR:1816 AET 18,* enclosing a miniature of a girl in Elizabethan costume. At the back, the inscription: *FRANCES: BOHUN: OB: 1 AUG: 1816: AET 15.*
ENGLISH: 1816.
Given by Dame Joan Evans, P.P.S.A.
M.117-1962

35 LOCKET
Silver-gilt frame enclosing a miniature of a woman standing by a tomb inscribed: *May Saints Embrace Thee with a Love Like Mine.*
ENGLISH: about 1780.
937-1888

36 LOCKET OR BROOCH
Engraved gold frame enclosing a miniature, embellished with gold wire and pearls, of a woman by a tomb inscribed: *Rest in Peace,* with a cherub above. At the back, the initials *ER* in seed pearls on hair.
ENGLISH: late 18th century.
925-1888

37 LOCKET
Gold frame edged with a serpent, enclosing a drooping rose bush and a butterfly in enamelled gold on a background of hair, surrounded by the inscription: *La Rose Flétrie le Papillon s'Envole* and *Napped it Fell to the Ground.* Engraved on the back: *And such I exclaim'd is the pitiless part, Some art by the delicate Mind, Regardless of Wringing and Breaking a Heart, already to sorrow resigned.*
ENGLISH: about 1810.
Given by Dame Joan Evans, P.P.S.A.
M.123-1962

38 LOCKET
Gilt metal frame enclosing a miniature of a woman visiting a tomb at night. The reverse with painted flowers and scrolling metal filigree.
ENGLISH: late 18th century.
947-1888

*39 LOCKET OR BROOCH
Engraved gold frame enclosing plaited hair and a shield with an urn bearing the initials *RM*. The reverse inscribed: *ROBT MULLIGAN OB. 16 DECR 1785 AET 60.*
ENGLISH: 1785-86.
976-1888

40 PIN
Engraved gold frame enclosing a miniature of a woman standing by a tomb beneath a willow. The tomb inscribed: *R D MORRIS OB JUY 19 1787, AE 70.*
ENGLISH: 1787.
968-1888

41 CLASP
Gold frame, set with seed pearls, enclosing the gold initials *MAR* on a background of plaited hair.
ENGLISH: about 1800.
986-1888

42 BROOCH
Chased gold frame enclosing an enamelled representation of a tomb. Engraved on the back: *C. ? CROSS OB. 18 MARCH 1818 AET 48.*
ENGLISH: 1818.
973-1888

43 BROOCH
Gold, enclosing the hair of Sir Marc Isambard Brunel (1769-1849) and his wife. The back inscribed: *Sir Marc Isambard Brunel died Decr 1849. Aged 80. Sophia Brunel, Died Jany 1855, Aged 79.*
ENGLISH: 1855.
Given by Miss A. Kelsey
M.21-1972

44 LOCKET
Gold frame, with the inscription: *In Memory of,* reserved on black enamel, and a row of seed pearls enclosing hair and seed pearls with gilt wire. The back machine-engraved.
ENGLISH: about 1830.
932-1888

45 BROOCH OR PIN
Enamelled gold frame enclosing a miniature of a woman seated by a tomb beneath a willow.
ENGLISH: late 18th century.
963-1888

46 SLIDE, MOUNTED AS A RING
Silver, set with chrysoberyls, with a gold surround.
About 1760.
Given by the Rt. Hon. Sir C.W. Dilke, in fulfilment of the wishes of Lady Dilke.
1538c-1904

47 BRACELET CLASP
Gold frame, set with seed pearls, enclosing a miniature of an urn embellished with hair.
ENGLISH: late 18th century.
985-1888

48 BROOCH
Gold, set with seed pearls.
Probably ENGLISH: about 1830.
975-1888

49 CLASP FOR A NECK-RIBBON OR BRACELET
Gold frame, set with seed pearls, enclosing a composition of a guitar within a wreath, in mother-of-pearl and seed pearls on glass.
? FRENCH: late 18th century.
988-1888

50 BRACELET
Enamelled gold and hair, with a pendant in the form of a padlock. Inscribed: *I.S.P. obt Augt 1 1846 aet 33, in memory of J.S. Parker.*
ENGLISH: 1846.
Given by Mrs. Bertha H. Parker
M.113-1933

CASE 27
SIDE A
NO. 41

CASE 27
SIDE A
NO. 45

161

CASE 27
SIDE A
NO. 14

CASE 27
SIDE B
NO. 39

CASE 27
SIDE A
NO. 48

Case 28

PENDANTS:
late 16th – 18th centuries

1 RELIQUARY PENDANT
Crystal mounted in enamelled gold,
enclosing paintings in *verre eglomisé*
(paintings under glass) of the
Assumption of the Virgin and St.
Peter; hung with pearls.
? SPANISH: early 17th century.
From the Treasury of the Cathedral
of the Virgin of the Pillar, Saragossa
338-1870

2 PENDANT (St. Lambert of Liège)
Enamelled gold, set with crystals.
NETHERLANDISH: late 17th
century.
Bequeathed by Captain Walter
Dasent, R.N.
M.349-1940

3 PENDANT
Enamelled gold, set with paintings in
verre eglomisé of the Annunciation
and Nativity; hung with pearls.
ITALIAN (Sicily): 17th century.
M.991-1910

4 PENDANT
Enamelled gold, set with paintings in
verre eglomisé of the Virgin and St
Francis; hung with pearls.
ITALIAN (Sicily): 17th century.
M.993-1910

5 PENDANT
Enamelled gold, set with paintings in
verre eglomisé of the Virgin and
Christ.
ITALIAN (Sicily): late 17th or 18th
century.
M.994-1910
Nos. 3-5, Murray Bequest

6 PENDANT
Enamelled gold, set with a painting
in *verre eglomisé* of the Virgin.
Reverse, a coloured engraving of
Christ; hung with pearls.
ITALIAN (Sicily): 17th century.
Alfred William Hearn Gift
M.56-1923

*7 PENDANT
Enamelled gold, set with garnets and
turquoises, with paintings in
verre eglomisé of the Flight into
Egypt and Christ among the Doctors,
inscribed; hung with pearls.
SPANISH or ITALIAN: early 17th
century.
From the Treasury of the Cathedral
of the Virgin of the Pillar, Saragossa
409-1873

*8 PENDANT (a ship)
Rock crystal hull, mounted in gold
with enamelled decoration.
? FRENCH: about 1600.
295-1854

*9 PENDANT
Crystal mounted in enamelled gold,
decorated with pearls, and set with
enamelled bas reliefs of the Crucifixion and the Virgin of the
Immaculate Conception in an
aureola; both under crystal.
Probably SPANISH: about 1620.
From the Treasury of the Cathedral
of the Virgin of the Pillar, Saragossa,
to which it was said to have been
presented by Louis XIII of France
332-1870

10 PENDANT
Gold, set with rose-cut diamonds;
with a relief of the Adoration of the
Magi in enamelled gold under
crystal.
SPANISH: about 1740.
From the Treasury of the Cathedral
of the Virgin of the Pillar, Saragossa
321-1870

11 PENDANT
Enamelled gold, set with paintings in
verre eglomisé of the Annunciation
and the Agony in the Garden.
SPANISH: 17th century. The loop
struck with a French import
mark introduced in 1893.
Alfred Williams Hearn Gift
M.63-1923

12 PENDANT
Enamelled gold, set with gouache
paintings of Christ and the Virgin.
SPANISH: about 1600.
Given by Mr. Robert G. Baird
M.120-1926

13 PENDENT CROSS
Table-cut topazes set in enamelled
gold; reverse, the Crucifixion in
painted enamel.
SPANISH: late 17th century.
213-1864

14 PENDANT (the Virgin of the
Immaculate Conception)
Enamelled gold figure of the
Virgin, in an enamelled gold
openwork frame set with
emeralds and a paste.
SPANISH: first half of 17th
century.
Webb Collection
396-1872

15 PENDANT (with cross in the
centre)
Table-cut crystals set in gold,
decorated with enamel; the cross,
flanked by palm branches, made
separately and inserted in the frame,
which is surmounted by a crown.
SPANISH: about 1630.
345-1870

16 PENDANT
Crystal mounted in enamelled gold,
set with two paintings in *verre
eglomisé* of the Virgin of Loreto and
an unidentifiable figure.
SPANISH (or perhaps ITALIAN):
about 1600.
347-1870
Nos. 15 & 16, from the Treasury of the
Cathedral of the Virgin of the Pillar,
Saragossa

CASE 28
NO. 7

CASE 28
NO. 8

CASE 28
NO. 9

Cases 29 and 30

Reserved for temporary displays, usually of modern works lent by the makers.

Case 31 Boards A-E

A collection of precious stones bequeathed by the Rev. Chauncey Hare Townshend (1798-1868), cleric and poet, with additional material given in 1913 by Sir A.H. Church, K.C.V.O., F.R.S., who compiled the first catalogue of the Townshend Bequest, *Precious Stones, A Guide to the Townshend Collection* (1882; new editions, 1905, 1908 and 1913).

All the stones were mounted as rings before they came to the Museum, mainly in a series of standardised gold settings, often of the coronet or galleried type. However, several specimens are set with greater elaboration, with diamond borders surrounding the central stone. Some of these were originally in the possession of Henry Philip Hope (d.1839), a brother of the novelist and antiquary Thomas Hope (*c.* 1770-1831). H.P. Hope formed a famous collection of diamonds and precious stones which was largely inherited by his three nephews. His collection, which included the Hope blue diamond, now in the Smithsonian Institution, Washington, was catalogued by B. Hertz in 1839. Townshend is recorded as having made purchases from it and his acquisitions are noted below. Townshend seems to have remounted several of his purchases, in whole or in part.

1 LAPIS LAZULI
1324-1869

2 EUCLASE
1291-1869

3 SPODUMENE
M.6-1913

4 ANDALUSITE
M.9-1913

5 LUMACHELLA or FIREMARBLE
1237-1869

6 MALACHITE
1334-1869

7 CONCHE PEARL
H.P. Hope Collection
1339-1869

8 PEARL
1340-1869

9 PEARL
1338-1869

10 PEARL
Flanked by two pear-shaped
brilliant-cut diamonds.
1337-1869

11 PYRITE
1335-1869

12 CHORASTROLITE
96-1870

13 APOPHYLLITE
1296-1869

14 TURQUOISE
1264-1869

15 TURQUOISE
Border of brilliant-cut diamonds.
1263-1869

16 TURQUOISE
Border of brilliant-cut diamonds, in a
setting of about 1850-60.
1262-1869

17 TURQUOISE
Cameo of a female head (? Medusa).
H.P. Hope Collection
1261-1869

18 TURQUOISE
1265-1869

19 TURQUOISE
Inlaid with gold in the manner of a
Persian seal with characters
(but a nonsense).
1266-1869

20 OPAL
Border of brilliant-cut diamonds.
1223-1869

21 OPAL
Border of brilliant-cut diamonds in a
setting of about 1850-60.
1221-1869

22 OPAL
1228-1869

23 OPAL
1225-1869

24 OPAL
Set in gold with a blue enamelled
border.
Late 18th century.
H.P. Hope Collection
1226-1869

25 BLACK OPAL
M.108-1913

26 OPAL
1229-1869

27 OPAL
1299-1869

28 OPAL
H.P. Hope Collection
1230-1869

29 OPAL
1235-1869

30 OPAL
Border of enamelled gold, with
brilliant-cut diamonds in a setting of
about 1850-60.
1222-1869

31 OPAL
Border of rose-cut diamonds in a
setting of about 1770.
1224-1869

32 OPAL
H.P. Hope Collection
1232-1869

33 OPAL
H.P. Hope Collection
1227-1869

34 OPAL
Border of brilliant-cut diamonds in a
setting of about 1850.
1220-1869

35 OPAL
H.P. Hope Collection
1234-1869

36 OPAL
H.P. Hope Collection (re-set by
Townshend)
1231-1869

37 FIRE OPAL
M.8-1913

38 OPAL
1236-1869

39 OPAL
H.P. Hope Collection
1233-1869

Case 31 Board B

1 DIAMOND
Border of brilliant-cut diamonds.
1175-1869

2 DIAMOND
Border of small rose-cut diamonds, in
a setting of about 1840, re-set by
Townshend.
H.P. Hope Collection
1176-1869

3 DIAMOND
Border of brilliant-cut diamonds, in a
setting of about 1825.
1179-1869

4 DIAMOND
Set about 1840-50.
1174-1869

5 DIAMOND
H.P. Hope Collection
1177-1869

6 DIAMOND
Border of brilliant-cut diamonds.
1173-1869

7 DIAMOND
Border of brilliant-cut diamonds;
the underside of bezel re-set by
Townshend.
H.P. Hope Collection
1178-1869

8 DIAMOND
1172-1869

9 SAPPHIRE
H.P. Hope Collection
1257-1869

10 SAPPHIRE
1242-1869

11 SAPPHIRE
1312-1869

12 SAPPHIRE
Border of rose and brilliant-cut
diamonds, about 1820. Hoop
replaced.
H.P. Hope Collection.
1247-1869

*13 SAPPHIRE
Flanked by two brilliant-cut
diamonds, in a setting of about 1830.
1239-1869

14 STAR SAPPHIRE
Border and shoulders of rose-cut
diamonds in a ?late 18th century
setting.
1245-1869

15 STAR SAPPHIRE
Border of rose-cut diamonds in a
setting of about 1830.
1244-1869

16 STAR SAPPHIRE
1246-1869

17 SAPPHIRE
H.P. Hope Collection; re-set by
Townshend.
1256-1869

18 SAPPHIRE
Flanked by brilliant-cut diamonds.
1240-1869

19 SAPPHIRE
Border of tiny rose-cut diamonds.
H.P. Hope Collection
1260-1869

20 SAPPHIRE
1290-1869

21 RUBY
Borders of brilliant-cut diamonds
in a setting of about 1830.
1249-1869

22 RUBY
Flanked by two brilliant-cut
diamonds.
1252-1869

23 SAPPHIRE
1277-1869

24 STAR RUBY
1250-1869

25 STAR SAPPHIRE
Border of rose-cut diamonds of about
1820. Hoop replaced.
H.P. Hope Collection
1251-1869

26 STAR SAPPHIRE
1243-1869

27 STAR SAPPHIRE
H.P. Hope Collection; re-set by
Townshend.
1258-1869

28 SAPPHIRE
Border of rose-cut diamonds in a
setting of about 1810-20. Swivel
ring.
H.P. Hope Collection
1259-1869

29 SAPPHIRE
H.P. Hope Collection
1238-1869

30 SAPPHIRE
Border of brilliant-cut diamonds in a
setting of about 1850.
1310-1869

*31 RUBY
Border of brilliant-cut diamonds in a
setting of about 1850.
1254-1869

32 RUBY
Border of rose- and brilliant-cut
diamonds in a setting of about 1850.
1253-1869

33 RUBY
Border of brilliant-cut diamonds in a
setting of about 1840.
1255-1869

34 CHRYSOBERYL CAT'S EYE
H.P. Hope Collection; setting
possibly adapted by Townshend.
1332-1869

35 CHRYSOBERYL CAT'S EYE
Border of brilliant-cut diamonds.
1328-1869

**36 CHRYSOBERYL VARIETY:
ALEXANDRITE CAT'S EYE.**
H.P. Hope Collection
1333-1869

37 CHRYSOBERYL CAT'S EYE
1329-1869

38 CHRYSOBERYL
1322-1869

166

39 SAPPHIRE
1314-1869

40 SAPPHIRE
1241-1869

41 SPINEL
Border of brilliant-cut diamonds in a
setting of about 1840.
1326-1869

42 SPINEL
Border of brilliant-cut diamonds in a
setting of about 1840.
1327-1869

43 SPINEL
1248-1869

44 SPINEL
1325-1869

45 SPINEL
Border of brilliant-cut diamonds.
1317-1869

46 CHRYSOBERYL CAT'S EYE
Border of brilliant-cut diamonds.
1330-1869

47 CHRYSOBERYL CAT'S EYE
1331-1869

48 CHRYSOBERYL
1297-1869

49 CHRYSOBERYL
1304-1869

50 CHRYSOBERYL
H.P. Hope Collection
1194-1869

1 QUARTZ: ROCK CRYSTAL
1180-1869

2 QUARTZ: CITRINE
H.P. Hope Collection
1182-1869

3 QUARTZ: CITRINE
1185-1869

4 QUARTZ: CITRINE
1183-1869

5 SMOKY QUARTZ: MORION
1181-1869

6 QUARTZ: AMETHYST
H.P. Hope Collection
1189-1869

**7 SMOKY QUARTZ AND
AMETHYST**
H.P. Hope Collection
1186-1869

8 QUARTZ: AMETHYST
H.P. Hope Collection (then set, as
now, as a swivel ring).
1187-1869

9 QUARTZ: AMETHYST
H.P. Hope Collection
1190-1869

10 QUARTZ: AMETHYST
H.P. Hope Collection
1191-1869

11 QUARTZ: AMETHYST
Cameo of a panther on one side; on
the other, a Bacchante.
H.P. Hope Collection (then set, as
now, as a swivel ring).
1208-1869

12 QUARTZ: CAT'S EYE
1218-1869

13 QUARTZ: CAT'S EYE
1217-1869

14 QUARTZ: CAT'S EYE
Border of brilliant-cut diamonds of
about 1800.
1219-1869

15 QUARTZ: HAWK'S EYE
1336-1869

16 AVENTURINE QUARTZ
Cameo of a monkey's head.
H.P. Hope Collection (then set, as
now, as a swivel ring).
1193-1869

17 AVENTURINE QUARTZ
1205-1869

18 CHALCEDONY
Intaglio of Zeus.
1204-1869

19 CHALCEDONY
1203-1869

20 CHALCEDONY
In a gothic bezel of about 1825.
1202-1869

**21 CHALCEDONY:
CHRYSOPRASE**
Cameo of a classical male bust
with laurel wreath.
1200-1869

**22 CHALCEDONY:
CHRYSOPRASE**
1199-1869

23 CHALCEDONY: PLASMA
Intaglio of Cupid holding a butterfly
over a torch.
1196-1869

**24 CHALCEDONY:
CORNELIAN**
Engraved with interlaced design of
flowers in the Persian manner.
1212-1869

**25 CHALCEDONY:
CORNELIAN**
Late Roman intaglio of Hercules,
signed (in Greek) *Pela,* in a 'Roman'
setting.
1825-1869

**26 CHALCEDONY:
CORNELIAN**
Early 19th century intaglio of
Omphale.
1824-1869

Case 31 Board D

27 CHALCEDONY: CORNELIAN
Roman intaglio of a quadriga (chariot of the sun), lettered: *INVICT/AUR* (*invictum aurum*, unconquered gold).
1823-1869

28 CHALCEDONY: SARD
Inscribed: *Khudabanda Mustafa.*
1814-1869

29 QUARTZ: JASPER
Roman intaglio of a satyr and a goat.
1829-1869

30 CHALCEDONY: BLOODSTONE
18th century intaglio of a scorpion, engraved on both sides.
1826-1869

31 CHALCEDONY: MOCHA STONE
H.P. Hope Collection; re-set by Townshend.
1215-1869

32 CHALCEDONY: MOCHA STONE
1214-1869

33 CHALCEDONY: AGATE
1207-1869

34 CHALCEDONY: AGATE
1206-1869

35 CHALCEDONY: MOSS AGATE
1213-1869

36 CHALCEDONY: EYE AGATE
H.P. Hope Collection
1210-1869

37 CHALCEDONY: ONYX
Roman intaglio of a Cupid and a bird.
1819-1869

38 CHALCEDONY: ONYX
H.P. Hope Collection
1211-1869

39 CHALCEDONY: ONYX
1209-1869

1 TOPAZ
H.P. Hope Collection; re-set by Townshend
1311-1869

2 TOPAZ
1315-1869

3 TOPAZ
1188-1869

4 TOPAZ
1195-1869

5 TOPAZ
1308-1869

*6 TOPAZ
Border of rose-cut diamonds.
H.P. Hope Collection; partly re-set by Townshend
1309-1869

7 TOPAZ
1316-1869

8 TOPAZ
1313-1869

9 TOURMALINE
1280-1869

10 TOURMALINE
H.P. Hope Collection; re-set by Townshend
1320-1869

11 TOURMALINE
H.P. Hope Collection; re-set by Townshend
1275-1869

12 TOURMALINE
1295-1869

13 TOURMALINE
M.4-1913

14 TOURMALINE
H.P. Hope Collection
1323-1869

15 TOURMALINE
M.3-1913

16 TOURMALINE
H.P. Hope Collection
1321-1869

17 TOURMALINE
1319-1869

18 ALMANDINE GARNET
1273-1869

19 ALMANDINE GARNET
H.P. Hope Collection
1271-1869

20 ALMANDINE GARNET
1278-1869

21 ALMANDINE GARNET
1270-1869

22 ALMANDINE GARNET
Border of brilliant-cut diamonds in a setting of about 1860.
1269-1869

23 ALMANDINE GARNET
1276-1869

24 ALMANDINE GARNET
Intaglio of a Bacchante.
H.P. Hope Collection
1272-1869

25 ALMANDINE GARNET
Border of rose-cut diamonds.
1192-1869

26 SPESSARTINE GARNET
Border of rose-cut diamonds.
H.P. Hope Collection; partly re-set by Townshend
1274-1869

27 HESSONITE GARNET
1279-1869

28 HESSONITE GARNET
? Renaissance cameo of a male bust.
1306-1869

29 HESSONITE GARNET
1307-1869

30 HESSONITE GARNET
H.P. Hope Collection
1318-1869

168

31 DEMANTOID GARNET
M.5-1913

32 ZIRCON
1281-1869

33 ZIRCON
1282-1869

34 ZIRCON
M.7-1913

35 ZIRCON
H.P. Hope Collection
1298-1869

36 ZIRCON
1305-1869

37 SPHENE
M.11-1913

38 IOLITE (CORDIERITE)
1268-1869

39 IOLITE (CORDIERITE)
1268-1869

40 FELDSPAR: MOONSTONE
M.10-1913

41 FELDSPAR: MOONSTONE
H.P. Hope Collection
1294-1869

42 FELDSPAR: SUNSTONE
1293-1869

**43 FELDSPAR:
LABRADORITE**
1292-1869

1 PERIDOT
1302-1869

2 PERIDOT
Intaglio of Apollo and a lizard,
signed (in Greek) by Giovanni
Calandrelli (d.1852), an Italian gem-
engraver who spent his last years in
Berlin, where he produced a number
of fake antique gems.
H.P. Hope Collection; re-set by
Townshend
1300-1869

3 PERIDOT
1303-1869

4 PERIDOT
1301-1869

5 BERYL: AQUAMARINE
H.P. Hope Collection
1286-1869

6 BERYL: AQUAMARINE
H.P. Hope Collection
1288-1869

7 BERYL: AQUAMARINE
H.P. Hope Collection
1287-1869

8 BERYL: HELIODOR
1184-1869

9 BERYL: AQUAMARINE
H.P. Hope Collection
1289-1868

10 BERYL: EMERALD
Border of brilliant-cut diamonds, in a
setting of about 1850.
1284-1869

11 BERYL: EMERALD
Inscribed: *Sir Jan Shurborunt
Bahadur, 1797.*
H.P. Hope Collection; re-set by
Townshend
1283-1869

12 BERYL: EMERALD
H.P. Hope Collection
1285-1869

CASE 31
BOARD B
NO. 13

CASE 31
BOARD B
NO. 31

CASE 31
BOARD D
NO. 6

ANCIENT EGYPTIAN AND PHOENICIAN RINGS:
about 1650 – 1st century BC

The large collection of rings shown in Cases 32-35 ranges from the Egyptian Middle Kingdom (about 2040-1633 BC) to the present day. The rings reflect many human pre-occupations: with personal embellishment, status, power, loyalty, affection, religion and magic. These themes have been interpreted in different ways in the course of three thousand years.

The V & A holdings are firmly based on the collections of two great nineteenth century antiquaries, Edmund Waterton (1830-1887) and Sir John Evans (1823-1908). Waterton sold most of his collection to the Museum in 1870; further major items, withheld at the time of the original sale, were purchased in 1899. Sir John Evans bequeathed the larger part of his collection to his son, Sir Arthur Evans (1851-1941), the excavator of Knossos. Sir Arthur made a number of additions to the collection, the bulk of which was inherited on his death by his half-sister, Dame Joan Evans (1893-1977), who again augmented it. Though Dame Joan gave generously to other museums, the V & A was the principal object of her benefactions, as is evident throughout the Gallery.

It may be puzzling, in the lists which follow, to see findplaces noted, especially in the case of medieval rings, which are not necessarily taken as establishing a country of origin. To accept, for instance, that everything discovered in England must be of English make would be to ignore the fact that jewellery played an important part in the elaborate international ritual of royal and diplomatic gifts and that, even more important, it was traded between country and country.

1 Gold. Revolving oval bezel set with a glazed steatite scarab with amuletic signs; not intended for use as a seal. Shoulders bound with wire.
EGYPTIAN: second Intermediate Period (Hyksos Kings), about 1650 BC.
407-1871

2 Silver. Revolving oval bezel set with a glazed steatite scarab; not intended for use.
EGYPTIAN: New Kingdom (Dynasty XVIII), about 1567-1320 BC.
411-1871

3 Gold. Revolving oval bezel set with a bloodstone scrab of Isis nursing the hawk-headed Horus; not intended for use.
PHOENICIAN: 6th century BC.
408-1871

4 Gold. Revolving bezel set with a jasper scarab of Isis nursing Horus.
PHOENICIAN: 6th century BC.
409-1871

5 Gold. Revolving oval bezel set with a lapis-lazuli scarab. Shoulders bound with wire.
EGYPTIAN: New Kingdom (Dynasty XIX/XX), about 1200 BC.
410-1871
1-5, Waterton Collection

6 Gold. Bezel engraved with a head of Isis.
EGYPTIAN: (Ptolemaic): 332-30 BC.
M.38-1963

7 Gold. Oval bezel engraved with Isis nursing Horus.
EGYPTIAN or MEDITERRANEAN.
412-1871

8 White metal. Revolving rectangular bezel with rounded corners, engraved with Isis nursing Horus; a papyrus border.
MEDITERRANEAN.
414-1871

9 Red-glaze (originally green-glaze) faience (quartz, powdered, fired and glazed. Oval bezel inscribed: *Neb-kheperu-re* (prenomen of Tut-ankh-amun).
EGYPTIAN: 1362-1353 BC.
406-1871

10 Silver. Bezel as in no. 8, engraved with a sphinx and human figures.
PHOENICIAN.
415-1871

11 Silver. Revolving cornelian bezel in the form of a *wedjet* eye of Horus, engraved with the sign for life *(ankh)*.
EGYPTIAN.
401-1871

12 Blue-glaze faience. Oval bezel with an ? onyx antelope.
EGYPTIAN: New Kingdom (late XVIIIth Dynasty), 14th century BC.
405-1871

13 Gold. Bezel as in no. 8, engraved with Horus holding the *ankh*.
EGYPTIAN or MEDITERRANEAN.
413-1871

*14 Glazed ware; *wedjet* eye of Horus in blue; yellow hoop.
EGYPTIAN: New Kingdom (late XVIIIth Dynasty), 14th century BC.
403-1871
Nos. 7-14, Waterton Collection

15 Glazed ware; *wedjet* eye of Horus.
EGYPTIAN: late New Kingdom, about 1200-1085 BC.
Circ. 28 & a-1935

169

Mainly GREEK AND
ETRUSCAN RINGS:
*about 8th century BC – 2nd
century AD*

ETRUSCAN RINGS:
8th-2nd century BC

170

1 Silver. Vesica-shaped oval bezel decorated with filigree (one pellet in gold).
GREEK: 8th or 7th century BC.
Waterton Collection
420-1871

2 Gold. Bezel chased in relief with a helmeted head.
GREEK: 5th century BC.
Given by Dame Joan Evans, P.P.S.A.
M.134-1962

3 Gold. Vesica-shaped bezel engraved with a female head in profile.
GREEK: late 5th or 4th century BC.
431-1871

4 Electrum. Revolving bezel set with a composition material. The shoulders bound with wire.
GREEK: 6th century BC.
Found at the necropolis of Camirus, Rhodes, by Auguste Salzmann.
421-1871
Nos. 3 & 4, Waterton Collection

5 Gold. Hollow hoop, bound with wires. Ram-head terminals.
GREEK: 5th or 4th century BC.
Given by Dame Joan Evans, P.P.S.A.
M.133-1962

6 Gold. Vesica-shaped bezel engraved with a seated woman holding a Victory who is offering a crown.
GREEK: early 4th century BC.
430-1871

7 Silver, with a plug of gold. Oval bezel engraved with a Victory binding her sandal.
GREEK: about 400 BC.
434-1871

8 Gold. Circular bezel engraved with a female figure standing at a tripod.
GREEK: 3rd or 2nd century BC.
429-1871
Nos. 6-8, Waterton Collection

9 Gold. Lozenge-shaped bezel set with a composition material; filigree border.
GREEK: 5th or 4th century BC.
Webb Collection
8773-1863

10 Bronze. Oval bezel engraved with Hercules crowned by Victory.
? GREEK: 4th or 3rd century BC.
459-1871

11 Silver. Oval bezel engraved with a woman fastening her sandal.
GREEK: 3rd century BC.
435-1871

12 Bronze. Vesica-shaped bezel engraved with a woman playing at knuckle-bones.
GREEK: 3rd century BC.
432-1871
Nos. 10-12, Waterton Collection

***13** Gold. Oval bezel engraved with a figure of Hera.
GREEK: 4th century BC.
Lent from the Salting Bequest
M.552-1910

14 Gold. Oval bezel set with a paste intaglio of a young woman.
GREEK: late 2nd or early 1st century BC.
8781-1863

***15** Gold. Beaded loop edged with twisted wires.
GREEK: 3rd century BC.
8770-1863
Nos. 14 & 15, Webb Collection

16 Silver. Circular bezel engraved with a galley between two dolphins.
GREEK: 3rd century BC.
458-1871

17 Bronze. Tapering hoop. Bezel engraved with Bacchic emblems.
GREEK: 3rd or 2nd century BC.
433-1871
Nos. 16 & 17, Waterton Collection

18 Gold. Swelling hoop set with a sard intaglio of a winged figure.
GRECO-ROMAN: 2nd century AD.
Given by Mr. Walter Child, A.R.S.M.
M.149-1909

1 Gold. Plain band widening into a bezel.
ETRUSCAN: 8th-7th century BC.
442-1871

2 Gold. Vesica-shaped bezel.
ETRUSCAN: 5th or 4th century BC.
444-1871

3 Gold. Large oval bezel.
ETRUSCAN: 5th or 4th century BC.
Webb Collection
8782-1863

4 White metal, plated with gold. Large circular bezel.
ETRUSCAN: 4th century BC.
Waterton Collection
447-1871

5 Gold. Rectangular bezel with rounded corners, engraved with a Siren, Oedipus with the Sphinx, and a ? winged star.
ETRUSCAN: 6th century BC.
Webb Collection
8779-1863

6 White metal plated with gold. Bezel as in no. 5, engraved with a deer, a lion and a ? scarab.
ETRUSCAN: 6th or 5th century BC.
Waterton Collection
437-1871

7 Gold hoop. Revolving onyx scarab; reverse, a seated male figure. Shoulders of hoop chased to imitate wires.
ETRUSCAN: 4th century BC.
8777-1863

8 Gold hoop. Revolving cornelian scarab; reverse, an ? antelope. Shoulders of hoop bound with wires.
ETRUSCAN: 4th century BC.
8769-1863
Nos. 7 & 8, Webb Collection

9 Bronze, plated with gold. Hoop flattened to form an oval bezel, stamped with a boar in intaglio.
ETRUSCAN: 4th century BC.
446-1871

ROMAN AND GRECO-ROMAN RINGS:
1st century-3rd century AD

10 Gold. Bezel as in no. 5, engraved with an ibis and a sphinx.
ETRUSCAN: 4th century BC.
Presented to Edmund Waterton by Cardinal Antonelli, 1857.
438-1871
Nos. 9 & 10, Waterton Collection

*11 Gold. Bezel as in no. 5, ? stamped' with a winged man between a sphinx and a panther.
ETRUSCAN: first half of 6th century BC.
Webb Collection
8775-1863

12 Gold. Hoop set with a composition scarab. Figures of Hercules and Juno Sospita chased on the shoulders.
ETRUSCAN: 4th century BC.
Found in the Maremma, 1856, this was thought to be a marriage ring.
Waterton Collection
445-1871

13 Gold. Vesica-shaped bezel engraved with a ? Victory with a palm branch.
ETRUSCAN: 3rd century BC.
Webb Collection
8767-1863

14 Bronze. Vesica-shaped bezel engraved with a man carrying ? fish
ETRUSCAN: 5th or 4th century BC.
Waterton Collection
441-1871

15 Gold. Oval bezel set with a foiled crystal; filigree border.
ETRUSCAN: 4th or 3rd century BC.
817-1902

16 Gold. Circular bezel set with a garnet; sun-rays engraved round the stone.
ETRUSCAN: 3rd century BC.
448-1871

17 Gold. Oval bezel set with a garnet intaglio of a dolphin.
ETRUSCAN: 3rd or 2nd century BC.
449-1871

18 Gold. Projecting oval bezel set with a paste intaglio.
ETRUSCAN: 2nd century BC.
456-1871

19 Gold. Oval bezel set with a garnet intaglio of a shoe.
ETRUSCAN: 3rd century BC.
It is suggested that the ring belonged to an actor.
454-1871

20 Gold. Oval bezel set with a garnet intaglio of the head of Mercury.
ETRUSCAN: 2nd century BC.
455-1871
Nos. 16-20, Waterton Collection

21 Bronze, silver plated. Circular bezel set with a paste intaglio of a man with an olive branch.
ETRUSCAN: 3rd century BC.
Given by Dr. W.L. Hildburgh, F.S.A.
M.158-1929

22 Bronze, plated with gold. Long oval bezel, set with a paste intaglio of Bacchus and Ampelus.
ETRUSCAN: 3rd century BC.
Waterton Collection
451-1871

23 Gold. Oval bezel with an empty setting; filigree border.
ETRUSCAN: 5th century BC.
Webb Collection
8768-1863

24 Silver. Circular bezel set with a paste in imitation of an eye.
ETRUSCAN: 3rd century BC.
450-1871

25 Gold. Six coils of double wire.
? ETRUSCAN.
436-1871
Nos. 24 & 25, Waterton Collection

1 Bronze. Oval bezel set with a paste intaglio of a man with two oxen.
ROMAN: 1st century AD.
Given by Dr. W.L. Hildburgh, F.S.A.
M.156-1929

2 Lead. Swelling hoop set with an onyx intaglio of a woman bathing.
? ROMAN: 1st century BC — 1st century AD.
492-1871

3 Gold. Oval bezel set with a cornelian intaglio of two horses; corded border.
ROMAN: 1st century AD.
575-1871

4 Cornelian. Hoop flattened to form a bezel, engraved with a figure of Aesculapius.
ROMAN: 1st or 2nd century AD.
566-1871

5 Gold. Swelling hoop set with a garnet intaglio of a crowned female head. Faceted shoulders.
GRECO-ROMAN: 2nd or 3rd century AD.
Given by Dame Joan Evans, P.P.S.A.
M.36-1967

6 Gold. Swelling hoop set with an onyx cameo of a child's head.
ROMAN: 1st-2nd century AD.
Webb Collection
8778-1863

7 Gold. Swelling hoop set with a cornelian intaglio of the head of the Emperor Augustus, cut to the shape of his head.
ROMAN: 1st century AD.
Found near Rome, 1857.
461-1871

8 Gold. Projecting circular bezel set with a sardonyx intaglio of Abundantia with cornucopia and an eagle with a wreath.
ROMAN: 1st or 2nd century AD.
460-1871

9 Plasma. Bezel in the form of a horned child's head in full relief. Hoop restored in gold.
ROMAN: 1st or 2nd century AD.
568-1871

172

10 Lapis-lazuli. Bezel in the form of a male head in full relief. Hoop restored in gold.
ROMAN: 1st century AD.
Found near Rome, 1857.
567-1871
Nos. 7-10, Waterton Collection

11 Brown glass with white twists. Bezel set with a mask in green.
ROMAN: 1st or 2nd century AD.
Fould and Waterton Collections
559-1871

12 Bronze. Near circular bezel engraved with a harpy.
ROMAN: 1st century AD.
Given by Mrs. Hamilton Evans
M.107-1913

13 Gold. Near circular bezel engraved with a caduceus within a laurel wreath.
ROMAN: 2nd century AD.
Webb Collection
8771-1863

14 Gold signet. Oval bezel inscribed in Greek: *ALETHI ZESAIS*. Shoulders chased with acanthus leaves.
ROMAN: 2nd century AD.
503-1871

15 Gold. Two bezels, inscribed: *POPOL/ARE* (for Popularis).
ROMAN: 1st century AD.
Found near Rome, 1851.
474-1871

16 Gold. Two bezels, each engraved with a palm branch.
ROMAN: 1st century AD.
473-1871

17 Gold. Rectangular bezel engraved with a palm branch.
ROMAN: 1st century AD.
467-1871

*18 Gold signet. Applied oval bezel inscribed: *ITERE FELIX* (good journey).
ROMAN: 2nd century AD.
502-1871
Nos. 14-18, Waterton Collection

19 Gold. Swelling hoop with applied comic mask in full relief.
ROMAN: 1st century AD.
Webb Collection
8780-1863

20 Gold. Swelling hoop with applied comic mask. Each shoulder engraved with a rosette.
ROMAN: 1st century AD.
Waterton Collection
463-1871

21 Bronze. Hoop set with a comic mask.
ROMAN: 1st or 2nd century AD.
Given by Mr. Harold Wallis from the Henry Wallis Collection
M.76-1917

22 Gold serpent ring. Bezel formed by the head and coiled tail; the eyes formerly set with stones.
ROMAN: 1st century AD.
Waterton Collection
476-1871

*23 Gold dragon ring. Triple coils. Eyes set with red stones.
GRECO-ROMAN: 1st-2nd century AD.
Sir Arthur Evans Collection
Given by Dame Joan Evans, P.P.S.A.
M.37-1967

24 Bronze. Hoop of seven wire coils.
ROMAN: 1st century AD.
Waterton Collection
552-1871

*25 Gold serpent ring. Two coils of wire ending in two chased cobra heads.
ROMAN: 1st or 2nd century AD.
Given by Dame Joan Evans, P.P.S.A.
M.135-1962

26 Silver serpent ring. Four coils of wire ending in two heads.
ROMAN: 1st or 2nd century AD.
477-1871

27 Silver serpent ring, ending in two heads; eyes formerly set with stones.
ROMAN: 1st or 2nd century AD.
478-1871

28 ? Child's ring. Gold. Octagonal hoop widening into the bezel, to which is applied a phallus.
ROMAN: 1st or 2nd century AD.
465-1871

29 ? Child's ring. Gold. Hoop widening into the bezel which is engraved with a phallus.
ROMAN: 1st or 2nd century AD.
464-1871

30 Gilt bronze. Oval bezel with a bust of Serapis in full relief.
ROMAN: 2nd century AD.
534-1871

31 Gold. Five flattened wire hoops set with garnets and sapphires, one inscribed: *E V M E* in reverse.
GRECO-ROMAN: 2nd century AD.
475-1871
Nos. 26-31, Waterton Collection

Case 32 Board E

ROMAN RINGS:
2nd – 5th century AD.

The intaglio designs, whether engraved on the metal or cut into a stone, are usually signets.

1 Gold. Circular bezel cast in relief with clasped hands, a love motif later known as *fede*, from Italian *mani in fede*, hands clasped in faith. The *fede* device was revived in the 12th century.
ROMAN: 2nd or 3rd century AD.
Given by Dame Joan Evans, P.P.S.A.
M.136-1962

2 Gold. Hoop flattened to form a bezel, engraved with clasped hands.
ROMAN: 2nd or 3rd century AD.
829-1871

3 Gold. Swelling hoop set with intaglio of a dancing girl cut in a convex onyx.
ROMAN: 2nd or 3rd century AD.
488-1871
Nos. 2 & 3, Waterton Collection

4 Gold. Bezel set with an onyx intaglio (damaged). Wide shoulders decorated with applied scrolling wires and pellets.
ROMAN: 3rd century AD.
Given (? to Sir John Evans) by Lord Grantley, 1905.
Given by Dame Joan Evans, P.P.S.A.
M.139-1962

5 Gold. Flat strip made into a tapering hoop, engraved with the Genius of Death.
ROMAN: 2nd or 3rd century AD.
Found at Rieti, 1856, with no. 13.
468-1871

6 Gold. Square bezel set with an oval garnet intaglio of the Genius of Death. The ring octagonal in section; hoop pierced with scrolls.
ROMAN: 3rd century AD.
469-1871

7 Lead. Oval bezel set with a cornelian intaglio of two conjoined masks.
ROMAN: 2nd or 3rd century AD.
541-1871

8 Gold. Swelling hoop set with a raised onyx intaglio of an ant.
ROMAN: 2nd or 3rd century AD.
487-1871

9 Gold. Swelling hoop set with an onyx intaglio of a male head with a wing behind the neck.
ROMAN: 3rd century AD.
486-1871

10 Iron. Swelling hoop set with a projecting onyx intaglio of two goats.
ROMAN: 2nd or 3rd century AD.
482-1871

11 Iron. Oval bezel engraved with a bust of Serapis above a griffin.
GRECO-ROMAN: 2nd century AD.
489-1871

12 Gold. Vesica-shaped bezel engraved with the head of Cybele and the letters *G or ? C R F*.
ROMAN: 2nd or 3rd century AD.
471-1871

13 ? A child's ring. Gold. Swelling hoop engraved with a Victory.
ROMAN: 2nd or 3rd century AD.
Found at Rieti, 1856, with no. 5.
470-1871

14 Gilt bronze. Swelling hoop engraved with a figure pouring a libation on to an altar.
ROMAN: 3rd century AD.
490-1871
No. 5-14, Waterton Collection

15 Bronze. Circular bezel engraved with a comic mask.
ROMAN: 3rd century AD.
Given by Dr. W.L. Hildburgh, F.S.A.
M.152-1929

16 Silver. Circular bezel inscribed: *LIBERI VIVAS* (? May you live carefree).
ROMAN: 3rd century AD.
505-1871

17 Silver. Square bezel inscribed: *APOLLINARES*.
ROMAN: 3rd century AD.
504-1871

18 Bronze. Octagonal bezel engraved with eight signs of the Zodiac.
ROMAN: 3rd century AD.
543-1871

19 Gold. Rectangular bezel set with an onyx cut with letters (indecipherable) in relief.
ROMAN: 3rd century AD.
485-1871

20 ? A child's ring. Gold. Circular bezel inscribed in stipple characters: *? MOMAM/M*.
ROMAN: 2nd century AD.
466-1871

21 Purple glass with white twists. The bezel set with a brown glass eye in a yellow surround.
ROMAN: 2nd or 3rd century AD.
560-1871

22 Brown glass paste with traces of black. Bezel with projecting disc.
ROMAN: 3rd century AD.
554-1871
Nos. 16-22, Waterton Collection

23 Gold. Ridged hoop with open collet (setting) for a stone (missing).
ROMAN: 2nd or 3rd century AD.
Webb Collection
8766-1863

24 Cornelian hoop with spiralling ridges and oval bezel; stone missing.
ROMAN: 3rd century AD.
565-1871

25 Brown glass paste with traces of black. Hoop flattened to form a bezel.
ROMAN: 2nd or 3rd century AD.
553-1871

26 Nielloed gold. Square bezel engraved with a dolphin. Grooved angular shoulders.
ROMAN: 3rd century AD.
499-1871

27 Nielloed gold. Bezel set with a sapphire. Angular shoulders inscribed: CIX/KXK.
ROMAN: 4th or 5th century AD.
498-1871
Nos. 24-27, Waterton Collection

ROMAN RINGS:
3rd-5th century AD
Most of these rings are signets.

174

*28 Gold. High pierced rectangular bezel set with a sapphire and an emerald.
ROMAN: 3rd century AD.
Fould and Waterton Collections
501-1871

1 Bronze. Projecting oval bezel engraved with a chariot and inscribed in capitals: *OSIMIUS BARBARUS*. A pair of flattened pellets on each shoulder.
ROMAN: 3rd century AD.
595-1871

2 Bronze. Projecting circular bezel engraved with a head. Angular shoulders.
ROMAN: 4th or 5th century AD.
497-1871

3 Bronze. Square bezel engraved with Abraxas, a cabalistic figure with the head of a bird, the arms and bust of a man, and the body and tail of a serpent.
GNOSTIC: 3rd or 4th century AD.
Used as an amulet by the Gnostics; Abraxas represented the 365 orders of spirits emanating from the Supreme Being.
609-1871

*4 Nielloed silver. Circular bezel inscribed: *AVE DAX*. Incised angular shoulders.
ROMAN: (? Early Christian): 4th or 5th century AD.
(The inscription means: Hail, the Dacian! but it may have been intended for *Ave Pax*).
Found at Cologne.
Senkler and Waterton Collections
601-1871

5 Nielloed silver. Octagonal bezel inscribed: *FAVS TINVS NICHA FRA*. Foliated scrolls on the shoulders.
ROMAN: 4th or 5th century. AD.
825-1871

6 Bronze. Bezel in the form of the sole of a sandal, inscribed: *FELIX*.
ROMAN: 3rd century AD.
544-1871

7 Bronze. Rectangular bezel inscribed: *LXII*: a star on one shoulder; unidentified device on the other.
ROMAN: 3rd century AD.
529-1871

8 Bronze. Rectangular bezel, inscribed: *XXV*. Incised symbols (one an omega) on the shoulders.
ROMAN: 3rd century AD.
97-1899

9 Silver. Oval bezel decorated with a plug of gold and inscribed: *NIKAS* and Omega, and engraved with a device of clasped hands.
ROMAN: 3rd century AD.
824-1871

10 Gold. Hexagonal bezel set with an onyx intaglio of a female head. A pair of flattened pellets on each shoulder.
ROMAN: 5th century AD.
614-1871

11 Gold. Ribbed bezel, set with an onyx intaglio of Ganymede. The shoulders inscribed: *TOT*.
ROMAN: 5th century AD.
Given by Dame Joan Evans, P.P.S. A
M.137-1962

12 Silver. Oval bezel set with a bloodstone intaglio of Abraxas, jackal-headed.
GNOSTIC: 3rd or 4th century AD.
Doubts have been expressed about this gem, as it seems to have been intended for a use as a seal, which was not a Gnostic custom.
Waterton Collection
608-1871

13 Silver. Bezel set with a cornelian intaglio of a man reaping corn.
ROMAN: 4th century AD.
Given by Dr. W.L. Hildburgh, F.S.A.
M.157-1929

14 Bronze. Oval bezel engraved with two confronted busts. Cusped shoulders.
ROMAN: 3rd or 4th century AD.
827-1871

*15 Bronze. Square bezel engraved with two heads and inscribed: *BENERAN DUS BARUL IA*.
ROMAN: 4th or 5th century AD.
828-1871

EARLY CHRISTIAN AND BYZANTINE RINGS:
4th – 16th century

16 Iron. Oval bezel engraved with a head and a Greek inscription.
ROMAN (Egypt): 4th or 5th century AD.
594-1871
Nos. 14-16, Waterton Collection

17 Gold wire hoop with a faceted paste bead.
ROMAN: ? 3rd or 4th century AD.
6580-1855

18 Gold. Hollow hoop, notched at the back for use as a whistle. Hollow head or bezel.
ROMAN: 3rd century AD.
93-1899

19 Jet. Projecting oval bezel. Notched shoulders.
ROMAN: 4th century AD.
564-1871
Nos. 18 & 19, Waterton Collection

20 Gold, set with an emerald.
ROMAN: 5th century AD.
Given by Dame Joan Evans, P.P.S.A.
M.138-1962

21 Bronze. Circular bezel decorated with *champlevé* enamel.
PROVINCIAL ROMAN: 3rd century AD.
630-1871

22 Bronze. Bezel in the form of a key.
? ROMAN.
551-1871
Nos. 21 & 22, Waterton Collection

*23 Bronze. Bezel in the form of a key.
ROMAN: 3rd century AD.
Given by Dr. W.L. Hildburgh, F.S.A.
M.151-1929

24 Bronze. Bezel in the form of a key.
ROMAN: ? 3rd century AD or later.
545-1871

25 Bronze. Bezel in the form of a key.
? ROMAN.
548-1871

26 Bronze. Bezel in the form of a key.
ROMAN: 3rd century AD or later.
546-1871
Nos. 24-27, Waterton Collection.

Many of the rings on this board are signets. The early Church, while discouraging extravagance in rings, recognised the use of signets as inevitable. Clement of Alexandria deprecated pagan subjects, favouring the use of definitely Christian devices. Thus, a lamb represents Christ; a dove, the Holy Ghost or the Christian soul; a ship, the voyage of the soul to eternity.

1 Gold. Oval bezel set with an inscribed bloodstone intaglio of St. John the Evangelist; border of engraved semi-circles.
BYZANTINE: 11th century.
616-1871

2 Bronze. Curved circular bezel engraved with the bust of a saint.
BYZANTINE: 6th-8th century.
619-1871

3 Nielloed gold. Circular bezel with a bust of the Virgin Mary between *M* and *A*.
BYZANTINE: 6th-8th century.
618-1871

4 Bronze. Two bezels, a large circular one engraved with a saint praying, and a smaller one with a cross.
BYZANTINE: 6th-7th century.
606-1871
Nos. 1-4, Waterton Collection

5 Gold. Bezel engraved with St. George and the dragon and inscribed: *BPATHA*.
BYZANTINE: 6th century.
C. Cote and Guilhou Collections.
Given by the National Art Collections Fund.
M.175-1937

6 Gilt bronze. Oval bezel engraved with the figure of a saint and the Greek inscription: + *KEROITHITOS O DOULO THEODIGI*. The shoulders inlaid with silver.
VENETO-GREEK: 16th century.
Waterton Collection
982-1871

7 Bronze. Projecting oval bezel engraved with the ? Visitation.
EARLY CHRISTIAN (Palestine): 5th or 6th century.
From Jerusalem.
1377-1904

8 Gold. Protecting square bezel engraved with Christ joining the hands of a husband and wife.
BYZANTINE: 7th century.
Guilhou Collection.
Given by Mr. Mosheh Oved
M.184-1937

9 Gold. Projecting oval bezel engraved with Christ joining the hands of a husband and wife.
BYZANTINE: 7th century.
Guilhou Collection
M.183-1937

10 Bronze. Roughly circular bezel engraved with a cross within circle.
EASTERN CHRISTIAN (Egypt): 5th or 6th century.
Found at Behnesa (Oxyrhynchus), 1896-97.
Given by the Egypt Exploration Fund
1894-1897

11 Bronze. Oval bezel engraved with a lamb and two branches.
Palm leaf hoop.
EARLY CHRISTIAN (Italy): 4th century.
604-1871

12 Bronze. Projecting octagonal bezel engraved with a dove, a branch and a star. Hoop of eight kernel-shaped sections.
Early CHRISTIAN (Italy): 4th century.
605-1871
Nos. 11 & 12, Waterton Collection

13 Bronze. Circular bezel set with a silver intaglio of two doves perched on a standing vase.
EARLY CHRISTIAN (Italy): 4th century.
Given by Dr. W.L. Hildburgh, F.S.A.
M.159-1929

*14 Gold. Bezel formed of two confronted peacocks modelled in the round (the peacock being a symbol of immortality in Christian iconography).
BYZANTINE: 6th-10th century.
615-1871

15 Circular silver signet in modern gold setting, engraved with ? two deer; two doves flanking a palm-tree; above, a lamb with the *Chi Rho* monogram (the first two letters of Christ's name in Greek). Inscribed: *IANVARI VIVAS*.
The signet EARLY CHRISTIAN (Italy): 5th or 6th century; the mount 19th century.
92-1899
Nos. 14 & 15, Waterton Collection

16 Bronze, with traces of silvering. Octagonal hoop, engraved with a lion and a partly erased inscription filled in with black lac.
EARLY CHRISTIAN (Palestine): 6th-7th century.
Said to have come from Mount Carmel.
M.1142-1926

17 Gold. Circular bezel engraved with an eagle and a monogram of an Omega and *M, A* and *K*.
EARLY CHRISTIAN (Egypt): 5th century.
621-1871

18 Bronze. Oval bezel engraved with a ship bearing the *Chi Rho* monogram on the sail. Inscribed: *STEPANVS HELENAE*.
EARLY CHRISTIAN (Italy): 5th century.
95-1899

19 Gold. Circular bezel set with a solidus of Constans II (641-668). The hoop inscribed: + *BARINOTA*.
BYZANTINE: 7th century.
617-1871
Nos. 17-19, Waterton Collection

20 Gold. Square bezel inscribed: *PEREGRINE VIVAS*.
EARLY CHRISTIAN (Italy): 5th century.
Guilhou Collection.
Given by the National Art Collections Fund
M.174-1937

21 Gold. Circular bezel engraved with a monogram.
BYZANTINE: 6th-7th century.
623-1871

22 Gold. Circular bezel engraved with a cross monogram including the letters *SIONA*.
BYZANTINE: 6th-7th century.
Fould Collection
622-1871
Nos. 21 & 22, Waterton Collection

23 Iron. Circular bezel engraved with a monogram and a cross.
EASTERN CHRISTIAN (Egypt): 6th century.
Found at Behnesa, 1896-97.
Given by the Egypt Exploration Fund
1894a-1897

24 Bronze. Oval bezel engraved with a cross monogram.
BYZANTINE: 10th or 11th century.
Given by Sir Otto Beit, Bart., K.C.M.G., who acquired it in Sicily.
M.251-1929

*25 Bronze. Circular bezel engraved with a cross monogram.
BYZANTINE: 10th or 11th century.
588-1871

ANGLO-SAXON and
VIKING RINGS:
*mainly 5th–11th century or
later*

26 Bronze. Circular bezel engraved with a cross monogram.
EARLY CHRISTIAN (Italy):
5th century.
589-1871

27 Bronze. Oval bezel inscribed in Greek: + *PETROU*.
BYZANTINE: 6th-10th century.
507-1871

28 Silver signet. Circular bezel engraved with a Greek inscription meaning: *O Lord, help the wearer.*
BYZANTINE: 10th-11th century.
506-1871

29 Bronze signet. Rectangular bezel inscribed: *VIVAS IN DIO* (live in God).
EARLY CHRISTIAN (Italy or Gaul):
4th century.
603-1871

30 Bronze. Circular bezel engraved with a monogram of *VIVAS IN DEO*.
EARLY CHRISTIAN (Italy or Gaul):
4th century.
591-1871

31 Silver. Oval bezel engraved with a monogram, perhaps of *VIVAS IN DEO*.
EARLY CHRISTIAN (Italy or Gaul):
4th century.
590-1871
Nos. 25-31, Waterton Collection

32 Nielloed gold. Oval bezel engraved with a Greek inscription meaning: *Lord, help Thy servant Nicetas captain of the imperial guard.*
BYZANTINE: 11th century.
Guilhou Collection.
Given by the National Art Collections Fund
M.173-1937

33 Gold. Rectangular bezel with a lion passant in relief. Shoulders engraved with reticulated ornament.
SICILIAN: 12th century.
26-1894

1 Bronze wire, the ends tapered and twisted into a bezel.
ANGLO-SAXON: 5th-7th century.
598-1871

2 Bronze wire, twisted as in no. 1.
ANGLO-SAXON: 5th-7th century.
597-1871

***3** Silver-gilt. Oval bezel with a dragon medallion flanked by four monster heads.
ANGLO-SAXON: late 8th or early 9th century.
Found in the Thames at Chelsea, 1856.
628-1871
Nos. 1-3, Waterton Collection

4 Gold. Hoop type with bands of beading alternating with plain and roped bands.
ANGLO-SAXON: 9th-11th century.
From York.
Given by Dame Joan Evans, P.P.S.A.
M.141-1962

***5** THE ALHSTAN RING
Nielloed gold. Birds and monsters in lozenges alternating with the name: *+A LH ST A* (and runic *N*) in roundels: stylised leaf edges.
ANGLO-SAXON: 9th century.
Found probably in 1753 at Llysfaen near Colwyn Bay, Wales. It has been suggested that the original owner was Ahlstan, Bishop of Sherborne (824-867).
Waterton Collection
627-1871

***6** Gold. Stirrup type. Bezel formed of a pellet issuing from two dragon heads in filigree.
ANGLO-SAXON: 9th century.
Found in the moat at Meaux Abbey, Yorkshire, 1867.
M.277-1920

7 Gold. Circular bezel set with a medallion in *cloisonné* enamel with a triskele device. Pelleted and toothed borders.
ANGLO-SAXON: 9th century.
Found in Ireland.
From the old Geological Museum, Jermyn Street
4917-1901

8 Gold plaited wires, tapering towards the back, where they are beaten flat.
VIKING: 9th-11th century.
632-1871

9 Gold twisted wires, tapering as in no.8 above.
VIKING: 9th-11th century.
631-1871

10 Gold. Set with a paste in a beaded bezel.
? ANGLO-SAXON: ?9th-11th century, but perhaps as late as the 15th century.
From Bury St. Edmunds
M.142-1962

11 Silver wire, plaited and flattened at the back.
VIKING: 9th-11th century.
From York.
Rev. W. Greenwell and Sir John Evans Collections
M.140-1962
Nos. 10 & 11, given by Dame Joan Evans, P.P.S.A.

12 Gold. A signet. Circular bezel engraved with the bust of a bearded man between the name +*AVF RET*. A pair of flattened pellets on each shoulder. Possibly 9th century.
This ring, previously described as Anglo-Saxon, was said to have been found in Rome with a hoard of coins of Alfred the Great (849-901). The story has recently been challenged, and the inscription cannot therefore be taken definitively to refer to King Alfred. The Anglo-Saxon attribution, which partly depended on the association with Alfred, has to be balanced against the general resemblance of the ring to Byzantine examples, which in turn derived from a Roman type. (See preceeding boards F, no. 10, for similar pelleted shoulders on a Roman ring, and G, nos. 21 and 22, for circular bezels on Byzantine rings).
Waterton Collection
629-1871

Case 32 Board I

GERMANIC RINGS:
6th-9th century

1 Gold. High circular bezel set with an onyx intaglio of a standing figure, surrounded by small drop-shaped collets for stones (missing).
MEROVINGIAN: probably 6th or 7th century.
Acquired (? by Sir John Evans) in the South of France, 1877.
Given by Dame Joan Evans, P.P.S.A.
M.143-1962

*2 Gold. Oval bezel set with an antique onyx intaglio of Bonus Eventus.
MEROVINGIAN: 6th or 7th century.
Waterton Collection
620-1871

3 Gold. Oval bezel set with a Roman nicolo intaglio of Arion on the Dolphin.
MEROVINGIAN: 6th century.
From Thennes, near Amiens.
M.173-1975

4 Gold. Oval bezel set with a classical jasper intaglio of a man.
MEROVINGIAN: 6th century.
Found near Compiègne.
M.174-1975
Nos. 3 & 4, given by Dame Joan Evans, P.P.S.A.

5 Gold. Circular bezel inlaid with garnets in a wheel pattern (some missing)
MEROVINGIAN: 6th or 7th century.
625-1871

6 Silver. Circular galleried and arcaded bezel for a stone (missing).
MEROVINGIAN or LOMBARD: 6th or 7th century.
952-1871
Nos. 5 & 6, Waterton Collection

7 Gold. Galleried and arcaded bezel, with filigree.
MEROVINGIAN: 6th or 7th century.
Guilhou Collection.
Given by the National Art-Collections Fund
M.176-1937

8 Gold. High pierced beaker-shaped bezel set with a sapphire; subsidiary tube-shaped mount for stone (missing). Three pellets on each shoulder.
MEROVINGIAN: 6th or 7th century.
Waterton Collection
624-1871

9 Gold. Lozenge-shaped arcaded bezel, set with a flat red paste.
MEROVINGIAN: 6th century.
From Thennes, near Amiens.
Given by Dame Joan Evans, P.P.S.A.
M.175-1975

10 Gold. Oval bezel inscribed: MAZNE. Nielloed shoulders.
MEROVINGIAN: 7th century.
525-1868

11 Gold. Circular bezel inlaid with garnets in a wheel pattern.
MEROVINGIAN: 6th-7th century.
626-1871

12 Bronze signet, chased with a monogram.
MEROVINGIAN: 6th-7th century.
730-1871
Nos. 11 & 12, Waterton Collection

13 Silver signet. Flat rectangular bezel engraved with a dove and leaves.
MEROVINGIAN: 6th-7th century.
Acquired at Amiens, 1877.
Given by Dame Joan Evans, P.P.S.A.
M.144-1962

14 Bronze signet. Projecting square bezel engraved with a monogram.
MEROVINGIAN: 6th or 7th century.
593-1871

15 Bronze signet. Projecting square bezel engraved with a monogram. Hoop inlaid with silver.
MEROVINGIAN: 6th or 7th century.
592-1871
Nos. 14 & 15, Waterton Collection

16 Gold. Circular bezel decorated with filigree and set with pastes.
LOMBARD: 6th-7th century.
Castellani Collection; transferred from the British Museum
M.123-1939

17 Gold. Swelling hoop set with two lozenges separated by beading.
LOMBARD: 6th or 7th century.
Waterton Collection
439-1871

18 Gold. Projecting cone-shaped bezel set with a garnet and pearls.
SOUTH ITALIAN: 7th century.
Guilhou Collection
M.178-1937

19 Gold. Projecting cone-shaped bezel set with a garnet intaglio of a man's head.
SOUTH ITALIAN: 7th century.
Guilhou Collection
M.177-1937
Nos. 18 & 19, given by the National Art-Collections Fund.

20 Silver-gilt. Projecting beaker-shaped bezel set with a glass mosaic.
CAROLINGIAN: 9th century.
Found in Lombardy.
Given by Sir James Hudson, K.C.B.
7442-1860

21 Gold. Oval bezel set with an amethyst, bordered by pellets at the junction with the shoulders. S-shaped wire filigree applied to hoop.
FRANKISH: 7th century.
From Andernach.
M.176-1975

22 Gold. Bezel set with a classical garnet intaglio surrounded by beading.
LOMBARD: 7th century.
From Benevento.
M.177-1975
Nos. 21 & 22, given by Dame Joan Evans, P.P.S.A.

Case 32 Board J

MEDIEVAL DECORATIVE RINGS:
13th-15th century

The stones are either roughly cut or are polished cabochons (flat-backed stones with a convex upper surface).

1 Gilt and nielloed bronze, set with a hexagonal sapphire. Stirrup ring (the hoop, flowing into the bezel, resembles a stirrup). Niello foliations on shoulders.
WEST EUROPEAN: 14th century.
636-1871

2 Gold, set with a sapphire. Stirrup type.
WEST EUROPEAN: 13th century.
634-1871

3 Gold, set with a sapphire. Stirrup type.
WEST EUROPEAN: 13th century.
633-1871
Nos. 1-3, Waterton Collection

4 Gold, set with a sapphire. Stirrup type.
WEST EUROPEAN: 13th century.
Found in the vicinity of the Chapel Royal, Windsor, about 1835.
Given by Dr. Harcourt
65-1871

5 Gold, set with a garnet. Inscribed in lombardic characters:
IESVIDUNDAM (I am a love gift).
The bezel may have come from a stirrup ring.
WEST EUROPEAN: 13th century.
Found near Bury St. Edmunds, Suffolk.
Joseph Warren and Sir John Evans Collections
Given by Dame Joan Evans, P.P.S.A.
M.286-1962

6 Gold. Double bezel (stones missing). Hoop inscribed in lombardic characters: + *PENSEZ DE LI PARKI SVI CI* (think of him through whom I am here).
WEST EUROPEAN: 13th century.
889-1871

7 Gold, set with a sapphire.
WEST EUROPEAN: 13th or 14th century.
637-1871

8 Gold, set with an emerald.
WEST EUROPEAN: 13th or 14th century.
638-1871

9 Gold. Hexagonal bezel set with a sapphire.
WEST EUROPEAN: 13th or 14th century.
639-1871
Nos. 6-9, Waterton Collection

10 Gold, set with a triangular sapphire. Stirrup type.
WEST EUROPEAN: 14th century.
From Rushford, Norfolk, 1850.
A.K. Creed and Crisp Collections
M.184-1962

11 Gold, small cup-shaped bezel set with a sapphire. Hoop inscribed in lombardic characters: + *DMO AIERVA-CLANSIE PA*.
WEST EUROPEAN: 14th century.
Found at Chester.
M.179-1975

12 Gold. Beaker-shaped bezel set with a sapphire. Engraved shoulders.
WEST EUROPEAN: early 14th century.
M.182-1962

13 Gold. Pentagonal bezel set with a sapphire. Pounced chevrons on shoulders.
WEST EUROPEAN: early 14th century.
Acquired (? by Sir John Evans), 1905.
M.185-1962

14 Gold. Pentagonal bezel set with a sapphire. Engraved saltires on shoulders.
WEST EUROPEAN: early 14th century.
Found near Mynchin Buckland Priory, Taunton, Somerset.
Rev. Thomas Hugo Collection
M.181-1962

15 Gold. Hoop inscribed twice in lombardic characters: + *IE S VI ICI EN LIV DAMI* (Je suis ici en lieu d'ami: I am here in place of a friend [or lover]).
WEST EUROPEAN: 13th century.
Found at Hemel Hempstead, 1865.
Sir Arthur Evans Collection
M.178-1962
Nos. 10-15, given by Dame Joan Evans, P.P.S.A.

16 Gold. Semicircular bezel set with a garnet.
WEST EUROPEAN: 13th or 14th century.
Waterton Collection
640-1871

*17 Gold. Foliated bezel with a sapphire. Dragon-head shoulders. Stirrup type.
WEST EUROPEAN: 13th century.
Guilhou Collection
M.183-1975

18 Gold. Oval bezel set with an irregular sapphire.
WEST EUROPEAN: 14th century.
M.178-1975
Nos. 17 & 18, given by Dame Joan Evans, P.P.S.A.

19 Gold. Oval bezel set with a sapphire. Chased foliated shoulders.
WEST EUROPEAN: 14th century.
Waterton Collection
641-1871

20 Gold. Hexagonal bezel set with an uncut sapphire.
WEST EUROPEAN: 14th century.
Acquired (? by Sir John Evans), Pressburg, 1886.
Given by Dame Joan Evans, P.P.S.A.
M.285-1962

21 Silver-gilt. Pyramidal bezel, imitating a diamond. Chased monsters on shoulders.
WEST EUROPEAN: 13th century.
Waterton Collection
937-1871

22 Gold, set with half a natural diamond crystal. Shoulders inscribed in black letter: *ave/mria*.
WEST EUROPEAN: late 14th or 15th century.
M.188-1975

180

23 Gold, set with a ruby (modern). The shoulders decorated with sixfoils. Partly defaced black letter inscription on the hoop: *qui* (me portera)/*a grant honneur venir* (he who wears me will achieve great honour).
? ENGLISH: late 14th or 15th century.
Acquired at Midgham by Dame Joan Evans, 1929.
M.287-1962

24 Gold. Hexagonal bezel set with a sapphire. Shoulders chased with dragon-heads. Hoop inscribed in lombardic characters: *+AVE MARIA GRACIA / + DNES AIV(T)VM MEAS.*
WEST EUROPEAN: late 13th century.
Sidney Churchill Collection (1934)
M.176-1962

*25 Gold, set a with green paste (one missing). The hoop terminates in a pair of hands holding a double bezel. Inscribed in lombardic characters: *+AVISITIVNVN/AVIORVRIOIOR.*
WEST EUROPEAN: early 14th century.
M.187-1962

26 Gold. Raised bezel set with an uncut ruby. The hoop inscribed *A/M/I/A/M*, the letters filled with black composition. Quatrefoils on shoulders.
? ENGLISH: 14th century.
The inscription may be the initial letters of: *Ave Maria* (et) *Iesus Ave Maria.*
Bought at Peterborough, 1926.
M.288-1962

27 Gold. Pentagonal bezel set with a sapphire; four small attached collets for emeralds (three missing). Engraved saltires on hoop.
WEST EUROPEAN: early 14th century.
Found in Durham.
Philip Nelson Collection
M.183-1962
Nos. 22-27, given by Dame Joan Evans, P.P.S.A.

28 Gold. Hexagonal bezel set with a sapphire. Chased dragon-head shoulders.
? FRENCH: 14th century.
Said to be from Amiens.
642-1871

29 Gold. Hexagonal bezel, set with a simple faceted sapphire. Chased dragon-head shoulders.
WEST EUROPEAN: 14th century.
647-1871

*30 Gold. Chased flower-shaped bezel set with a sapphire. The shoulders have settings for stones, one holding a ruby, the other empty. An episcopal ring, said to have been found in the tomb of a French bishop.
WEST EUROPEAN: 14th century.
Given to Edmund Waterton by the Hon. Robert Curzon.
90-1899
Nos. 28-30, Waterton Collection

31 Silver-gilt. Hexagonal bezel set with blue paste. Faceted shoulders.
WEST EUROPEAN: late 14th or 15th century.
M.34-1971

1 Gold. Projecting 4-claw bezel set with a sapphire.
WEST EUROPEAN: 12th or 13th century.
Waterton Collection
644-1871

2 Gold. Projecting 4-claw bezel set with a sapphire. Foliated hoop with lozenges.
WEST EUROPEAN: 13th century.
M.180-1975

3 Gold. Projecting 4-claw bezel set with a sapphire. Lion-mask shoulders. The hoop inscribed in lombardic characters: *AVE MA RIA GRA* and *AMOR VI NCI(T) O(M)NIA.* The second inscription (love conquers all) adorned the brooch worn by the Prioress on pilgrimage, in the Prologue to Chaucer's *Canterbury Tales,* written about 1387.
WEST EUROPEAN: 13th century.
M.181-1975

4 Gold. 4-claw bezel set with a sapphire. Lion-mask shoulders. The hoop inscribed in lombardic characters: *AVE MARIA G/RACIA PLENA.*
WEST EUROPEAN: 13th century.
M.182-1975
Nos. 2-4, given by Dame Joan Evans, P.P.S.A.

*5 Gold. 4-claw bezel set with a sapphire, flanked by small amethysts in individual tube-shaped settings.
WEST EUROPEAN: 13th century.
Found at Epsom.
Harman-Oates Collection
M.7-1929

6 Gold. Projecting 4-claw bezel set with a sapphire. Forked shoulders.
WEST EUROPEAN: 13th century.
645-1871

7 Gold. 4-claw bezel, the stone missing. Foliated shoulders with Hercules (reef) knots.
WEST EUROPEAN: 15th century.
653-1871

8 Gold. Projecting bezel set with an emerald. Open quatrefoils and rope decoration on hoop.
WEST EUROPEAN: 15th century.
652-1871

9 Gold. Projecting 4-claw bezel set with a piece of green porphyry. Heart motifs on shoulders. Hoop inscribed in black letter: *god. help. anna. maria.*
ENGLISH: late 14th century.
675-1871
Nos. 6-9, Waterton Collection

10 Gold. 3-claw bezel set with a sapphire. Foliated shoulders; black letter inscription on hoop: *saunz+ departier* (without division).
WEST EUROPEAN: 15th century.
M.206-1975

*11 Gold. 6-cusped setting with a drilled octagonal sapphire. Ridged shoulders chased with floral sprays. Inscribed inside in black letter: *wllms wytlesey.*
ENGLISH: between 1362 and 1374. Said to have been found in the grave of William Wytlesey, Archbishop of Canterbury (d. 1374).
Pierced stones were said to have more 'virtue', that is, they possessed enhanced curative or talismanic properties.
Sir Arthur Evans Collection
M.191-1975
Nos. 10 & 11, given by Dame Joan Evans, P.P.S.A.

12 Gold. Projecting 4-claw bezel set with an carbuncle.
WEST EUROPEAN: 13th century.
650-1871

13 Gold. 4-claw bezel set with an antique plasma bust.
WEST EUROPEAN: 13th century.
Found at Canmore Place, near Oxford.
646-1871
Nos. 12 & 13, Waterton Collection

14 Gold, the bezel cast with a sun in splendour, the badge of the Yorkists.
ENGLISH: third quarter of the 15th century.
The badge commemorates the omen of a triple sun that appeared in the sky on the day that Edward IV (1442-1483) defeated the Lancastrian army at the battle of Mortimer's Cross, 1461, afterwards proclaiming himself king.
Found between Yeovil and Athelney, Somerset.
Philip Nelson Collection; acquired by Dame Joan Evans.
M.191-1962

15 Gold. The bezel set with a relief of St. George and the dragon. Sprigs engraved on shoulders. Inscribed in black letter: *nul/si bien.*
? ENGLISH: late 14th century.
Found at King's Langley, Hertfordshire, 1866.
M.235-1962
Nos. 14 & 15, given by Dame Joan Evans, P.P.S.A.

*16 Latten. Projecting bezel re-set with an amethyst. Roses stamped on shoulders. Hoop inscribed in black letter: *par/grant/amour.*
WEST EUROPEAN: about 1400.
Found at Cardiff.
Harman-Oates Collection
M.10-1929

17 Gold, originally enamelled. Cusped and clawed setting with a dark sapphire.
WEST EUROPEAN: 15th century.
Found in the Seine at Rouen, 1876; acquired by Sir John Evans.
M.180-1962

18 Gold. 4-claw bezel set with ruby.
WEST EUROPEAN: 14th century.
Said to have been found in Tours; acquired by Sir John Evans.
M.186-1962

19 Gold. Hoop, rosettes and scrolls inscribed in black letter: *?en bien/ame/vanv/ame.*
WEST EUROPEAN: 15th century.
Acquired by Sir John Evans, 1886.
M.65-1960

20 Gold. Hoop, inscribed in lombardic characters: *+GE/ VOVLDROY* (I would like ...)
WEST EUROPEAN: 14th century.
Sir John Evans and Mrs C.J. Longman Collections
M.61-1960
Nos. 17-20, given by Dame Joan Evans, P.P.S.A.

21 Gold. Tranverse fluted hoop, chased with sprigs; traces of enamel.
WEST EUROPEAN: 15th century.
894-1871

182

22 Silver-gilt. Applied bezel with a heart between two death's heads. Hoop engraved with a worm and inscribed in black letter: +*iohes godefroy.*
ENGLISH: second half of 15th century.
According to Charles Oman, *British Rings,* 1974, this is the earliest surviving example of an English mourning ring.
900-1871
Nos. 21 & 22, Waterton Collection

23 Silver-gilt. Projecting bezel set with a pearl.
? MEDITERRANEAN: 14th century.
94-1899

24 Silver-gilt. Chased bezel, twisted hoop.
WEST EUROPEAN: 15th century.
Waterton Collection
682-1871

25 Silver. Hoop, inscribed in black letter: + *aimis. ames. aimie. ave* (love, my love, you have a lover).
WEST EUROPEAN: 15th century.
Philip Nelson Collection; acquired by Dame Joan Evans.
M.63-1960

*26 Silver-gilt. Hoop, shaped panels flanked by pearls and inscribed in black letter with the letter *m* repeated.
WEST EUROPEAN: 15th century.
M.229-1962
Nos. 25 & 26, given by Dame Joan Evans

27 Nielloed silver. Bezel with the bust of a woman; rosettes on shoulders.
ITALIAN; 15th century.
7550-1861

28 Nielloed silver. Circular bezel, with initials *IL* in a 6-pointed star.
? ITALIAN: 15th century.
887-1871

29 Silver. Hoop, inscribed in lombardic characters: + *AMOVR + MERCI.*
WEST EUROPEAN: 14th century.
888-1871
Nos. 28 & 29, Waterton Collection

30 Silver-gilt openwork. Cast bezel formed of openwork branches encasing a stag.
GERMAN: ? 15th-16th century.
1204-1903

31 Silver-gilt. 4-claw bezel set with a turquoise. Openwork floriated hoop.
WEST EUROPEAN: 15th century.
1205-1903

32 Silver-gilt. Double bezel, engraved with flower heads.
WEST EUROPEAN: 15th century.
6769-1860

33 Gilt bronze. Hoop, set with antique paste cameos of Marcus Aurelius and Hadrian. Inscribed in black letter: *mur.*
WEST EUROPEAN: 15th century.
654-1871

34 Gilt bronze. Rectangular bezel set with a pyramidal crystal over foil.
WEST EUROPEAN: 15th century.
656-1871
Nos. 33 & 34, Waterton Collection

35 Gilt bronze. Cusped setting with square projecting green paste. Shoulders also cusped.
ITALIAN: late 15th century.
Given by Dr. W.L. Hildburgh, F.S.A.
M.160-1929

36 THUMB-RING. Gold. Hoop, set with a point-cut diamond and rubies. Inscribed in black letter: *rv* and, inside, *for a caufe.*
ENGLISH: 15th century.
Ashburnham Collection
M.253-1921

These rings, their name deriving from poesy, or poetry, are engraved with tags, amatory and otherwise. Some of the earlier examples are gem rings, but from the fifteenth century at least they mainly took the form of hoops.

1 Gold. Hoop, inscribed in lombardic characters: +*WEL:WERE:HIM:YAT: WISTE:*TO:WHOM:HE MIGTE: TRISTE* (well for him who knows whom he can trust).
ENGLISH: about 1300.
Found at Park Street, near St. Albans. Sir Arthur Evans Collection
M.184-1975

2 Gold. Hoop, inscribed in lombardic characters: +*IOSVI:DE:DRVERIE: NE:ME:DVNE:MIE* (I am a love token, do not give me away).
ENGLISH: early 14th century.
Sir Arthur Evans Collection
M.60-1960

3 Gold. Hoop, inscribed in lombardic characters: + *IESVS.*
WEST EUROPEAN: 14th century.
M.223-1962
Nos. 1-3, given by Dame Joan Evans, P.P.S.A.

4 Gold. Hoop, engraved with sprigs and inscribed in black letter: *Vous et nul autre* (you and no other).
WEST EUROPEAN: early 15th century.
M.57-1946

5 Brass. Hoop, possibly cast or stamped, with black letter inscription: *Amie+aimes+envie* (?my love dispels judgement).
? FRENCH: 15th century.
Bought by Sir John Evans at Amiens, 1890.
M.62-1960

6 Gold. Hoop, inscribed inside (largely) in black letter: +*god be my help At nede.*
ENGLISH: 15th century.
M.66-1960
Nos. 5&6, given by Dame Joan Evans, P.P.S.A.

7 Gold. Hoop, engraved with sprigs and inscribed: *in bone foy.*
ENGLISH: 15th century.
Waterton Collection
891-1871

8 Gold. Hoop, engraved with sprigs and inscribed: *Autre ne vueil* (desire no other).
WEST EUROPEAN: 15th century.
7125-1860

9 Gold. Hoop, engraved with sprigs and inscribed: *Por tous jours* (for always).
WEST EUROPEAN: 15th century.
892-1871

10 Silver-gilt. Hoop, engraved with sprigs and inscribed in black letter: *Cest mon plesir* (it is my pleasure).
WEST EUROPEAN: 15th century.
898-1871
Nos. 9 & 10, Waterton Collection

11 Gold. Hoop with pearled and raised border, inscribed in black letter: *De bon coer.*
WEST EUROPEAN: 15th century.
Rev. C.L. Marson and Sir Arthur Evans Collections
Given by Dame Joan Evans, P.P.S.A.
M.219-1962

12 Silver. Hoop, with 21 concave facets, inscribed in lombardic characters: *+AVE MARIA GRATIA PLENA DO.*
WEST EUROPEAN: 15th century.
Miss E.M. Begg Bequest
M.336-1975

13 Silver. Hoop, inscribed in black letter: *+quant. dieu. plera. melior. sera.* (when God pleases, things will be better).
WEST EUROPEAN: 15th century.
Waterton Collection
899-1871

14 Nielloed silver. Hoop, inscribed: *+ZARAGEINELEVE.*
WEST EUROPEAN: early 15th century.
Miss E.M. Begg Bequest
M.335-1975

15 Gold. Stirrup type; the bezel is missing. Hoop inscribed in black letter: *+si: ergo.me.qieritis.sinite. eos.babire.* (a corruption of the Vulgate. John 18, 8: if therefore ye seek me, let these go their way).
? ENGLISH: 15th century.
Found near Hastings, 1881, and acquired by Sir Arthur Evans.
Given by Dame Joan Evans P.P.S.A.
M.188-1962

16 Gold. Hoop, chased with foliage, birds and a scroll inscribed: *Myn. Genyst (?my consort).*
GERMAN: 15th century.
Guilhou Collection
Given by the National Art Collections Fund
M.182-1937

17 Gold. The bezel inscribed with the Sacred Monogram in black letter and the hoop with: *MARIA. ?JOHANNIS* in lombardic characters.
WEST EUROPEAN: 15th century.
Waterton Collection
677-1871

18 Gold. Raised square bezel with vacant hole. Faceted hoop, inscribed inside in black letter: *+ioe+saunz+ fine* (joy without end).
WEST EUROPEAN: 15th century.
M.224-1962

19 Gold. Hoop, engraved with sprigs and inscribed in black letter: *+ioie+ sans fin.*
WEST EUROPEAN: 15th century.
M.68-1960
Nos. 18 & 19, Philip Nelson Collection; acquired by Dame Joan Evans, P.P.S.A.

*20 Gold. Hoop, engraved with sprigs and a heart, inscribed in black letter: *+pense, de moy* (think of me).
WEST EUROPEAN: 15th century.
M.222-1962

21 Gold. Hoop, inscribed inside in black letter: *+buro+berto+beriara* (a magical charm against toothache).
ENGLISH: early 15th century.
Sir John Woodford Collection
M.90-1960
Nos. 18-21, given by Dame Joan Evans, P.P.S.A.

22 Gold. Hoop, inscribed inside in black letter: *+my.wordely.ioye+alle. my.trust+hert.thought.lyfe.and.lust.*
ENGLISH: early 16th century.
895-1871

23 Gold. Hoop, engraved with *C* and *M* flanking a true lovers' knot and inscribed in Roman capitals: *DEVX. CORPS.VNG.CVER.* (two bodies, one heart).
? ENGLISH: 16th century.
Found at Glastonbury Abbey.
897-1871

24 Gold. Hoop, engraved inside with a heart pierced by an arrow, and the names *Eygen* and *Uwer* in black letter.
GERMAN: early 16th century.
896-1871
Nos. 22-24, Waterton Collection

25 Gold. Hoop, engraved with sprigs and inscribed inside in floriated capitals: *+I.AM.YOURS.K:S.*
English; 16th century.
J.W. Singer and Sir John Evans Collections
Given by Dame Joan Evans, P.P.S.A.
M.67-1960

26 Gold. Hoop, chased with sprigs and scrolls and inscribed in black letter on the outside: *?Nul.Sans.Peyn* (nothing without effort) and inside, *Sans mal desyr* (without evil wishes)
WEST EUROPEAN: early 16th century.
Waterton Collection
893-1871

27 Gold. Hoop, set with an onyx cameo of a female bust. Hoop inscribed inside in black letter: *+dung+seul+regart+vous+doibt+ suffire (you must be satisfied with one glance).*
FRENCH: 15th century.
Pichon and Guilhou Collections
M.190-1962

28 Gold. Four-lobed or petal setting with a turquoise. Hoop inscribed inside in black letter: *en bon an* (I wish you a good year. A New Year's gift.)
? ENGLISH: 14th century.
M.77-1969

29 Gold. Lozenge-shaped bezel set with a small sapphire. Hoop inscribed in lombardic characters: *AVE MARIA GI.*
? FRENCH: late 13th century.
Pichon and Guilhou Collections
M.179-1962
Nos. 27-29, given by Dame Joan Evans, P.P.S.A.

CASE 32
BOARD D
NO. 18

CASE 32
BOARD D
NO. 25

CASE 32
BOARD A
NO. 14

CASE 32
BOARD B
NO. 13

CASE 32
BOARD E
NO. 28

CASE 32
BOARD F
NO. 23

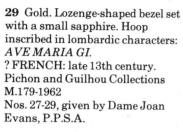

CASE 32
BOARD B
NO. 15

CASE 32
BOARD F
NO. 4

CASE 32
BOARD G
NO. 14

CASE 32
BOARD C
NO. 11

CASE 32
BOARD F
NO. 15

CASE 32
BOARD G
NO. 25

CASE 32
BOARD G
NO. 32

CASE 32
BOARD I
NO. 2

CASE 32
BOARD K
NO. 5

CASE 32
BOARD H
NO. 3

CASE 32
BOARD J
NO. 17

CASE 32
BOARD K
NO. 11

CASE 32
BOARD H
NO. 4

CASE 32
BOARD J
NO. 25

CASE 32
BOARD K
NO. 16

CASE 32
BOARD H
NO. 6

CASE 32
BOARD J
NO. 30

CASE 32
BOARD L
NO. 20

Case 33 Board A

ENGLISH ICONOGRAPHICAL RINGS:
late 14th-early 16th century

This particularly English type of ring, introduced in the late fourteenth century, is characterised by one of more Christian figures engraved on the bezel or head of the ring, and, often, on the shoulders. Traces of enamel are discernable in several specimens. A few items with the Sacred Monogram and other religious devices are also included on this board.

1 Gold. St Christopher and St Paul. The shoulders inscribed in black letter: *pre ... / ? cuore;* with engraved sprigs.
15th century.
Guilhou Collection
M.240-1962

2 Gold. The Annunciation and St Mary Magdalene. Engraved sprigs on transverse fluted shoulders. Inscribed inside in black letter: *en bon an;* traces of enamel.
15th century.
M.208-1975

3 Gold. St. Margaret.
15th century.
M.238-1962
Nos. 1-3; given by Dame Joan Evans, P.P.S.A.

4 Gold. Plain circular bezel. St Barbara and ? St Catherine on fluted shoulders, flanked by sprigs. Inscribed inside in black letter: *de bon cor* (be of good heart).
15th century.
Waterton Collection
902-1871

5 Gold. The Five Joys of Our Lady on the shoulders. The bezel and table-cut amethyst modern.
About 1500.
Engraved on the inside with an inscription recording the presentation of the ring on 12 March 1924 to the Rt. Rev. William Brown on his consecration as Bishop of Pella. Bequeathed by the Rt. Rev. William Brown.
M.27-1952

6 Gold. St Catherine. Traces of sprigs engraved on the shoulders.
15th century.
691-1871

7 Silver-gilt. Figures and busts of saints.
15th century.
683-1871
Nos. 6 & 7, Waterton Collection

8 Gold. ?St Margaret. Hoop inscribed outside in black letter: *pur/bone* (pure and good); traces of white enamel.
15th century.
Found at West Ham; acquired by Sir Arthur Evans.
Given by Dame Joan Evans, P.P.S.A.
M.212-1975

9 Gold. St Christopher. Engraved sprigs on transverse fluted shoulders. Hoop inscribed inside in black letter: *de bon cor.*
15th century.
Waterton Collection
692-1871

*10 Gold. St Christopher. Hexagonal hoop inscribed outside in black letter: *en/(n.e.u.?)e/a/ne* (for the new year).
15th century
Philip Nelson Collection; acquired by Dame Joan Evans.
M.239-1962

11 Gold. The Trinity and St Catherine. Inscribed behind in black letter: *de bon cuer* (be of good heart). Engraved sprigs on transverse fluted shoulders.
15th century.
Guilhou Collection
M.193-1975

12 Gold. The Virgin and Child, St John the Baptist, and St Edmund. Hoop inscribed outside in black letter: *+bone/+fyne/bon ioye,* and inside: *god+help;* traces of white enamel.
Late 14th century.
Guilhou Collection; acquired by Dame Joan Evans.
M.192-1975
Nos. 10-12, given by Dame Joan Evans, P.P.S.A.

13 Gold. The Trinity; the Pietà, and St Anne with the Virgin.
Early 16th century.
Waterton Collection
693-1871

*14 Silver-gilt. St Anthony and St John the Baptist. Engraved sprigs on double-fluted shoulders.
15th century.
Acquired at Dunwich, Suffolk, 1869, presumably by Sir John Evans.
Given by Dame Joan Evans, P.P.S.A.
M.244-1962

15 Silver-gilt. Three saints. Engraved sprigs on ridged shoulders.
15th century.
Waterton Collection
680-1871

16 Gold. The Trinity, St Margaret and St Catherine. Inscribed behind in black letter: *en bon an.* Engraved sprigs on ridged shoulders.
15th century.
Given by Dame Joan Evans, P.P.S.A.
M.241-1962

17 Gold. Virgin and Child; traces of enamel. The hoop inscribed in lombardic characters: *+GAVDE VIRGO MATER XPI* (rejoice in the Virgin, Mother of Christ).
Late 14th century.
Rosenheim and A.G.B. Russell Collection
M.8-1956

18 Gold. St George, on foot, transfixing the Dragon. Cross-hatched triangles on shoulders.
Early 15th century.
Rosenheim Collection
Given by Dame Joan Evans, P.P.S.A.
M.237-1962

19 Gold. The Sacred Monogram in a heart-shaped bezel.
Early 16th century.
740-1877

*20 Gold, formerly enamelled. Hoop, with oval reliefs of Christ as the Man of Sorrows and Instruments of the Passion.
Early 16th century.
Acquired in Leicester by Sir Arthur Evans.
Given by Dame Joan Evans, P.P.S.A.
M.243-1962

21 Silver. Three saints. Engraved sprigs on triple fluted shoulders.
15th century.
M.818-1926

TALISMANIC AND DEVOTIONAL RINGS:
13th-17th century.

22 Silver-gilt. St Catherine and St Joseph with the Infant Christ. Engraved sprigs on transverse fluted shoulders.
15th century.
686-1871

23 Silver-gilt. St. Barbara and another saint. Engraved sprigs on transverse fluted shoulders.
15th century.
685-1871
Nos. 22 & 23, Waterton Collection

24 Gold. St Bartholomew, St George and St Paul. Engraved sprigs on transverse fluted shoulders. Inscribed behind in black letter: *ffor euer.*
15th century.
From Lincolnshire, 1886; acquired by Sir Arthur Evans.
M.242-1962

25 Gold. St Paul; traces of enamel. Engraved sprigs on transverse fluted shoulders; twisted hoop. Inscribed behind in black letter: *sans+de+ partir.*
15th century.
From Fenham Hall, Essendine.
M.194-1975

26 Gold. St John the Evangelist and St Barbara. Engraved sprigs on the twisted shoulders; traces of white enamel.
15th century.
Found at Pitstone, near Tring, Bucks.
M.198-1975

27 Gold. St George. Engraved sprigs on wrythen hoop. Inscribed behind in black letter: *+ ioe + sanz + fin* (joy without end).
15th century.
Acquired (? by Sir John Evans), 1875.
M.236-1962
Nos. 24-27, given by Dame Joan Evans, P.P.S.A.

28 Gold. Hoop chased with the Five Wounds and the Instruments of the Passion.
15th century.
Found at Titchfield Abbey, Hants.
Given by the daughters of the late Captain G. Spencer-Smith
M.430-1936

29 Silver-gilt. St. Barbara, St John the Baptist and another saint; traces of enamel. Tau crosses on the shoulders.
15th century.
Waterton Collection
681-1871

30 Silver-gilt. Three figures, possibly representing St Peter between the Virgin Mary and St Ethelreda, to whom Ely Cathedral was dedicated in 1252. Engraved sprigs on transverse fluted shoulders; traces of black enamel.
Late 15th or early 16th century.
Found in Ely Cathedral, 1772, allegedly near the grave of Bishop Northwold.
M.245-1962

31 Gold. The Annunciation and the Virgin Mary. Shoulders inscribed in black letter: *tout/pur/vous* (all for you).
15th century.
Found near Colchester.
Philip Nelson Collection; acquired by Dame Joan Evans, P.P.S.A.
M.195-1975

32 Gold. St John the Baptist and St. Catherine. Transverse fluted hoop with sprigs. Inscribed behind in black letter: *tut. pur. un*
(all for one); traces of enamel.
15th century.
Sir Arthur Evans Collection.
M.211-1975
Nos. 30-32, given by Dame Joan Evans, P.P.S.A.

The inscriptions on many of these rings illustrate the medieval (and later) readiness to accommodate both religion and magic. Piety and the hope of salvation in the after-life did not preclude the desire to ward off sickness and other troubles in this world. Some of the materials used in the rings, such as toadstones, which were thought to come from the heads of toads, were credited with magical properties. It must also be remembered that gemstones were also believed to have prophylactic qualities. In the Middle Ages the sapphire, for instance, was said to dispel envy, detect fraud and witchcraft and cure snake bites.

The last rings on the board, decade rings, have ridged or knobbed hoops and are so called because they were used as miniature rosaries, an *ave* being said for each knob and a *pater noster* for the bezel. Normally the rings have ten projections; some however have additional ones for other prayers.

*1 Gold. Heart-shaped bezel set with a tooth. Shoulders decorated with stiff-leaf foliage rising from crowns in openwork circles. Later black letter inscription inside the hoop: *buro+berto+berneto+consumatm/e* (the first three words a magical charm against toothache; the last, an abbreviation of Christ's final words on the Cross, calmed storms).
ENGLISH or FRENCH: 13th century. The inscription probably added in the late 14th or 15th century.
816-1902

2 Silver. Circular cusped bezel set with a toadstone (the fossilized tooth of a fish called *Lepidotes*, common, for instance, in the Oolitic and Wealden strata of England, which was held to be effective against kidney disease).
WEST EUROPEAN: 16th century.
Waterton Collection
713-1871

3 Silver. Circular cusped bezel
with a toadstone. Applied pellets on
the shoulders. Hoop inscribed inside:
Whom I kiss hir I cure, with the
initials *I.P.*
ENGLISH: 17th century.
Given by Dame Joan Evans, P.P.S.A.
M.325-1975

4 Horn (? or hoof) mounted with
silver. Circular cusped setting with a
toadstone.
ENGLISH: 15th or 16th century.
Ass's hoof was considered efficacious
against epilepsy.
712-1871

5 Horn (? or hoof) with outer band of
silver. Octagonal silver bezel with a
toadstone in a cusped setting.
ENGLISH: 15th or 16th century.
Found at Richmond, Yorks.
711-1871
Nos. 4 & 5, Waterton Collection.

6 Silver-gilt. Bezel set with pearls,
amethysts and other stones and a
wolf's tooth (the latter a hunting
charm which later also ensured
successful teething in a baby).
WEST EUROPEAN: 17th century or
later.
Probably a peasant piece.
Formerly in the Londesborough
Collection
Lent anonymously

7 Iron. Small circular bezel set with
a conical piece of fossil tooth; scale
ornament on hoop.
WEST EUROPEAN: 16th century.
Waterton Collection
721-1871

*8 Silver. Bezel with a piece of
trochus shell in a serrated setting.
Hoop inscribed in Roman capitals:
AGIOS+ OEOS+EATANATOS: a
pellet on each shoulder.
SPANISH: 17th century.
Given by Dame Joan Evans, P.P.S.A.
M.249-1962

9 Gold encasing horn in hoop form.
WEST EUROPEAN: ? 17th century.
Waterton Collection
718-1871

10 Gold. Circular bezel set with
toadstones. Hoop inscribed in italic:
All is thyn on this side time.
ENGLISH: 17th century.
Given by Dame Joan Evans,
P.P.S.A.
M.250-1962

11 Gold. Circular bezel set with a
toadstone.
?ENGLISH: 17th century.
Brooke Gift
389-1864

12 Gold. Circular bezel set with a
toadstone. Inscribed: *A friend at need
doth gould exceed.*
ENGLISH: 17th century.
715-1871

13 Enamelled gold. Circular bezel
set with a toadstone.
? ITALIAN: second half of 17th
century.
The toadstone is unbacked, in order
to warm the skin when in the
presence of poison (see Anselmus
Boetius de Boot, *Gemmarum et
Lapidum Historia,* p.303).
716-1871

14 Silver. Three oval bezels each set
with a wolf's tooth. Applied flowers
on shoulders.
GERMAN: 16th century.
Waterton Collection
720-1871

15 Silver-gilt. Double bezel set with
two wolf's teeth, the shoulders with
pastes.
GERMAN: 18th century.
Probably a specimen of peasant
jewellery.
170-1872

16 Twisted strands of brass and
iron, formed into a hoop and lined
with silver-gilt inscribed in black
letter: *+iaspar.melchiar.baltazar.*
GERMAN: 14th century.
The names of the Magi, or the three
Kings of Cologne, may be of Mithraic
origin. Belief in their amuletic
powers persisted after the passing of
the Middle Ages.
719-1871

17 Silver. Inscribed inside in black
letter: *+ai.ebel diabel+gugul+gugul.*
WEST EUROPEAN: 15th century.
705-1871
Nos. 16 & 17, Waterton Collection

18 Silver-gilt. Ridged hoop inscribed
in lombardic characters: *+AVE
MARIA GRATIA.*
ENGLISH: 15th century.
Given by Dame Joan Evans, P.P.S.A.
M.232-1962

19 Nielloed silver. Oval bezel
engraved with a cross pattée. Hoop
inscribed outside in lombardic
characters: *T.E.A.L.E.V.T.A.V.X.Y.
+A.P.* and inside: *O.E.R.O.
S.5.A.P.H.I.E.L.X.D.A.P.*
ITALIAN: 14th century.
708-1871

20 Silver. Square bezel engraved
with the Sacred Monogram and a
cross. Flat hoop inscribed in
lombardic characters: *+HCER+S+
DIA+BIZ+SA+SI,* and inside:
ABIZ+SAN+HCBERBN (part of the
Zacharias blessing).
ITALIAN: 15th century.
710-1871
Nos. 19 & 20, Waterton Collection

21 Silver. Applied small circular
disc, a signet engraved with *h*
in black letter. Hoop inscribed
in black letter: *iacper.melchior.
baltacar.*
ENGLISH: 15th century.
Acquired by Sir John Evans, 1892.
Given by Dame Joan Evans, P.P.S.A.
M.257-1962

22 Nielloed silver. Shaped bezel
engraved with the Sacred Monogram.
ITALIAN: 16th century.
The hoop struck with a French
warranty mark for 1838 onwards.
Waterton Collection
697-1871

23 Silver hoop with raised borders
and cinquefoils, inscribed in black
letter: *iaspur melcior baltasar.*
ENGLISH: 15th century.
Found at Great Yarmouth and
acquired by Joseph Warren, 1860.
Given by Dame Joan Evans, P.P.S.A.
M.248-1962

24 Gold. Circular bezel engraved with an heraldic rose, subsequently scored with a cross, presumably to cancel its use as a signet. Hoop inscribed outside in black letter: *+ihesus nasarenus rex ivdeorum**, and inside: *+iaspar melchior baltasar*. The two inscriptions, used together, were a charm against cramp (epilepsy). *Ihesus Nazarenus* etc, used independently, was a precaution against sudden death.
ENGLISH: late 15th century.
Waterton Collection
701-1871

25 Bronze. Buckle type. The hoop inscribed: in lombardic characters: *MATER.DEI.MEMANTO.* [MEI] (Mother of God, be mindful of me).
ENGLISH: 15th century.
Sir John Evans Collection
Given by Dame Joan Evans, P.P.S.A.
M.225-1962

26 Silver. Oval bezel set with an antique onyx intaglio of a scorpion. The setting ITALIAN: 15th century; the intaglio 2nd or 1st century BC.
It was widely believed in the Middle Ages that intaglios of scorpions gave protection against fevers.
724-1871

27 Silver.
IRISH: 18th century.
Said to have been worn as a charm against rheumatism.
722-1871

28 Silver. Inscribed in Roman capitals outside and inside: *+EC+ EBER+DIABIR+SABAVC.*
ITALIAN: early 16th century.
704-1871
Nos. 26-28, Waterton Collection

29 Gold. Inscribed in black letter: *iasper.melchior.baltazar.*
ENGLISH: early 15th century.
Given by Dame Joan Evans, P.P.S.A.
M.91-1960

30 Gold. Oval bezel chased with the Sacred Monogram. Shoulders chased with terminal figures and volutes.
? GERMAN: 16th century.
1582-1902

31 Gold. Decade ring. Iconographical bezel, with Saint Barbara and St. Christopher. Inscribed behind in black letter: *a ma vye.*
ENGLISH: 15th century.
Waterton Collection
690-1871

32 Brass. Decade ring. Oval bezel engraved with St. Catherine.
ENGLISH: 15th century.
From the old Geological Museum, Jermyn Street
5575-1901

33 Silver. Decade ring. Oval bezel engraved with the Sacred Monogram.
? ENGLISH: 17th century.
Croft Lyons Bequest
M.816-1926

34 Gold. Decade ring. Oval bezel engraved with St. Christopher.
ENGLISH: 15th century.
Waterton Collection
689-1871

35 Bronze. Decade ring. Shaped oval bezel with the letter *S* in relief.
ENGLISH: early 16th century.
775-1871
Nos. 34 & 35, Waterton Collection

36 Bronze. Decade ring. Oval bezel engraved with the Sacred Monogram and a cross.
ENGLISH: 17th century.
Given by Mr. B. Philips
M.98-1952

37 Silver, parcel-gilt. Decade ring. Circular bezel with a cast relief of the Virgin of the Rosary and the raised letters: *R.S/R.*
ITALIAN: 17th century.
Croft Lyons Bequest
M.815-1926

38 Silver. Decade ring. Circular bezel engraved with the Sacred Monogram. Inscribed inside: *? God ... to follow* and *VB.*
WEST EUROPEAN: 17th century.
M.817-1926

39 Gold. Decade ring. Oval bezel set with a Roman amethyst cameo of a veiled woman's head
WEST EUROPEAN: 17th century.
Ready Bequest
M.12-1959

40 Gold. Decade ring.
WEST EUROPEAN: 18th century.
M.234-1962

41 Silver-gilt. Decade ring. Crucifix bezel forming a receptacle for a relic.
WEST EUROPEAN: 16th-18th century.
It has been claimed that these crucifix rings were used solely by the Knights of Malta.
M.233-1962
Nos. 40 & 41, given by Dame Joan Evans, P.P.S.A.

42 Silver. Decade ring. Oval bezel engraved with Crucifixion.
WEST EUROPEAN: 17th century
Illegible mark.
M.814-1926

A. FEDE RINGS:
15th and 16th centuries

190

The term *fede*, as is described in Case 32, Board E, no. 1, is derived from the Italian *mani in fede* (hands clasped in faith). The love symbol of clasped hands, dating at least from Roman times, was revived in the twelfth century, remaining popular for several centuries thereafter.

1 Silver-gilt. Two bezels, a *fede* and an applied quatrefoil enclosing a heart. Shoulders inscribed in black letter: *ihc/help*.
ENGLISH: 15th century.
Harman-Oates Collection
M.8-1929

2 Silver-gilt. Two applied bezels, one a *fede*, the other a crowned lombardic *T* enclosing a heart inscribed *I*. Hoop engraved with x's.
ENGLISH: 15th century.
Found at Canterbury, 1854.
Given by William Burges, the architect, to Edmund Waterton.
A ring designed by Burges is shown in Case 34,Board K, no. 3.
858-1871

3 Silver-gilt. Two bezels, a *fede* and an applied quatrefoil with a heart. Hoop inscribed in black letter: *bindit as findit*.
? SCOTTISH: 15th century.
Sir Arthur Evans Collection
Given by Dame Joan Evans, P.P.S.A.
M.64-1960

4 Silver, formerly gilt. Hoop inscribed in black letter: *+in+on+is+al+*.
ENGLISH: 15th century.
845-1871

5 Silver-gilt. Hoop inscribed in black letter: *+ihc+nazaren*.
WEST EUROPEAN: 15th century.
842-1871

6 Silver-gilt. Double ridged bezel with a *fede* and a heart between two quatrefoils. Shoulders inscribed in black letter: *ave: ch ihs/et maria*.
ENGLISH: 15th century.
M.247-1962

7 Silver-gilt. Two bezels, a *fede* and foliage in quatrefoil. Hoop inscribed in lombardic characters: **IHS/N:R:I*.
ENGLISH: 15th century.
Found at Hempstead, Essex, 1849.
Joseph Warren and Whincopp Collections
M.230-1962
Nos. 6 & 7, given by Dame Joan Evans, P.P.S.A.

8 Silver-gilt. Hoop engraved with an unintelligible inscription.
WEST EUROPEAN: 15th century.
843-1871

9 Silver-gilt. Hoop inscribed in lombardic characters: *I/H/E/S/V/S*.
? GERMAN: 15th century.
846-1871
Nos. 8 & 9, Waterton Collection

10 Silver-gilt. Hoop inscribed in lombardic characters: *AVEMARE*.
WEST EUROPEAN: 15th century.
Miss E.M. Begg Bequest
M.329-1975

11 Silver. Two bezels, one a *fede* and the other two hands clasping a heart.
ITALIAN: 15th century.
Acquired by Edmund Waterton in Rome, 1857.
848-1871

12 Silver-gilt. Ridged hoop inscribed in lombardic characters: *+IH'C. NAZAREN.REX./IVDEORVM+ IASPAR*.
ENGLISH: 15th century.
844-1871

13 Nielloed silver.
NORTH ITALIAN: 15th century.
Acquired by Edmund Waterton in Rome, 1860.
835-1871

14 Nielloed silver. Hoop inscribed in lombardic characters: *ERVNT DVO IN CARNE VNA*.
NORTH ITALIAN: 15th century.
834-1871

15 Nielloed silver. Simulated inscription.
NORTH ITALIAN: 15th century.
849-1871

*16 Nielloed silver. Two bezels, one a *fede* and the other circular, with a female bust and a rose. Shoulders decorated with rosettes.
NORTH ITALIAN: 15th century.
873-1871
Nos. 11-16, Waterton Collection.

17 Silver-gilt. Inscribed in black letter: *ihc. naza. renus*.
WEST EUROPEAN: 16th century.
Miss E.M. Begg Bequest
M.330-1975

18 Silver-gilt. Inscribed in lombardic characters: *SAS. ?BT*.
WEST EUROPEAN: 16th century.
Miss E.M. Begg Bequest
M.331-1975

19 Silver. The hands cast. A term on each shoulder.
WEST EUROPEAN: 16th century.
Waterton Collection
850-1871

20 Gold. The hands cast and inscribed in black letter: *gi* in rosettes on each wrist. The hoop inscribed inside: *sauns faileir*.
ENGLISH: 15th century.
Found near Peterborough; acquired by Sir Arthur Evans.
Given by Dame Joan Evans, P.P.S.A.
M.204-1975

B. MISCELLANEOUS SILVER RINGS

SIGNET RINGS:
13th-16th century

21 Silver, parcel-gilt. Lobed hoop type, chased in black letter: *je le de sir* (je le désir, I desire him), alternating with crowns.
ENGLISH: 15th century.
890-1871

22 Nielloed silver. The transverse octagonal bezel inscribed in lombardic characters: *+CATARINA NICOLA* surrounding ?a coat of arms. Ridged and scrolling shoulders.
ITALIAN: 15th century.
833-1871

23 Nielloed silver. The circular bezel with a female bust and the inscription: *VENIRA;* the shoulders foliated.
Bought by Edmund Waterton at Monte di Pieta, Rome, 1857.
879-1871

24 Nielloed silver. The transverse oval bezel with a full-face female head. The hoop inscribed: *LA VIRTV FA.* On the shoulders, *AG* and floral scrolls.
NORTH ITALIAN: 15th century.
Bought by Edmund Waterton at Rome, 1857.
880-1871

25 Nielloed silver. The transverse bezel with a woman's head in profile. The hoop inscribed: *+A VE MA RIA.*
NORTH ITALIAN: 15th century.
882-1871
Nos. 21-25, Waterton Collection

1 Gold. Oval bezel set with a spinel ruby intaglio of a crowned head and engraved in black letter: *tel il nest* (there is none like him). Shoulders engraved with sprigs; traces of enamel. The intaglio may be the one described in the 1379 inventory of Charles V of France: *The signet of the King which is the head of a king without beard; and is (made) of a fine oriental ruby; this is that which the King seals the letters which he has written with his (own) hand.*
The setting ENGLISH: 15th century; the intaglio FRENCH: second half of 14th century.
Arundel and Marlborough Collections
Lent from the Salting Bequest
M.554-1910

2 Gold. Rectangular bezel set with a Roman cornelian intaglio of a bearded head. Inscribed behind in black letter: *Mielx a moy.* Engraved sprigs on shoulders.
WEST EUROPEAN: about 1380.
Given by the Alkali Division of Imperial Chemical Industries Ltd.
M.46-1954

3 Gold. Oval bezel set with a Roman jasper intaglio with a *fede* device and the initials: *CCPS/IPD,* and inscribed in lombardic characters: *SIGILLU.THOMASII.DE. ROGERII S.DESUESSA.* (The seal of Thomas de Rogerii, priest of Suessa). The hoop inscribed: *+ET VERBU:CARO. FACTU:E:ET ABITANT:/NOB/* (and the word was made Flesh and dwelt among us; John I, 14) and: *+XPS VINCIT X XPS X REGNAT X XPS:IMPERA* (Christ conquers, Christ reigns, Christ rules).
ITALIAN: 14th century; the intaglio 3rd century AD.
It has been suggested that the owner may have been a member of the Neapolitan family Roggieri. Said to have been found in the church of Santa Maria in Comedia, Suessa Arunca (near Naples), 1845.
George Barrett, Guilhou Collections; acquired by Dame Joan Evans.
M.275-1962

4 Gold. Oval bezel set with a sard intaglio of a classical male head and inscribed in lombardic characters: *IOHANNES:EST:NOMEN:EIVS.* (John is his name).
ENGLISH: 13th century.
Philip Nelson Collection; acquired by Dame Joan Evans.
M.290-1962
Nos. 3 & 4, given by Dame Joan Evans, P.P.S.A.

*5 Gold. Oval bezel, open-backed, set with a sapphire intaglio of a hooded head and inscribed: *TECTA. LEGE. LECTA.TEGE.* (read what is written, hide what is read).
? FRENCH: 13th century.
The engraving of sapphires was a French speciality.
Found in a well in Hereford, 1824.
Waterton Collection
89-1899

6 Nielloed gold. Octagonal bezel set with an onyx intaglio of a lion rampant; initial *P* behind. Hoop inscribed in lombardic characters: *+IN MANUS:TUAS:DOMINE: COMENDO:SPIRITUM:MEUM.* (into thy hand O Lord I commend my spirit).
ITALIAN: 15th century.
Sidney Churchill Collection
M.190-1975

7 Gold. Oval bezel engraved with a stag couchant and inscribed in black letter: *Edmund;* behind: *tout ma vie.* The shoulders engraved with Tau crosses and flowers; traces of white enamel.
ENGLISH: 15th century.
The Tau cross was associated with St Anthony, whose intervention was sought to protect against the erysipelas and other diseases.
M.202-1975

8 Gold. Circular bezel engraved with a hand holding five flowers, and inscribed in black letter: *iohn: devereux.* Shoulders engraved with Tau crosses and sprigs; traces of black enamel.
ENGLISH: late 15th or 16th century.
M.215-1975
Nos. 6-8, given by Dame Joan Evans, P.P.S.A.

*9 Gold. Circular bezel engraved with a cradle. Inscribed behind in black letter: *my wille were*.
ENGLISH: 15th century.
903-1871

10 Gold. Circular bezel engraved with a rebus (a tree, perhaps an elm, between *wy* and *ot* with *r* below in black letter), for ? R. Wylmot.
ENGLISH: first half of 16th century.
794-1871

11 Gold. Circular bezel engraved with a hound on a leash, couchant beneath a tree, and *IL* in lombardic characters.
? ENGLISH: 16th century.
795-1871
Nos. 9-11, Waterton Collection

12 Gold. Circular bezel engraved with a ? falcon in a fetterlock.
ENGLISH: 15th century.
The badge of falcon and fetterlock is associated with the House of York, but the ring is too late to have a direct connection with Edmund de Langley, Duke of York (1341-1402).
M.205-1975

13 Gold. Circular bezel engraved with a stag running and the name *Edmund* in black letter. Shoulders engraved with Tau crosses above foliage.
ENGLISH: 15th century.
M.201-1975
Nos. 12 & 13, given by Dame Joan Evans, P.P.S.A.

14 Gold. Shoulders engraved with the Virgin and Child and St. Christopher. Inscribed inside in black letter: *en bon an*.
An iconographical ring converted into a signet with the addition of a flat plate applied to the bezel, engraved with a castle.
ENGLISH: 15th century, with a mid 18th century bezel.
Found under London Bridge, about 1720; described and illustrated by William Cole in a manuscript catalogue of Horace Walpole's Collection at Strawberry Hill, 3 September 1762.
Walpole and Waterton Collections
695-1871

15 Gold. Circular bezel engraved with a lion couchant and *p* and *lemys* in black letter and inscribed behind in black letter: *nul sy buen* (nothing as good). Shoulders engraved with ? St. Mary Magdalene and St. John the Baptist between flowers and leaves.
ENGLISH: 15th century.
M.199-1975

16 Bronze, heavily gilt. Circular bezel engraved with a coat of arms and the inscription in black letter: *s.iohis? Newport*.
ENGLISH: 15th century.
M.213-1975

17 Gold. Circular bezel engraved with the name *thomas atherton* in black letter. Inscribed behind: *honour et ioe*. Shoulders engraved with sprigs.
ENGLISH: 15th century.
M.251-1962

18 Gold. Circular bezel engraved with a triskele motif, the shoulders with sprigs.
ENGLISH: 15th or early 16th century.
M.216-1975
Nos. 15-18, given by Dame Joan Evans, P.P.S.A.

19 Gold. Octagonal bezel engraved with a pelican in its piety; behind, *TS* in monogram. Hoop reduced in size.
ENGLISH: early 16th century.
An almost identical ring in the possession of Corpus Christi College belonged to the founder, Richard Foxe, Bishop of Winchester (d.1528). It is possible, therefore, that this is a standard signet of the Bishops of Winchester.
Waterton Collection
792-1871

20 Gold. Rectangular bezel engraved with a coronet and a loop of rope, enclosing a device. Plaited hoop.
ENGLISH: about 1500.
M.214-1975

21 Gold. Octagonal bezel engraved with a sleeping dog and the inscription in black letter: *muet* (dumb).
? FRENCH: 15th century.
M.200-1975
Nos. 20 & 21, given by Dame Joan Evans, P.P.S.A.

22 Gold. Octagonal bezel engraved with St. James the Great and inscribed in black letter: *iaques bouchier*.
FRENCH: 15th century.
688-1871

23 Gold. Octagonal bezel engraved with a crowned *I*. Entwined ribbon hoop.
ENGLISH: 15th century.
773-1871

24 Gold. Long hexagonal bezel engraved with the arms of Lounsdon of Suffolk or Scott of Camberwell and ? *ivd* in black letter. The hoop inscribed outside: *san ta: anna. ora. pro. me*, and in Roman capitals: *HELP + SANT + ANNA. SELLEF + OBVR* and inside: *CASPAR. MELCHIAR. BALTASAR.*
ENGLISH: early 16th century.
702-1871
Nos. 22-24, Waterton Collection

Case 33 Board E

SIGNET RINGS:
13th-15th century

1 Gold. Oval 4-claw bezel set with an antique Roman plasma intaglio. FRENCH: 13th century.
649-1871

2 Gold. Oval bezel set with a Roman cornelian intaglio of Ceres and inscribed in lombardic characters: +*S HEMERICI*.
? FRENCH: 13th century.
727-1871
Nos. 1 & 2, Waterton Collection

3 Gold. Oval bezel set with a sapphire intaglio of a man with a sword on horseback and inscribed in lombardic characters: +*A.E. ? MARIA TM.*
? FRENCH: about 1300.
Bequeathed by Mrs. Cecil Firth
M.189-1937

4 Gold. Oval bezel set with a red cornelian intaglio of ? Jupiter Ammon, with the letters *MA* and inscribed: +*S' CONRADI. DE. COMITE*. The hoop modern.
ITALIAN: 13th century.
Waterton Collection
726-1871

5 Silver. Oval bezel set with a Roman red jasper intalio of a janiform head and inscribed in lombardic characters: +*S'NOT RICCARDI BVSSONI*. The hoop modern.
ITALIAN: 14th century.
4099-1857

6 Silver-gilt. Oval bezel set with a Roman red jasper intaglio of two masks, a scorpion, a star and a serpent and inscribed in lombardic characters: *S. F R DE COLUMPNA*. The hoop modern.
ITALIAN: 13th century.
725-1871
Nos. 1-6, Waterton Collection

7 Gold. Octagonal bezel set with a sapphire intaglio of a bearded head and inscribed in lombardic characters: *VERBUM: CARO: FACT*. Tear-shaped shoulders with scrolling flowers. Ridged hoop inscribed: +*DEVS:/IN NOMI:/NE+ TVO/SALVVM*.
. ? FRENCH: 14th century.
M.186-1975

8 Gold. Oval bezel set with a medieval agate intaglio of a male head and inscribed in lombardic characters: +*.AHERRICI D. SVESSA.CACELLARII LEGATI*. The hoop inscribed: + *VERBUM X CARO X FACTUM X EST X ET: ABITAB //: INOBIS + ET: VIDIMUS X GLORIAM X EIUS X GLORIAM*.
ITALIAN: 14th century.
See also no. 3 above.
Guilhou Collection; acquired by Dame Joan Evans
M.189-1975

9 Silver. Oval bezel set with a cornelian intaglio of the heads of Julia, daughter of Augustus, and her sons Caius and Lucius, and inscribed in lombardic characters: + *S. ANDREOCTI. D' S' RA*. The hoop modern.
ITALIAN: 14th century; the intaglio Ist century AD.
Probably once in the possession of the Neapolitan family of Serra.
ITALIAN: 14th century.
723-1871

10 Gold. Projecting bezel set with a Roman cornelian intaglio of ? Juno (Hera). Dragon-head shoulders.
WEST EUROPEAN: 14th century.
651-1871

11 Gold. Octagonal bezel engraved with a coat of arms with mantling and inscribed in lombardic characters: *? ARCAMO A BOART*.
ITALIAN: 14th century.
798-1871

12 Silver. Octagonal bezel engraved with a coat of arms and inscribed in lombardic characters: +*ANNTONII. DE. MARI*. Shoulders inscribed with the letters *A* and *N*.
ITALIAN: 14th century.
797-1871

13 Silver. Octagonal bezel engraved with a coat of arms and inscribed: + *S. SANTILLO D. PAHOLO*.
ITALIAN: 14th century.
803-1871
Nos. 9-13, Waterton Collection

14 Gold. Octagonal bezel engraved with a coat of arms with the initial *R* and inscribed in lombardic characters: *A. ROGERII. GAVTANO*. Inscribed inside the hoop: *IHS.E.M. IHS +*.
Possibly ITALIAN: about 14th century.
Pichon and Guilhou Collections; acquired by Dame Joan Evans, P.P.S.A.
M.185-1975

15 Silver. Circular bezel engraved with a coat of arms and inscribed in lombardic characters: + *N NOTAR ANGELIS ACC*. Ridged hoop inscribed: + *MORTUUS. FUERAM. A. REVIT/+PERIERAM ET INVENTUS SUM* (I was dead, I was brought to life, I was lost and I was found).
WEST EUROPEAN: 14th century.
Acquired by Edmund Waterton in Rome.
805-1871

16 Gold. Circular bezel engraved with a coat of arms and inscribed in lombardic characters: + *S: MENTO: SASO*. Applied shields on shoulders.
? SPANISH or ITALIAN: early 14th century.
Given by Dame Joan Evans, P.P.S.A.
M.277-1962

17 Bronze. Octagonal bezel engraved with a human-headed monster wearing a hat.
WEST EUROPEAN: 14th century.
Given by Dr. W.L. Hildburgh, F.S.A.
M.169-1929

18 Silver-gilt. Circular bezel engraved with a coat of arms.
WEST EUROPEAN: 14th century.
Miss E.M. Begg Bequest
M.334-1975

19 Gold. Circular bezel engraved with the arms of Borischi, Rome and inscribed in black letter: + *illi x coli x ceruo + fidem*, repeated inside the hoop.
WEST EUROPEAN: 15th century.
M.252-1962

194

20 Gold. Engraved with a coat of arms and inscribed in lombardic characters: *+A:NOTI:RICCI D CLVS.*
ITALIAN: 15th century.
M.210-1975
Nos. 19 & 20, given by Dame Joan Evans, P.P.S.A.

*21 Nielloed silver. Projecting octagonal bezel engraved with a dragon. Ridged shoulders.
Probably ITALIAN: 15th century.
785-1871

22 Silver. Octagonal bezel engraved with the Agnus Dei and *G*.
ITALIAN: 15th century.
602-1871

23 Silver. Octagonal bezel engraved with a crowned *M* and *+MARTINNI ?DT*.
ITALIAN: 15th century.
762-1871

24 Silver. Octagonal bezel engraved with an arm holding a sword and the motto, in lombardic characters: *PER. ARDIMENTO.*
ITALIAN: 15th century.
788-1871
Nos. 21-24, Waterton Collection

25 Silver. Octagonal bezel engraved with a coat of arms and: *+?NUCIA.*
ITALIAN: 15th century.
Given by Dr. W.L. Hildburgh, F.S.A.
M.236-1926

26 Gold. Octagonal bezel engraved with a coat of arms and inscribed in lombardic characters: *.PETRVS.. NOVARINO.*
ITALIAN: 15th century.
Pichon and Guilhou Collections; acquired by Dame Joan Evans.
M.276-1962

27 Nielloed gilt bronze. Octagonal bezel engraved with a wyvern segreant. Mock inscription on hoop.
ITALIAN: 15th century.
Given by Dr. W.L. Hildburgh, F.S.A.
M.237-1926

28 Silvered and nielloed copper. Octagonal bezel engraved with the arms of Orsini.
ITALIAN: 15th century.
799-1871

29 Silver, parcel-gilt. Octagonal bezel engraved with a coat of arms. *A* and *R* engraved on the shoulders.
? ITALIAN: 15th century.
The arms (two oxen affronted) may be a simplified rendering of those of the Vitelleschi family of Corneto.
789-1871

30 Gold. Oval bezel engraved with unidentified arms and inscribed in black letter *?iohanni loupsht.*
WEST EUROPEAN: 15th century.
804-1871
Nos. 28-30, Waterton Collection.

1 Silver. Lozenge-shaped bezel engraved with the arms of Lovell, Co. Norfolk, for William Lovel (d.1476). Applied details on shoulders.
ENGLISH: late 15th century.
Found at Morley, Norfolk, 1777.
Philip Nelson Collection; acquired by Dame Joan Evans.
M.264-1962

2 Silver. Circular bezel engraved with *I* and *W* in monogram. Tau cross and bell engraved on shoulders.
? ENGLISH: 15th century.
Found at Winchester.
M.255-1962
Nos. 1 & 2, given by Dame Joan Evans, P.P.S.A.

3 Silver. Rectangular bezel engraved with a crowned *W*.
? ENGLISH: 15th century.
? A religious confraternity ring (see Nos. 6, 7 & 13).
Waterton Collection
767-1871

4 Silver. Circular bezel. Hoop inscribed in black letter: *god x help x williem* with the initial *W*.
ENGLISH: late 15th or early 16th century.
Given by Dame Joan Evans, PPSA
M.256-1962

5 Brass, formerly gilt. Octagonal bezel, inscribed: *N.S.* over a tournament shield. The arms appear to be those of the Counts Spreti, Italy and Bavaria.
? ITALIAN: second half of 15th century.
Miss E M Begg Bequest
M.341-1975

6 Silver. Octagonal bezel engraved with a crowned *I*, flanked by two branches.
ENGLISH: 15th century.
? A religious confraternity ring (see Nos. 3 & 7).
? Found at Chichester.
1374-1903.

SIGNET RINGS:
15th and 16th centuries

*7 Silver. Octagonal bezel engraved with a crowned *I* flanked by two branches.
ENGLISH: 15th century.
? A religious confraternity ring (see Nos. 3, 6 & 13).
Given to Edmund Waterton by Major Darell of Cole Hill.
Waterton Collection
771-1871

8 Silver. Octagonal bezel engraved with *r* & *g* at right angles in black letters; pearled border.
ENGLISH: late 15th or early 16th century.
Found in Taunton Priory.
Given by Dame Joan Evans, P.P.S.A.
M.260-1962

9 Nielloed silver. Octagonal bezel engraved with a cross and sickle moon, which can also be read as *IP*. Fluted shoulders, inscribed in black letter *i h e merci* and *ladi help*.
ENGLISH: mid-15th century.
Miss E M Begg Bequest
M.339-1975

10 Silver. Circular bezel engraved with ? a rebus, containing the letter *U*. Fluted shoulders, beaded edges.
WEST EUROPEAN: early 16th century.
Waterton Collection
754-1871

11 Silver. Circular bezel engraved with a coat of arms and *MA*.
WEST EUROPEAN: 15th century.
Given by Lady Norah Hodgson
M.32-1951

12 Silver. Circular bezel, engraved with a bird, a sexfoil beneath its tail and *S*.
ENGLISH: early 16th century.
Given by Dame Joan Evans, P.P.S.A.
M.259-1962

13 Brass bezel inscribed with a crowned *I*.
WEST EUROPEAN: 15th century.
? A religious confraternity ring (see Nos. 3, 6 & 7).
Miss E M Begg Bequest
M.340-1975

14 Silver. Circular bezel engraved with a coat of arms and the letters *IOI*.
? ENGLISH: early 16th century.
Found at Tattershall, Lincs.
Given by Dame Joan Evans, P.P.S.A.
M.261-1962

15 Bronze. Octagonal bezel engraved with the letter *B*.
WEST EUROPEAN: 15th century.
903-1904

16 Bronze. Oval bezel engraved with a crowned *n* in black letter.
WEST EUROPEAN: 15th century.
Found in the fens near Cambridge.
Waterton Collection
769-1871

17 Silver. Oval bezel engraved with a tree; above, *H.S.*
WEST EUROPEAN: mid 16th century.
Miss E M Begg Bequest
M.342-1975

18 Horn. Circular silver bezel engraved with the arms of Pietrorch beneath initials *PP*. Hoop mounted with a copper wire.
GERMAN: 16th century.
Waterton Collection
717-1871

1 Silver. Octagonal bezel engraved with *I* (? a tau cross) between two stars. Fluted shoulders.
? GERMAN: 16th century.
Waterton Collection
779-1871

2 Silver. Octagonal bezel engraved with the coat of arms of a knight of St. John of Jerusalem and inscribed in lombardic characters: *+H.IO.DIA. BEIE.*
ENGLISH: 15th century.
Given by Dame Joan Evans, P.P.S.A.
M.253-1962

3 Silver. Oval bezel engraved with couchant hound and inscribed in black letter: *iame s'geein* ('perhaps for *j'aime songeant,* 'I love in my dreams') Hoop engraved with an illegible inscription.
? FRENCH: 15th century.
143-1907

4 Silver. Octagonal bezel engraved with *I* crowned, flanked by branches. The shoulders fluted.
? GERMAN: 16th century.
768-1871

5 Silver. Octagonal bezel engraved with a crowned eagle; on the shoulders, the initials *AI*.
GERMAN: 15th century.
786-1871

6 Silver-gilt. Oval bezel engraved with the initials *AN*. Hoop inscribed with a magical sequence of letters: *+EADC.EU.PH.RUNASKHR+*.
GERMAN: 15th century.
782-1871

7 Silver. Octagonal bezel engraved with a black letter monogram. Twisted ribbon hoop.
GERMAN: early 16th century.
777-1871
Nos. 4-7, Waterton Collection

8 Silver. Octagonal bezel engraved with a coat of arms band inscribed in black letter with the name: *iuhanis de lasu.*
FRENCH: 15th century.
142-1907

195

9 Silver. Octagonal bezel engraved with a black letter monogram.
GERMAN: early 16th century.
778-1871

10 Silver. Rectangular bezel engraved with *IS* in monogram.
? GERMAN: early 16th century.
776-1871

11 Silver. Circular bezel engraved with *IR* in black letter.
GERMAN: late 15th century.
781-1871

12 Silver-gilt. Octagonal bezel engraved with a coat of arms.
ITALIAN: 16th century.
800-1871
Nos 9-12, Waterton Collection

13 Nielloed silver. Octagonal bezel engraved with a coat of arms and inscription in black letter variant.
HUNGARIAN: 15th century.
M.471-1936

14 Gold. Octagonal bezel engraved with the arms of Jouanniere (Bretagne) and inscribed in black letter: *qant.qe.soit.* Fluted shoulders engraved with sprigs.
FRENCH: 15th century.
Guilhou Collection
Given by the National Art Collections Fund
M.181-1937

15 Gold. Octagonal bezel set with a garnet intaglio of a female bust. Shoulders engraved with sprigs and inscribed in black letter: *pour bien.*
? FRENCH: early 16th century; the intaglio ITALIAN: 15th century.
Waterton Collection
901-1871

16 Gold. Circular bezel engraved with a coat of arms and inscribed:
MARIA/N/VS.MR. Shoulders chased with foliated scrolls.
ITALIAN: 15th century.
Guilhou Collection
Given by the National Art Collections Fund
M.179-1937

17 Gilt bronze. Circular bezel engraved with a coat of arms between *F* and *R.*
ITALIAN: 16th century.
791-1871

18 Nielloed silver. Circular bezel engraved with a transverse initial *R* between two flowers. A pseudo-signet, as the letter is not in reverse.
? GERMAN: 16th century.
780-1871

19 Gilt bronze. Oval bezel engraved with a coat of arms.
? ITALIAN: 16th century.
790-1871
Nos. 17-19, Waterton Collection

20 Copper, with traces of gold and niello inlay. Engraved with a coat of arms beneath a crowned helmet.
ITALIAN: 15th century.
Miss E.M. Begg Bequest
M.332-1975

21 Nielloed silver. Circular bezel engraved with a slipped trefoil. Shoulders decorated with palmettes.
ITALIAN: 16th century.
Waterton Collection
746-1871

22 Nielloed silver. Oval bezel set with a late Roman intaglio. Shoulders decorated with foliage. Hoop inscribed lombardic characters: *+VERBUMxCHARO+.*
ITALIAN: 15th century.
Given by Dame Joan Evans, P.P.S.A.
M.192-1962

23 Silver. Hexagonal bezel engraved with a chalice and wafer between *f* and *c* in black letter. Shoulders engraved with a Tau cross and a flower. Hoop inscribed inside: *ana+m+aria.*
WEST EUROPEAN: late 15th century.
Harman-Oates Collection
M.9-1929

24 Gold. Oval bezel set with a crystal with two engraved shields mounted over foil with the Sacred Monogram, forget-me-nots and a fleur-de-lis, and the initials: *FGMN (fergiss mein nicht — forget me not).*
GERMAN: late 16th century.
Waterton Collection
815-1871

*25 Silver. Square bezel engraved with *W* crowned. The Sacred Monogram engraved in black letter on one shoulder and a Tau cross on the other.
WEST EUROPEAN: 15th century.
Waterton Collection
772-1871

SIGNET AND
SENTIMENTAL RINGS:
15th-17th century

With the arrival of the Renaissance, the main types of medieval lettering, lombardic and black letter, began to give way to roman capitals and italic script. Their use became so wide-spread that their incidence is not noted.

1 Gold. Shaped octagonal bezel engraved with the arms of Muti and inscribed in lombardic characters: *+SIGILLVM. ANGNILI. D.MVTIS.* Pearled border. Shoulders incised with rosettes; volute terminals. Hoop inscribed: *+SPERO.IN/.DOMINO.* (my hope is in the Lord).
ITALIAN: early 16th century.
Given by Dame Joan Evans, P.P.S.A.
M.279-1962

2 Gold. Circular bezel engraved with the arms of Contarini. Shoulders chased with acanthus.
ITALIAN: 16th century.
Waterton Collection
806-1871

3 Enamelled gold, set with an oval sapphire intaglio of the head of Medusa. Shoulders decorated with arabesques.
The setting WEST EUROPEAN: about 1600. The intaglio ROMAN: 1st century A.D.
Arundel and Marlborough Collections
Lent from the Salting Bequest
M.553-1910

4 Nielloed silver. Oval bezel set with a cornelian intaglio of Hercules resting. Sides of bezel, shoulders and hoop nielloed with flowers.
ITALIAN: about 1600.
Waterton Collection
968-1871

5 Enamelled gold. Oval box bezel set with an emerald intaglio, perhaps a replacement, of a coat of arms. Deeply chased, shoulders with head and volutes, enamelled.
WEST EUROPEAN: about 1580.
Given by Dame Joan Evans, P.P.S.A.
M.211-1962

6 Enamelled gold. Oval box bezel set with a sard intaglio of ? Hercules playing a lyre. Back of bezel chased in sunflower form. Shoulders chased with volutes.
? ITALIAN: 16th century.
Waterton Collection
960-1871

*7 Enamelled gold. Oval bezel with a bloodstone intaglio of the head of St. John the Baptist set in a footed cup. The bezel opens; inside, a compass and dial with an enamelled cover.
GERMAN or ITALIAN: about 1580.
Guilhou Collection: acquired by Dame Joan Evans, P.P.S.A.
M.218-1975

8 Gold, with traces of enamel. Bezel with an antique intaglio of a young warrior's head with a helmet forming the face of an old man. Shoulders chased with foliated strapwork.
SOUTH GERMAN: late 16th century.
Said to have been found in the garden of Llandulas Rectory, North Wales.
M.102-1920

9 Gold, formerly enamelled. Hollow bezel set with an agate intaglio of a female head. Shoulders chased with foliated decoration.
SOUTH GERMAN: late 16th century.
Given by Dame Joan Evans, P.P.S.A.
M.262-1962

10 Gold. Oval bezel engraved with a mythical animal which when turned becomes a crested helmet between *M* and *P*. Spreading ribbed shoulders.
WEST EUROPEAN: late 15th century. Pichon and Guilhou Collections; given by the National Art Collections Fund
M.180-1937

11 Gold. Oval bezel engraved with a coat of arms with an indecipherable inscription in lombardic characters. Hoop inscribed: *am.gratia.pena.*
? GERMAN: early 16th century.
Given by Dame Joan Evans, P.P.S.A.
M.217-1975

*12 Gold. Oval bezel set with a red-foiled crystal engraved with a warrior's head; gold details of the helmet painted underneath.
GERMAN: late 16th century.
737-1871

13 Gold. Oval bezel set with a gold-foiled crystal engraved with a shield bearing two clasped hands with a bunch of forget-me-nots; also inscribed: *VMN (vergiss mein nicht,* forget me not).
GERMAN: dated 1572.
Said to have been found in the Seine at Paris, 1859.
736-1871
See also Board G, no. 24 above

14 Gold. Oval bezel set with a foiled crystal engraved with a coat of arms.
? GERMAN: dated 1597.
French warranty marks for 1838 onwards.
817-1871
Nos. 12-14, Waterton Collection

15 Gold, once enamelled. Oval bezel set with a foiled crystal engraved with a coat of arms bordered by scrollwork. Bezel and shoulders chased in high relief with an animal head, strapwork and scrolls.
? GERMAN: mid 16th century.
Given by Dame Joan Evans, P.P.S.A.
M.219-1975

16 Gold. Oval bezel set with a foiled crystal engraved with an escutcheon bearing *A V* in monogram; above, the initials *WG*. Underneath, the date 1555 in gold foil.
? ENGLISH: 1555.
819-1871

17 Gold. Oval bezel set with a foiled crystal engraved with the arms of Erskine of Balgowrie; tinctures underneath.
BRITISH: late 16th century.
818-1871

19 Gold. Octagonal bezel engraved with a coat of arms, below *I.C.*
WEST EUROPEAN: 16th century.
M.222-1975

20 Gold. Octagonal bezel set with a panel of *verre eglomisé*, depicting clasped hands holding three flowers (forget-me-nots) between *A W* and *GH.* Inscribed: *ANNO/1634/12 IVNI.* Masks on shoulders.
GERMAN: the goldsmiths' work probably late 16th century. Mark, a fascis. The bezel later.
M.229-1975
Nos. 19 & 20, given by Dame Joan Evans, P.P.S.A.

21 Gold. Oval bezel set with a chalcedony intaglio of Henry VIII (1491-1574) between *H* and *R.*
ENGLISH: mid 16th century.
The ring predates 31 October 1576, on which date it was used as a seal on a deed by Dorothy, wife of John Abington of Hindlip, Worcs., cofferer to Queen Elizabeth I (PRO, Ancient Deed, pp/103).
Fellons, Webster and Holbrooke Collections
Frank Ward Bequest
M.5-1960

*22 THE LEE RING
Gold. Oval bezel set with a foliated crystal engraved with the arms of Sir Richard Lee (d.1575) of Sopwell, near St. Albans. Behind the bezel is engraved a grasshopper, enamelled in green, the badge of the financier Sir Thomas Gresham (d.1579), and the motto: *FLAME ET.FAME.*
ENGLISH: about 1554-1575.
Sir Thomas Gresham gave a number of these rings to his friends, all bearing his grasshopper badge but each having the arms of the recipient.
Bought with the aid of funds provided by Mr. L.C.G. Clarke
M.249-1928

*23 Gold. Hexagonal bezel engraved with an eagle displayed, the shoulders with the Virgin and Child, and St. John the Divine. Behind, *J* and *K* joined by a true-lover's knot.
WEST EUROPEAN: early 16th century.
694-1871

24 Silver, formerly gilt. Oval bezel engraved with *I* and *S* joined by a true-lover's knot.
? ENGLISH: second half of 16th century.
838-1871

*25 THE 'DARNLEY' RING
Gold. Circular bezel engraved with *H* and *M* joined over a true-lover's knot. Behind, a crowned shield with a lion rampant, and the inscription: *HENRI.L.DARNLEY./1565.*
Foliated shoulders.
The ring ENGLISH: 16th century.
The inscription probably early 19th century.
The date on the ring is that of the betrothal and marriage of Mary Queen of Scots (1542-1587) and her second husband Henry, Lord Darnley (1545-1567). The engraving however is sharp and distinct, while the ring itself and the engraved border of the bezel show signs of wear. The initials on the bezel are badly spaced, and the outer lower serif of the letter *M* impinges on the whipped border. Said to have been found at Fotheringay Castle, the ring was in the possession of Edmund Waterton by 1857.
841-1871
Nos. 22-25, Waterton Collection

26 Gold. Oval bezel engraved with a hand holding a sunflower, between *T* and *S;* pearled border.
WEST EUROPEAN: late 16th century.
M.221-1975

27 Gold, engraved with three flowers between *R* and *S.*
ENGLISH: 16th century.
M.227-1975
Nos. 26 & 27, given by Dame Joan Evans, P.P.S.A.

28 Gold. Oval bezel engraved with the arms of Baker, Co. Devon; inside, *CB* in monogram. Shoulders chased with terms.
ENGLISH: late 16th century.
807-1871

29 Gold. Oval bezel engraved with a lion rampant with initials, above, *AH.*
WEST EUROPEAN: late 16th century.
793-1871
Nos. 28 & 29, Waterton Collection

30 Gold. Oval bezel engraved with a coat of arms.
ENGLISH: late 16th century.
129-1865

31 Gold. Revolving oval bezel with arms and crest of Sir Nicholas Throckmorton, assumed by him after 1607 in right of his wife, the heiress Anne Carew of Beddington. The Throckmortons changed their name to Carew when Lady Throckmorton inherited Beddington.
ENGLISH: early 17th century.
Waterton Collection
808-1871

32 Gold. A skull. Circular bezel engraved with a skull surrounded by the name: *EDWARDxCOPE.* Behind, a fragment of a bone, presumably a talisman or relic.
ENGLISH: early 17th century.
Designed as a signet, with letters in reverse, the ring clearly relates to *memento mori* (keep death in your thoughts) in the form of rings embellished with skulls (see Case 34, Board F, nos. 1 & 2), but it also functioned as a talisman.
Henry Willett Collection
Given by Dame Joan Evans, P.P.S.A.
M.273-1962

SIGNET RINGS:
16th and 17th centuries

1 Silver. Rectangular bezel engraved with *IA* crowned.
WEST EUROPEAN: early 16th century.
765-1871

2 Silver. Clipped rectangular bezel engraved with *IB* crowned.
WEST EUROPEAN: early 16th century.
770-1871

3 Gold. Oval bezel engraved with the arms of Pipart and, above, *CP*.
ENGLISH: late 16th century.
809-1871
Nos. 1-3, Waterton Collection

4 Gold. Oval bezel engraved with a true lovers' knot, three sprigs and *AF*.
ENGLISH: 16th century.
Given by Dame Joan Evans, P.P.S.A.
M.228-1975

5 Bronze. Circular bezel engraved with a vine and *cent* in black letter, probably a rebus for Vincent. Shoulders chased with flowers; traces of gilding.
ENGLISH: 16th century.
796-1871

6 Gold. Oval bezel engraved with a rose bush, with *W* and *C,* and inscribed in Roman capitals: *EX DONO ROBERTI BRADLEY* (the gift of Robert Bradley).
ENGLISH: 17th century.
740-1871

*7 Gold. Oval bezel engraved with a coat of arms.
WEST EUROPEAN: 17th century.
Found at Caer Gys, Wales.
810-1871

8 Gold. Oval bezel engraved with a hand between *A* and *R*.
ENGLISH: 17th century.
738-1871
Nos. 5-8, Waterton Collection

9 Gold. Oval bezel engraved with the mantled arms of Mortimer, Co. Norfolk.
ENGLISH: 17th century.
Maker's mark C in a shield.
Given by Mrs. Lucy S. Jarman (née Mortimer)
4-1874

10 Gold. Oval bezel engraved with the crest of Toovey, between *S* and *T*. Behind, rough initials *R.P.*
ENGLISH: 17th century. Maker's mark, IY in a rectangle.
1583-1902

11 Gold. Octagonal bezel engraved with a ship in full sail. Behind, the pricked initials *T./I.R.*
ENGLISH: 16th century. Struck with an indecipherable mark.
Given by Dame Joan Evans, P.P.S.A.
M.226-1975

12 Gold. Octagonal bezel engraved with a coat of arms.
ENGLISH: late 16th century.
Waterton Collection
812-1871

13 Bezel engraved with a coat of arms, and inscribed behind: *Memoriae/Sacrum,* with a skull between *A* and *L* in black enamel.
ENGLISH: post 1660.
Court Collection
Given by Dame Joan Evans, P.P.S.A.
M.269-1962

14 Gold. Oval bezel engraved with a skull and, behind, with the initials *A.B.*
? ENGLISH: early 17th century.
Waterton Collection
921-1871

15 Gold. Octagonal bezel engraved with a skull and inscribed: *IB (sic) MEMENTO.MORI.*
ENGLISH: 17th century.
Given by Mr T.B. Clarke-Thornhill
M.378-1927

16 Gold. Oval bezel chased with a heart and inscribed with the initials *WR.*
ENGLISH: 17th century.
Possibly found at Cromer, Norfolk.
Waterton Collection
739-1871

17 Gold. Octagonal bezel engraved with the arms of Brooke impaling another.
ENGLISH: 17th century.
Brooke Gift
390-1864

18 Gold. Oval bezel engraved with the arms of Leigh of Addington, Co. Surrey, granted 1609.
ENGLISH: 17th century.
Given by Dame Joan Evans, P.P.S.A.
M.267-1962

19 Gold. Oval bezel engraved with the arms of Willmott.
ENGLISH: 17th century.
Waterton Collection
91-1899

20 Gold. Oval bezel engraved with the arms of Rous, of Great Clacton, Co. Essex.
ENGLISH: 17th century.
Court Collection
Given by Dame Joan Evans, P.P.S.A.
M.266-1962

21 Brass. Oval bezel engraved with the crest of ? Harley.
ENGLISH: about 1630.
Given by Mr. H. Vincent Harley
M.25-1945

22 Gilt bronze. Circular bezel inscribed: *+BE.STEDFAST.IN. FAITH.* and *RL.*
ENGLISH: 17th century.
Given by Mr. B.L.F. Potts
507-1894

23 Brass. Oval bezel engraved with a lion rampant.
ENGLISH: 17th century.
Brooke Gift
391-1864

24 Gilt bronze. Oval bezel engraved with a crest of a griffin's head erased ducally gorged between *I* and *R*.
ENGLISH: 17th century.
Given by Mr. L.A. Lawrence, F.R.C.S.
M.374-1923

200

25 Silver-gilt. Oval bezel engraved with an implement in a shield beneath *RK*. Shoulders chased with acanthus ornaments.
Probably GERMAN: late 16th century.
7753-1863

26 Gilt bronze. Circular bezel engraved with the initial *W* surmounted by a crown. Gadrooned shoulders and hoop.
GERMAN: 16th century.
766-1871

27 Gilt bronze. Octagonal bezel engraved with *A* within a tressure counterfleury. The shoulders and hoop fluted.
WEST EUROPEAN: 17th century.
783-1871

28 Copper-gilt. Circular bezel with a shield charged with the initial *S*, surrounded by the inscription: *GRAF SI FW URM* (Count Siegfried Wurm). Dragon-heads on the shoulders.
GERMAN: 17th century.
741-1871
Nos. 26-28, Waterton Collection

29 Bronze. Octagonal bezel engraved with a lion rampant holding a flower, above *MK* and a quatrefoil.
WEST EUROPEAN: late 16th century.
Given by Dr. W.L. Hildburgh, F.S.A.
M.168-1929

30 Bronze. Oval bezel engraved with a double-headed eagle. Hoop with a projecting tobacco tamper.
? GERMAN: 17th century.
743-1871

*31 Bronze. Oval bezel engraved with a fleur-de-lis. Hoop with a tobacco tamper.
? GERMAN: 17th century.
745-1871

32 Gilt bronze. Oval bezel engraved with a hand holding an object.
WEST EUROPEAN: first half of 17th century.
836-1871
Nos. 30-32, Waterton Collection

33 Gilt bronze. Bezel engraved with a coat of arms and inscribed: *PONE DNE SIGNVM SALVTIS.*
? SPANISH: 17th century.
Given by Dr. W.L. Hildburgh, F.S.A.
M.203-1930

1. Gold. Oval bezel engraved with the arms of Rolle, Co. Devon. Inscribed behind, *GR*.
ENGLISH: 17th century.
Waterton Collection
811-1871

2 Gold. Oval silver-gilt bezel engraved with a coat of arms. Rose-cut diamonds set on forked and foliated shoulders.
GERMAN: late 17th century.
628-1872

3 Gold. Octagonal bezel engraved with a coat of arms. Inscribed behind with the initial *E*.
WEST EUROPEAN: 17th century.
Waterton Collection
813-1871

4 Gold. Oval bezel engraved with a coat of arms, perhaps of Sampson or Fletcher.
ENGLISH: 17th century.
M.265-1962

5 Gold. Oval bezel engraved with the arms of John Collins of Batterton, Co. Berks. Inscribed behind: *in mem./I.C./10 dec. 85.*
ENGLISH: 1686. Maker's mark, AW in monogram.
John Collins bequeathed 'twenty shillings for a ring memoriall' to his brother-in-law in his will, and to his wife, 'all rings . . . of her closet.'
M.268-1962

6 Gold. Oval bezel engraved with the arms of Bard, North Kelsey, Lincs., impaling another.
ENGLISH: late 17th century.
Court Collection
M.270-1962
Nos. 4-6, given by Dame Joan Evans, P.P.S.A.

7 Gold. Circular bezel inscribed with *S* and *G* bound by a true-lovers' knot and inscribed: *ELIZABET EDOLFF.*
ENGLISH: 17th century
There was a Kentish family of the name of Edolphe at the time of James I.
840-1871

8 Silver. Square bezel engraved with *L* enclosing a heart (a pseudo-signet). Lion masks on the shoulders.
ITALIAN: 17th century. Maker's mark, IG.
923-1871
Nos. 7 & 8, Waterton Collection

9 Enamelled gold, set with a late Roman garnet intaglio of a caduceus, Inscribed: *PIETAS*.
WEST EUROPEAN: late 16th century.
Ready Bequest
M.9-1959

10 Gold. Oval bezel, with a scalloped edge, set with a cornelian intaglio; arms of ? Rushe, Co. Essex. Engraved behind with a skull and inscribed: *I/R/Obijt Sep. t/13th.52. etat.63.*
ENGLISH: about 1652.
Given by Dame Joan Evans, P.P.S.A.
M.271-1962

11 Gold. Oval bezel set with a cornelian intaglio; arms of Baduley.
ENGLISH: about 1650-60.
Said to have belonged to John Baduley, still living in 1675.
Given by Miss Anna Newton
1644-1903

12 Enamelled gold. Oval bezel set with a bloodstone (? Gnostic) intaglio of a falcon, snake and ibis.
The enamelled setting ? GERMAN: first quarter of 18th century.
Given by Dame Joan Evans, P.P.S.A.
M.232-1975

13 Gold. Octagonal bezel set with a sapphire intaglio; arms of Pio di Savoia of Carpi. Fluted back.
ITALIAN: 17th century.
The arms include the insignia of the Gonfalonier of the Holy Roman Church.
Waterton Collection
820-1871

14 Gold, with traces of enamel on the shoulders. Octagonal bezel set with a blue glass intaglio; a coat of arms, with initials *F./W.*
GERMAN: late 17th century.
Given by Dame Joan Evans, P.P.S.A.
M.230-1975

15 Enamelled gold. Octagonal bezel set with a sapphire intaglio; monogram *IL* below a coronet; lobed and enamelled back.
FRENCH: early 17th century.
Ready Bequest
M.10-1959

16 Oval bezel (a 'Roman setting') with an amethyst intaglio; a coat of arms below a coronet. Forked shoulders.
? GERMAN: 18th century.
822-1871

*17 Gold. Rectangular bezel engraved with a merchant's mark and inscribed in lombardic characters with the name: + *GALGANO D'CICHO*. Hoop inscribed: + *IESUS. AUTEM. TRANSIENS. PER. MEDIUM. ILLORUM. IBAT.* (but He (Jesus) passing through the midst of them went His way; Luke, 4, 30).
ITALIAN (? Sienese): 14th century.
The verse from St Luke's Gospel seems to have been used by travellers as a charm against sudden dangers, such as attacks by robbers.
88-1899
Nos. 16 & 17, Waterton Collection

18 Silver. Octagonal bezel engraved with a merchant's mark between *I* and *H*. On each shoulder, a crown in relief.
ENGLISH: 15th century.
783-1877

*19 Silver. Circular bezel engraved with a merchant's mark. Shoulders ornamented with five projections (one wanting).
ENGLISH: 15th century.
Waterton Collection
756-1871

20 Gold. Octagonal bezel engraved with a cruciform merchant's mark between *R* and *S*. Corded border.
ENGLISH: 15th century.
From Stamford.
Given by Dame Joan Evans, P.P.S.A.
M.203-1975

21 Silver. The round bezel engraved with a merchant's mark, *P* and *W* and a sprig.
ENGLISH: 15th century.
Miss E.M. Begg Bequest
M.337-1975

22 Silver. Circular bezel engraved with an open pair of shears, with *g/ra/c/e* in black letter between. Fluted and beaded shoulders.
ENGLISH: late 15th or early 16th century.
Possibly made for a Merchant-Taylor named Grace.
Given by Dame Joan Evans, P.P.S.A.
M.258-1962

23 Silver. The circular bezel engraved with a merchant's mark.
WEST EUROPEAN: early 16th century.
Laking and Harman-Oates Collections
M.11-1929

24 Silver. The long octagonal bezel engraved with a merchant's mark.
ENGLISH: early 16th century.
753-1871

25 Silver. Hexagonal bezel engraved with a merchant's mark and foliage.
? IRISH: 16th century.
Found near Cork in 1844 and formerly in the possession of Mr Edward Hare of that city.
755-1871

26 Gilt bronze. Octagonal bezel engraved with a merchant's mark. Hoop spirally gadrooned.
WEST EUROPEAN: 16th century.
752-1871
Nos. 24-26, Waterton Collection

27 Silver. Circular bezel engraved with a merchant's mark and *MI* with sketchy foliage.
WEST EUROPEAN: 16th century.
Miss E.M. Begg Bequest
M.338-1975

28 Gold. Oval bezel engraved with a merchant's mark.
Shoulders chased with leaves.
ENGLISH: 16th century.
759-1871

29 Silver. Oval bezel engraved with a merchant's mark. Shoulders chased with leaves and scrolls.
WEST EUROPEAN: 16th century.
758-1871
Nos. 28 & 29, Waterton Collection

30 Gold. Raised circular bezel engraved or re-engraved with a merchant's mark and *D G A* (not in reverse); inscribed behind with the date: *MDXL*. Shoulders chased with terms.
ENGLISH: ? 1540; the bezel probably engraved in the 19th century.
6807-1860

31 Enamelled gold. Elaborate 2-stage drum bezel engraved with a merchant's mark between *B* and *B* (not in reverse). Behind, an enamelled heart and crossed arrows below a crown. Shoulders decorated with strapwork in relief.
ENGLISH: mid 16th century.
M.193-1962

32 Gold. The oval bezel engraved with a merchant's mark of a double barred cross between *G* and *S*.
ENGLISH: ? mid 16th century.
M.223-1975
Nos. 31 & 32, given by Dame Joan Evans, P.P.S.A.

33 Silver. Oval bezel engraved with a shield charged with a merchant's mark; above, *G* (not in reverse) and *B*. Shoulders chased with figures of Adam and Eve.
ENGLISH: second half of 16th century.
1375-1903

34 Gold. Revolving circular bezel enamelled with a skull on one side; reverse, a merchant's mark. On the edge, the inscription: *NOSSE TE IPSUM* (Know yourself). Volutes on shoulders.
? ENGLISH: late 16th century.
Found at Guildford.
Harman-Oates Collection
M.18-1929

35 Gold. Circular bezel set with a white cornelian intaglio with a merchant's mark, the monogram *EM* surmounted by a double cross.
ENGLISH: late 16th century.
Found in Bolford churchyard, Lincs., 1849.
761-1871

36 Gold. The bezel set with a cornelian intaglio with a merchant's mark.
ENGLISH: early 17th century.
760-1871
Nos. 35 & 36, Waterton Collection

37 Gold. Octagonal bezel engraved with a shield with two notches, a merchant's mark with *D* and *R* attached, a skull above and the inscription: *RICORDATI.IL.TUO. FINN.*
? ENGLISH: early 17th century.
Maker's mark, MF conjoined in a shield.
It has been suggested that the inscription is a literary conceit.
Acquired by Dame Joan Evans in London in 1932.
Given by Dame Joan Evans, P.P.S.A.
M.272-1962

38 Silver-gilt. Oval bezel engraved with a merchant's mark and *MPS*, surmounted by a flower. The shoulders foliated.
WEST EUROPEAN: 17th century.
733-1871

39 Brass. Octagonal bezel engraved with a merchant's mark and *PW*, impaling a double-headed eagle.
GERMAN: 17th century.
757-1871
Nos. 38 & 39, Waterton Collection

RINGS SET WITH STONES:
16th and 17th centuries

1 Gold, with traces of enamel on the shoulders. Bezel formed of two oval collets each with 4-cusp setting, with a triangular-cut diamond and a ruby. Fluted shoulders with volutes and foliage.
GERMAN: about 1500.
Guilhou Collection; acquired by Dame Joan Evans, PPSA.
M.1-1959

2 Enamelled gold. Cusped 4-petal setting with a ruby, with interlaced work. Double scroll shoulders.
WEST EUROPEAN: mid 16th century.
M.200-1962

3 Gold, set with a table-cut diamond in a 4-petal setting.
WEST EUROPEAN: 1st half of 16th century.
M.194-1962
Nos. 1-3, given by Dame Joan Evans, P.P.S.A.

4 Enamelled gold. Hexagonal bezel with a turquoise in a cusped setting.
WEST EUROPEAN: 16th century.
19th century Roman mark.
A small ring, like no. 5 below, perhaps to be worn on the first joint of the finger.
956-1871

5 Enamelled gold, Hexagonal bezel set with a turquoise. Imbricated hoop.
WEST EUROPEAN: 16th century.
955-1871
Nos. 4 & 5, Waterton Collection

6 Enamelled gold. Lozenge-shaped bezel on a cushion; cusped setting with faceted hog-back diamond. Volutes on shoulders.
WEST EUROPEAN: 16th century.
730-1904

7 Gold. 4-petal bezel, with double cusps, set with a turquoise.
WEST EUROPEAN: mid 16th century.
Waterton Collection
954-1871

8 Enamelled gold. 4-petal bezel, with double cusps, re-set with a ruby. Volutes on shoulders.
WEST EUROPEAN: mid 16th century.
4397-1857

9 Enamelled gold. 4-petal bezel, with double cusps, set with a jacinth. Scrolls on shoulders.
? ITALIAN: mid 16th century.
948-1871

10 Enamelled gold. 4-petal bezel, with double cusps, set with a ruby. Volutes on shoulders.
WEST EUROPEAN: mid 16th century.
949-1871

*11 Enamelled gold. Sexfoil bezel with double cusps, set with a turquoise engraved with an *F*, surrounded by garnets. Volutes on shoulders.
WEST EUROPEAN: mid 16th century.
Said to have belonged to King Frederick the Great of Prussia (1712-1786).
953-1871
Nos. 9-11, Waterton Collection

*12 Enamelled gold. 4-petal bezel, with double cusps, set with a table-cut diamond. Volutes on shoulders.
WEST EUROPEAN: mid 16th century.
Lent from the Salting Bequest
M.556-1910

13 Enamelled gold. 4-petal bezel set with a table-cut sapphire. Volutes on shoulders.
WEST EUROPEAN: mid 16th century.
201-1906

14 Enamelled gold. 4-petal bezel reset with a ruby. Chased shoulders.
WEST EUROPEAN: mid 16th century.
597-1892

15 Gold, originally enamelled. Box bezel set with a ruby. Scrolled shoulders.
WEST EUROPEAN: late 16th century.
Acquired (presumably by Sir John Evans), Agincourt, 1870.
Given by Dame Joan Evans, P.P.S.A.
M.198-1962

16 Gold. Square box bezel on cushion set with an emerald. Volutes on shoulders.
WEST EUROPEAN: late 16th century.
193-1864

17 Enamelled gold. Square box bezel set with a paste. Rosettes on shoulders.
WEST EUROPEAN: late 16th century.
Waterton Collection
947-1871

18 Enamelled gold square box bezel on cushion set with a paste. Rosettes on shoulders.
WEST EUROPEAN: late 16th century.
30-1894

19 Crystal. Carved to resemble a 4-petal setting. Chased shoulders.
GERMAN: later 16th century.
Given by Dame Joan Evans, P.P.S.A.
M.204-1962

20 Gold. Rectangular box bezel set with a rose-cut sapphire.
WEST EUROPEAN: second half of 16th century.
Found in the City of London.
Harman-Oates Collection
M.15-1929

21 Enamelled gold. Box bezel on cushion set with ruby. Shaped shoulders.
WEST EUROPEAN: late 16th century.
731-1902

DECORATIVE RINGS:
16th and 17th centuries

204

22 Enamelled gold. Box bezel on cushion set with a cabochon ruby. Volutes and rosettes on shoulders.
WEST EUROPEAN: late 16th century.
7143-1860

23 Enamelled gold. Box bezel on cushion set with a point-cut diamond.
WEST EUROPEAN: late 16th century.
934-1871

24 Enamelled gold. Box bezel on cushion set with a point-cut diamond. Chased shoulders.
WEST EUROPEAN: late 16th century.
935-1871
Nos. 23 & 24, Waterton Collection

25 Gold. Square box bezel set with a table-cut crystal.
ENGLISH: second half of 16th century.
M.195-1962

26 Enamelled gold. Octagonal box bezel on cushion set with a rose-cut amethyst. Chased shoulders.
WEST EUROPEAN: late 16th century.
Acquired (presumably by Sir John Evans), London, 1870.
M.197-1962

27 Enamelled gold. Bezel set with a point cut diamond; 4 pellets. Enamelled shoulders. Heavily restored.
WEST EUROPEAN: early 17th century.
Acquired by Dame Joan Evans, 1932.
M.201-1962
Nos. 25-27, given by Dame Joan Evans, P.P.S.A.

1 Enamelled gold. Oval bezel set with an amethyst cameo of a child's head. Shoulders chased with cartouches.
WEST EUROPEAN: 16th century.
Waterton Collection
940-1871

*2 Enamelled gold. Oval bezel set with an onyx cameo head of Medusa. The shoulders and bezel cushion chased with cartouches, masks and foliage.
SOUTH GERMAN: about 1580.
Lent from the Salting Bequest
M.555-1910

3 Enamelled gold, set with an onyx cameo of Queen Elizabeth I. Hoop with painted enamel of pansies and eglantines.
ENGLISH: the cameo after 1575, the setting about 1600.
Loria and Desmoni Collections; lent by Mr. and Mrs. A. Kenneth Snowman

4 Onyx. Oval bezel set with a cameo of a river god in a white stratum; ?Neptune surprising Caenis. Shoulders engraved with terms.
ITALIAN: 16th century.
Waterton Collection
957-1871

5 Gold. Bezel formed as a lion's head, set with a ruby and emeralds.
ITALIAN: 16th century.
Acquired by Sir Arthur Evans, Talemone Maremma, Italy, 1888.
M.206-1962

6 Gold. Almost circular bezel, face pierced and set with shaped turquoises leaving a heart, scrolls and the initials *FDA* reserved in metal.
GERMAN: mid 16th century.
M.2-1959
Nos. 5 & 6, given by Dame Joan Evans, P.P.S.A.

7 Enamelled gold. Box bezel with a ruby in talons.
WEST EUROPEAN: early 17th century.
Waterton Collection
945-1871

8 Enamelled gold. Box bezel set with a jacinth.
WEST EUROPEAN: early 17th century.
4398-1857

9 Enamelled gold. Octagonal box bezel re-set with a smoked quartz.
Probably SPANISH: first half of 17th century.
967-1871

10 *Fede* ring. Enamelled gold. Lozenge-shaped bezel set with pearls surrounding a ruby engraved with clasped hands; back of bezel engraved with a red flower.
ITALIAN: early 17th century. Later Roman mark for gold (1815-1870).
857-1871
Nos. 9 & 10, Waterton Collection

11 Enamelled gold. Sexfoil bezel with a garnet in talons, surrounded by six turquoises.
WEST EUROPEAN: 17th century.
733-1902

12 Enamelled gold, set with a green pearl between two cinquefoils. A fleur-de lis and quatrefoil on shoulders.
? ENGLISH: about 1575.
Given by Dame Joan Evans, P.P.S.A.
M.202-1962

*13 Enamelled gold. Box bezel set with a diamond. Inscribed: *AIN* and *RIC*.
WEST EUROPEAN: early 17th century.
732-1902

*14 Enamelled gold. Box bezel set with an emerald.
WEST EUROPEAN: early 17th century.
194-1864

15 Enamelled gold. Octagonal bezel set with a garnet.
ENGLISH: 17th century.
Brooke Gift
1112-1864

CASE 33
BOARD A
NO. 10

16 Enamelled gold. Square bezel re-set with a paste and rose-cut diamonds in silver collets.
ITALIAN: early 17th century.
Given by Mr. Walter Child
638-1906

17 Gold. Bezel based on a cross fitchee, set with point-cut pastes.
SPANISH (Andalusia): late 16th or early 17th century.
1215-1871

18 Enamelled gold. Star-shaped bezel, the points alternating with talons; set with point-cut pastes.
WEST EUROPEAN: early 17th century.
M.20-1929

19 Enamelled gold. Octofoil bezel set with cabochon emeralds (two missing). Enamel decoration behind and on shoulders, the latter outlined in filigree.
ENGLISH: about 1625.
Found in the City of London, with no. 20 below. Similar in date and treatment to rings in the Cheapside Hoard, Museum of London.
M.16-1929

20 Enamelled gold. Sexfoil bezel set with red pastes. Behind, 6-petal flower in enamel outlined in filigree.
ENGLISH: early 17th century.
M.17-1929
Nos. 18-20, Harman Oates Collection

21 Gold, set with green pastes and crystals.
SPANISH (Andalusia): early 17th century.
M.142-1937

22 Gold, set with crystals and pastes
SPANISH (Andalusia): early 17th century.
M.141-1937
Nos. 22 & 23, given by Dr. W.L. Hildburgh, F.S.A.

23 Gold, set with pastes and crystals.
SPANISH (Andalusia): early 17th century.
331-1864

24 Enamelled gold. Circular bezel set with a pearl and amethysts held by talons. Forked shoulders.
? ENGLISH: early 17th century.
M.208-1962

25 Enamelled gold. Cross-shaped bezel set with rubies and a table-cut diamond. Behind, flowers in enamel.
DUTCH: mid 17th century.
M.212-1962
Nos. 24 & 25, given by Dame Joan Evans, P.P.S.A.

26 Gold hoop, with painted enamel. Decorated with groups of figures in 17th century costume and with the inscription: *R.L. to T.* and *T to K:L.*
ENGLISH: mid 17th century.
Maker's mark illegible.
M.15-1968

27 Enamelled gold. Oval bezel set with a turquoise inlaid with a Persian inscription.
WEST EUROPEAN: first half of 17th century.
965-1871

28 Gold. Oval bezel with revolving turquoise intaglio of Venus and Cupid, having a Gnostic inscription on the reverse. Hoop formed by three chains decorated with faceting and rosettes.
ITALIAN: 17th century.
613-1871
Nos. 27 & 28, Waterton Collection

*29 Enamelled gold. Pyramidal square bezel set with a crystal; scrolls reserved on black enamel on the underside and hoop.
ITALIAN: about 1660.
Given by Dame Joan Evans, P.P.S.A.
M.225-1975

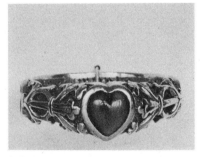

CASE 33
BOARD A
NO. 20

CASE 33
BOARD B
NO. 1

CASE 33
BOARD B
NO. 8

CASE 33
BOARD C
NO. 16

CASE 33
BOARD G
NO. 25

CASE 33
BOARD H
NO. 23

CASE 33
BOARD D
NO. 9

CASE 33
BOARD H
NO. 7

CASE 33
BOARD H
NO. 25

CASE 33
BOARD E
NO. 21

CASE 33
BOARD H
NO. 12

CASE 33
BOARD I
NO. 7

CASE 33
BOARD F
NO. 7

CASE 33
BOARD H
NO. 22

CASE 33
BOARD I
NO. 31

206

CASE 33
BOARD J
NO. 17

CASE 33
BOARD L
NO. 2

CASE 33
BOARD J
NO. 19

CASE 33
BOARD L
NO. 13

CASE 33
BOARD K
NO. 11

CASE 33
BOARD L
NO. 14

CASE 33
BOARD K
NO. 12

CASE 33
BOARD L
NO. 29

Case 34 Board A

DECORATIVE RINGS
(including rings with stones):
16th-early 18th century

208

*1 Gold. Bezel cast in the form of a crouching hound among branches.
? GERMAN: 16th century.
Given by Dame Joan Evans, P.P.S.A.
M.38-1967

*2 Enamelled gold. Bezel cast in the form of a man struggling with a unicorn. Shoulders with cast volutes.
GERMAN: about 1575.
963-1871

3 Enamelled gold. Pyramidal bezel with squared top and talons (the stone missing).
WEST EUROPEAN: late 16th century.
944-1871
Nos. 2-3, Waterton Collection

4 Gold. Bezel with cast pineapple and pins for pearls or stones. Shoulders with cast volutes and strapwork in high relief.
WEST EUROPEAN: about 1575.
Acquired by Dame Joan Evans, 1920.
M.207-1962

5 Enamelled gold. Bezel acting as a base for a reclining Cupid. Shoulders with cast volutes. Inscribed inside:
QVIS RESISTET (who can resist him). Behind, a heart transfixed by an arrow.
SOUTH GERMAN: about 1575.
Acquired by Dame Joan Evans, 1920.
M.210-1962

6 Gold. In the form of a buckled belt. Chased foliated scrolls. Inscribed inside: *SERVIS.NVLLA.QVIES* (S's reversed) (No rest for slaves).
ENGLISH: 16th century.
From Wymondham, Norfolk.
Sir Arthur Evans Collection
M.228-1962
Nos. 4-6, given by Dame Joan Evans, P.P.S.A.

7 Gold, formerly enamelled. Bezel cast in the form of a frog. Shoulders cast and chased.
WEST EUROPEAN: late 16th century.
Waterton Collection
938-1871

8 Enamelled gold. Bezel cast in the form of a Cupid. Rosettes on shoulders.
GERMAN: late 16th century.
216-1870

*9 Enamelled gold. Bezel cast in the form of a Cupid having a red paste on his breast.
WEST EUROPEAN: early 17th century.
191-1864

10 Enamelled gold. Oval bezel cast and chased with a female bust, shoulders with leaves.
WEST EUROPEAN: first half of 17th century. French provincial mark 1838-1919 (horse's head) on shank.
Waterton Collection
939-1871

11 Gold, once enamelled. Square box bezel set with a point-cut diamond in a cusped setting. Shoulders with chased scrollwork.
WEST EUROPEAN: mid 16th century.
Found at Stamford.
Given by Dame Joan Evans, P.P.S.A.
M.220-1975

12 Enamelled gold. Square box bezel set with a crystal. Shoulders chased in broken lines.
WEST EUROPEAN: about 1600.
23-1865

13 Gold. Pyramidal bezel set with a table-cut crystal.
WEST EUROPEAN: late 16th or early 17th century.
Given by Dame Joan Evans, P.P.S.A.
M.246-1962

14 Gold. Pyramidal oval bezel set with a turquoise.
WEST EUROPEAN: early 17th century.
943-1871

15 Gold. Pyramidal bezel set with an almandine garnet; talons below.
WEST EUROPEAN: late 16th or early 17th century.
941-1871

16 Gold. Square pyramidal bezel set with a crystal. Scrollwork on shoulders.
WEST EUROPEAN: late 16th or early 17th century.
942-1871
Nos. 14-16, Waterton Collection

17 Enamelled gold. Rounded pyramidal bezel set with a garnet; talons below. Behind, enamelled roses. Baluster shoulders. Hoop decorated in relief with swag of husks and foliage.
WEST EUROPEAN: late 16th or early 17th century.
Given by Dame Joan Evans, P.P.S.A.
M.203-1962

*18 Enamelled gold, set with a turquoise and garnets.
? ITALIAN: early 17th century.
Waterton Collection
966-1871

19 Enamelled gold. Pyramidal bezel set with a ruby; talons below. Sides of bezel and shoulders cusped and enamelled.
WEST EUROPEAN: early 17th century.
6826-1860

20 Enamelled gold. Rectangular bezel set with a garnet. Sides of bezel and hoop enamelled.
WEST EUROPEAN: about 1620.
190-1864

21 Enamelled gold. Rectangular box bezel, set with a garnet. Sides of bezel and shoulders enamelled.
WEST EUROPEAN: 17th century.
Two indecipherable marks on hoop.
Waterton Collection
951-1871

*22 Enamelled gold, set with table-cut diamonds. Bezel in the form of three overlapping lozenges, set with seven diamonds. Bezel and shoulders enamelled.
WEST EUROPEAN: about 1700.
192-1864

A. STONE-SET AND FANCY RINGS:
18th century

*23 Enamelled gold. Oval bezel set with a spinel in a border of rose-cut diamonds in silver collets. Enamelled flutes behind.
ENGLISH: late 17th century.
Brooke Gift
1116-1864

24 Gold. Convex oval bezel set with an emerald in a border of table-cut diamonds. Shoulders chased with acanthus leaves. Engraved on the back of the bezel, the crowned monogram of King James II (1685-88), by whom it is said to have been given to his chaplain.
ENGLISH: 1685-88.
Given in memory of the late Mr Martin A. Buckmaster
M.10-1970

25 Enamelled gold. Rectangular bezel set with a jacinth. Table-cut diamonds in silver collets on the shoulders.
ENGLISH: late 17th century.
Brooke Gift
1113-1864

26 Gold. Oval bezel set with an onyx in a border of diamond sparks. A spark also on each shoulder.
WEST EUROPEAN: late 17th century.
Bequeathed by Miss Birkenruth
M.20-1937

27 Enamelled gold. In the form of an articulated snake, set with table-cut diamonds.
WEST EUROPEAN: 17th century.
Waterton Collection
961-1871

28 Enamelled gold. Bezel in the form of a skull and cross-bones.
WEST EUROPEAN: 17th century.
172-1872

29 Enamelled gold. Bezel in the form of a skull and cross-bones. Rose-cut diamonds set on the shoulders.
WEST EUROPEAN: 17th century.
528-1868

30 Enamelled gold. Bezel in the form of a skull and cross-bones in a border of rubies. Enamelled rosette behind.
NORTH-WEST EUROPEAN: third quarter of 17th century. Two marks: CC and ? AL in monogram.
Given by Dame Joan Evans, P.P.S.A.
M.280-1962

*31 Enamelled gold. Bezel in the form of a skull and cross-bones, set with rose-cut diamonds.
WEST EUROPEAN: 17th century.
Waterton Collection
922-1871

32 Enamelled gold. Hoop painted with flowers over apertures containing hair.
NORTH-WEST EUROPEAN: mid-late 17th century.
Given by Mrs. Leonora Carr
M.2821-1931

1 Gold, set with emeralds and rose-cut diamonds in silver collets. Bezel in the form of a shell filled with Masonic emblems. Shoulders set with emeralds.
ENGLISH: mid 18th century.
212-1870

2 Gold. Circular bezel set with an onyx and rubies. Openwork shoulders.
WEST EUROPEAN: third quarter of 18th century.
8546-1863

3 Gold. Octagonal bezel with a monogram in gold wire on foil, under crystal. Hoop inscribed inside: *HOPES.*
ENGLISH: early 18th century.
Brooke Gift
1109-1864

4 Gold, set with a square ruby and crystals in silver collets. Openwork shoulders.
WEST EUROPEAN: late 18th century.
M.370-1923

5 Gold, set with a garnet between two- rose-cut diamonds in silver collets. Chased openwork hoop.
GERMAN: 18th century.
959-1872

6 Gold. Octagonal bezel set with an amethyst.
ENGLISH: 18th century.
Brooke Gift
1111-1864

7 Gold. Octagonal bezel with faceted border, set with an amethyst. Radiating flutes behind. Hoop chased with diagonal mouldings.
? ENGLISH: mid 18th century.
M.205-1962

8 Gold. Heart-shaped bezel, set with an amethyst in a border of brilliant-cut diamonds in 11 clawlets. Forked shoulders.
? ENGLISH: 18th century.
M.214-1962
Nos. 7 & 8, given by Dame Joan Evans, P.P.S.A.

210

*9 Gold. Heart-shaped openwork bezel set with a brilliant-cut diamond and a ruby surrounded by emeralds in silver collets. Chased flowers and leaves on shoulders.
WEST EUROPEAN: third quarter of 18th century.
8543-1863

10 Enamelled gold. Heart-shaped bezel set with turquoises in a ruby border (two missing). Radiating gadroons behind. Forked shoulders.
Hoop inscribed: *A/PLEDGE/.OF. MY/LOVE.*
ENGLISH: mid 18th century.
Acquired by Dame Joan Evans in Oxford, 1938.
M.173-1962
Given by Dame Joan Evans, P.P.S.A.

11 Gold. Lozenge-shaped openwork bezel set with rose-cut diamonds in silver collets.
WEST EUROPEAN: late 18th century.
8544-1863

12 Gold. Octofoil bezel set with table-cut diamonds. Radiating gadroons behind. Forked shoulders. Pierced foliated hoop.
SPANISH: first half of 18th century.
Given by Dame Joan Evans, P.P.S.A.
M.213-1962

13 Gold. Circular bezel set with emeralds and pastes in a cluster. Forked shoulders, each branch set with a leaf.
SPANISH: 18th century.
Purchased by J.C. Robinson for the Museum at Baza or Murcia.
206-1864

14 Gold. Oval bezel set with amethysts in a cluster. Shoulders chased with acanthus ornament.
SPANISH: 18th century.
241-1864

15 Gold. Circular bezel set with emeralds in a cluster. Forked shoulders.
SPANISH: late 18th or early 19th century.
200-1864

16 Gold. Vesica-shaped (marquise) openwork bezel set with emeralds.
SPANISH or ITALIAN: late 18th century.
1214-1871

17 Gold. Marquise openwork bezel set with emeralds.
SPANISH or ITALIAN: late 18th century.
336-1864

18 Gold. Shaped circular bezel and shoulders set with emeralds.
? SPANISH: 18th century.
Given by Miss Ball
M.2-1974

These flower rings, so-called after the Italian word for 'little gardens', enjoyed an international vogue and passed into the repertory of the makers of traditional jewellery (see Case 35, Board B, nos. 25-28). Most of the specimens shown here belong to the early phase of the style, having the scrolling hoops characteristic of Rococo design of the mid 18th century.

19 Gold. Openwork bezel in the form of a bunch of flowers, set with rose-cut diamonds in silver collets.
Second third of 18th century.
214-1870

20 Gold. Openwork bezel in the form of a fleur-de-lis, set with a brilliant-cut diamond, a ruby, emeralds and sapphires in silver collets.
Second third of 18th century.
8549-1863

21 Gold. Openwork bezel in the form of a flower spray, set with rose-cut diamonds and rubies in silver collets. Spirally-gadrooned shoulders.
? SPANISH: second third of 18th century.
234-1864

22 Gold. Openwork bezel in the form of a flower set with a table-cut yellow diamond, rubies and emeralds. Chased scrolling openwork shoulders, each set with a brilliant-cut diamond.
Second third of 18th century.
8548-1863

23 Enamelled gold. Bezel in the form of a pierced heart, inscribed: *DOUX ET SINCERE*, framing a tulip set with rubies.
? ENGLISH: second third of 18th century.
Sir John Evans Collection.
Given by Dame Joan Evans, P.P.S.A.
M.170-1962

24 Gold. Openwork bezel in the form of a vase of flowers, set with a ruby and brilliant-cut diamonds in silver collets.
Second third of 18th century.
8547-1863

Case 34 Board C

ENGLISH AND
CONTINENTAL RINGS
WITH MOTTOES AND
INSCRIPTIONS:
16th-18th century

A. POSY RINGS (see introduction to Case 32, Board L). These are later rings, all hoops.

25 Gold. Openwork bezel in the form of a vase of flowers, set with an amethyst, table-cut diamonds and rubies in silver collets. Pierced hoop.
Second third of 18th century.
8551-1863

*26 Gold. Openwork bezel in the form of a vase of flowers, set with rose-cut diamonds, rubies and emeralds in silver collets.
Second third of 18th century.
Waterton Collection
970-1871

27 Gold. Openwork bezel in the form of a flower, set with a ruby and rose-cut diamonds in silver collets.
Second third of 18th century.
8541-1863

28 Gold. Openwork bezel in the form of a vase of flowers, set with rubies and table- and rose-cut diamonds in silver collets. Chased flowers and leaves on shoulders.
Second third of 18th century.
8550-1863

29 Gold. Openwork bezel in the form of a basket of flowers, set with rubies, emeralds and pastes in silver collets.
Second third of 18th century.
Pfungst-Reavil Bequest
M.50-1969

30 Gold. Openwork circular bezel set with rubies and rose-cut diamonds in a floral design.
Second third of 18th century
M.86-1913

1 Gold. Inscribed: *+MVLIER.VIRO/ SVBIECTA.ESTO.* (Woman is to be subject to man).
WEST EUROPEAN: mid 16th century.
Sir John Evans and Mrs. C.J. Longman Collections
M.3-1959

2 Gold. Inscribed outside: *VNG TEMPS* VIANDRA* (a time will come); inside: *+MON*DESIR*ME* VAILLE* (my longings keep me awake).
? FRENCH: early 16th century.
M.221-1962

3 Gold. Inscribed: *+SPERANDO* MVLTO/MERITANDOxNVLLA* (hoping for much/worthy of no woman).
WEST EUROPEAN: late 16th century.
Acquired by Sir Arthur Evans at Warwick, 1900.
M.76-1960

4 Enamelled gold. Inscribed inside: *.yf.fortune.will. I.shall.*
ENGLISH: 2nd quarter of 17th century.
Sir John Evans Collection
M.89-1960

5 Gold, enamelled with sprigs. Small hinged lid around the circumference conceals amatory mottoes, beginning: *JE T'AIME.*
FRENCH: late 18th century.
M.172-1962
Nos. 1-5, given by Dame Joan Evans, P.P.S.A.

6 Stained gut and white quill. Lettered: *ANN CHILCOTT*, with a heart.
ENGLISH: 18th century.
Given by Miss E.A. Chilcote
374-1908

7 Stained gut and white quill. Lettered: *EHRENBREITSTEIN.*
GERMAN: 18th century.
A souvenir of a German town, connected to Coblenz by bridge over the Rhine.
Lent anonymously

8 Gold. Inscribed: *No joy in life to a verteous wife* ('to' means 'like to').
ENGLISH: early 18th century.
Given by Dame Joan Evans, P.P.S.A.
M.94-1960

9 Gold. Inscribed: *Let us Share in joy and Care.*
ENGLISH: 18th century. Maker's mark, BU.
Brooke Gift
379-1864

10 Gold. Inscribed: *My promise past shall always last.*
ENGLISH: 18th century.
Waterton Collection
914-1871

11 Gold. Hebrew inscription: *Simon and Sarah, ? May Zion our City be rebuilt.*
WEST EUROPEAN: 18th century.
M.21-1933

12 Gold. Converted into a mourning ring, chased with flowers and foliage enamelled in black. Inscribed: *Joined in one by God alone. E.W. 1729.*
ENGLISH: dated 1729. Maker's mark, DE in gothic script.
M.83-1960
Nos. 11 & 12, given by Dame Joan Evans, P.P.S.A.

13 Gold. Inscribed: *Vnited hearts death:only:parts.*
ENGLISH: 18th century.
378-1864

14 Gold. Inscribed: *A faithful wife preser(v)eth life.*
ENGLISH: 18th century.
380-1864
Nos. 13 & 14, Brooke Gift

B. MISCELLANEOUS SENTIMENTAL RINGS

C. GIMMEL RINGS

15 Gold. Oval bezel set with a crystal engraved with a heart with, inset, a classical head, and inscribed: *TIS.ALL.HER.OWN.*
ENGLISH: 17th century.
Given by Dame Joan Evans, P.P.S.A.
M.171-1962

*16 Enamelled gold, set with rose-cut diamonds in silver collets. A *fede* ring, with a crowned heart held by two hands. Inscribed: *Dudley & Katherine united 26. Mar. 1706.*
ENGLISH: dated 1706.
302-1867

17 Enamelled gold, set with a ruby. The bezel in the form of a Cupid flying off with a heart. Hoop inscribed: *STOP THIEF.*
ENGLISH: mid 18th century.
215-1870

18 Gold, set with brilliant-cut diamonds in silver collets. The bezel a crowned heart.
ENGLISH: late 18th century.
8545-1863

19 Gold, set with table- and brilliant-cut diamonds. A cluster ring, the central portrait crystal set over plaited hair. Behind, a ridged rosette.
ENGLISH: 18th century.
Brooke Gift
1117-1864

*20 Enamelled gold, set with diamond sparks. The bezel in the form of an urn. Hoop inscribed: *.IT.SHAKES.A.STEADY MIND.* Behind, a hinge conceals a locket fitting for hair.
ENGLISH: late 18th century.
Given by Dame Joan Evans, P.P.S.A.
M.85-1960

21 Enamelled gold. The swelling hoop inscribed with interlaced Y's and the hoop: *SOYEZ HEUREUX.*
ENGLISH: 1791.
A souvenir of the marriage in Berlin on 29 September 1791 of Frederick Augustus, Duke of York (1763-1827), second son of George III, and Princess Frederica of Prussia. Presented by the bridegroom to John Marling, a guest at the wedding.
Given by Mrs. F.J. Halse
325-1907

The gimmel ring (from Latin *gemellus*, a twin) was worn in Roman times and revived in the Middle Ages. It was made with two interlacing or pivoted hoops capable of division so that each lover might wear half. In practice they do not seem often to have been so divided. Examples with three or more hoops are not uncommon and are merely an extension of the earlier idea. Most of the examples shown here are gimmel *fede* rings, combining double (or triple) hoops with the clasped hand motif.

22 Enamelled gold, set with table-cut diamonds and a ruby. *Fede* ring.
WEST EUROPEAN: 17th century.
852-1871

23 Enamelled gold; rose-cut diamonds in silver collets on shoulders.
WEST EUROPEAN: 17th century.
Illegible mark.
112-1871
Nos. 22 & 23, Waterton Collection.

*24 Gold. Bezel in the form of a bust of a blackamoor, enamelled and set with table-cut diamonds, an emerald and rubies, on a pivot holding the two hoops together. The latter enamelled outside and inscribed inside: *TAL QVAL ME MIRI, IO FVI SEMPRE PER TE* (to you I have always been as I saw myself).
ITALIAN: late 17th century.
Though not a proper gimmel ring, as the bezel does not divide, this specimen is clearly inspired by the gimmel type.
M.231-1975

25 Enamelled gold, set with a triangular-cut diamond. Triple gimmel *fede* ring, the two hands clasping an enamelled heart with the diamond. First hoop inscribed: *MEIN. ANFANCK. VND. ENDE* (my beginning and end); second: *WAS. GOTT. ZVSAMEN. FVGET. SOLL.;* third: *KEN. MENSCH. SCHEIDEN.* (What God has joined together let no man put asunder). Volutes on shoulders.
GERMAN: 3rd quarter of 16th century. The second quotation, from the marriage service, indicates that the ring was used as a marriage ring.
M.224-1975
Nos. 24 & 25, given by Dame Joan Evans, P.P.S.A.

26 Enamelled gold. Gimmel *fede* ring. Hoop inscribed: *CLEMEN. KESSELER. DEN-25 AUG. AO.1607.*
GERMAN: dated 1607.
854-1871

27 Enamelled gold. Gimmel *fede* ring, the lower hand with a red heart enamelled on the palm. Hoop inscribed: *QVOD. DEVS. CONIVNXIT./HOMO. NON. SEPARET.* (What God has joined together let no man put asunder).
? GERMAN: about 1600.
851-1871
Nos. 26 & 27, Waterton Collection

28 Enamelled gold, set with turquoises. Gimmel *fede* ring, one head with a heart. Strapwork on shoulders. Hoop inscribed: *SYMON. CORNELISZ./CORNELISIE ENGELS.D.*
DUTCH: late 16th century.
Acquired by Dame Joan Evans, 1930.
M.281-1962
Given by Dame Joan Evans, P.P.S.A.

*29 Enamelled gold. *Fede* ring. Scrolls on shoulders.
ITALIAN: early 17th century.
Murray Bequest
M.1015-1910

30 Gold. Gimmel *fede* ring.
WEST EUROPEAN: 18th century.
Waterton Collection
859-1871

POSY AND SENTIMENTAL RINGS:
16th-19th century

Most posy rings are inscribed inside.

31 Gold. *Fede* ring. Pyramidal bezel divisible into two, cusped and enamelled with moresques on the sides (and shoulders) and set with a table-cut diamond, a ruby and a green and blue paste. Two hoops inscribed: *WER MICH VA—ER DENCK SEINIT* (who (verb) let him think of it) and *DECHTER S SOV—OSER MEIN* (were he to think it he would ... of me).
GERMAN: late 16th or early 17th century.
22-1865

1 Gold. Hoop engraved with scrolls and inscribed outside: + *OBSERVE WEDLOKE*: inside, + *MEMENTO MORI* with motif.
ENGLISH: 16th century.
Waterton Collection
905-1871

2 Gold. Hoop with 12 (? stamped) foliate lozenges. Inscribed inside *NO. CVTE. TO. VNKINDNES.*
ENGLISH: 16th century.
Sir John Evans and Mrs C J Longman Collections
M.75-1960

3 Gold. Hoop inscribed: **CONTINNVE*FAITHFVLL.*
ENGLISH: late 16th century.
Sir John Evans Collection
M.69-1960

4 Gold. Hoop inscribed: *KEPE* FAYTH* TEIL* DETHE.*
ENGLISH: early 17th century.
Sir John Evans and Mrs C J Longman Collections
M.71-1960

5 Gold. Hoop inscribed: *LET + VERTV + GVD + THE* (Let virtue guide thee)
ENGLISH: early 17th century.
Nos. 2-5, given by Dame Joan Evans P.P.S.A.

6 Gold. Hoop chased with scrolls. Inscribed inside: *TIME. DEVM. ME. AMA. QD.* (fear God, love me. QED) with the initials *R/E.*
ENGLISH: 17th century.
Waterton Collection
904-1871

7 Gold. Hoop chased with scrolls. Inscribed inside: +*ESPOIR. EN. DEEV.* (hope in God).
? ENGLISH: late 16th century.
J W Singer; Sir John Evans; Mrs. C J Longman Collections
Given by Dame Joan Evans, P.P.S.A.
M.70-1960

8 Gold. Inscribed inside: *MB/ remember, the* (heart) *that.is.in payne.*
ENGLISH: 17th century.
Waterton Collection
910-1871

9 Gold. Hoop chased with four panels of strapwork. Inscribed: *NEVER TO CHANGE.*
ENGLISH: early 17th century.
Sir John Evans and Mrs C J Longman Collections
Given by Dame Joan Evans, P.P.S.A.
M.92-1960

10 Gold, with traces of enamel. Hoop chased with a hare pursued by two hounds. Inscribed: *TIME LESSENETH NOT MY LOVE.*
ENGLISH: 17th century.
Waterton Collection
911-1871

11 Gold. Inscribed: **SEITHE.GOD. HATHE WROUGHT THIS. CHOICE. .IN.THE./SO.FRAME. THYSELFE. TO.COMFOVRTH.ME.*
ENGLISH: early 17th century.
Brooke Gift
384-1864

12 Silver. Hoop inscribed: *Love and obay.*
ENGLISH: about 1660. Maker's mark, R.
Given by Miss Mary Barnaby
M.43-1960

13 Enamelled Gold. Hoop enamelled in black outside with *EC* and *EH* separated by 4 hearts and inside with the arms of Chibnall, Haselwood, Wilmer and Andrews.
ENGLISH: 17th century.
Presumably commemorates a marriage of a Chibnall and a Haselwood.
Given by Dame Joan Evans, P.P.S.A.
M.157-1962

14 Gold. Hoop inscribed: *AS GOD DECREED SO WE AGREED.*
ENGLISH: 17th century.
Brooke Gift
377-1864

15 Gold. Hoop inscribed: *Godlines. is.great.gaine.*
ENGLISH: mid 17th century.
Sir John Evans and Mrs. C J Longman Collections
Given by Dame Joan Evans, P.P.S.A.
M.93-1960

16 Gold. Hoop inscribed: *GODS PROUIDENC IS OUR INHERITANC I/EA.*
ENGLISH: mid 17th century.
M.369-1923

17 Gold. Hoop inscribed inside: *WHERE (heart)TS AGREE GOD WILL BEE.*
ENGLISH: 17th century.
Brooke Gift
381-1864

18 Gold. Hoop inscribed: *Alway affect what gets respect*
ENGLISH: 2nd half of 17th century.
Maker's mark, HN conjoined.
Sir John Evans and Mrs C J Longman Collections
Given by Dame Joan Evans, P.P.S.A.
M.77-1960

19 Gold. Hoop inscribed: *CAREFULL I'LE BE TO COMFORT THEE.*
ENGLISH: 17th century.
Brooke Gift
382-1864

20 Gold. Hoop inscribed: *E.G.I am blacke but comely.*
ENGLISH: second half of 17th century.
Sir John Evans and Mrs. C J Longman Collections
M.82-1960

21 Gold. Inscribed: *Fear God and lye Abed till Noone.*
ENGLISH: about 1660.
M.87-1960
Nos 20 & 21, given by Dame Joan Evans, P.P.S.A.

22 Silver. Inscribed: *LOUE THE TRUTH.*
ENGLISH: 17th century.
Waterton Collection
913-1871

23 Enamelled gold. Double trefoil-shaped bezel set with point-cut diamonds theirs tops cut off, in silver collets. Inscribed behind: *LOVE FOR LOVE.* Hoop engraved with foliage.
ENGLISH: late 17th century.
8540-1863

24 Enamelled gold. Hoop inscribed: *AS TRUE TO THEE AS DEATH TO ME.*
ENGLISH: 17th century. Maker's mark, R.
Brooke Gift
662-1864

25 Enamelled gold. Hoop engraved with a skeleton and hour glass. Inscribed: *God above increase our love.* The external decoration presumably the result of conversion into a mourning ring.
ENGLISH: about 1695. Maker's mark, DM.
Given by Dame Joan Evans, P.P.S.A.
M.80-1960

26 A child's ring. Gold. Small circular bezel set with a cut diamond. Inscribed: *THIS SPARK WILL GROW.*
ENGLISH: 17th century.
908-1871

27 Gold. Two hoops, pivoted. Inscribed inside: *ACCEPT.THIS. GIFT/OF.HONEST.LOVE.WHICH. NEVER.COVLD/NOR.CAN. REMOVE.* Outside: *1 HATH.TIDE/ 2 MEE.SVRE/3 WHILST.LIFE/ 4 DOTH.LAST.*
ENGLISH: 17th century.
Acquired by Waterton at Bury St Edmunds, 1854.
909-1871
Nos. 26 & 27, Waterton Collection

*28 Gold. Hollow openwork hoop, enclosing hair. Inscribed: *In thy brest my heart doth rest.*
ENGLISH: about 1700. Maker's mark: PH.
Sir John Evans and Mrs C J Longman Collections.
Given by Dame Joan Evans, P.P.S.A.
M.84-1960

29 Gold, with traces of enamel. Hoop engraved with a hare, a hound, a hind, a fly and plants. Inscribed inside: *LOYALTE NE PEUR.*
ENGLISH or FRENCH: 17th century.
Given to Waterton by Henry Cholmley in Rome, 1865.
906-1871

*30 Gold. *Fede* ring. Inscribed: *Never to change.*
ENGLISH: mid 17th century.
M.74-1960

31 Enamelled gold. *Fede* ring, the two hands clasping a heart. Inscribed: *Let virtue by they guide.* Hoop formed of lozenges and ? forget-me-nots.
ENGLISH: about 1660.
M.86-1960
Nos. 30 & 31, given by Dame Joan Evans, P.P.S.A.

32 Gold. Claddagh ring, inscribed inside: *JMM.* A variety of *fede* ring, with two hands clasping a crowned heart, traditional to the Claddagh district of Galway.
IRISH: late 18th century. Mark of Andrew Robinson, Galway.
Given by Mrs. K Ticher
M.12-1961

*33 Gold. *Fede* ring. Three hoops, the two outer each with a hand, the centre with two hearts inscribed *F* and *M*.
WEST EUROPEAN: 18th century. A late example of the type, a marginal candidate for the Local and Traditional board (see Case 35, Board B).
Waterton Collection
856-1871

34 Gold and carved jet. Hoop, with flowers, leaves and, in the centre, clasped hands.
ENGLISH: about 1825.
Given by Miss M I Courtenay
M.90-1952

Case 34 Board E

LOYALIST, COMMEMORATIVE AND PORTRAIT RINGS:
16th-19th century

Most of these rings have royal connotations. Some were distributed by royal families; others, including certain of the Jacobite rings, which are not of high quality, were produced in quantity to meet public demand.

1 ? Pewter. Circular bezel with a double medallion portrait of the Emperor Charles V (1500-1558) and his brother and successor as Holy Roman Emperor, the Archduke Ferdinand (1503-1564). Bezel and hoop pierced to form a whistle.
GERMAN: 2nd half of 16th century. Probably inspired by a circular boxwood carving in the Kunsthistoriches Museum, Vienna.
919-1871

2 Gold. Oval bezel set with a crystal enclosing a profile portrait in gold and enamel of Gustavus Adolphus (1594-1632), King of Sweden. Behind the motto: *SIC REDIT* (thus he returns).
WEST EUROPEAN: probably post 1632.
Based on a medal of the King by the German Sebastian Dadler (1586-1657), this ring was probably among the souvenirs of Gustavus Adolphus, who died championing the Protestant cause at the Battle of Lutzen.
925-1871
Nos. 1 & 2, Waterton Collection

*3 Enamelled gold. Oval bezel with revolving centre; obverse, a portrait of Anne of Austria (1601-1666); reverse, her son Louis XIV (1638-1715). Hoop enamelled with coloured flowers on white.
? FRENCH: mid 17th century.
103-1865

4 Enamelled gold. Oval bezel set with an enamel miniature of Charles I (1600-1649): border of rose-cut diamonds in silver collets. Back of bezel and hoop enamelled in black with floral ornament. Shoulders set with a brilliant-cut diamond.
ENGLISH: mid 17th century
A souvenir of the executed King (see also Case 14 Board H).
Waterton Collection
924-1871

5 Enamelled gold. Oval bezel set with a crystal enclosing a miniature on vellum of Charles I; reverse, an enamelled white skull below a crown between *C* and *R*. Palm in black enamel and a crystal on shoulders. Hoop inscribed inside: *sic transit gloria mundi* (thus passes the vainglory of the world).
ENGLISH: mid 17th century.
Sir John Evans Collection
Given by Dame Joan Evans, P.P.S.A.
M.145-1962

*6 Gold. Oval bezel set with a crystal enclosing a miniature of Charles I.
ENGLISH: the miniature ? 17th century; the setting 18th century.
Bequeathed by Miss A. Cameron
M.1-1909

7 Gold. Oval bezel set with a crystal enclosing a miniature of Charles I, between two brilliant-cut diamonds in silver collets.
ENGLISH: mid 18th century.
M.207-1930

8 Enamelled gold. Oval bezel with a revolving centre; obverse, an intaglio portrait of Charles I; reverse, a skull between a coronet and a royal crown; inscribed: *GLORIA* and *VANITAS*. Border inscribed behind: *IA: the 30/1648*. Hoop engraved inside: *Emigravit gloria Angl:* (the glory of England has departed).
ENGLISH: mid 17th century.
Acquired by Sir John Evans at Christie's, 1895.
Given by Dame Joan Evans, P.P.S.A.
M.274-1962

9 Enamelled gold. Oval bezel enamelled in white with a skull above *CR* in black. Shoulders chased with masks and enamelled black.
ENGLISH: mid 17th century.
Harman-Oates Collection
M.22-1929

10 Gold, formerly enamelled. Oval bezel set with a faceted crystal enclosing plaited hair and *CR KR* below a crown in gold wire. Foliated hoop; traces of black enamel.
ENGLISH: probably 1685-1705. Commemorates Charles II (1630-1685), but may not have been made until after the death of his Queen, Catherine of Braganza (1638-1705), whose cipher (with *K* instead of *C*) appears with his.
Waterton Collection
927-1871

11 Enamelled gold. Octagonal bezel, set with a faceted crystal over a royal crest, probably for Charles II. Foliated shoulders, traces of black enamel.
ENGLISH: about 1685.
Given by Mr. Alfred Spero
M.2-1946

12 Gold. Oval bezel set with a crystal enclosing a watercolour miniature of James, Duke of York (1633-1701), later James II. Openwork shoulders.
ENGLISH: probably about 1675.
J.L. Propert Collection
Given by Dame Joan Evans, P.P.S.A.
M.146-1962

13 Gold. Oval bezel set with a faceted crystal enclosing the monogram *JR* in gold wire below a crown supported by two angels in silk. Foliated shoulders enamelled in black.
ENGLISH: about 1701. Commemorates James II, who died in exile in 1701.
Harman-Oates Collection
M.21-1929

14 Gold. Oval bezel set with a crystal enclosing a miniature on vellum of Prince James Francis Edward Stuart (1688-1766), the Old Pretender, son of James II. Openwork shoulders.
? ENGLISH: about 1740.
6-1899

15 Gold, Octagonal bezel set with a table-cut crystal enclosing a portrait of the Old Pretender on ivory.
? ENGLISH: about 1740.
926-1871

16 Gold. Oval bezel set with an onyx cameo of Prince Charles Edward (1720-1788), the Young Pretender, eldest son of the Old Pretender.
The cameo ITALIAN: 18th century; the setting probably 19th century.
932-1871
Nos. 14-16, Waterton Collection

17 Gold. Revolving silver bezel set with a Gnostic bloodstone intaglio; on one side Abraxas and *WAI*; on the other, Venus with *AT ITA*.
The stone ROMAN: 3rd century. The setting 18th century.
Bequeathed by Lieut.-Col. E.A. Belford, whose great-grandfather is said to have taken it from the baggage of Prince Charles Edward at Culloden.
M.86-1933

18 Gold and silver. Oval bezel set with a faceted crystal enclosing a miniature of Queen Anne (1665-1714), second daughter of James II by his first wife.
ENGLISH: 1714.
Joseph Mayer and Sir John Evans Collection
M.147-1962

19 Gold. Oval bezel set with an agate cameo of George I (1660-1727).
The cameo ENGLISH: about 1720; the setting about 1800.
M.148-1962

20 Gold. Oval bezel set with an enamelled miniature of John Wilkes (1727-1797). Behind, the inscription: *Friendship/without/Interest*
ENGLISH: about 1770.
A souvenir of a politician whose championship of the freedom of the Press and his opposition to the government over the American War of independence earned him great popularity in England and abroad.
Sir John Evans and Sir Arthur Evans Collections
M.152-1962
Nos 18-20, given by Dame Joan Evans, P.P.S.A.

21 Silver-gilt. Circular bezel set with a faceted crystal enclosing a gold medal of Pope Innocent XI (1676-1689). Garnets set on shoulders.
? ITALIAN: late 17th century.
928-1871

22 Iron and silver. Oval silver bezel engraved with four portrait busts divided by clasped hands holding a caduceus. Below, the inscription: *BORBONVM FOEDVS*. The busts are (from left), Ferdinand IV (1751-1825), King of the Two Sicilies, Philip, Duke of Parma, Louis XV (1710-1774), King of France, and Charles III (1716-1788), King of Spain.
ITALIAN: about 1761.
All were members of the Bourbon family, and it appears that the ring commemorates their family compact of 1761.
930-1871
Nos. 21 & 22, Waterton Collection

23 Gold. Oval bezel set with a Tassie paste cameo of George, Prince of Wales (1762-1830), later George IV.
ENGLISH: about 1786.
James Tassie (1735-1799) was well-known for his vitreous cameos.
M.55-1950

24 Enamelled gold. Oval bezel set with a silhouette of a woman. Border inscribed: *JE CHERIS JUSQU'A SON OMBRE*
FRENCH or ENGLISH: about 1780.
M.174-1962
Nos. 23 & 24, given by Dame Joan Evans, P.P.S.A.

25 Gold. Octagonal bezel set with a crystal enclosing a *grisaille* miniature of a young man.
FRENCH: about 1785.
527-1868

26 Gold. Oval bezel set with a Tassie paste cameo of George III (1738-1820).
ENGLISH: about 1775.
M.149-1962

27 Gold. Oval revolving bezel set with crystal over a relief portrait of King Frederick the Great (1740-86); border inscribed: *Sein Andenken ist unvergeslich* (His memory is unforgettable); *ges 1786* (died in 1786). Reverse, King Frederick William II (1786-97) of Prussia.
GERMAN (Prussia): about 1786-97.
M.153-1962
Nos 26 & 27, given by Dame Joan Evans, P.P.S.A.

28 Enamelled gold. Oval bezel set with a Tassie paste cameo of a man.
ENGLISH: dated 1778.
Major W.F. St. Clair Bequest
M.93-1969

29 Gold. Marquise-shaped bezel set with an onyx cameo bust of an elderly man wearing a coat with two diamond buttons (one missing).
Signed: *WHITLEY F* (ecit).
ENGLISH: about 1790.
W. Whitley, medallist and gem-engraver, worked in Old Bond Street in the late 18th and early 19th centuries.
Given by Col Guthrie
7128-1860

30 Gold. Heart-shaped bezel set with a crystal enclosing hair said to be that of King Charles II; garnet border.
ENGLISH: late 18th century.
Bequeathed by Miss Laura and Miss Mary Metford Badcock
M.98-1935

31 Gold. Oval bezel set with a crystal over a hair monogram: *MM* under a heart; border of garnets. Trifid shoulders.
Given by Mrs. Penryn Milsted
M.107-1930

32 Silver. Applied bezel stamped with portraits of Jean-Paul Marat (murdered 13 July 1793) and Louis Michel Lepelletier de Saint Fargeau (murdered 20 January 1793).
FRENCH: late 18th century.
A mass-produced souvenir
The assassination of the implacable Jacobin, Marat, by Charlotte Corday, intensified the Terror of 1793-94.
Waterton Collection
931-1871

33 Gold. Rectangular bezel set with a silhouette of a woman by John Miers (1758-1821), under glass.
ENGLISH: about 1800.
Given by Mrs. Nevill Jackson, in memory of her friend, Basil Somerset Lond.
M.27-1939

ENGLISH *MEMENTO MORI* AND MOURNING RINGS:
16th-18th century

34 Gold. Bezel in the form of a royal crown, set with rubies, a brilliant-cut diamond, and decorated with enamel. Locket fitting at the back containing hair. Hoop inscribed: *Hair cut from the head of George III, 1 Apr., 1816.*
ENGLISH: dated 1816.
M.218-1930

*35 Copper. Shaped rectangular bezel set with a paste cameo of Queen Charlotte (1744-1818), consort of George III. Shoulders split into four strands.
ENGLISH: about 1810.
Given by H.M. Queen Mary
M.589-1936

36 Enamelled gold. Oval bezel with a crowned *A* on black bordered by the motto: *REMEMBER ME* on a white border. Hoop inscribed: *Pss AMELIA.DIED 2 NOV: 1810 AGED 27.*
ENGLISH: 1810.
Princess Amelia (1783-1810) was the youngest daughter of George III.
Crisp Collection; acquired by Sir John Evans from the sale of the Duke of Cambridge's Collection
M.151-1962

37 Enamelled gold. Squared oval bezel with the royal crown enamelled in red and white. Hoop with chased floral border. Central band inscribed in gold letter reserved on blue: *HONI. SOIT.QUI.MAL.Y.PENSE.*
Inscribed inside: *GEO:3rd born 4 June 1738/Acceeded 25 Oct 1760/Married 8 Sep 1760/Crowned 22/died 29 Jan 1820 Aged 81.*
ENGLISH: London hallmarks for 1819-20. Maker's mark, SW.
Sir John Evans Collection
M.150-1962

*38 Enamelled gold. Shaped oval bezel with a Viscount's and a Duke's coronet over *N* and *B* in gold letter with, below: *TRAFALGAR*, reserved on black enamel. Hoop inscribed outside with Nelson's motto: *PALMAM QVI MERUIT FERAT* (Let him who earned it bear the palm (of victory)). Inside: *Lost/to his Country/21:Octr:1805/Aged 47.*
ENGLISH: about 1805. One of more than a hundred such rings made by Salter of the Strand.
Admiral Lord Nelson, who died at the Battle of Trafalgar, was also Duke of Bronte, a title conferred upon him by Ferdinand IV of the Two Sicilies.
M.234-1975

39 Enamelled gold set with diamonds. Oval bezel, with rose-cut diamond cipher of King Louis Philippe of France (reigned 1830-1848) below a crown over blue enamel. Openwork brilliant-cut diamond border.
FRENCH: about 1840.
A presentation ring.
M.154-1962
Nos.36-39, given by Dame Joan Evans, P.P.S.A.

40 Enamelled gold. Oval bezel with applied silver shield bearing the arms of Poland and Lithuania with the motto: *Usque ad finem.* Shoulders enamelled blue and decorated with a sword, axe, bill and scythe.
WEST EUROPEAN: about 1863
Probably made abroad for a Polish resistance group.
Rev. Chauncy Hare Townshend Bequest
1831-1869

41 Bronzed copper. Hoop; a raised frieze of laurel, a crowned shield with the monogram *AM* and the inscription: *TOUS/AUX/DANGERS/TOUS/A L'HONNEUR/1870-1871*
FRENCH: about 1871. The name of the maker stamped inside: *FROMENT-MEURICE.* A mass-produced ring, perhaps relating to General J.-A. Margueritte.
Given by Mrs. K. Greenwood-Wynne
M.35-1962

Memento mori jewellery (Latin, Keep death in your thoughts) was widespread in the sixteenth century. No.1 below appears to fall in this category, but a similar ring, no. 2, may combine the two functions of *memento mori* and mourning ring, in view of the two initials bound by a true lovers' knot.
The practice of bequeathing rings as souvenirs to relatives and friends is an ancient one. Documented evidence survives from the Middle Ages, though most such bequests probably took the form of the fashionable shapes of the day. The earliest surviving English mourning ring with an inscription and appropriate motifs dates from the fifteen century (see Case 32, Board K, no. 22).

1 Enamelled gold. Hexagonal bezel with incurving sides, enamelled (in white) with a skull surrounded by the inscription: *+NOSSE TE. PSUM* (know thyself). On the edge: *+DYE TO LYVE.* Volutes and foliated shoulders enamelled in black, 2nd half of 16th century.
Waterton Collection
920-1871

2 Enamelled gold. Hexagonal bezel with incurving sides, enamelled in white with a skull surrounded by the inscription: *+BEHOLD. THE. ENDE.* On the edge: *X RATHER. DEATH THEN FALS.FAYTH.*
Behind, *M* and *L* bound by a true-lovers' knot. Volutes and foliated shoulders, enamelled in black.
2nd half of 16th century.
Said to have been presented by Charles I on the day of his execution in 1649 to Bishop Juxon (1582-1663), later Archbishop of Canterbury.
Given by Miss Charlotte Frances Gerard
13-1888

3 Gold, with openwork enamel ornament underlaid with hair. Hoop, the outside enamelled in black and white with skulls and two coats of arms, one of Nicholets, Co.Herefordshire. Inscribed inside: *Samuell Nicholets obijt 7 July (1661) Christ is my portion.*
Given by Dame Joan Evans, P.P.S.A.
M.156-1962

217

4 Enamelled gold, set with rose-cut diamonds, some in silver collets. Bezel enamelled in white with a skull and cross-bones. Shoulders set with a diamond. Hoop, pierced with floral designs.
Late 17th century.
211-1870

5 Enamelled gold. Hoop, with a skull reserved in black enamel. Inscribed: *Non hic Sr. N.S. obt 30 June 86.* Dated (16) 86. Mark (struck twice), G in pelta shield.
Sir John Evans Collection; given by Dame Joan Evans, P.P.S.A.
M.88-1960

6 Gold. Oval bezel set with a faceted crystal enclosing a gold wire monogram over red foil. Foliated Shoulders, enamelled in black.
Early 18th century.
Brooke Gift
1114-1864

7 Gold, formerly enamelled. Circular bezel set with a faceted crystal enclosing *CP* in gold wire. Foliated shoulders, enamelled.
Late 17th or early 18th century.
M.95-1913

8 Enamelled gold. Oval bezel set with a bevelled crystal over plaited hair and *S-J* in gold wire. Foliated shoulders, enamelled in black.
Late 17th or early 18th century.
Brooke Gift
1110-1864

*9 Enamelled gold. Oval bezel set with a faceted crystal enclosing a monogram in gold wire. Hoop with a skeleton and cross-bones reserved on black enamel. Inscribed inside: *M Frend obt 9' May 1709 aeta. 59.*
Given by Miss Anna Newton
1639-1903

10 Enamelled gold. Octagonal bezel set with a faceted crystal enclosing a gold wire monogram on yellow silk. Foliated shoulders, enamelled in black.
Early 18th century.
Brooke Gift
1124-1864

11 Enamelled gold. Oval bezel set with a faceted crystal in a silver collet, enclosing a gold wire monogram on blue silk. Behind, the initials *IMS*. Foliated shoulders, enamelled in black.
Early 18th century.
526-1868

12 Gold. Hoop set with three rose-cut diamonds. Inscribed inside: *MB obt 16 Augt 1720.*
1118-1864

13 Enamelled gold. Hoop set with an oval faceted crystal enclosing a skull and cross-bones. Hoop enamelled in black with floral patterns. Inscribed inside: *MB obt. 16 Augt 1720 aeta: 63* (see no. 12 above).
Maker's mark, RU.
1119-1864

14 Enamelled gold, decorated as in no. 13 above. Inscribed inside: *CMB Obt. 21 Nov. 1721.*
Maker's mark, DE.
Probably for Mary Catherine Brooke (born Hammond), wife of Walter Brooke (see no. 15 below).
1120-1864

15 Enamelled gold. Hoop set with an oval faceted crystal enclosing *MCB* in gold wire. Hoop with three flowers in black enamel. Inscribed inside: *MCB obt.21 Nov:1721 aeta 24* (see no.14 above).
1121-1864
Nos. 12-15, Brooke Gift

16 Enamelled gold. Hoop, set with an oval crystal enclosing a piece of black silk. Hoop with a skeleton and bones reserved on black enamel. Inscribed outside: *MEMENTO MORI;* inside: *S. Spiller ob.14 May 1719 aet.39*
Maker's mark, T.T.
M.371-1923

17 Enamelled gold. Hoop set with an oval faceted crystal enclosing *WB* in monogram, in gold wire. Hoop enamelled in black with floral patterns. Inscribed inside: *WB obt. 15 Nov: 1722 aet 27.*
Maker's mark, RU.
Brooke Gift
1122-1864

18 Gold. Square bezel set with paste. Hoop of six scrolls inscribed in reserve on black enamel: *RACH BRAIN OB 26 JUN 1746 AE:3.* This ring is an exception to the popular convention of the time that those who died unmarried were commemorated with rings in white enamel.
M.373-1923

19 Gold, with silver heart-shaped bezel set with a rose-cut diamond. Hoop of six scrolls, formerly enamelled, inscribed: *RICH D PERRY OB 22 APR: 1754 AE 76.*
Given by Mr. C.B. Farmer
138-1906

20 Enamelled gold. Hexagonal bezel set with a crystal enclosing a skull. Hoop of five scrolls, inscribed in reverse on white enamel: *ELIZ: HORS.MAN OB: 7 JUNE 1740 AE:3.*
Given by Mr Martin Travers
M.351-1927

21 Enamelled gold. Octagonal bezel set with an emerald, held by clawlets. Behind, flutes. Hoop of five scrolls, inscribed in reserve on black enamel: *JONAS PAUL OB: JUNE 6: 1722.AE 36.*
Given by Dame Joan Evans, P.P.S.A.
M.160-1962

22 Enamelled gold. Hoop of five scrolls, inscribed in reserve on black enamel: *ROB: POCKLEY.AR.OB 19. NOV. 1744. AE 53.*
661-1864

*23 Enamelled gold. Hoop of five scrolls, inscribed in reserve on white enamel: *ROBINSON MORLEY ARM: OB 28 SEP: 1756 AET 22.*
660-1864
Nos. 22 & 23, Brooke Gift

24 Enamelled gold. Hoop of five scrolls, inscribed in reserve on black enamel: MARY SELLAR OB: 21 MAR: 1761 AE 65.
M.372-1923

25 Enamelled gold. Wavy hoop inscribed in reserve on black enamel: *ANNA MITFORD OB: 6 MAY 1763 AE 38.*
655-1864

26 Enamelled gold. Scroll-edged bezel inscribed in reserve on black enamel: *MEMENTO*. Hoop inscribed *RICH: EPIS: LONDON.OB: 15.MAY 1764 AET.75*.
Commemorates Richard Osbaldeston, Bishop of London 1690-1764).
654-1864
Nos 25 & 26, Brooke Gift

*27 Enamelled gold. Openwork silver scroll-edged bezel set with rose-cut diamonds and an amethyst in the form of a cross. Hoop of six scrolls, inscribed in reserve on black enamel: *RICH: PETT.DI:23 FEB: 1765 AG: 76*. Commemorates Richard Pett, master cooper at the Victualling Office, Plymouth, whose will provided for mourning rings at 5 and 3 guineas each.
Crisp Collection
Given by Dame Joan Evans, P.P.S.A.
M.159-1962

28 Enamelled gold. Hoop inscribed in reserve on white enamel: *W: OSBALDESTON: ESQ: OB: 5.SEP: 1766.AE 79*.
Commemorates an M.P. for Scarborough.
659-1864

29 Enamelled gold. Hoop inscribed in reserve on white enamel: *THO: MORLEY. ESQ: OB: 20 AUG: 1766 AE 30*.
658-1864
Nos. 28 & 29, Brooke Gift

30 Enamelled gold. Oval bezel set with a crystal enclosing a landscape executed in hair on white enamel. Hoop inscribed in reserve: *RICHD. TOWNSEND. ESQ: OB: 12 MAR: 1768. AE 44*.
1630-1903

31 Enamelled gold, sit with a rose-cut diamond. Hoop inscribed in reserve on black enamel: *S.E: BROOKE:OB: 27 FEB: 1769.AE 85*.
1123-1864

32 Enamelled gold, set with a rose-cut diamond. Hoop inscribed in reserve on white enamel: *F.W. OSBALDESTON.ESQ: OB:10. JUNE.1770 AE 76*.
657-1864

33 Enamelled gold. Hoop inscribed in reserve on black enamel: *BOYNTON.LANGLEY.ESQ:OB: 5. JAN 1772 AE 32*.
Boynton Langley lived at Wycombe Ubley, Yorkshire.
647-1864
Nos.31-33, Brooke Gift

The compositions executed in enamelled gold and hair are protected by crystal, as is the other hairwork.

1 Gold, enamelled in white, set with pearls and rose-cut diamonds. Oval bezel, half-pearl border. Centre, blue paste ground with applied urn, set with diamonds. Inscribed behind: *Wilm/Fauquier/Esqr./obt. Decr. 15/1788/aet. 80*.
Fauquier was a Director of the East India Company and a Fellow of the Royal Society.
849-1888

2 Gold, enamelled in blue and white. Convex oval bezel, set with an urn and pedestal lettered *EP*, over plaited hair.
Inscribed behind: *In Memory/of Mrs. Elizth./Partridge/Obt. 30 May/1789/Aet:27*.
Mrs Partridge was the wife of Joseph Partridge, merchant, of Fenchurch Street, London.
919-1888

3 Gold. Shaped oval bezel set with an urn and plinth in hair and gold, over hair.
Inscribed behind: *Lady/Mawbey/Ob. 19th Aug:/1790/aet: 45*.
Lady Mawbey was the wife of Sir Joseph Mawbey, (1730-1798), of Bottley's, Surrey.
855-1888

4 Gold, enamelled in blue and white. Shaped oval bezel set with urn and plinth over hair. Border inscribed: *GABL. WIRGMAN. DIED. 12.SEP: 1791. AGED 53*. Inscribed behind: *Thos. Garle. /Arm:/Obt. 5 Sepr. 1789 Aet 67*.
Gabriel Wirgman was a jeweller, goldsmith and enameller, working in London, 1767-91.
907-1888

5 Gold, enamelled in white. Shaped oval bezel set with star-dotted border and a composition of a budding rose on opalescent ground, inscribed: *NIPT IN THE BUD*. Inscribed behind: *Butterfield/Harrison/Obt 14 March/1792./Aet. 2 ys/9 Mos/& 14 ds*.
Acquired by Dame Joan Evans, 1918.
M.162-1962

6 Gold, enamelled in black. Hoop with shoulders and bezel formed of two hands grasping an urn hinged to reveal a locket fitting for hair. London hallmark for 1791-92. Maker's mark. WK.
M.167-1962
Nos. 5 & 6, given by Dame Joan Evans, P.P.S.A.

7 Gold. Octagonal bezel set with a sepia miniature on ivory of a veiled woman seated by an urn, the pedestal inscribed: *NOT LOST/BUT ../GONE.- BEFORE*; cherub holds scroll inscribed: *TO BLISS.* Inscribed behind: *Harriot/Willock/Ob 18 Decr./1788/Act. 15.*
902-1888

8 Gold, enamelled in black and white. Octagonal bezel with *MW* in monogram. Border inscribed: *MARY.WHITE./OB: 10.FEB. 1798: AE:73.*
883-1888

9 Gold, enamelled in black and white. Convex circular bezel set with plaited hair. Hoop inscribed: *ELIZ: DENMAN. OB: 7.NOV: 1781. AE: 59.*
868-1888

10 Gold, enamelled in blue and set with seed pearls. Convex circular bezel with *JSH* in monogram over plaited hair, bordered by half-pearls. About 1780-90.
Given by Mr S P Avery
585-1892

11 Gold, enamelled in black and white. Convex circular bezel with *EH* in seed pearls in monogram over plaited hair.
Inscribed: *EDWARD.HARPER. DIED. 20.MAY 1795. AGED. 58.*
886-1888

12 Gold, enamelled in black and white. Dished circular bezel with white enamelled urn. Inscribed behind: *Jno Brown/Ob.24.Novr/1795/Aet:66.*
877-1888

13 Gold, enamelled in black and white. Convex oval bezel set with *MG* in monogram in gold over hair. Border inscribed: *In MEMORY.OF./MARY.GRISSIN.* About 1795-1800.
879-1888

*14 Gold, enamelled in black and white. Convex oval bezel with a miniature of a woman seated by an urn on a pedestal inscribed *IH.* The border inscribed: *Mr ISAAC.HITCHIN.OB: 14.JAN: 1796: AET 71.*
913-1888

15 Gold, set with pearls. Shaped convex rectangular bezel set with woven hair, bordered by half-pearls. Inscribed behind: *Thomas/Berrow. /died 9 Augt./1783/Aged 62.* Forked shoulders with leaf centre.
869-1888

16 Gold, set with black garnets and pearls. Shaped convex square bezel set with woven hair, bordered by half-pearls with garnets inside. Forked shoulders.
About 1790.
896-1888

17 Gold, set with pearls. Shaped convex rectangular bezel set with woven hair, bordered by half-pearls. Forked shoulders with trefoil centre.
About 1790.
887-1888

18 Gold, enamelled in black and white, set with black garnets. Convex oval bezel set with plaited hair, bordered by garnets.
Inscribed behind: *Barbara Towneley/Ob. 25 Decr./1797/Aet: 66.*
899-1888

19 Gold, enamelled in black. Convex oval bezel set with woven hair, bordered by half-pearls. Inscribed behind: *Wm Raven, obt. 22./Augt. 1804. Aet: 39.* Shoulders enamelled with radiating lines.
888-1888

20 Gold, enamelled in black and white set with black garnets. Convex oval bezel set with *AW* in monogram over hair, bordered by garnets.
Inscribed behind: *Mrs. Ann Watts./Ob. 8 May 1804./Aet: 59.*
Bequeathed by Mrs Margaret Watts
M.50-1972

21 Gold, enamelled in black and white. Rectangular revolving bezel, inscribed on one side: *SARAH/WYMER/OB: 14/APR. 1807/AE: 15.* The other side fitted with a locket containing hair. Forked wire shoulders.
Given by Miss Mary I Courtenay
M.66-1949

22 Gold enamelled in black and white. Shaped rectangular bezel, with a willow tree reserved on white enamel with a small glazed locket containing hair. Inscribed behind: *Anna/Seward./Ob. 25 March, 1809./Aet. 66.*
Anna Seward, authoress, was known as the 'Swan of Lichfield'.
Given by Mr. Cecil Crofton
M.326-1922

23 Gold enamelled in black and white. Shaped rectangular bezel set with plaited hair. Border inscribed: *W M GODSELL. OB: 12.OCT: 1810 AET: 39 YS.*
889-1888

24 Gold enamelled in black, white, red and blue. Oval bezel with the Union Flag surrounded by a serpent. Inscribed behind: *Captn. James Newman Newman, lost off the Haak in the Hero 74. Dec. 24, 1811, aged 46.*
Given by Mrs. G H Goodman
M.314-1926

25 Gold, enamelled mainly in black. Square bezel with a baron's coronet over T in gothic lettering. Hoop inscribed: *EDWD. LORD. THURLOW. OB: 12 SEP: 1806.AE.76.*
Edward Thurlow, first Baron Thurlow (1731-1806), Lord Chancellor.
Crisp Collection
M.165-1962

ENGLISH MOURNING RINGS

All the miniatures are painted in sepia, often admixed with snippets of hair, and all are set under crystal.

26 Gold enamelled in dark blue, white and light blue. Hoop inscribed on intertwined ribbons: *ETTY/ SAVORY/OB:23.FEB/1792.AE.70 and: HENRY/SAVORY/OB: 30.DEC/1798:AE:86.*
Crisp Collection
M.161-1962

27 Gold, enamelled in black. Hoop inscribed outside: *RT.HON: SPENCER.PERCEVAL.OB: 11.MAY. 1812.AE.49.* Inside: *died by the hand of an Assassin.*
London hallmarks for 1812-13.
Maker's mark, SG.
Spencer Perceval, Prime Minister, assassinated in 1812 in the lobby of the House of Commons.
Sir John Fleming Leicester, Lord de Tabley Collections; acquired by Sir John Evans, 1888.
M.166-1962
Nos. 25-27, given by Dame Joan Evans, P.P.S.A.

28 Gold, enamelled in black. The hoop cast with anchors, sea horses and an urn with plaited hair under a crystal. Inside, an illegible inscription.
London hallmarks for 1810-11.
M.10-1973

29 Gold, enamelled in black and white. Hoop inscribed in gothic lettering: *IN.MEMORY.OF.:* chased floral borders. Inscribed inside: *James Selby Pennington Obt. Novr. 1st 1831. Ac 88.*
York hallmarks for 1824-25. Made by Barber, Cattle & North.
Brooke Gift
653-1864

30 Gold, enamelled in black. The hoop inscribed *IN.MEMORY.OF.:* chased floral borders. Inscribed inside: *Esther Ferriman. Obt. April 20th 1817.Act 42.*
Given by Mrs. Virginia Ferriman
M.8-1974

31 Gold enamelled in black. A snake, with diamond sparks for eyes. Under, locket fitting with plaited hair. Inscribed inside: *George Edward Earl of Waldegrave. Obt. 28 Sepr. 1846 Aet 30.*
Lord Waldegrave's widow inherited his estates; a well-known London hostess, she also restored Horace Walpole's Strawberry Hill.
Given by Dame Joan Evans, P.P.S.A.
M.169-1962

32 Gold, enamelled in black. Bezel rounded rectangular inscribed: *AEI* (for ever) in diamond sparks. Inscribed inside: *Hannah Darby died 20th Decr 1860. Aged 77.*
London hallmarks for 1860-61.
Maker's mark, GI
M.20-1970

33 Gold, enamelled in black. The bezel in the form of a shield inscribed: *G.C.* The hoop bound outside with plaited hair.
About 1860. Maker's mark, H.H. & S.
Given by Mrs Mary I. Courtenay
M.67-1949

1 Gold. Vesica-shaped (marquise) bezel with a miniature on ivory of a woman seated by an urn on a pedestal inscribed: *REST IN PEACE.* Inscribed behind: *Mick l Norton.died 13th Feby.1770. Aged 60. Ann Norton. died 14th. Novb 1768. Aged 60.*
905-1888

2 Gold. Marquise bezel with a miniature on ivory of a woman standing by an urn worked in hair, on a pedestal inscribed: *EVER TO BE REMEMBER'D.* Inscribed behind: *Amos Angles ob.9.June 1782.Aet.73.*
917-1888

3 Gold. Marquise bezel with a miniature of a woman standing by an altar inscribed: *ASD.* Inscribed behind: *Samuel Durrant died Sepr 4 1783 aged 62.*
857-1888

4 Gold, enamelled in blue and white. Marquise bezel with an enamelled urn and a weeping willow worked in hair. Inscribed behind: *John Davys Esqr. Ob.22 April 1783 Aet.70 Eliz. Davys Obt. 7 Dec 1784 Aet.55.*
911-1888

5 Gold, enamelled in black. Marquise bezel with a miniature of an urn on a pedestal. Hoop inscribed: *FRANCES. CRABTREE OB: 27. SEP: 1783 AE:72.*
853-1888

6 Gold. Marquise bezel with an urn worked in hair with gold fittings. Inscribed behind: *E.Tempest.Ob: July:3:1784 A(et.) ?76.*
871-1888

7 Gold. Marquise bezel with a miniature of a woman standing by an urn on a pedestal inscribed *HM.* Inscribed behind: *Martha Holworthy Ob 13 Sep. 1785 Aet 64.*
915-1888

*8 Gold, enamelled in black and white. Marquise bezel with a painting of Hope seated by an urn on a pedestal inscribed: *SACRED TO FRIENDSHIP*, bordered by laurel. Inscribed behind: *John Chalmers Esq. Ob. 28 Mar 1786 Aet.57.*
909-1888

9 Gold, decorated with seed pearls. Marquise bezel with *SWH* and willow leaves partly worked in hair, over plaited hair. Inscribed behind: *Sarah Hetherington Ob: 7 Apr.1786 Aet. 7 Ms Wm Hetherington Ob 31 July 1786 Aet 8 Yrs 9 Ms.*
864-1888

10 Gold. Marquise bezel with a miniature of a woman standing by an urn on a pedestal inscribed *WB*. Inscribed behind: *Wm.Barber Ob: 26 Jan 1787 Ae 71.*
916-1888

11 Gold. Marquise bezel with a miniature of a seated woman holding a plaque inscribed: *NOT.LOST.BUT. GONE.BEFORE.* Inscribed behind: *John Griffiths Esqr. Obt. 9 Aug 1788 Ae 50.*
Given by Miss Marie Langton
364-1890

12 Gold. Marquise bezel with a miniature of a woman standing by an urn, inscribed: *T.D.* Inscribed behind: *Thos. Darvill Ob 16 Apl 1788 Aet 25.*
860-1888

13 Gold. Marquise bezel with a miniature of a woman seated by an urn on a pedestal inscribed: *NOT LOST BUT GONE BEFORE.* Inscribed behind: *Ann Scurfield Ob 20 Octr 1790 Aet 59.*
858-1888

14 Gold. Marquise bezel with a miniature of a weeping willow and an urn on a pedestal inscribed: *SACRED TO LOVE.* Inscribed behind: *Ino. Amey Ob 18 Mar 1791 Aet 64.*
John Amey, Master of the Greenwich and London Packets, died at Berwick-on-Tweed.
872-1888

15 Gold. Marquise bezel, with a miniature of a girl seated by an obelisk inscribed: *TO JOY & HAPPINESS I RISE ELIZA CLARK OB: 9 OCT 1792 AE 15 YRS.*
Her spirit, rising from the monument, is about to be crowned by an angel.
918-1888

16 Gold, enamelled in black. Hoop inscribed: *EDWD.LORD.HAWKE OB: 17 OCT:1781.AE:76.*
Lord Hawke married a member of the family of the donor.
Brooke Gift
650-1864

17 Gold, enamelled in black. Hoop, inscribed: *THOS GAINSBOROUGH ESQ.OB . . . AUG: 1788.AE:61.*
Maker's mark, HC.
Thomas Gainsborough (1727-1788), the painter, was born in Sudbury, Suffolk.
M.141-1978

18 Gold, enamelled in black. Oval bezel enamelled with an urn inscribed: *DANL. DANIEL* surrounded by *MARTHA. MYERS. OB: 8.OCT: 1779.AET 58.* Hoop inscribed: *SAML.MYERS.OB: 10.AUG: 1777.AET:62.* Inscribed behind: *Obt 25 Augt (erased) Ae 61.*
852-1888

*19 Gold, enamelled in white. Oval bezel with a miniature of a woman weeping by an urn. Hoop inscribed: *JOHN.PRINCE.OB: 11 SEP: 1779. AE:7 WS.*
875-1888

20 Gold. Oval bezel with a miniature of a youth standing by an urn and pedestal worked in hair and inscribed: *WB 1777 EB 1779.* Inscribed behind: *W. Ballantine Ob.29 Mar.1777 Ae.82. Eliz Ballantine Ob 19 Octr. 1779 Ae 68.*
904-1888

21 Gold, enamelled in black. Oval bezel with a miniature of a woman weeping by an urn. Inscribed behind: *E.Davy.Ob:28 Octr.1779.Aet:71.*
876-1888

22 Gold. Oval bezel with an urn worked in hair. Inscribed behind: *Frances Blake Ob.5 July 1780. Aet 14.*
850-1888

23 Gold, enamelled in brown. Oval bezel with a brown enamel urn mounted with gold. Inscribed behind: *James Stewart Ob: 9 May 1780 Ae 29.*
854-1888

24 Gold. Oval bezel with an urn of plaited hair and gold. Inscribed behind: *Gabriel Brooke Esqr. Ob. 12 Apr. 1781. Aet.71.*
Brooke Gift
1125-1864

25 Gold. Oval bezel with a miniature of a woman standing by an urn on a pedestal with *EM* in monogram. Inscribed behind: *EM Mar (rie)d.14 May 1779 Ob 23 Aug.1783 A't 25.*
903-1888

26 Gold. Oval bezel with an urn surrounded by the inscription: *NOT.LOST.BUT.GONE BEFORE.*
About 1780-90.
848-1888

27 Gold. Oval bezel with a miniature of an urn surrounded by the inscription: *SAML.CHARLSON OBT.MAY 23RD 1788 AGED 72.*
851-1888

28 Gold, enamelled in black. Hoop inscribed: *ELIZ:CARTER.OB:31 DEC 1797 AE . . .* Added bezel with a miniature of a woman standing by an urn inscribed *CEH*, under a willow.
London hallmarks for 1791-92.
Maker's mark, IP.
862-1888

29 Gold, set with rose-cut diamonds and coloured pastes. Oval bezel, bordered by amethyst pastes. Centre, a silver vase of flowers on a white ground. Inscribed behind: *Cease/thy tears/Religion/points on high/CS. . ob. . 25 Jan:/1787.aet.70/IS.ob. . 18 Sep:/1792./aet:72.*
M.164-1962

Case 34 Board I

A. FANCY AND SENTIMENTAL RINGS:
18th century

30 Gold, set with rose-cut diamonds and coloured pastes. Composition similar to no. 29 above, and damaged inscription also as above.
Acquired by Dame Joan Evans, 1930.
M.163-1962
Nos. 29 & 30, given by Dame Joan Evans. P.P.S.A.

31 Gold, enamelled in blue. Oval bezel with a miniature of a woman and girl weeping beside an urn on a pedestal inscribed: *SACRED TO THE BEST OF HUSBANDS,* surrounded by: *WM. HEMBROW. OB:8.OCT:1792.AET:31.*
908-1888

32 Gold. Oval bezel with a miniature of a woman seated by an urn on a pedestal inscribed: *WW.* Inscribed behind: *WM WARRINGTON OBT. 1794 AET 54.*
Warrington died at Heckington, Lincolnshire.
906-1888

33 Gold, enamelled in white and set with rose-cut diamonds. Oval bezel with an enamelled urn on a pedestal set with diamonds and inscribed *MR.* Inscribed behind: *Maurice Randle Obt.7 Octr.1796 aet 48.*
912-1888

34 Gold, enamelled in white and set with amethyst pastes. Shaped oval bezel with urn decorated in translucent enamel on white. Inscribed behind: *GEO/NASSAU/ ARM/OB:18.AUG 1823/AET: 66.*
George Richard Savage Nassau (1756-1823), bibliophile, of Easton, Suffolk.
Given by Dame Joan Evans, P.P.S.A.
M.168-1962

*1 Gold. Four pivoted hoops, in the form of a miniature armillary sphere, but apparently unusable as such.
? ENGLISH: late 18th century.
M.368-1923

*2 Silver. Square bezel overlaid with two modelled cannon. Shoulders and hoop chased with scrolls.
GERMAN: 18th century.
987-1871

3 Silver. A puzzle-ring; three hoops, each set with a square plaque engraved with a cross between four ovoid devices. The three plaques, each united by three pellets, form a bezel.
WEST EUROPEAN: 18th century.
861-1871

*4 Enamelled copper. Broad hoop, with painted enamel scenes of three musicians, a man and woman dancing, three gamblers and two savages.
AUSTRIAN (probably from the Tyrol): mid 18th century.
1003-1871
Nos. 2-4, Waterton Collection

5 Enamelled gold. Hoop, decorated with a hunting scene in gold on a blue enamel ground.
GERMAN: early 19th century.
M.233-1975

6 Gold. Circular bezel, in the form of a vinaigrette; hinged crystal cover, set in gold. Pierced radiating panels on sides.
ENGLISH: late 18th century.
M.20-1933
Nos. 5 & 6, given by Dame Joan Evans, P.P.S.A.

7 Gold. Oval bezel set with a sardonyx intaglio bust of Paris, after the statue by Antonio Canova (1757-1822). Forked shoulders. The engraved gem attributed to Luigi Pichler (1773-1854); unsigned.
ITALIAN SCHOOL: late 18th or early 19th century.
Given by Messrs. S.J. Phillips Ltd.
M.336-1977

8 Gold. Swivel ring. Heart-shaped crystal bezel enclosing a monogram over plaited hair.
? ENGLISH: early 18th century.
Given by Mrs O.C. Leveson-Gower
M.50-1974

9 Gold, enamelled in blue. Shaped rectangular bezel with a miniature on ceramic of a girl with a dove. Enamelled border.
? FRENCH: late 18th century.
French and Dutch marks.
910-1888

*10 Gold, set with pearls. Vesica- (marquise-) shaped bezel with a composition in seed pearls of a dove bearing an olive branch, perched on a tree, over plaited hair; crystal cover.
WEST EUROPEAN: about 1775-85.
863-1888

11 Gold, set with pearls. Marquise bezel with a composition in hair of two doves perched on an urn, set with half-pearls, below the inscription: *AMITIE;* crystal cover. Inscribed behind: *SS/JLH* in monogram, and *1787.*
? ENGLISH: 1787.
As in most of the hairwork and pearl pieces, the pearls appear at least in part to be artificial.
856-1888

12 Gold, set with pearls. Marquise bezel with a sepia painting under crystal of a woman holding a garland over a pair of doves perched on an altar bearing the initials *MB,* executed in hairwork and decorated with pearls and gold details. Half-pearl border.
WEST EUROPEAN: about 1785.
861-1888

13 Pair of hair hoops.
Gold bezels with initial *D.*
ENGLISH: about 1840.
Given by Miss O.C. Leveson-Gower
M.46 & a-1974

224

*14 Gold, set with zircons. Oval bezel with a carved ivory scene under crystal of two dancers and a musician in a landscape.
WEST EUROPEAN: second half of 18th century. This may be French, English, German or Swiss. The firm of Stephany & Dresch, of Bath and London, specialised in carved ivory jewellery and knick-knacks.
Bequeathed by Mr. F.W. Daniels
21-1883

15 Gold. Oval bezel with a Roman onyx cameo of a male head in a 'Roman' setting.
The setting WEST EUROPEAN: mid 18th century.
The 'Roman' setting, in which metal raised from a depression in the border secured the stone, was much favoured for cameos and intaglios.
The Rev. Chancey Hare Townshend Bequest
1801-1869

16 Gold. Oval bezel with a Roman lapis-lazuli intaglio of a warrior with spear and shield, in a 'Roman' setting. A diamond spark in a silver collet on each shoulder.
? ITALIAN: mid 18th century.
Ready Bequest
M.13-1959

17 Gold. Oval bezel with an onyx cameo of Theseus and the slain Minotaur in a 'Roman setting'.
Signed with the initials in Greek *(IP)* of Giovanni (Johann Anton) Pichler (1734-1791), after a gem of the 1st century BC by Philemon in the former Imperial Collections, Vienna. Forked and foliated shoulders.
ITALIAN: about 1760. French import mark introduced in 1893.
Given by Dame Joan Evans, P.P.S.A.
M.218-1962

18 Gold. Marquisé bezel with a Wedgwood jasper cameo of a seated youth and a standing girl. Forked shoulders with central leaf.
ENGLISH: about 1780.
The two figures adapted from a larger Wedgwood composition of a scene with a sacrifice, used on a patch box.
621-1894

19 Gold. Octagonal bezel with an antique burnt sard intaglio of the heads of a horse and a lion-gryphon (or ? goat) addorsed. Ridged sides.
The setting ENGLISH: about 1790.
The gem ? Gnostic. Said to have been mounted, with no. 12 below, for the writer and antiquary William Beckford (1759-1844), but a similar deep octagonal bezel is to be seen on a mount in the Townshend Collection (Case 31, Board C, no. 11).
Southesk Collection
M.41-1980

20 Gold. Setting as in no.19 above, with a burnt sard intaglio of a winged figure within a finger-ring, with two fighting cocks above.
Southesk Collection
M.42-1980

From at least the fifteenth century, candidates called to be admitted to the ranks of Serjeants-at-Law (from whom judges were appointed) were required to present rings bearing a suitable motto to the monarch and various dignitaries. They frequently also gave further rings as souvenirs to their friends. The practice came to an end when the office was abolished by the Judicature Act of 1875.
New mottoes were chosen at each call; the rings differed in value according to the rank of their recipients. With the exception of no. 25 (Brooke Gift), all the rings shown here were presented by Dame Joan Evans. Most (if not all) had been in her father's collection. They are all gold hoops, with the mottoes engraved on the outside.

21 Inscribed: + *REX EST A [N] I [M] A LEGIS* (The King is the soul of the Law). General call of 1531.
Found at Hethersett, Norfolk, 1843; Warren Collection
M.52-1960

22 Inscribed: +*VIVAT. REX. ET. LEX.* (Long live the King and the Law). Second quarter of 16th century.
M.51-1960

23 Inscribed. *LEX. REGIS. PRAESIDIUM.* (Law is the King's protection).
General call of 1577.
Maker, ? Richard Pindar.
M.53-1960

24 Inscribed: + *LEX. EST. ARMA. REGUM.* (Law is the armour of Kings).
General call of 1555.
Supplied by Nicholas Deering.
M.54-1960

25 Inscribed: *LEX LEGIS TVTAMEN.* (Law is the defence of Law).
Used at the call of 17 Serjeants in November 1669.
Brooke Gift
388-1864

C. ENGLISH SIGNETS:
19th century

A. STONE SET AND CAMEO RINGS:
19th century

26 Inscribed: *Secundis dubiisq. rectus* (Unswerving through success and doubts).
Call of Sir William Blackstone, 1770.
Maker's mark of Edmund Prince.
M.58-1960

27 Inscribed: *Mos et Lex* (Custom and Law).
Call of William de Gray, etc., 1771.
Maker's mark of Edmund Prince.
M.55-1960

28 Inscribed: *Vis temperatam* (Power kept within due bounds).
Call of F. Buller, 1777.
Maker's mark of Edmund Prince.
M.56-1960

29 Inscribed: *Reverentia legum* (Respect for the Law — Juvenal).
Call of Sir A. Thomson and S. Le Blanc, 1787.
Maker's mark of R. Dipple.
M.57-1960

*30 Inscribed: *Bonis legibus judiciis gravibus* (By good laws and weighty judgments).
Call of S. Gaselee and R. Spankie.
London hallmarks for 1824-25.
Maker's mark of William Parker.
M.59-1960

31 Inscribed: *Aliud nobis est agendum* (Our role is to act as subordinates).
London hallmarks for 1861-62.
Maker's mark of Thomas Bartlett.
M.50-1960

32 Gold. Square bezel set with a garnet engraved with a crest; an arm embowed in armour brandishing a scimitar.
About 1830.
M.53-1974

33 Gold. Circular bezel set with a bloodstone intaglio of a colt.
About 1860.
M.54-1974

34 Gold. Circular bezel set with a bloodstone intaglio of the crest and motto of Gower. Hoop inscribed inside: *A.L.G.* and *1869*.
Possibly owned by Arthur Frederick Gresham Leveson-Gower (1851-1922).
M.48-1974
Nos. 32-34, given by Mrs. O.C. Leveson-Gower

35 Gold. Oval bezel set with a cornelian intaglio of the crest and motto of Lieut.-Colonel G.B. Croft-Lyons, F.S.A.
About 1870.
Croft Lyons Bequest
M.853-1927

36 Gold. Oval bezel engraved with the arms of Henry Charles Howard, 13th Duke of Norfolk (1791-1856), impaling those of his wife, Charlotte Leveson-Gower (married 1814, died 1870).
ENGLISH: about 1840.
Croft-Lyons Collection.
Given by Mill Stephenson, Esq., F.S.A.
M.848-1927

*1 Gold. Diagonal bezel with scrolling ends set with rubies and brilliant-cut diamonds in gold and silver collets.
? ENGLISH: late or early 19th century.
8542-1863

2 Gold. Half-hoop bezel set with garnets, half-pearl border.
ENGLISH: about 1790.
Cory Bequest
M.112-1951

3 Gold. Shaped rectangular bezel with a crystal enclosing plaited hair; half-pearl border. Loop at back, holding seven hoops of alternately fluted and plaited gold.
WEST EUROPEAN: early 19th century.
Given by Miss Crawford
M.70-1979

4 Gold. Lozenge-shaped bezel set with a garnet, pearls and pastes. Five pivoted hoops, alternately beaded and plain.
WEST EUROPEAN: about 1800.
113-1870

5 Gold. Rectangular openwork bezel set with brilliant-cut diamonds in silver, lined with gold. Openwork forked shoulders
? FRENCH: late 18th or early 19th century.
M.215-1962

*6 Gold. Quatrefoil bezel set with a brilliant-cut diamond and pearls. Forked shoulders set with emeralds and half-pearls.
ENGLISH: about 1810.
M.217-1962
Nos. 5 & 6, given by Dame Joan Evans, P.P.S.A.

7 Gold. Square bezel set with an emerald surrounded by brilliant-cut diamonds in silver collets. Openwork shoulders set with roses and brilliant-cut diamonds.
ENGLISH: early 19th century.
Lent by Mrs. L M Bosanquet (4).

8 Gold. Square bezel set with an emerald. Forked shoulders set with rose-cut diamonds in silver collets.
? ENGLISH: early 19th century.
199-1864

9 Gold. Projecting circular bezel enclosing a watch by W. Hughes under glass; amethyst border.
ENGLISH (London): early 19th century.
Given by Miss G M Pratt
M.14-1957

10 Gold. Half-hoop bezel set with rubies, with diamond sparks on the edges.
ENGLISH: about 1840.
779-1902

11 Gold, set with an opal flanked by two brilliant-cut diamonds held by claws.
ENGLISH: mid 19th century.
778-1902
Nos. 10 & 11, given by Mr George A H Tucker

12 Gold. Tall shaped openwork bezel with shell above and below; set with an emerald and brilliant-cut diamonds. Forked and foliated shoulders.
ENGLISH: about 1860.
Bequeathed by Mr Cecil Crofton to whom it was bequeathed by Dame Genevieve Ward
M.4-1936.

13 Gold. Half-hoop bezel, set with brilliant-cut diamonds over a gallery.
ENGLISH: about 1880.
Bequeathed by Miss D B Simpson
M.98a-1978

14 Gold. Oval coronet bezel, set with an opal.
WEST EUROPEAN: about 1860.
Given by Mrs. Bodinnar
M.19-1970

*15 Gold. Oval bezel with an antique onyx cameo of a Cupid lighting a torch, in a 'Roman' setting.
The setting ? ENGLISH: about 1825.
One of the standardised settings in the bequest made by the Rev. Chauncey Hare Townshend (see introduction to Case 31).
1812-1869

16 Gold. Shaped oval antique cameo of a crouching cat in a setting similar to the above.
1811-1869

17 Gold. Oval coronet bezel set with an onyx cameo of a head of a negro wearing a cap. One of the standardised settings in the Townshend Bequest.
ENGLISH: mid 19th century.
1810-1869

18 Gold. Oval bezel set with a shell cameo of the bust of a classical woman. Fluted shoulders and hoop.
WEST EUROPEAN: about 1830.
1800-1869
Nos. 16-18, Townshend Bequest

19 Gold. Projecting circular bezel with a paste cameo of a head of a woman.
WEST EUROPEAN: about 1860.
Given by Miss Margaret Evans
M.59-1980

20 Plaited gold wire. Large oval bezel set with a malachite cameo of two cherubs with a garland.
ITALIAN: late 19th century.
Given by Mrs. K E Sargeant
M.41-1961

21 Gold. Large oval bezel set with an opal cameo of the bust of a woman in Elizabethan costume.
WEST EUROPEAN: late 19th century.
Arthur Hurst Bequest
M.202-1940

22 Gold. Circular bezel with a paste intaglio of a lion rampart in a shield, inscribed: *SPERANZA*
? ITALIAN: mid 19th century.
Given by Dame Joan Evans, P.P.S.A.
M.278-1962

*23 Enamelled gold. Shaped square bezel set with a miniature of a man painted in enamel. Foliated shoulders, also enamelled.
Probably ENGLISH: about 1840.
Given by Miss Jane Dear
M.33-1968

24 Gold. Revolving bezel in the form of a cast gold scarab; underside hinged as a locket fitting.
FRENCH (Paris): about 1850-60.
Paris warranty marks for 1838 onwards.
In the ancient Egyptian style (see Case 32, Board A.
M.40-1980

B. SERPENT RINGS:
19th century

C. MISCELLANEOUS

D. ANTIQUARIAN/ FAKE

These rings, based on a Roman design (see Case 32, Board D, nos. 24-27), were internationally popular throughout the nineteenth century.

25 Gold. Hoop, the outside with three coils in the manner of a serpent. A hinged locket fitting inside enclosing hair.
? ENGLISH: early 19th century.
Given by Miss E M Anderson
M.99-1952

26 Gold. Single serpent with three coils; eyes set with rubies.
ENGLISH: early 19th century.
Said to have been a favourite ring of King George IV (1762-1830), who is perhaps wearing it in a portrait by Sir Thomas Lawrence in the Wallace Collection, London (559).
Bequeathed by Mrs A B Woodcroft
476-1903

*27 Gold. Single serpent, one coil, the head set with a brilliant-cut diamond; eyes set with cabochon rubies.
? ENGLISH: mid 19th century.
Given by Mr George A H Tucker
776-1902

28 Gold. Single serpent, four coils.
ITALIAN: mid 19th century.
Probably made by Castellani of Rome.
Bought from the sale of Alessandro Castellani's effects in Italy, 1884, as a genuine Roman piece
642-1884

29 A doll's ring. Gold. Single serpent, its tail in its mouth.
WEST EUROPEAN: late 19th century.
M.119-1978

30 Gold. A signet ring for a baby or a very small child, engraved with the monogram *FHC*.
WEST EUROPEAN: late 19th century.
M.120-1978

31 Jet. Hoop, engraved with flowers; in the centre, a recumbent hound.
? ENGLISH: about 1825-35.
Given by Miss E M Begg.
M.85-1957

A selection of some of the rings once thought to date from the fifteenth to the seventeenth century, but now believed to have been made in the nineteenth century. (See also No. 28 above, for a specimen of a ring bought as Roman)

32 Gold. High 4-claw bezel set with a sapphire. Cast hoop with scrolls; double scrolls on shoulders pierced with fleurs-de-lis.
WEST EUROPEAN: about 1825.
Acquired as ITALIAN: 15th century.
A ring of somewhat similar design is in the British Museum (Dalton cat. 2006) and other related rings are in existence.
4377-1857

33 Enamelled gold. Oval bezel; hinged cover set with a ruby in a border of rose-cut diamonds; below, a compass dial. Volutes and strapwork on shoulders.
? GERMAN: mid 19th century.
Acquired as ITALIAN: 16th century.
4300-1857

34 Enamelled gold. Rectangular box bezel with 6 cusps, set with an emerald. Strapwork on shoulders.
? GERMAN: second half of 19th century. French import mark introduced in 1864. Acquired as ITALIAN: 16th century.
65-1896

35 Enamelled gold. Rectangular box bezel, set with a garnet. Openwork scrolling shoulders.
? GERMAN: second half of 19th century.
Acquired as GERMAN: early 17th century.
456-1873

36 Enamelled gold. Oval bezel set with a Roman paste intaglio.
WEST EUROPEAN: 19th century.
Acquired as 17th century.
Ready Bequest
M.11-1959

A RINGS BY ARTISTS AND ARTIST-SMITHS:
19th and 20th centuries

228

37 Enamelled gold. Shaped square bezel set with an amethyst in a border of diamond sparks. Arcaded enamel border. Pierced scrolling shoulders.
WEST EUROPEAN: second half of 19th century.
Acquired as late 17th century, but recognised as 19th century by Charles Oman in his catalogue of rings (1930, no. 377).
454-1873

38 Gold. Openwork foliate bezel set with an oval quartz, artificially coloured pink, flanked by two lions resting on the shoulders. Foliated hoop.
WEST EUROPEAN (? FRENCH): about 1830.
Originally acquired by Dame Joan Evans as a 19th century piece, but after an addition had been removed from the bezel, she suggested that it might date from the 17th century.
Given by Dame Joan Evans, P.P.S.A.
M.196-1975

*1 Steel and gold. The bezel in the form of a niche, in which sits a Muse attended by two cherubs, cast and chased. The gold figures probably modelled by J.B. Klagmann.
FRENCH: about 1856. Made in the workshops of F.-D. Froment-Meurice.
Acquired by the Museum from the Paris Universal Exhibition, 1855 (see also Case 20, Boards C & D).
2658-1858

2 Parcel-gilt iron hoop, chased with leaves and female terms. Lined with gold.
? SPANISH: mid 19th century.
Presumably made by Eusebio Zuloaga (1808-1898), Royal armourer and metal-worker, of Madrid and Eibar, or his son Plácido (1833-1910). Both father and son exhibited works at successive international exhibitions.
Given by Dame Joan Evans, P.P.S.A.
M.199-1962

3 Gold. Oval bezel set with a cabochon sapphire in a serrated collet. Applied stiff-leaf ornament on shoulders.
Designed by the architect and antiquary William Burges (1827-1881).
ENGLISH: about 1870. Made by an unknown goldsmith.
M.281-1975

*4 Enamelled gold. Oval bezel with a painted enamel plaque of Psyche by Charles Lepec; border of brilliant-cut diamonds.
FRENCH (Paris): about 1870.
Lepec, an enamelist, won a gold medal at the Paris Universal Exhibition of 1867. His work was sold in London by Robert Phillips of Cockspur Street.
Bolckow Bequest
746-1890

*5 Enamelled gold. Rectangular bezel set with a sapphire held by claws over an enamelled border; chased edge above a gallery. Openwork trellis shoulders.
ENGLISH (London): about 1875.
Made by Carlo Giuliano. Unmarked.
M.327-1922

6 Enamelled gold. Shaped circular bezel set with rose-cut diamonds in gold collets in the form of a cross. Further diamonds on the shoulders.
ENGLISH (London): about 1875.
Made by Carlo Giuliano. Unmarked. The information about the maker came from the donor. (See also No. 5 above and case 20, Board I).
M.328-1922
Nos. 5 & 6, given by Mr Cecil Crofton

*7 Gold. The bezel in the form of a facade of a church, set with a amethyst, an emerald and a sapphire, with a sapphire flanked by rubies below. Designed by the architect W R Lethaby (1857-1931), as a marriage present for his wife, Edith Crosby of New York, in 1901.
ENGLISH (London): 1901. Made by Henry Wilson. The hoop struck with Wilson's monogram. (See Case 21, Boards I & J).
Two drawings of this ring, annotated by both designer and maker, are in the V & A Print Room.
Given by M. Crosby
M.6-1934

*8 Chiselled iron. Bezel with reversed heads of Neptune and Amphitrite. Dolphin shoulders; one unfinished.
ENGLISH (Birmingham): late 19th century. Designed and made by Thomas Spall, who worked for Elkington's of Birmingham.
(See Case 6, Board N no. 89).
538-1903

9 Gold. Bezel in the form of a domed turret, the dome a cabochon ruby. Buttressed shoulders. Designed by Charles Ricketts for May Morris (see introduction to Case 21, Board D).
ENGLISH (London): 1899-1903.
? Made by Carlo Giuliano. The original drawings are in an album lettered 'Jewellery, 1899' in the British Museum.
May Morris Bequest
M.35-1939

10 Gold. Shaped bezel in the form of a female figure at the side of an opal.
ENGLISH: about 1901. Designed and made by A.C.C. Jahn (1865-1947), then Headmaster of Wolverhampton School of Art.
M.80-1947

11 Gold. Shaped bezel in the form of a mermaid clasping an opal mirror. Designed and made by A.C.C. Jahn. (See No. 10 above and Case 21, Board E, no. 2 & 3).
M.79-1947
Nos. 10 & 11, Jahn Bequest

12 Gold. The bezel set with a cabochon sapphire flanked by six brilliant-cut diamonds in separate raised collets. Traceried shoulders.
ENGLISH: about 1912. Designed and made by the artist Edmund Ware (1883-1960), as an engagement present for his future bride.
M.240-1977

13 Gold. Circular galleried bezel set with a sapphire, flanked by two pearls on the shoulders. Volutes and pellets on shoulders. Inside hoop, in wire, *SGW* and *1919*.
ENGLISH: 1919. Designed and made by Ethel Williamson Wyatt while a pupil at the Manchester School of Art for her mother, Mrs Sophia Gertrude Wyatt.
Given by Miss A L Wyatt
M.23-1974

14 Silver. Rectangular bezel set with transverse baguette amethysts. Pierced stepped shoulders.
ENGLISH: about 1928. Designed and made by Fred Partridge for his daughter Joan.
Fred Partridge formerly worked for the Guild of Handicraft. (See Case 21, Board F, no. 9).
Given by Miss Joan Partridge
M.15-1976

15 Platinum and gold. The bezel a convex section of amber. Shoulders set with black onyx (stained chalcedony) flanked by jadeite.
FRENCH (Paris): about 1930-35. French warranty mark for gold from 1838 onwards and for platinum from 1912 onwards. Signed: *G. FOUQUET* and stamped *22715* and *24364*. (See also Case 22, Board B, no. 9).
M.4-1980

16 Platinum. Stepped shoulders each side of three brilliant-cut diamonds arranged vertically. Designed and made, using diamonds from an engagement ring of 1913, by H G Murphy (1884-1939), for Mrs James Ardern Grant (1887-1965).
ENGLISH (London): 1932.
Mrs Grant's husband, an artist, worked with H G Murphy at the Central School of Arts and Crafts in London.
M.229-1977

*17 Gold. Abstract form originally carved in rosewood by Yves Tanguy (1900-1955), and first cast in gold in 1937.
The original FRENCH: 1937. New casting by H J Company, Ltd. London hallmarks for 1961. A ring of this design shown in the International Exhibition of Modern Jewellery, 1890-1961, Goldsmiths' Hall, 1961.
Circ. 10-1962

18 Gold wire bezel and hoop, with applied pellets. Designed and made by E R Nele.
GERMAN: 1957-60.
E R Nele was a contemporary of Gerda Flöckinger at the Central School of Arts and Crafts, London, in the 1950s.
Circ. 476-1960

19 Silver. The bezel in the form of a bird with outstretched wings and a long beak.
ENGLISH: about 1955. Designed and made by Alan Davie.
Circ. 374-1961

20 Silver-gilt. Flower bezel. Inscribed inside hoop: *151/2 J C Champagnat*.
FRENCH: 1961. A second edition of a ring designed and executed by Jean-Claude Champagnat which was shown at the International Exhibition of Modern Jewellery, 1961.
Circ. 195-1963

*21 Oxidised silver and gold. Hoop expanding into a bezel decorated with applied pellets and other motifs and set with a carved citrine and tourmaline; pendant with a disc set with an opal and a long tail.
ENGLISH: 1969. Designed and made by Gerda Flöckinger; shown in the Flöckinger exhibition, V & A Museum, 1971.
Circ. 118-1971

*22 Oxidised silver and gold. Drum-shaped bezel pierced and decorated with pellets and trailing applied wires, and a fragment of Persian turquoise.
ENGLISH: 1969. Designed and made by Gerda Flöckinger. Shown in the exhibition cited in No 21 above.
Circ 117-1971

23 Double ring (a pair of rings, designed to be worn together). One of oxidised silver, the other of gold, textured and decorated with pellets.
ENGLISH: 1976. Designed and made by Gerda Flöckinger. Both pieces bear the applied initials of the artist.
M.178-1979

24 Ring with pendants. Silver and gold hoop decorated with wires and pellets and set with three pendants, two long tails headed by grey pearls and a small gold disc set with a brilliant-cut diamond.
ENGLISH: 1980. Designed and made by Gerda Flöckinger.
M.60-1980
Nos. 23 & 24, Christmas presents from the artist to the V & A in 1979 and 1980

25 Silver. Bezel in the form of a tall building.
ENGLISH: London hallmarks for 1975. Maker's mark of Michael Burton.
Together with nos. 7 and 9 above, probably inspired by Jewish marriage rings (see Case 5, Board C).
Purchased from the first Loot Exhibition, Goldsmiths' Hall, 1975.
M.296-1975

B. MORE ART DECO

A. PAPAL RINGS
15th — early 16th century

230

26 Three rings. Broad silver hoops variously inlaid and overlaid with ebony.
ENGLISH: London hallmarks for 1976. Maker's mark of Julia Manheim.
M.33-6-1982

27 Two rings. Swelling hoops of blued steel, set with gold mask medallions and lined with silver.
ENGLISH: 1977. Designed and made by Mary Lloyd.
Acquired from the Royal College of Art Degree exhibition and given by the Hon. A. McAlpine through the V & A Associates.
M.402-1977

28 Silver wire, almandine garnets, amethysts, nephrite and red pastes.
ENGLISH: 1981. Designed and made by Frances Bendixson.
M.36-1982

29 Watch ring. Platinum and rose- and brilliant-cut diamonds surrounding the watch face.
ENGLISH (London): about 1925. Made by Nathan Fishberg in his factory at 201 Commercial Road. Given by his son, Mr Harry Fishberg, in response to the V & A appeal for Art Deco jewellery.
M.241-1977

30 Platinum. The bezel set with an opal; the shoulders with baguette rubies and brilliant-cut diamonds.
? CENTRAL EUROPEAN: about 1927.
M.235-1977

Under this heading are grouped rings decorated with the names or insignia of Popes, Cardinals, Bishops and European sovereigns. The distinctive features of these rings are massiveness and low intrinsic worth. They are made of gilt bronze or copper and are set with pastes or stones of very little value. Examples appear to have been discovered all over Europe.

Their function is a matter still unresolved, but the balance of opinion inclines to the view that they were worn as credentials by mounted couriers between Popes and other ecclesiastics and sovereigns. The great size of the rings made them suitable for use by couriers over gloved fingers and thumbs, and their lack of value helped to preserve their wearers from attacks by robbers on the road.

1 Gilt bronze. The original stone replaced by a signet. Engraved on one side, the crown and column of the Colonna family, for Pope Martin V (1417-1431); on the other, the Papal tiara. On either side of the bezel, *P* and *M* (for Papa Martinus).
Waterton Collection
87-1899

2 Gilt bronze. Re-set with an amethyst. Shoulders engraved with a mitre, crossed keys and a cardinal's hat between two mitres.
15th century.
Given by Dr. W.L. Hildburgh, F.S.A.
M.161-1929

3 Gilt bronze, set with a stone. Shoulders engraved with a crown, *RAGONAS* (Aragon), and the arms of Aragon. Applied symbols of the Four Evangelists around the bezel.
Mid 15th century.
Probably for Alfonso, King of Aragon and Sicily (1416-1458) and Naples (1442-1458).
663-1871

4 Gilt bronze, set with green chalcedony. Shoulders with the arms of Alfonso the Magnanimous (see no.3 above). Hoop inscribed: *RX RAGONA*.
Mid 15th century.
664-1871

5 Gilt bronze. Square bezel set with a point-cut crystal. Shoulders engraved with tiara and a cross above a coat of arms. Symbols of the Four Evangelists around the bezel.
15th century.
660-1871

6 Gilt bronze. Rectangular bezel set with a ? tourmaline. Shoulders with the tiara and crossed keys in low relief. Symbols of the Four Evangelists around the bezel.
15th century.
Possibly intended for the arms of Pope Nicholas V (1447-1455) who, lacking family arms, used the crossed keys of St Peter, the Papal emblem.
661-1871

7 Gilt bronze. Square bezel set with a table-cut crystal. Behind, two crowns. Shoulders with the arms of Condulmero in relief and a ? cardinal's hat with tassels.
15th century.
Attributable either to Gabriele Condulmero, Cardinal 1408-1431 and afterwards Pope Eugenius IV, or to his nephew Francesco, Cardinal 1431-1453.
658-1871

8 Gilt bronze. Rectangular bezel set with a table-cut crystal. Shoulders with the tiara, the crossed keys and *PAPA PIVS* divided by the arms of Pope Pius II (1458-1464). Symbols of the Four Evangelists around the bezel.
667-1871

9 Gilt Bronze. Rectangular bezel set with a paste. Shoulders with the crossed keys above the arms of Pope Pius II (1458-1864), *PAPA PIO* and the tiara. Symbols of the Four Evangelists around the bezel.
666-1871

*10 Gilt bronze. Rectangular bezel set with a green paste. Decorated as no. 9 above.
665-1871
Nos. 3-10, Waterton Collection

11 Gilt bronze. Rectangular bezel set with a table-cut crystal in a 6-cusp collet. Shoulders with the tiara and arms of Pope Sixtus IV (1471-1484) in relief and inscribed: *SIXTVS. PAPA. QUARTVS*. Symbols of the Evangelists on front and back of bezel.
Bernal Collection
2107-1855

12 Gilt bronze. Rectangular bezel set with a point-cut crystal. Shoulders with the Virgin and Child with a flower pot containing a lily in low relief and a half-figure of an abbess with a book. A hat with tassels on front and back of bezel. Hoop inscribed: *EPISC. LVGDVN*.
15th century.
Perhaps relating to an Archbishop of Lyons, or a Bishop of Laon or St. Bertrand de Cominges.
741-1871

13 Gilt bronze. Rectangular bezel set with a yellow paste. Shoulders with a mitre above a coat of arms in relief and a ? cardinal's hat with tassels. Second half of 15th or early 16th century.
Perhaps the arms of the Genoese family of Cibo, attributable either to Giovanni Battista Cibo, Cardinal 1473, afterwards Pope Innocent VIII (1484-1492), to his nephew Lorenzo, Cardinal 1488, or grandson Innocentio, Cardinal 1515.
659-1871

14 Gilt bronze. Rectangular bezel re-set with a paste. Shoulders with a mitre in relief above the engraved arms of della Rovere, and a ? cardinal's hat with tassels. On back and front of bezel, the inscription: *PAPA SISTVS* for Pope Sixtus IV (1471-1484).
669-1871
Nos. 13 & 14, Waterton Collection

15 Silver-gilt. Pierced box bezel set with a cabochon crystal and pastes. Hoop inscribed: *s: andreas*.
WEST EUROPEAN: early 16th century.
Not a Papal ring: probably a votive ring for a statue of St Andrew in a church.
Given by Dame Joan Evans, P.P.S.A.
M.175-1962

16 Silver-gilt. Large circular bezel set with a cabochon crystal in a cusped collet. Engraved behind with the Crucifixion. Shoulders with applied cherubs and foliations.
? ITALIAN: 17th century.
673-1871

17 Gilt bronze. Rectangular bezel set with a garnet. Shoulders chased with vine scrolls.
WEST EUROPEAN: 16th century.
671-1871
Nos. 16 & 17, Waterton Collection

C. MISCELLANEOUS:
16th-19th century

232

Four rings bearing the cross of St John (nos.18-21) are usually associated with the Knights of Malta. The remaining three rings are episcopal.

18 Enamelled gold. Oval bezel enamelled with the cross in white on black (the bezel perhaps a replacement). Shoulders decorated with terms.
WEST EUROPEAN: 16th century.
Waterton Collection
958-1871

19 Enamelled gold. Rectangular bezel enamelled with the cross as above.
WEST EUROPEAN: 17th century.
Given by Dame Joan Evans, P.P.S.A.
M.282-1962

20 Enamelled gold. Oval openwork bezel enamelled in white with the cross within two wreaths.
MALTESE: late 18th century. Marks, a bell, and A.V.
1059-1905

21 Enamelled gold. Openwork oval bezel enamelled in white with the cross.
MALTESE: late 18th century.
1060-1905
Nos. 20 & 21, given by the Rev. George Smith

22 A Cardinal's ring. Gold. Rectangular bezel set with a sapphire. Behind, the enamelled arms of Pope Benedict XIV (1740-1758). Openwork shoulders. Chased hoop, hinged and opening with a spring.
Waterton Collection
674-1871

23 A Cardinal's ring. Gold. Cusped oval bezel set with a ? sapphire. Behind, the enamelled arms of Pope Pius IX (1846-1878).
Given by Dame Joan Evans, P.P.S.A.
M.155-1962

*24 A Bishop's ring. Gold. Oval bezel engraved with the arms of William Thomson, Archbishop of York 1862-1890, surrounded by a crozier, mitre and cross.
ENGLISH: 1862.
Presented to the Archbishop by his Oxford friends.
Given by Lady Thomson
M.111-1945

1 RING SET. Three gold rings decorated with red enamel, on a transparent acrylic stand. Each with a different turned bezel, set with garnet or cornelian.
ENGLISH (London): 1971. Designed and made by Wendy Ramshaw. One of the innovative works turned on a lathe which won the artist a Council of Industrial Design award in 1972 (see also Case 24, no. 11).
M.34-b-1982

2 RING AND BOX. Blue ring in a grey box; acrylic and gold.
ENGLISH (London): 1976. Designed and made by Roger Morris.
M.257-1977

3 THREE RELATED RING SETS. White and yellow gold rings on turned nickel stands on separate plinths.
ENGLISH (London): 1981. Designed and made by Wendy Ramshaw for the tenth anniversary exhibition of the Electrum Gallery, London. The sets are designed to develop a theme in an increasingly complex manner.
M.45-47e-1981

CASE 34 BOARD A NO. 1	CASE 34 BOARD A NO. 2	CASE 34 BOARD A NO. 9	CASE 34 BOARD A NO. 18

233

CASE 34
BOARD A
NO. 23

CASE 34
BOARD A
NO. 32

CASE 34
BOARD B
NO. 9

CASE 34
BOARD B
NO. 26

CASE 34
BOARD C
NO. 16

CASE 34
BOARD C
NO. 20

CASE 34
BOARD C
NO. 24

CASE 34
BOARD C
NO. 29

CASE 34
BOARD D
NO. 28

CASE 34
BOARD D
NO. 30

CASE 34
BOARD D
NO. 33

CASE 34
BOARD E
NO. 3

CASE 34
BOARD E
NO. 6

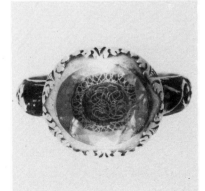

CASE 34
BOARD E
NO. 35

CASE 34
BOARD E
NO. 38

CASE 34
BOARD F
NO. 9

234

CASE 34
BOARD F
NO. 23

CASE 34
BOARD F
NO. 27

CASE 34
BOARD G
NO. 14

CASE 34
BOARD H
NO. 19

CASE 34
BOARD I
NO. 1

CASE 34
BOARD I
NO. 2

CASE 34
BOARD I
NO. 4

CASE 34
BOARD I
NO. 10

CASE 34
BOARD I
NO. 14

CASE 34
BOARD I
NO. 30

CASE 34
BOARD J
NO. 1

CASE 34
BOARD J
NO. 6

CASE 34
BOARD J
NO. 23

CASE 34
BOARD J
NO. 27

CASE 34
BOARD K
NO. 1

235

CASE 34
BOARD K
NO. 4

CASE 34
BOARD K
NO. 5

CASE 34
BOARD K
NO. 7

CASE 34
BOARD K
NO. 8

CASE 34
BOARD K
NO. 17

CASE 34
BOARD K
NO. 21

CASE 34
BOARD K
NO. 23

CASE 34
BOARD L
NO. 10

LOCAL AND
TRADITIONAL RINGS
(1)

236

This group is characterised by the use of impure gold and silver, with pastes or semi-precious stones. Some of the examples follow contemporary types, such as the version of gimmel *fede* rings (no. 33). Others, including the Norwegian ring with the Virgin and Child (no. 24), are based on earlier medieval designs.

1 Silver-gilt.
SCANDINAVIAN.
Given by J.H.E. Allen, Esq.
397-1896

2 Silver-gilt.
SCANDINAVIAN.
Waterton Collection
974-1871

3 Silver.
SCANDINAVIAN.
1327-1873

4 Silver-gilt. A stag.
MID-EUROPEAN.
292-1902

5 Silver-gilt.
SCANDINAVIAN.
6754-1860

6 Silver-gilt. A stag.
MID-EUROPEAN.
28-1894

7 Silver. For use as a weapon.
MID-EUROPEAN.
Waterton Collection
971-1871

8 Gold, with applied filigree.
MID-EUROPEAN.
Given by Miss Alma F. Oakes
M.2820-1931

9 Silver.
MID-EUROPEAN.
Waterton Collection
986-1871

10 Enamelled silver, set with a paste.
MID-EUROPEAN.
457-1873

11 Silver-gilt, set with pastes and garnets.
MID-EUROPEAN.
1207-1903

12 Silver-gilt, set with pastes.
MID-EUROPEAN.
29-1894

13 Silver-gilt, set with garnets.
MID-EUROPEAN.
27-1894

14 Silver, set with garnets.
MID-EUROPEAN.
927-1872

15 Silver-gilt, set with a paste and a garnet.
MID-EUROPEAN.
6768-1860

16 Enamelled silver, set with a turquoise.
MID-EUROPEAN.
Waterton Collection
980-1871

17 Silver-gilt, set with garnets.
MID-EUROPEAN.
939-1872

18 Silver-gilt, set with garnets.
MID-EUROPEAN.
940-1872

19 Silver, set with a paste.
Perhaps RUSSIAN.
115-1866

20 Silver-gilt, set with mother-of-pearl.
MID-EUROPEAN.
116-1866

21 Enamelled silver, set with ? bone.
MID-EUROPEAN.
Waterton-Collection
975-1871

22 Enamelled brass, set with a satin-stone.
Perhaps RUSSIAN.
112-1866

23 Silver, parcel-gilt, set with mother-of-pearl.
EAST EUROPEAN.
114-1866

24 Silver-gilt. The Virgin and Child.
NORWEGIAN.
Given by Dame Joan Evans, P.P.S.A.
M.22-1933

25 Silver-gilt. Symbol of St. Luke.
SCANDINAVIAN.
Given by Miss E.M. Begg
M.7-1956

26 Silver-gilt. The Crucifixion.
NORWEGIAN.
Given by Dame Joan Evans, P.P.S.A.
M.23-1933

27 Silver-gilt. The Virgin and Child.
SCANDINAVIAN.
Given by Mr. J.H.E. Allen
398-1896

28 Silver-gilt. The Annunciation.
MID-EUROPEAN.
Waterton Collection
973-1871

29 Silver, parcel-gilt. St. Michael and the Devil.
GERMAN.
46-1872

30 Silver-gilt. The Virgin and Child.
MID-EUROPEAN.
Waterton Collection
972-1871

31 Silver-gilt.
SCANDINAVIAN.
949-1902

32 Silver. St. Anthony of Padua with the Infant Christ.
MID-EUROPEAN.
Given by Mr. Walter Child
M.135-1909

33 Gimmel *fede* ring. Silver-gilt, set with garnets.
MID-EUROPEAN.
Waterton Collection
855-1871

34 Silver, parcel-gilt, set with garnets.
? FRENCH.
Waterton Collection
860-1871

Case 35　Board B

LOCAL AND
TRADITIONAL RINGS (2)

The Castellani collection, a small part of which is shown on this board, was put together by Alessandro Castellani in his guise as a dealer. He bought specimens of regional jewellery from all over Italy and showed them at the Paris Universal Exhibition of 1867. The collection was acquired by the Museum the following year.

1 Gold, set with a paste.
ITALIAN.
Castellani Collection
476-1868

2 Gold, set with pearls.
ITALIAN.
Waterton Collection
1006-1871

3 Gold filigree.
? MALTESE. Maker's mark: G 4 A.
M.13-1912

4 Gold, set with pearls.
ITALIAN.
Castellani Collection
482-1868

5 Gold, set with pearls.
ITALIAN.
Waterton Collection
969-1871

6 Gold, set with crystals in silver collets.
ITALIAN.
457-1868

7 Gold, silver bezel set with pastes.
ITALIAN. Maker's mark: P.C.C.U.
436-1868

8 Gold, set with crystals in silver collets.
ITALIAN.
428-1868

9 Gold, set with a turquoise.
ITALIAN.
459-1868
Nos. 6-9, Castellani Collection

10 Silver.
MALTESE: about 1870.
1459-1873

11 Gold. Gimmel ring.
ITALIAN.
Castellani Collection
435-1868

12 Gold, set with garnets.
MID-EUROPEAN.
Given by Mr. Walter Child
131-1909

13 Gold, set with a paste and crystals in silver collets.
ITALIAN.
Castellani Collection
461-1868

14 Gold, set with pastes.
SPANISH.
1217-1871

15 Gold, set with crystals and pastes in silver collets.
ITALIAN.
462-1868

16 Gold, set with pastes.
ITALIAN.
441-1868

17 Gold, set with a paste and crystals.
ITALIAN.
449-1868
Nos. 15-17, Castellani Collection

18 Gold, set with crystals.
SPANISH.
697-1870

19 Gold, set with pastes in silver collets.
ITALIAN.
427-1868

20 Gold, set with pastes.
ITALIAN.
471-1868

21 Gold, set with a pearl and garnets.
ITALIAN.
481-1868

22 Gold, set with turquoises.
ITALIAN.
Nos. 19-22, Castellani Collection

23 Gold, set with pastes.
MID-EUROPEAN.
1000-1903

24 Gold, set with turquoises.
ITALIAN.
440-1868

25 Gold, set with an emerald, a topaz, crystals, and garnets in silver collets.
A giardinetti ring, but coarser than the examples in Case 34, Board B.
478-1868

26 Gold, set with pastes in silver collets.
A giardinetti ring.
ITALIAN.
455-1868
Nos. 24-26, Castellani Collection

27 Gold, set with emeralds.
A giardinetti ring.
? SPANISH.
M.144-1937

28 Gold, set with emeralds.
A giardinetti ring.
? SPANISH.
M.143-1937
Nos. 27 & 28, given by Dr. W.L. Hildburgh, F.S.A.

29 Gold. A crucifix.
MID-EUROPEAN.
1462-1873

30 Gold, set with pastes in silver collets. Centre, Virgin of the Pillar, Saragossa.
SPANISH.
235-1864

31 Silver. A crucifix.
ITALIAN.
Castellani Collection
431-1868

32 Silver-gilt, set with a crystal enclosing a painting of the Crucifixion.
SPANISH: 18th century.
Waterton Collection
699-1871

JEWISH MARRIAGE RINGS

238

33 Gold, set with pastes.
MID-EUROPEAN.
204-1864

34 Gold, set with a painting under glass.
ITALIAN.
483-1868

35 Enamelled silver, set with pastes.
ITALIAN.
429-1868

36 Enamelled gold, set with diamonds in silver collets.
484-1868
Nos. 34-36, Castellani Collection

The earliest known examples of these rings seem to date from the fourteenth century, but most of them belong to the sixteenth century and later and are probably of Central European and Mediterrean origin. They were intended to be used only at the actual ceremony and not to be worn afterwards. The buildings which appear on some examples have been variously thought to represent the Temple of Jerusalem or the synagogues of the Diaspora, but may also allude to the Talmudic saying, 'His house is his wife' Most examples of these rings bear the inscription Mazal Tov (Good luck) either in full or in an abbreviated form.

1 Gold.
864-1871

2 Enamelled gold. Hebrew inscription for Good Luck.
866-1871
Nos. 1 & 2, Waterton Collection

3 Gold. Hebrew initials for Good Luck.
2746-1855

*4 Enamelled gold. Hebrew inscription for Good Luck.
4100-1855

5 Gold. Hebrew inscription for Good Luck.
Waterton Collection
865-1871

*6 Enamelled gold. Hebrew initials for Good Luck.
32-1894

7 Enamelled gold. Hebrew inscription for Good Luck.
Waterton Collection
868-1871

*8 Enamelled gold. Hebrew inscription for Good Luck.
80-1872

9 Gold.
Waterton Collection
863-1871

10 Gold. Hebrew initials for Good Luck.
453-1873

11 Gilt bronze. Hebrew inscription for Good Luck.
17th century.
Waterton Collection
870-1871.

12 Gold.
Given by Mrs. Eugenie Klugman.
M.25-1952

13 Gilt-bronze. Hebrew inscription for Good Luck.
Waterton Collection
867-1871

14 Silver-gilt. Hebrew inscription for Good Luck.
Waterton Collection
869-1871

15 Gilt bronze. Hebrew initials for Good Luck.
81-1872

CASE 35
BOARD C
NO. 4

CASE 35
BOARD C
NO. 8

CASE 35
BOARD C
NO. 6

Reserved for new acquisitions

Case 36

Reserved for loaned objects

Case 37

SCANDINAVIAN LOCAL AND TRADITIONAL JEWELLERY

Two Bridal Crowns

Board A

Silver, parcel-gilt.
SWEDISH: 18th or 19th century.
1354-1873

Board B

Silver-gilt.
NORWEGIAN: 18th or 19th century
2-1879

1 BROOCH   239
Silver-gilt, with figure of an angel.
NORWEGIAN: 18th or 19th century.
371-1907

2 TWO BODICE-FASTENERS
From a set of four. Silver-gilt, with
filigree decoration.
SWEDISH (Ystad hallmark):
about 1830. Maker's mark of P.M.
Wallengren.
537b, c-1886

3 BELT-ENDS
Silver-gilt filigree, set with pastes.
NORWEGIAN: 18th or 19th century.
620-1872

4 CLASP
Silver-gilt, with figure of St. Olave.
NORWEGIAN: 18th or 19th century.
M.498-1911

5 CLASP
Silver-gilt, with figure of an angel.
NORWEGIAN: 18th century.
M.36-1920

6 BROOCH
Silver-gilt, with filigree decoration.
NORWEGIAN: 19th century.
372-1907

7 BROOCH
Silver-gilt.
NORWEGIAN: 18th century.
Given by Miss E.M. Begg.
M.22-1957

8 BROOCH
Silver.
NORWEGIAN: 18th century.
Given by Mr. Walter Child
1002-1905

9 BROOCH
Silver-gilt.
NORWEGIAN: 18th or 19th century.
Wimborne Collection
Given by Dr. W.L. Hildburgh, F.S.A.
M.54-1955

10 BROOCH
Silver, parcel-gilt.
NORWEGIAN: ? 18th century.
Given by Miss E.I. Begg.
M.23-1957

FRENCH LOCAL AND
TRADITIONAL
JEWELLERY

240

11 BROOCH
Silver-gilt, with figure of the Virgin
and Child.
NORWEGIAN: 18th or 19th century.
38-1894

12 PENDANT
Silver-gilt, set with pastes.
NORWEGIAN: 18th or 19th century.
M.1003-1905

13 BROOCH
Silver-gilt. From Molde.
NORWEGIAN: ? 18th century.
M.447-1910
Nos. 12 & 13, given by Mr. Walter
Child

14 BROOCH
Silver.
NORWEGIAN: ? 19th century.
M.26-1957

15 BROOCH
Silver-gilt.
NORWEGIAN: 18th or 19th century.
M.24-1957

16 BROOCH
Silver.
NORWEGIAN: ? 18th century.
M.25-1957
Nos. 14-16, given by Miss E.M. Begg

17 BROOCH
Silver-gilt, with filigree decoration.
NORWEGIAN: 19th century.
M.530-1924

18 BROOCH
Silver filigree.
NORWEGIAN: 19th century.
Maker's mark, IÖ.
M.531-1924
Nos. 17 & 18, given by Dr. G.F. Hill

19 BROOCH
Silver-gilt, with filigree decoration.
NORWEGIAN: 19th century.
373-1907

20 TWO BODICE-FASTENERS
Silver-gilt.
SWEDISH: 18th or 19th century.
M.567, 567a-1911

21 CLASP
Silver-gilt filigree.
NORWEGIAN: 19th century.
Maker's mark, V.T.N.
Given by Dr. G.F. Hill
M.532-1924

**1 CROSS AND PAIR OF
EARRINGS**
Silver.
FRENCH (Normandy): early 19th
century.
Given by Miss Edith J. Hipkins
M.428-428b-1911

2 CLASP
Silver.
FRENCH: Evreux mark for 1819-38.
Maker's mark, ? RF.
91, 91a-1869

3 CLASP
Silver.
FRENCH: warranty mark for 1838
onwards. Maker's mark, P B with
a stork.
93, 93a-1869

4 CLASP
Silver.
FRENCH: Rouen mark for 1781-9.
Maker's mark: J F R.
94, 94a-1869

5 CROSS
Silver, set with crystals.
FRENCH (Normandy): warranty
mark for 1798-1809. Maker's mark,
JF.
70-1869

6 CROSS
Silver, set with crystals.
FRENCH (Normandy): early 19th
century.
98-1869

7 PENDANT
Silver, set with crystals.
FRENCH (Normandy): northern
mark for 1819-38. Maker's mark, E.C.
265, 265a-1869

8 SILVER CROSS
FRENCH (Normandy): early 19th
century.
Given by Miss Edith J. Hipkins
M.429-1911

9 CROSS
Gold, set with crystals.
FRENCH (Normandy): northern
mark for 1819-38. Maker's marks, J C
(cross), H P (heart).
261, 261a-1869

RUSSIAN AND ALBANIAN LOCAL AND TRADITIONAL JEWELLERY AND OTHER OBJECTS.

10 CROSS
Gold.
FRENCH (Normandy): warranty mark for 1798-1809. Maker's mark, O L M.
60-1869

11 PENDANT
Gold, set with crystals.
FRENCH (Normandy): warranty mark for 1809-19. Maker's mark, J.H.
264, 264a-1869

12 CROSS
Gold, set with crystals.
FRENCH (Normandy): warranty mark for 1809-19. Maker's mark, D.G.
69-1869

13 CROSS
Gold, set with crystals.
FRENCH (Normandy): warranty mark for 1809-19. Maker's mark, J C.
63-1869

14 CROSS
Gold, set with crystals.
FRENCH (Normandy): 1781-1789. Marks, G C crowned and a leaf.
M.350-1910

15 CROSS
Silver, set with crystals and garnets.
FRENCH: early 19th century.
80-1869

16 EARRING
Gold, set with crystals.
FRENCH (Normandy): early 19th century.
268-1869

17 EARRING
Gold, set with crystals.
FRENCH (Normandy): early 19th century.
269-1869

18 CROSS
Silver, set with crystals.
FRENCH (Normandy): early 19th century.
85-1869

1 CROSS
Jasper, mounted in silver, parcel-gilt.
RUSSIAN: 19th century.
101-1866

2 CROSS
Glass, mounted in silver-gilt.
RUSSIAN: 18th or 19th century.
102-1866

3 SILVER CROSS
RUSSIAN: Kostroma mark for 1857.
514-1869

4, 5 CROSS AND CHAIN
Silver-gilt.
RUSSIAN: the cross probably 18th century, the chain 19th century.
134-1866, 513-1869

6 AMULET-CASE
With chain. Silver, embossed with St. George and the Dragon.
ALBANIAN: 19th century.
1421-1873

7 CROSS
Enamelled silver.
RUSSIAN: 19th century.
106-1866

8 TINDER-BOX
Silver, with silver-mounted steel.
ALBANIAN: 19th century.
169-1894

9 CROSS
Silver, parcel-gilt, enriched with enamelled filigree and set with turquoises and a paste.
RUSSIAN: 18th or early 19th century.
98-1866

10, 11 CHAIN AND FRAME FOR AN IKON
Enamelled silver-gilt.
RUSSIAN: 19th century.
San Donato Collection
159, 233-1889

12 EARRING
Silver-gilt, hung with coral beads.
ALBANIAN: 18th or 19th century.
1477-1873

13 PAIR OF SILVER BUTTONS
ALBANIAN: 19th century.
1484, 1484a-1873

14 BREAST-ORNAMENT
Silver, set with glass beads.
ALBANIAN: 19th century.
1436-1873

15 EARRING
Silver-gilt, filigree, with corals, stones and pastes, and portion of a chain.
ALBANIAN: 18th century.
580-1868

16 PENDANT AND CHAIN
An imperial eagle of gold filigree-work, set with emeralds, rubies and pearls. The chain, strings of seed pearls with cylindrical beads of *cloisonné*-work filled with coloured mastic.
ALBANIAN: possibly 17th century.
Gibson-Carmichael Collection
607-1902

17 PENDANT AND CHAIN
Silver, set with glass and coral.
ALBANIAN: 19th century.
535-1862

18 CLASP-KNIFE
Nielloed silver handle.
ALBANIAN: 18th or 19th century.
Given by Mr. Walter Child
M.130-1909

GERMAN LOCAL AND TRADITIONAL JEWELLERY

GERMAN, FLEMISH AND SCANDINAVIAN GIRDLES

242

1 SILVER CROSS OF ST. ULRICH
GERMAN (Augsburg): 18th century.
929-1872

2 PENDANT
Silver-gilt filigree, set with black pastes.
GERMAN or SWISS: 19th century.
89-1872

3 PENDANT
Silver-gilt filigree, set with black pastes.
GERMAN or SWISS: 19th century.
85-1872

4 NECKLACE
Silver filigree, with silver and garnet beads.
GERMAN (Bavarian): probably 18th century.
165-1872

5 ROSARY
Coral and silver-gilt filigree, with pendent medallion commemorating the Peace of Ryswick, dated 1697.
SOUTH GERMAN: 18th century.
151-1872

6 CHAIN
Silver, with two filigree pendants.
GERMAN (Stuttgart hall-mark): second half of 17th century or early 18th century.
101-1872

7 ROSARY
Amber and silver filigree, with two pendants enclosing gilt medals of the Virgin of Altötting.
SOUTH GERMAN: late 17th century.
155-1872

8 SILVER CROSS OF ST. ULRICH
GERMAN (Augsburg): 18th century.
Given by Mr. L.A. Lawrence, F.S.A.
M.122-1926

9 CHILD'S BAUBLE
Silver-gilt, set with a wolf's tooth.
SOUTH GERMAN: probably 17th century.
104-1872

10 NECKLACE
Enamelled silver.
GERMAN: 18th or 19th century.
153-1872

1 GIRDLE
Leather, with brass mounts over green parchment.
GERMAN: about 1500.
1599-1901

2 GIRDLE
With pendent scent-case. Silver, parcel-gilt.
SCANDINAVIAN: 17th century.
534-1893

3 GIRDLE
Silver, parcel-gilt, with cast filigree work.
GERMAN: second half of 16th century.
190-1872

4 GIRDLE
Silver, parcel-gilt.
GERMAN: second half of 16th century.
163-1899

5 GIRDLE
Silver-gilt.
FLEMISH: 16th century.
1610-1855

6 GIRDLE-END
Silver-gilt.
GERMAN: early 18th century.
Bernal Collection
2304-1855

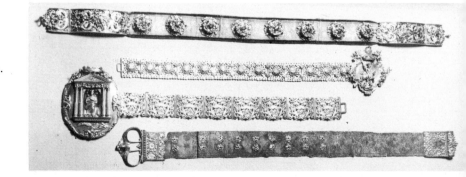

CASE 38
BOARD D
NO. 1-4

Case 38 Board B

GERMAN AND SCANDINAVIAN GIRDLES

1 GIRDLE
Silver, parcel-gilt.
GERMAN (Bavarian): 17th century
934-1872

2 GIRDLE
Silver-gilt, mounted on modern velvet.
Said to have belonged to Queen Christina of Sweden (1626-89).
SWEDISH: dated 1546. Marks, N T in monogram and 98.
745-745a-1897

3 GIRDLE
Silver, parcel-gilt.
? DANISH: late 16th century.
Mark, S V X in monogram.
M.126-1900

4 GIRDLE
Silver-gilt, chased with figures of Temperance and Bacchus. On the clasp, Aesculapius and Mars with a shield inscribed *ABI LIVOR TIBI NON SPIRAT* (May envy not breathe on you)
SWEDISH: dated 1745. Marks, ? STS and the date 1745. Modern velvet mounting.
Given by Mr. Walter Child
2061, 2061a-1900

5 GIRDLE
The buckle and various ornaments in silver-gilt, mounted on modern velvet.
NORWEGIAN: 17th century.
164-1899

Case 38 Board C

SCANDINAVIAN, GERMAN AND TRANSYLVANIAN GIRDLES

1 BUCKLE AND BELT-END
Silver-gilt.
NORWEGIAN: mid 16th century.
Wimborne Collection
Given by Dr. W.L. Hildburgh, F.S.A.
M.5-1948

2 PART OF A GIRDLE
Silver-gilt. Inscribed with portions of the Angelic Salutation to the Virgin.
SCANDINAVIAN: mainly early 16th century.
M.75-1910

3 GIRDLE
Silver-gilt, with enamelled clasp.
SOUTH GERMAN: early 17th century.
Zschille Collection
162-1894

4 GIRDLE
Silver, parcel-gilt.
GERMAN: 17th century.
Zouche Collection
771-1891

5 GIRDLE
Silver-gilt.
TRANSYLVANIAN-SAXON: about 1730. Mark of Martinus Regis of Sibiu.
Given by Dr. W.L. Hildburgh, F.S.A.
M.17-1953

6 GIRDLE-END
Silver-gilt, engraved with a figure of Fortune.
NORWEGIAN: about 1600.
Given by Mr. Walter Child
1004-1905

Case 38 Board D

ITALIAN AND TRANSYLVANIAN GIRDLES

*1 GIRDLE
Silver-gilt clasp and bosses with pastes, on gold brocade.
TRANSYLVANIAN-SAXON: 18th or 19th century. Struck with the Austro-Hungarian warranty mark (possibly added later) for 1866-1937.
Maker's mark: L.H.
Given by Dr. W.L. Hildburgh, F.S.A.
M.18-1953

*2 GIRDLE
Worn at festivals by peasants of Piana dei Greci, Palermo, Sicily.
SICILIAN (Palermo mark): second half of 18th century.
Marks, ?SCC and AM (buckle); PC 710 (girdle).
Given by Mrs. Richards
M.65-1949

*3 GIRDLE
Silver, parcel-gilt.
Worn at festivals by peasants of Piana dei Greci, Palermo, Sicily.
SICILIAN: early 19th century.
Marks, G.G.B. and Sicilian marks.
Given by Mr. T.B. Clarke-Thornhill
M.130 & a-1916

*4 GIRDLE
Gold brocade, the buckle and end of gilt metal with enamel and nielloed silver.
ITALIAN: 15th century.
4278-1857

COLOMBIAN COPPER AND GOLD ALLOY OBJECTS:
about 9th-15th century AD, from the Quimbaya Area

(acc. nos. 697-786-1872)

244

1 NOSE PIECES

2 EAR PIECES
Worn, inserted in the lower part of the ear.

3 EAR PIECES
Hung from gold wire.

4 PROBABLE EAR PIECES

COLOMBIAN COPPER AND GOLD ALLOY OBJECTS:
about 9th-15th century AD, from the Quimbaya Area, and other objects

(acc. nos. 697-876-1872)

1 NECKLACE BEADS
Zoomorphic.

2 NECKLACE BEADS
Abstract.

*3 NECKLACE BEADS
Anthropomorphic.

4 ? HAIRPINS

5 AXE
Perhaps for metalworking.

6 ? BUTTONS

7 FLAT ORNAMENTS

8 PENDANT
Made from a Spanish coin: colonial period.

*9 GOLD ALLOY OBJECTS
Probably from Panama.

GOLD OBJECTS OF THE ASHANTI (GHANA):
mainly before 1874

1 ORNAMENT
Gold, perhaps a bead.
376-1874

2 ORNAMENT
Repoussé gold, for attachment to furniture or clothing.
377-1874

3 ORNAMENT
Cast gold, in the form of a bird, probably from a ceremonial hat.
M.454-1936

4 BADGE
Cast gold, worn by the Asantehene's 'soul washer' as a badge of office.
7-1883

5 BADGE
Cast gold, worn by the Asantehene's 'soul washer' as a badge of office.
370-1874

6 BADGE
Cast gold, worn by the Asantehene's 'soul washer' as a badge of office.
369-1874

7 BADGE
Cast gold, worn by the Asantehene's 'soul washer' as a badge of office.
371-1874

8 ORNAMENT
Repoussé gold, feather shaped, for attachment to furniture or clothing.
378-1874

*9 ORNAMENT
Repoussé gold, disc-shaped, for attachment to furniture or clothing.
369-1874

10 PART OF AN ORNAMENT
Repoussé gold, for attachment to furniture or clothing.
375-1874

Case 39 Board D

GOLD AND SILVER OBJECTS OF THE ASHANTI (Ghana):
mainly before 1874

1 CEREMONIAL PIPE
Cast and repoussé gold, bound with gold wire.
368-1874

2 ORNAMENT
Repoussé gold, diadem-shaped, for attachement to clothing or furniture.
89-1875

3 PART OF AN ORNAMENT
Repoussé gold, shaped as a strip, for attachment to clothing or furniture.
374-1874

4 PENDANT
Repoussé gold, perhaps for attachment to clothing.
373-1874

5 PAIR OF ANKLETS
Silver.
380 & a-1874

6 RING
Gold.
Given by Mr. Victor Ames
M.256-1951

Case 39 Board E

IRISH AND CELTIC JEWELLERY

1 OBJECT WITH TRUMPET-SHAPED TERMINALS
Gold.
IRISH: bronze Age.
Received with a label inscribed: *Armagh*, where it was presumably found.
Ready Bequest
M.14-1959

*2 RING
Gold. Openwork bezel chased with two masks.
CELTIC (? North Italian): 5th century BC.
Waterton Collection
419-1871

*3 GORGET
Gold, repoussé.
IRISH: about 7th century BC.
Found near Shannongrove, County Limerick, in the mid 18th century, and formerly an heirloom of the Earls of Charleville.
Given by Colonel C.K. Howard Bury, D.S.O.
M.35-1948

4 MOULD FOR JEWELLERY
Mudstone.
IRISH: medieval.
Bequeathed by Dr. W.L. Hildburgh, F.S.A.
M.352 & a-1956

5 BRACELET
Gold.
IRISH: Dowris Phase (about 700 BC).
5612-1901

Case 39 Board F

ABYSSINIAN

*CROWN
Gold, worn by the Abuna or head of the Abyssinian Christian Church. It was subsequently appropriated by Theodore, King of Abyssinia (reigned 1855-68).
ABYSSINIAN: date uncertain.
Loan

246

*1 CHALICE

Gold, hammered, with details cast
and chased.
Beneath the lip and on the foot are
incised inscriptions in Ethiopic, the
former to the effect that the chalice
was given by King Joshua (1682-
1706) and his Queen to the sanctuary
of Quesquâm.
ABYSSINIAN: ? 17th century.
Loan

2 RING

Gold, in the form of a berry.
ABYSSINIAN: 19th century.
643-1884

CASE 39
BOARD B
NO. 3

CASE 39
BOARD B (1 only)
NO. 9

CASE 39
BOARD C
NO. 9

CASE 39
BOARD E
NO. 2

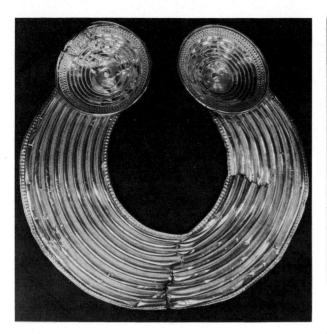

247

CASE 39
BOARD E
NO. 3

CASE 39
BOARD F
LOAN

CASE 39
BOARD G
NO. 1

SPANISH LOCAL AND TRADITIONAL JEWELLERY AND OTHER OBJECTS

248

1, 2 PENDANT AND PAIR OF EARRINGS
Gold, set with table- and rose-cut diamonds and crystals.
SPANISH: 18th or 19th century.
Bequeathed by Mrs. Geoffrey Webb
M.17-18a-1962

3 EARRING
Gold, with filigree decoration.
SPANISH (Madrid hall-mark): about 1870.
1076-1873

4 EARRING
Gold, with filigree.
SPANISH: about 1870.
1078-1873

5 EARRING
Rose-cut diamonds, set in gold.
SPANISH: 18th or 19th century.
237-1864

6 EARRING
Emeralds, set in gold.
SPANISH: 18th or 19th century.
333-1864

7 CHILD'S BAUBLE
Silver.
SPANISH (Saragossa hall-mark): possibly early 19th century. Marks, a head, PC, and a lion rampant.
From the Treasury of the Cathedral of the Virgin of the Pillar, Saragossa
331-1870

8 PENDANT
Silver-gilt, set with pastes.
SPANISH: 18th century.
233-1864

9 PAIR OF EARRINGS
Enamelled gold, set with pearls.
SPANISH: probably early 19th century.
Murray Bequest
M.1025, 1025a-1910

10 NECKLACE
Gold, set with pearls.
SPANISH (Salamanca): about 1870.
1374-1873

11 PAIR OF EARRINGS
Gold filigree, set with pearls.
SPANISH (Salamanca): about 1870.
1376, 1376a-1873

12 PENDANT
Gold, set with rose-cut diamonds, pastes and a large emerald.
SPANISH: probably early 19th century.
Given by the Rt. Hon. Sir C.W. Dilke, in fulfilment of the wishes of Lady Dilke.
1537-1904

13 NECKLACE
Silver, parcel-gilt, set with crystals and emeralds in gold collets.
SPANISH: probably 19th century.
Bequeathed by Miss Winifred Mary Bompas
M.100-1935

14 PENDANT
Gold filigree, set with pearls.
SPANISH (Salamanca): about 1870.
1375-1873

15 PENDANT AND TWO NECKLACE ORNAMENTS
Gold, set with rose-cut diamonds and pastes.
SPANISH: 18th century. Marks, D (pendant); AV (ornaments).
Given by Dr. Joan Evans, P.P.S.A.
M.53 to 53b-1962

16 BROOCH
Gold filigree, set with pearls.
SPANISH (Balearic Islands): about 1870.
115-1870

17 EARRING
Gold filigree, set with pearls.
SPANISH: early 19th century.
196-1864

18 PENDANT
Gold. A unicorn.
SPANISH: 17th century.
M.146-1937

19 PENDANT
Copper-gilt.
SPANISH: possibly early 19th century.
M.147-1937
Nos. 18 & 19, given by Dr. W.L. Hildburgh, F.S.A.

20 PENDANT
Silver-gilt, set with table-cut diamonds and pastes.
SPANISH: late 18th or early 19th century.
227-1864

21 PAIR OF EARRINGS
Copper, hung with pearls and set with a paste and garnets.
SPANISH: early 19th century.
Given by Miss A.V. Hammond
M.115, 115a-1953

22 CHILD'S BAUBLE
Silver.
SPANISH: probably early 19th century.
543-1905

Case 40 Board B

SPANISH LOCAL AND TRADITIONAL DEVOTIONAL JEWELLERY

1 PENDANT
Silver-gilt, set with paintings under glass of a female saint and the Instruments of the Passion.
SPANISH: probably 18th century.
M.59-1923

2 PENDANT
Silver-gilt, set with paintings under glass of the Annunciation and the Crucifixion.
SPANISH: 17th century.
M.53-1923
Nos. 1 & 2, Alfred Williams Hearn Gift

3 PENDANT
Silver-gilt, set with pastes and a porcelain plaque with the badge of the Carmelites.
SPANISH: 18th century.
426-1873

4 PENDANT
Silver-gilt, set with plaques of painted enamel.
SPANISH (Aragon): the enamel 16th century, the setting perhaps later.
Alfred Williams Hearn Gift
M.55-1933

5 PENDANT
Silver filigree work, set with a medal of St. Peter and St. John the Baptist.
SPANISH or ITALIAN: 18th century.
Murray Bequest
M.1028-1910

6 CROSS
Silver filigree.
SPANISH or ITALIAN: 18th century.
338-1890

7 PENDANT
Silver filigree, enclosing a medallion with St. Jeanne Françoise de Chantal on the obverse, and St. François de Sales on the reverse.
SPANISH: 19th century.
317-1890

8 PENDANT
Silver-gilt. The Virgin of Sagrario.
SPANISH: 19th century.
1232-1871

9 ROSARY WITH CRUCIFIX
Pink coral and gold filigree.
SPANISH: 19th century.
Bolckow Bequest
741-1890

10 FRAME
Silver-gilt filigree, set with pastes.
SPANISH (Astorga): 1800.
1378-1873

11 CROSS
Gold filigree. From Gibraltar.
SPANISH: 18th century.
221-1881

12 PENDANT
Silver, set with emeralds and rose-cut diamonds, with a gold figure of the Virgin under glass.
SPANISH: early 18th century.
Alfred Williams Hearn Gift
M.64-1923

13 PENDANT
Silver, set with rock crystal covering paintings over foil of the head of Christ and the Instruments of the Passion.
SPANISH: 18th century.
Given by Dr. W.L. Hildburgh, F.S.A.
M.2-1948

14 PENDANT
Gold, with reliefs of the Annunciation and the Holy Family under crystal.
SPANISH: first half of 18th century.
6-1866

15 PENDANT
Silver-gilt, set with pastes and a porcelain plaque of the Virgin of the Pillar.
SPANISH: early 19th century.
Mark, 9 D.
468-1864

16 CROSS PENDANT
Silver-gilt filigree rosettes.
SPANISH: 18th century.
341-1890

17 PENDANT
Silver, engraved with the Sacred Monogram and a cross.
SPANISH: 18th century.
521-1898

18 PENDANT
Silver filigree, parcel-gilt, enclosing paintings under crystal of the Emblems of the Passion, St. Barbara, and St. Anthony of Padua.
SPANISH: 18th or 19th century.
Alfred Williams Hearn Gift
M.62-1923

19 PENDANT
Silver-gilt filigree, with coloured engravings under glass.
SPANISH (Cordova): about 1870.
1170-1871

Case 41 Board A

A. PORTUGUESE LOCAL AND TRADITIONAL JEWELLERY

1 PENDANT
Gold, set with rose-cut diamonds.
NORTH PORTUGUESE: probably
19th century.
13-1866

2 PENDANT
Gold, set with rose-cut diamonds.
NORTH PORTUGUESE: probably
19th century.
14-1866

3 EARRING
Gold, set with rose-cut diamonds.
(Moorish type).
PORTUGUESE: late 18th century.
19-1866

4 PAIR OF EARRINGS
Gold, set with rose-cut diamonds.
(Moorish type).
PORTUGUESE: late 18th century.
Acquired at Lisbon.
591 & a-1908

5 PAIR OF EARRINGS
Gold, set with pastes.
(Moorish type).
PORTUGUESE: late 18th century.
Acquired at Oporto.
592 & a-1908

6 PENDANT
Gold, set with rose-cut diamonds.
PORTUGUESE: 18th century.
Acquired at Funchal, Madeira.
593-1908
Nos. 4-6, given by Mr Walter Child

7 PAIR OF EARRINGS
Gold, set with emeralds and pearls.
PORTUGUESE: probably early 19th
century.
Given by Mrs. Mary Houghton of
Florence
M.22 & a-1948

8 PENDANT
Gold, set with rose-cut diamonds.
NORTH PORTUGUESE: Probably
19th century.
15-1866

9 SLIDE AND PENDANT
Rose-cut diamonds set in gold.
SPANISH or PORTUGUESE:
18th century.
M.82-1913

10 NECKLACE AND PENDANT
Rose-cut diamonds, foiled topazes,
emeralds, rubies and foiled
crystals, set in silver and gold.
PORTUGUESE: 18th century.
M.1-1912

11 AGNUS DEI
An impression made in wax from the
remains of the paschal candle,
blessed by the Pope for distribution
to the faithful. With titles of Clement
XI and date 1714. Gold case, set with
pearls and rock crystal.
PORTUGUESE: early 18th century.
17-1866

12 PENDANT
Gold, set with rose-cut diamonds.
PORTUGUESE: 18th century.
749-1893

13 PAIR OF EARRINGS
Gold, set with emeralds.
Probably PORTUGUESE: late 18th
or early 19th century.
Given by Mrs. Mary Houghton of
Florence
M.21 & a-1948

14 EARRING
Silver, set with chrysolite.
PORTUGUESE: 18th century.
Given by Dr. Joan Evans, P.P.S.A.
M.73-1962

15 PENDANT
Gold filigree.
PORTUGUESE: about 1870. Maker's
mark, J.M.R.
1073-1873

16 PENDANT AND EARRINGS
Gold, set with rose-cut diamonds.
PORTUGUESE: late 18th century.
804-b-1902

17 EARRING
Gold, set with diamonds.
PORTUGUESE: 18th century.
21-1866

B. SWISS LOCAL AND TRADITIONAL JEWELLERY

18 ARMBAND
Silver filigree, parcel-gilt, with
garnets.
SWISS (Schwyz): 19th century.
161-1870

19 NECKLACE
Gold filigree, decorated with enamel.
SWISS (Zurich): probably 19th
century.
182-1870

20 BUCKLE
Gold filigree, enamelled.
SWISS (Zurich): probably 19th
century.
114-1872

**21, 22 NECKLACE WITH
PENDANT AND EARRINGS**
Silver-gilt filigree-work, decorated
with enamel.
SWISS (Zurich): probably 19th
century.
184, 185, 185a-1870

23 NECKLACE
Gold filigree-work, enriched with
enamel, pearls, and sapphires.
SWISS (Zurich): 18th or early 19th
century.
33-1894

24 NECKLACE
Silver-gilt, set with garnets.
SWISS or BOHEMIAN: possibly
19th century.
162-1870

25 PENDANT
Gold filigree, decorated with enamel.
SWISS (Zurich): probably 19th
century.
1557-1856

26 PENDANT
Silver-gilt filigree, decorated with
enamel.
SWISS (Zurich): probably 19th
century.
1558-1856

27 PENDANT
Gold filigree, enamelled, hung with a
pearl. The Sacred Monogram
crowned.
SWISS: probably early 19th century.
9082-1863

ITALIAN LOCAL AND TRADITIONAL JEWELLERY

28 BOSS FROM A HEADBAND
Silver filigree, parcel-gilt.
SWISS (Engadin): probably 19th
century.
165-1870

1 CRUCIFIX
Enamelled gold, set with rubies.
ITALIAN: 19th century.
9080-1863

2 CROSS PENDANT
Gold, set with rubies and emeralds.
SICILIAN (Palermo): possibly early
19th century.
Given by Mr. Walter Child
641-1906

3 CROSS
Gold, set with point- and rose-cut
diamonds.
ITALIAN: 19th century.
Mark, fleur-de-lis above F.
Murray Bequest
M.1026-1910

4 EARRING
Silver, set with emeralds and
rose-cut diamonds.
ITALIAN: 19th century.
M.25-1948

5 EARRING
Silver, set with rubies and modified
point- and rose-cut diamonds in gold
collets.
ITALIAN: 19th century.
M.24-1948

6 BROOCH
Silver, set with crystals.
ITALIAN: late 18th or early 19th
century.
M.23-1948
Nos. 4-6 given by Mrs Mary
Houghton of Florence

7 POCKET MIRROR
Glass, in ebony frame mounted with
enamelled gold, set with pearls.
VENETIAN: probably early 19th
century.
489-1897

8 PAIR OF EARRINGS
Gold, hung with seed pearls.
(Adriatic type).
VENETIAN: early 19th century.
163 & a-1895

9 PAIR OF EARRINGS
Enamelled gold, hung with seed
pearls.
(Adriatic type).
VENETIAN: 18th century.
238 & a-1894

10 PAIR OF EARRINGS
Silver-gilt, set with garnets; hung
with seed pearls.
(Adriatic type).
VENETIAN: 18th century.
M.79 & a-1909

11 PAIR OF EARRINGS
Gold, hung with seed pearls.
(Adriatic type).
VENETIAN: early 19th century.
M.78 & a-1909.

12 PAIR OF EARRINGS
Gold filigree.
VENETIAN: 18th or early 19th
century.
Given by Miss Victoria Leveson-
Gower
M.13-a-1962

**13 PAIR OF PENDANTS FOR
EARRINGS**
Gold, hung with pearls.
Patmos type, but perhaps
VENETIAN: 18th century.
889 & a-1900

**14 BREAST ORNAMENT WITH
PENEANT CROSS**
Gold, set with garnets and crystals.
ITALIAN: 19th century.
998-1903

15 PAIR OF EARRINGS
Gold, set with garnets and crystals.
ITALIAN: 19th century.
999 & a-1903

16 COLLAR
Gold filigree links.
ITALIAN: 19th century.
14-1893

17 NECKLACE
Gold filigree studded with enamelled
flowers, set with rubies and
emeralds.
ITALIAN: early 19th century.
2753-1852

18 NECKLACE
Silver, partly encrusted with gold
and set with rubies and rose-cut
diamonds.
ITALIAN (Sicily): 19th century.
Given by Miss Susan H. Sterling.
M.13-1942

Case 42
Jewellery in acrylics, refractory
metals and other materials.

**19 NECKLACE WITH
PENDANT AND EARRINGS**
Gold openwork and mother-of-pearl.
Possibly ITALIAN: 18th century.
1172-c-1901

20 PAIR OF EARRINGS
Enamelled gold, set with pastes.
ITALIAN: 18th or early 19th century.
236 & a-1894

21 PAIR OF EARRINGS
Enamelled gold, set with pearls.
ITALIAN (Sicily): 18th century.
M.985 & a-1910

22 PAIR OF EARRINGS
Enamelled gold, hung with pearls.
ITALIAN (Sicily): 18th century.
M.989 & a-1910

23 CRUCIFIX
Enamelled gold, hung with pearls,
and garnets.
ITALIAN (Sicily): 18th century.
M.1000-1910

24 CRUCIFIX
Enamelled gold, hung with pearls.
ITALIAN (Sicily): 18th century.
M.999-1910
Nos. 21-24, Murray Bequest

25 NECKLACE
Enamelled gold, set with garnets;
hung with pearls.
SOUTH ITALIAN: probably early
19th century.
2754-1853

26 PAIR OF EARRINGS
Gold, set with pearls.
ITALIAN: early 19th century.
Given by Miss Jane I. Auty in
memory of her mother
M.108 & a-1929

27 PAIR OF EARRINGS
Enamelled gold, hung with pearls.
ITALIAN (Sicily): 17th century.
Murray Bequest
M.988 & a-1910

28 PAIR OF EARRINGS
Gold openwork, enriched with pearls
and rubies.
ITALIAN: 19th century.
J.C. Robinson Collection
148, 148a-1879

29 PAIR OF EARRINGS
Enamelled gold, hung with pearls.
ITALIAN (Sicily): 18th century.
Murray Bequest.
M.990 & a-1910

30 PAIR OF EARRINGS
Enamelled gold, set with pearls.
ITALIAN: late 18th century.
Mark, ON.
Given by Dr. Joan Evans, P.P.S.A.
M.52 & a-1962

31 NECKLACE
Gold and coral beads, strung with
pearls.
ITALIAN: early 19th century.
183-1870